D1568866

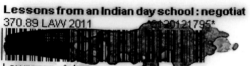

LESSONS FROM AN
INDIAN DAY SCHOOL

LESSONS FROM AN INDIAN DAY SCHOOL

Negotiating Colonization in
Northern New Mexico, 1902–1907

ADREA LAWRENCE

UNIVERSITY PRESS OF KANSAS

Published by the University Press of Kansas (Lawrence, Kansas 66045), which was organized by the Kansas Board of Regents and is operated and funded by Emporia State University, Fort Hays State University, Kansas State University, Pittsburg State University, the University of Kansas, and Wichita State University

Publication was made possible, in part, by a grant from the Charles Redd Center for Western Studies at Brigham Young University.

Library of Congress Cataloging-in-Publication Data

Lawrence, Adrea.
  Lessons from an Indian day school : negotiating colonization in northern New Mexico, 1902–1907 / Adrea Lawrence.
     p.   cm.
  Includes bibliographical references and index.
  ISBN 978-0-7006-1807-1 (cloth : alk. paper)
  1. Indians of North America —Education —Pueblo of Santa Clara, New Mexico —History. 2. Indian students —Pueblo of Santa Clara, New Mexico — Social conditions. 3. Teachers, White —Pueblo of Santa Clara, New Mexico —Attitudes. 4. Racism in education —Pueblo of Santa Clara, New Mexico —History. 5. Pueblo of Santa Clara, New Mexico — History. 6. Pueblo of Santa Clara, New Mexico — Social conditions. 7. Pueblo of Santa Clara, New Mexico —Race relations. I. Title.
  E97.65.N6L39 2011
  370.8909789'52 —dc23   2011022657

British Library Cataloguing-in-Publication Data is available.

Printed in the United States of America

10 9 8 7 6 5 4 3 2 1

Contents

Acknowledgments

I feel very lucky to be able to do what I do, and this would certainly not be possible without the care of those around me, of archivists around the country, of the staff at the University Press of Kansas, and of course of those at Santa Clara Pueblo. Writing a book—a history—is a test of endurance and often involves bouncing between the poles of frustration and joy. It is an educational process, and working on this project for the last six years, for me, has been more than educational—it has been educative. It has changed the way I look at the world and the questions I ask. Had the people and places studied in this book not existed, and had Clara D. True's letters not surfaced in an online search when they did, this study would not have ever begun. Such is the serendipitous life of the researcher.

I am very fortunate to have been able to work with stellar archivists and librarians around the country. My research began at the National Archives and Records Administration facility in Denver. Marene E. S. Baker, Eric Bittner, Richard A. Martinez, and David Miller all helped me find sources that I otherwise might not have requested. Their collective knowledge of the vast Bureau of Indian Affairs collections for the Rocky Mountain Region is remarkable, and many of the sources featured in this book reflect their expertise. Coi Drummond-Gehrig and Abby Hoverstock at the Denver Public Library's Western History and Genealogy collection guided me through a number of photographic images from New Mexico and through the permissions process. Samuel Sisneros at the State Records and Archives for the State of New Mexico talked with me at length about this project, offering suggestions about which sources I might fruitfully consult. He was also kind enough to correspond with me through e-mail and set me straight when I attempted to locate burned-up court documents. At the Palace of the Governors, Daniel Kosharek and Tomas Jaehn helped me locate documents and photographs that were instructive for this study. At the Laboratory of Anthropology at the Museum of Indian Arts and Culture in Santa Fe, Diane Bird shared with me not only her vast and deep knowledge of the collections but also her insight into how Indian pueblos and their members interacted with non-Native Indian Office officials at the turn of the twentieth century. I am grateful for the time she has shared with me on this project and in other ventures.

I am at a loss to express the gratitude I feel for the generous guidance given to me by Wanda Dozier and Robert Jenkins at Santa Clara Pueblo. I continually reflect on the time I have spent with them, and I appreciate their kindness, hospitality, and patience with me. I hope I have done justice to their forebears. I am likewise thankful for the insight of Chris Crandall, Gordon Crandall, Gratia Griffith, and Barbara E. Hannan—Clinton J. Crandall's descendents. Their e-mail correspondence with me has helped me to understand C. J. Crandall better. Gordon Crandall and Gratia Griffith, grandchildren of C. J. and Minnie Crandall, shared several of their family photographs with me, and two of them are featured in the pages that follow. I hope that I have done justice to their forebears as well.

The School of Education, Teaching & Health (SETH) and the College of Arts and Sciences at American University have generously supported me throughout the creation of this book. Deans Sarah Irvine Belson, Kay Mussell, Peter Starr, and Phyllis Peres have ensured that I had the means to do my research and put this book together through summer research awards and a faculty research award over the course of the 2010–2011 academic year. This support has meant that the project benefited from the expertise of the archivists in New Mexico and Colorado. Within SETH and the history department, Sarah Irvine Belson, Charles A. Tesconi, and Robert Griffith have mentored me and advised me in ways too many to count. They have served as sounding boards on this project and are models of good judgment and living examples of what the life of the mind can be.

In writing this history, I have relied on the advice of several people. David Wallace Adams and K. Tsianina Lomawaima reviewed the initial manuscript, and their rich feedback, without a doubt, helped me improve the argument and prose of this study significantly. Their time and their expertise are gifts, and I am thankful for them. I am likewise indebted to my writing group at American University. Susan Shepler, Elizabeth A. Worden, Brenda Werth, Kate Haulman, Kristin Smith Diwan, and Rachel Sullivan Robinson each read multiple drafts of each chapter and showed me how I might sharpen arguments and use evidence in different ways from multiple disciplinary perspectives. Their care with this manuscript made me want to continually improve it, and our friendships with one another have become foundational for me. Going into this book project, I had very little idea of how the publishing world worked, and the University Press of Kansas, with its expert and affable staff, has been an absolute delight to work with over the last couple of years. Ranjit Arab, Robin DuBlanc, Susan Schott, and Jennifer Dropkin have all helped me craft this book. They have made me a better writer, and they have walked me through every step of the process. Special thanks goes to Ranjit Arab, who had the foresight to apply for a publication grant, and to the Charles Redd Center for Western Studies at Brigham Young University, which awarded this book such a grant. I am deeply grateful for and honored to receive this support.

This study is reflective, I think, of my personal intellectual genealogy. Though I did not realize it at the time, the guidance of Philip J. Deloria and Vine Deloria Jr. during my undergraduate years and their interdisciplinary scholarship have transformed into an epistemological cornerstone of sorts for me. I consult their work in ways that are too many to count. Vine Deloria Jr.'s discussion of place-based history, or spatial history, in *God Is Red* has haunted me now for a good fifteen years. Keith Basso's published work illustrating spatial history among the Western Apache has made me ask questions of and apply maps and satellite imagery to documentary sources in ways that I otherwise would not have considered. Christopher J. Frey and Felipe Vargas have listened to me talk about this ad nauseam. Their questions, whether they realize it or not, have pushed me to hone my methods. So, too, have those of Lawrence J. Friedman and Donald Warren. They were my mentors and continue to advise me. Perhaps my greatest debt is to Don Warren. His fearlessness, sense of humor, demand for nuance, and friendship have meant the world to me over the last nine years. He has continually pushed against my hesitations and insisted that I create and try out theories and methodological tools that did not jibe with education policy scholars or education historians. His primary assumption, I now understand, is that education can and does exist outside of the school. This assumption has become another epistemological cornerstone for me, as this study demonstrates.

And finally, my family has been a source of support that wrapped around me as I worked on this project. My parents, Bill and Karen

Lawrence, and my sister, Lisa Lawrence, have always regarded Native peoples and their histories as others regard more quotidian American characters—as infinitely creative and intriguing. This position makes me respond to people who ask, "Why are *you* interested in American Indians?" with "How can *you* not be?" I attribute the tone to my grandmother, Mabel Cunningham, who sternly advised me when I began this project shortly before her passing, "Honey, don't screw this up." I have been very lucky to find a partner and mother-in-law who respond similarly. My spouse, Brett Rosenberg, has listened to me talk and walk through arguments and pieces of evidence to an extent that now surprises me. His unconditional support, curiosity, and intellect are tinder for me. And Bev Haskins, his mother, has only fanned the flames. Lastly, I am grateful for my son, Reid, whose impending birth meant that I had to stick to my deadlines.

Introduction

This book is an education history, but it is not about the school. Rather, it uses a school as a prism for looking at the educative processes associated with colonization and racialization in the New Mexico Territory at the turn of the twentieth century. Specifically, this book is a microhistory, or an ethnographic reconstruction, of how Office of Indian Affairs school personnel, Pueblo Indians, and Hispanos carried out and appropriated federal Indian policy in the northern Rio Grande valley, a nexus for a number of colonial policies.[1] Drawing from the correspondence between Clara D. True, an Office of Indian Affairs (OIA) day school teacher stationed at Santa Clara Pueblo,[2] and Clinton J. Crandall, the superintendent of the Santa Fe Indian School and the acting agent for the Northern Pueblos District, I demonstrate how school sites and school personnel were respectively hubs and intermediaries for a variety of issues, including land, public health, citizenship, schooling, and education writ broadly, that extended well beyond the schoolhouse walls. In fact, these issues were what True, Crandall, Santa Clarans, and neighboring Hispanos discussed most frequently. To be sure, True, Crandall, and other OIA school personnel were concerned with the officially sanctioned *Course of Study for the Indian Schools of the United States, Industrial and Literary* (also known as the *Uniform Course of Study*), but they were also responsible for making a range of decisions related to other, seemingly disparate concerns. This is what True's and Crandall's letters reflect. Individuals and groups who had a stake in these issues and their related policies thus navigated and constructed the educative processes that shaped the colonization and racialization of the American West.

Pueblo Indian communities and the Hispano, or former Mexican,[3] populations in the New Mexico Territory confounded the U.S. government's attempts to colonize the region in the late nineteenth and early twentieth centuries. Pueblo Indian communities presented a colonization paradox for Anglo federal employees like True and Crandall: Pueblo Indians offered an alternative form of "civilized" living that aligned with European-derived markers of "civilization," including sedentary agriculturalism and Christian affiliation. At the same time, Pueblo Indians maintained pre-Spanish social, political, and religious beliefs and practices. Anglo OIA representatives likewise found Hispano communities paradoxical. Once the New Mexico Territory, among other regions, became part of the United States with the conclusion of the U.S. war with Mexico and the passage of the Treaty of Guadalupe Hidalgo in 1848, Hispanos' status shifted from that of the colonizer to the colonized. In spite of the fact that the U.S. government officially regarded Hispanos as "White," Indian Office officials and the courts regarded Hispanos as "Other" in practice, disregarding their European lineage. The story of how these distinctions came to be reflects New Mexico's land and its peoples' centuries-long experiences with colonization.

HISTORIES OF COLONIZATION

According to Tewa histories, Montezuma, otherwise known as the elusive Poseyemu, prophesied the Spanish incursion into Pueblo Indian territory. In a variation of the story recounted by Elsie Clews Parsons, an Anglo anthropologist, an anonymous source told her:

> "From the south they are going to come in, Mexicans. Next will come the White people from the north." That is the way he talked, that man. He said, "Those Mexicans coming from the south are going to rule us. We are going to stand under the flag they are going to raise up. Next White people are going to take us and we are going to stay under their flag." . . . "Clothes we have not seen here are going to be brought in and you are going to wear them."[4]

According to the source, Poseyemu showed the Pueblo Indians how the Spanish and Anglos would be dressed and told them to take their religious ceremonials literally underground, saying, "You have to keep on this way until I come back."[5] Poseyemu then left, going south, to return one day when the Pueblo peoples would live in their country without interlopers. Clara D. True recounted a similar version of the history that she had been told by Francisco Naranjo, a prominent Santa Claran, to folklorist Clara Kern Bayliss: "He began to prophesy changes,—the coming of new, noisy conveyances, and of a strange, all-conquering race. The Indians would be subdued by people coming from the South."[6] Montezuma created a test for the Tewa Indians at San Juan Pueblo:

> He gathered all the principal men about him. Then he disappeared. Presently he reappeared, coming through the trap-door in the roof, strangely garbed, booted, and spurred (like a Spanish cavalier). With him came an assemblage of attendants, similarly dressed; and following these came a company of beautiful women, in queer, gay attire. At the sight of all of this, the Indians were so terrified that they fell over each other trying to escape from the house.[7]

Montezuma knew this would happen, and he left, heading south, noting that he would return after a time of "peace and prosperity" that would ensue when episodes of persecution had passed. He told the Tewa, "Endure all things, and keep the peace."[8]

And then the Spanish came into Pueblo country and stayed. Unlike many of their nomadic or seminomadic counterparts in what is now the Southwest, Pueblo Indians are distinguished for their permanent farming communities, their unique architecture, their extensive network of irrigation canals, their linguistic families, and their sociocultural organization. Spanning the northern half of the Rio Grande basin in New Mexico and its tributaries to the west, Indian Pueblos with speakers from six language groups dot the valleys. The two Western Pueblos of Hopi and Zuni lie along the present-day border between New Mexico and Arizona. Just west of the border are the Hopi, whose language is distinct but part of the larger Uto-Aztecan language group; and to the east of the border, near Gallup, is Zuni Pueblo. There, Shiwi'ma, or Zuni, a language isolate, is spoken. Following the San José River east and fanning out along the Rio Grande are the Eastern Pueblos. Two of these Pueblos, Laguna and Acoma—both of the Keresan language group—lie along the San José River. The majority of the remaining Pueblos belong to the Tanoan language group, which includes three different tongues: Tiwa, Towa, and Tewa. The majority of these Pueblos are located in the mountains north of Santa Fe. Closest to the Colorado border are two of the Tiwa Pueblos, Taos and Picuris. Further south, close to where the Chama River meets the Rio Grande, sit the Tewa Pueblos of San Juan (Ohkay Owingeh), Santa Clara, San Ildefonso, Pojoaque, Nambé, and Tesuque. The only remaining Towa Pueblo—Jemez—lies along the river

Indian Pueblos and Language Groups of New Mexico. Map by author.

that shares its name to the west of the Rio Grande. Two more Tiwa Pueblos, Isleta and Sandia, sit close to Albuquerque, separated from the other Tanoan societies by the Keresan Pueblos of San Felipe, Santo Domingo, Cochiti, Santa Ana, and Zia. Although some Pueblos share the same language family, similar sociocultural organizations, and belief systems, each Pueblo is a unique society with its own attributes and history. What the Rio Grande Pueblos do share unequivocally is the Spanish incursion into their country.[9]

Beginning with Francisco Vázquez de Coronado and his entourage in the 1540s, the Spanish sent expedition parties into what we now know as New Mexico and Arizona. According to Edward P. Dozier, an anthropologist and Santa Clara Pueblo member, these conquistadors "made themselves feared and distrusted" as they established colonial outposts in the Rio Grande valley. Their goal, writes historian Robert Galgano, was to create new sources of revenue for Spain through silver and gold mines as well as through cattle ranches and farming. Initially, the Spanish thought Indian Pueblos would be instrumental in establishing these new business enterprises: the Pueblos had sociopolitical systems that were familiar to the Spanish, they understood the geographic particularities of the region, and they were sources of free labor. Additionally, they were heathen souls in need of saving.[10] Or so it would seem.

The Spanish settlement of New Mexico did not begin in earnest until the 1590s with Juan de Oñate's party of 500 colonists. Until then, the most frequent visitors—Franciscan friars—simply disappeared. When Oñate came with settlers and livestock to establish ranches, he also instituted a rigid form of governance both over his legions and the nearby Pueblo Indian communities. He demanded allegiance from Pueblo peoples in the form of monetary tribute and labor; when allegiance was not given, as with the rebellion at Acoma Pueblo in 1598, Oñate responded with violence. Such resistance, though, was not uncommon as the Spanish colonies experienced intermittent hostile confrontation well into the late sixteenth century, necessitating ongoing "negotiated accommodations" between the Spanish settlers and established Pueblo Indian communities. Over the next eighty years, Spanish colonial rule was marked by political contests between Franciscan missionaries, whose goal was to build churches and convert the Native population, and Spanish governors, whose goal was to produce goods to augment Spain's economic position in Europe. In these sometimes bloody internal Spanish struggles, Spanish colonial factions often used Pueblo peoples as pawns. Under the early Spanish regime, Pueblo Indians experienced famine, forced labor, and forced religious conversion. But in 1675 the Spanish went too far, arresting forty-seven Pueblo Indian shamans. Pueblo frustration and anger percolated, reaching a boiling point in 1680.[11]

In 1680 the Pueblos united and initiated what was to be a twelve-year revolt against the Spanish. Under the leadership of Popé, a shaman from San Juan Pueblo who had been among those arrested in 1675, the Pueblos north of Isleta participated in a five-day uprising against the Spanish, beginning with the execution of Franciscan friars and ending with the recapture of Santa Fe. The Pueblo Indians held off the Spanish until 1692, when Diego de Vargas began his four-year "reconquest" of the area. Though documentary evidence of the Pueblo Revolt is scarce, limiting our understanding of what happened, the coexistence of Pueblo peoples and Spanish settlers after 1696 appears to have been relatively nonviolent. The Spanish Crown awarded land grants to Pueblo Indian communities and Spanish colonists in the region, which for the most part were respected. The Crown also imposed a colonial political structure on each Pueblo community.[12]

Under the Spanish regime, Pueblo Indians were deemed wards of the Crown who had certain privileges that were not bestowed on other Indigenous groups. Although Pueblo Indians were not considered full citizens, the Spanish government did grant each Pueblo 17,000 acres, which included the village and the land immediately surrounding it. By law, Spanish settlers could not live at the Pueblos, nor were they supposed to stake ranches within 3.9 miles of Pueblo villages. The Spanish government also required Pueblo communities to select political officers each year from within the village to liaise with colonial representatives in the region. Ironically, as anthropologists Barbara Aitken and W. W. Hill argue, these new political offices created by the Spanish strengthened the traditional position of power and authority within eastern Rio Grande Pueblos because traditional leaders determined who would hold the colonial offices. The men selected to serve in the positions took their orders from those traditional local leaders. While Pueblo Indians still use both the Spanish and Indigenous political structures today, anthropologists agree that the Indigenous political organization is the default source of power and authority within each Pueblo. The Spanish offices, however, remained useful in dealing with people and colonial government entities on the outside long after the end of the Spanish regime.[13]

When Mexico became a sovereign state in 1821 after its war for independence against Spain, colonial rule over Indian Pueblos transferred to the Mexican government. In the twenty-seven years that followed, life at the Pueblos appears to have remained relatively unchanged. Though Pueblo Indians became full citizens of Mexico and were granted voting rights, they did not necessarily see themselves as Mexican citizens. As the population in the north grew, the Mexican government recognized and protected land grants awarded by the Spanish Crown to both

Indigenous and Hispano populations. Pueblo citizenship and protected land rights, however, would become contentious and murky under the U.S. regime.[14]

Between 1846 and 1848, the United States and Mexico were engaged in a war over land and the expanding westward settlement of American citizens. The Treaty of Guadalupe Hidalgo, which ended the U.S. war with Mexico in 1848, ceded 529,000 square miles—roughly the northern half—of Mexico to the United States. In addition to concluding negotiations between the U.S. and Mexican governments, the treaty also served as the primary agreement between the U.S. government and Indigenous tribes living in the annexed region, even though the latter were not part of the official treaty-making process. For Native and Hispano peoples who remained in the area, sorting out citizenship and land claims was confusing and difficult. Those of Spanish descent found their status had changed from "colonizer" to "colonized" virtually overnight. Not only did they have to work through an unfamiliar legal system to prove their long-standing land claims, they found that their very identities were nebulous. While they might have preferred to call themselves "Spanish" or "Hispano," Anglo newcomers referred to them as "Mexicans," despite Hispanos' legal status as "White."[15] For American Indians, the annexation of the region meant that they were to experience yet another episode of colonization. Broadly, the U.S. acquisition of lands in North America formerly under Indigenous control and the issue of what to do with the Native peoples now being dispossessed of those lands became known as "the Indian problem." What the United States had, though, like Mexico and Spain before it, was a colonization problem. That is, the troublesome issues that developed in association with American Indians existed then, as they exist today, because of the colonizing policies of the U.S. government.[16]

Scholars argue that nineteenth-century reformers assumed one of two positions regarding the future of American Indians in the United States: some, like the French political observer Alexis de Tocqueville, believed that Natives would soon become extinct, and others, like Thomas Jefferson, believed that Indians' survival depended on their assimilation into Euro-American society and culture.[17] After the U.S. Civil War ended in 1865, many policy makers pushed for the assimilation of American Indians, as extermination no longer seemed a viable or ethical option. Speaking to the Friends of the Indian society at its annual meeting at Lake Mohonk, New York, Henry Dawes, the author of the General Allotment Act (1887), stated, "The Indian problem has always been with us. From our earliest history as a people and as a Government it has troubled us." Missouri senator Carl Schurz, like many other reformers, argued for assimilation: "To civilize them, which was once only a benevolent fancy, has now become an absolute necessity, if we mean to save them." Even with the push toward civilization through assimilation, policy makers and settlers saw the continued presence of American Indians in the United States as a problem, and that is precisely how they approached federal Indian policy. Part of the "civilizing" mission of non-Indian U.S. reformers was to inculcate the values of the privileged Euro-American population, which included individualism, private property, self-support, a monogamous nuclear family, Christianity, and citizenship through individual land ownership and schooling. The goal of assimilation in the Euro-American mainstream was central to federal Indian policy and manifested itself in a variety of ways.[18]

THIS STUDY

The setting for this study is the Santa Clara Pueblo in the northern Rio Grande valley of New Mexico from 1902 to 1907, the years that frame Clara D. True's tenure as the Office of Indian Affairs day school teacher there. True was responsible for teaching Santa Claran children under the age of twelve how to read, write, and speak English as well as basic mathematics and home economics. True was an Anglo woman from Kentucky whose career in the Office of Indian Affairs took her to government schools for American Indian children around the country. She and her family appear in the 1880 U.S. census. The oldest of three girls, Clara was born in 1868, when her father, George, was twenty-seven and her mother, Frances, was twenty-two. The census data indicate that George True was a store clerk and that Frances True kept house. Clara's younger sisters, Lizzie and Johan, trailed her in age by three and five years, respectively. Each member of the True household was born in Kentucky; by 1880, though, the family had moved west to Fulton, Missouri, approximately twenty miles east of Columbia and seventy miles west of St. Louis.[19]

Miss True carrying a boy, 1907. Courtesy of the National Anthropological Archives, Smithsonian Institution, Negative Inventory number 2337800.

True's letters to Crandall and her personnel file reveal that she held several teaching posts in the Office of Indian Affairs. Prior to her appointment at the Santa Clara day school, True served at the Haskell Indian School in Kansas, the Colville Indian School in Washington State, the Lower Brulé Indian School in South Dakota, and the Chilocco Indian School in Oklahoma. Her longest stint as an OIA teacher before her transfer to the Santa Clara day school was at Lower Brulé; and it was there, in the mid-1890s, that True and Crandall worked together until he was relocated to the Santa Fe Indian School in 1900. In her first year of service—1894—True was disciplined at the Chilocco School for "borrowing" money and leaving to recruit students in Kansas; according to Benjamin Coppock, the superintendent of the school, True neither recruited a single student nor repaid the money. After her five years at Santa Clara, True was promoted to the position of superintendent and transferred to southern California, first to the Potrero Indian School and then to the nearby Malki Indian School. There she met

Mary Bryan, who became True's secretary-cum–lifelong companion. True resigned in 1910 and returned to the Rio Grande valley to settle permanently on her ranch near Santa Clara Pueblo. In total, she spent sixteen years as a teacher and superintendent in OIA Indian schools.[20]

Evidence suggests that True used her professional ties to secure posts for family members at least twice. In late 1902, soon after her arrival at Santa Clara, she appears to have convinced Crandall to recommend her mother, Frances, for the position of housekeeper at the school. Several years later, through the same process, True had her sister Lizzie Randall hired as housekeeper at the nearby San Juan day school after Randall's husband and son had apparently died. Although her letters do not provide details, court documents indicate that True and her mother either purchased or were given a ranch located on San Ildefonso Pueblo land. When True and her companion Mary Bryan quit the Indian School Service and returned to New Mexico from California in 1910, they converted the ranch into an apple orchard. There they remained into the 1930s.[21]

Crandall's letters illuminate the larger policy context of both his own and True's experiences. Spanning several collections, Crandall's letters were meticulously kept, unlike many of the Indian Office records, which are scant, unorganized, and damaged by water and age. Like True, Clinton J. Crandall had a long career in the Office of Indian Affairs, spanning the last two decades of the nineteenth century to 1927, just three years before he died. Crandall worked as the superintendent of the Santa Fe Indian School from 1900 to 1912; he also served as the superintendent of the Northern Pueblos Agency beginning in 1923, four years after the agency was created, to 1927. Born in Ohio in 1857 or 1858, Crandall spent much of his childhood in Rockford, Minnesota. Though his motives for joining the Indian Office are not described in the letters examined in this study, his careful record keeping and his attention to legal and procedural detail in his work as the Santa Fe Indian School superintendent suggest that he took his position quite seriously. Like True, Crandall was transferred in 1911 as a part of a disciplinary action; he was accused of running a liquor ring out of a drug store he co-owned in Santa Fe. Though the Indian Office found him innocent of the charges, the commissioner of Indian Affairs nevertheless reassigned Crandall to the Pierre Indian School in South Dakota.[22]

Clinton J. Crandall. Courtesy of Gratia H. Griffith, Family Collection.

True's and Crandall's letters together, along with corresponding documents from Pueblo Indians, periodicals, legal cases, statutes, Indian Office circulars, and anthropological studies conducted by both Native and non-Native scholars, create a microhistorical glimpse into what the world along the northern Rio Grande was like at the turn of the twentieth century. Indeed, these sources cast diffuse light on learning and education outside of the schoolhouse, leaving classroom learning and behavior in the shadows. As an education history, this book cuts across the disciplines of history, anthropology, and American Indian studies as well as several of their subfields in substantive and methodological ways. My approach to the research has been inductive, breaking with many of the mainstream histories of education that have been published in the last forty years. Rather than begin with a definition of "education," as noted historians Lawrence Cremin and Bernard Bailyn did in the early 1960s, I have elected to follow instead the methodological recommendation of historian Richard Storr: to search broadly and inductively for evidence of learning, avoiding a cogent definition of "education" so as to avoid in turn "teleology in reverse creep."[23] And I have found learning in many manifestations, nearly all of them outside of the classroom. By beginning with the goings-on that True and Crandall describe, it has been possible to track both backward and forward in time what patterns of learning existed among groups in the Rio Grande valley and where they deviated for particular individuals. Checked against the archival and anthropological records, these patterns—through consistency and repetition—emerged as educative processes among individuals and groups of people. As these educative processes came to the fore in each of the topical episodes that True and Crandall discuss—land, disease, citizenship, institutions, and education via travel—missed lessons also emerged. Those educative processes and missed lessons are the metanarrative of this particular study. Even as these educative processes surface, though, a pithy definition of education does not. Rather, the evidence presented here describes features of education for the Santa Clarans, Hispanos, and Anglos in northern New Mexico: it was social and communicative, it was structured through individuals' and groups' interactive experiences and the meaning they created around those experiences, and it was cumulative, often over generations.

As education historian Donald Warren has noted, Bailyn's definitional and Storr's methodological approaches to broadening what constitutes the history of education have wreaked intellectual havoc on the field, with scholars arguing that such sweeping inquiry is nearly impossible. Boundaries are needed. For this study, True's tenure as the day school teacher at Santa Clara Pueblo serves as a temporal boundary—1902–1907—as does the delimited geographic location—New Mexico's northern Rio Grande. Too, True's and Crandall's letters frame the scope of this study. They documented their concerns, and perhaps unwittingly their learning, as well as the concerns of Santa Clarans, other Pueblo Indian communities, and Hispanos.[24] That the nascent point of this study rests in letters from OIA school personnel feels somewhat serendipitous; presumably, they could have come from other Indian Office employees who lived and worked among Pueblo Indians in New Mexico. But they do not. Instead, the correspondence between True and Crandall reveals, unexpectedly, the multitude of roles OIA day school teachers and superintendents were expected to assume. What they wrote about most intensely and most frequently were the issues that pressed Santa Clara Pueblo and its neighbors: land, disease, citizenship, and multiple modes of formal and informal education. Not only were True and Crandall school keepers, they were the eyes and ears of the OIA, whose political arms literally reached into Native communities. They were also public health officials, demographers, arbiters, legal consultants, and gatekeepers. Their varying roles depended on what was happening within tribal communities and within the territorial and federal government arms. In this respect, relationships between OIA officers and Pueblo Indians were formalized. But this binary relationship did not formally account for other groups with whom True, Crandall, and Pueblo Indians regularly interacted: neighboring Hispanos and Jicarilla Apaches, both of whom had long-standing relationships with the Santa Claran and other Pueblo Indian communities.

One of the constraints of this study is the relatively scant source material from Santa Clarans and other Pueblo Indians. Where possible I have incorporated the research of Native scholars, notably Edward P. Dozier from Santa Clara, Alfonso Ortiz from Ohkay Owingeh (San Juan Pueblo), and Joe Sando from Jemez Pueblo. Likewise, I have included archival documents from Santa Clarans and other Pueblo Indians as they were available. Over the last several years, I have been in conversation with members of Santa Clara Pueblo. I have made digital copies of my notes, sources, and published work for the Santa Clara library. At the request of the Pueblo, I have tagged the most recent batch of digital documents I have collected by the names of people mentioned, the topic at hand, and specific places to make the sources searchable by Santa Clarans who want to do research. I have had regular conversations with those involved in research at Santa Clara about the sources I was finding and how I was incorporating them into my study. Those conversations for the most part have remained off the record. In the summer of 2009, I conducted archival research at the Anthropology Lab in Santa Fe and had the opportunity to talk extensively with Diane Bird, the archivist there, who is from Cochiti and Santo Domingo. Her insight and long understanding of Pueblo and Bureau of Indian Affairs history in New Mexico have made me rethink relationships between individuals and questions concerning land. Any errors in the pages that follow are my own and likely stem from my own epistemological limitations as a non-Native scholar.

In spite of these limitations, the educative processes and missed lessons illuminate several learnings about the colonization and racialization in New Mexico 100 years ago. First, although the U.S. government officially charged OIA school faculty and staff with carrying out directives relating to federal Indian policy, these employees did not have an exclusive hold on the particularities of how such directives were actually realized. Pueblo Indians and Hispanos actively interpreted and appropriated policies tied to citizenship, land use, and social customs. Second, central to this process of appropriation were the relationships individuals and groups created with one another and their environments. These relationships, in fact, reflect the assumptions individuals and groups had about themselves and others, which in turn organized modes of interaction. Third, the interactions and performed assumptions of different individuals and groups demonstrate that colonization and racialization were tandem processes, which in the Southwest did not have a binary colonizer-colonized structure. By the time the region was within U.S. boundaries, Pueblo Indians had already experienced two waves of colonization, with the Spanish and the Mexican regimes. Hispanos, who were descended from Spanish colonists, found that their sociopolitical position had shifted from the colonizer to the colonized under the U.S. regime, leaving their status ambiguous.

Each of the chapters in this book illustrates a lesson or series of lessons centered on a concrete sequence of episodes or issues that True and Crandall repeatedly referenced in their letters. These instances double as learnings for particular individuals or educative processes for particular groups; they are identified by a one-word descriptor—land, disease, citizen, institutions, education—that we commonly associate with the European colonization of the Americas. Several recurring themes are traced through each chapter, each oscillating between the foreground and the background of the events that unfold: colonization as negotiation, policy appropriation as educative, place as a participant, True's and Crandall's notions of "good" and "bad" Indians, and the significance of the relationships between Pueblo Indians, Hispanos, and Anglos. Throughout these chapters learning and educative processes manifest in a multitude of ways.

Chapter 1, "Land," centers on the paradoxical creation of the Santa Clara Reservation. In order for Santa Clara to maintain its traditional landholdings and prevent Anglo and Hispano encroachment, tribal leaders determined that the Pueblo had to cede title to its land grants to the U.S. government. Doing so would compel the federal government to patrol and protect the land within the reservation. Disputed land claims between Santa Clarans, their Hispano neighbors, and Anglos interested in creating a national park in the area prompted Crandall to lobby for the creation of the reservation in order to defend Pueblo land. In the process of moving from landowners to people who lived on a reservation, Santa Clarans bypassed customary land use practices with nearby Hispanos and shifted their traditional land management practices to accommodate Crandall in his role as the new administrator of the reservation. The Pueblo's new status likewise forced Hispanos living close to change their practices of grazing livestock and cutting timber.

Chapter 2, "Disease," examines the 1903 diphtheria outbreak at Santa Clara Pueblo and how True learned the sociopolitical organization of the community during this event. Intense letters between True and Crandall written during the outbreak make clear the limits of Santa Clarans' trust in the OIA physician as well as the limits of True's authority within the Pueblo and the Indian Office. In analyzing the responses of Santa Clarans, True, and the OIA physician to the biomedical disease, we learn how the sociopolitical structure of the Pueblo might have shaped the reactions of individual Santa Clarans and affected the sociocultural health of the community. Gender roles among the Santa Clarans and Anglos figure prominently in the chapter, illuminated most clearly in instances of resistance or acquiescence to the physician's treatment of sick children. Finally, this chapter documents the schism between True and Crandall that developed in the first months of her tenure at Santa Clara Pueblo and that continued until she left in 1907.

Chapter 3, "Citizen," examines the changing status of Pueblo Indian citizenship through several court cases and the responses to them by Pueblo Indians and Crandall. During the first decade of the twentieth century, Pueblo Indians' legal status as citizens was in flux. Through a series of citizenship cases hinging on land, liquor, and taxes, the courts, Congress, and the president of the United States curbed Pueblo Indian citizenship rights and responsibilities, changing their status from that of full citizen to that of federal ward. This particular trajectory of moving from citizen to ward was the opposite of what other American Indian tribes experienced; but Santa Clarans and other Pueblo Indians had good reason to push for this change in status—it offered protection of their lands and property. These moves, coupled with the right to buy and sell alcohol, not only highlight how federal authorities determined Indian citizenship, they also underscore differing perceptions of "good" and "bad" Indians as well as significant cultural gaps between Anglos and those who had been in New Mexico for centuries—American Indians and Hispanos.

Chapter 4, "Institutions," considers how the twin organizations of federal Indian schools and the Office of Indian Affairs itself shaped interactions and perceptions among Indian Office employees and the Native communities they served. Caught in the beginning of Progressive reforms to streamline curricula and managerial practices, the OIA attempted to strictly and hierarchically regulate what went on in its schools through the *Uniform Course of Study* and by controlling how its employees conducted themselves within the agency. Federal Indian schools and the Indian Office as colonial institutions defined Indigenous populations as those to be colonized, and each institution enforced a rigid chain of command on its would-be colonizers, its employees. Through instances where True pushed Crandall to make exceptions to the rules or where she attempted to circumvent "proper" procedure, Crandall's view of his own role became clearly delineated. Too, the OIA reliance on superintendents becomes apparent through the reporting procedures and the latitude given to superintendents in the management of their districts.

Chapter 5, "Education," has two purposes: to synthesize the educative processes and missed lessons drawn out in previous chapters and to present two additional examples of learning through Santa Clarans' participation in the 1904 Louisiana Purchase Exposition in St. Louis and Anglo tourists' visits to Indian Pueblos and Hispano communities in New Mexico. The chapter reveals, in the words of historian Bernard Bailyn, how "education reflects and adjusts to society; once formed, it turns back and acts on itself."[25] In the two cases of cultural tourism for the express purpose of learning something about the "Other," Santa Clarans' demonstrate their savvy understanding of how and when to present themselves as "Indian" or as "civilized" according to circumstance and to suit their own ends.

CHAPTER ONE

Land; or, Relearning Place in a New Colonial Era

INTRODUCTION

"New Mexico is known as the land of the turquoise sky," remarked Frederic J. Haskins in a 1910 newspaper article appealing for New Mexican statehood;[1] it is also called the "land of enchantment," as present-day license plates announce. In her 1987 *Roadside Geology of New Mexico*, Halka Chronic describes New Mexico as "a land of contrasts: arid deserts and forested highlands, salty playas and blowing dunes, rugged volcanic uplands, and colorful plateaus, and a great river flowing unperturbed through a rift valley that quite literally slashes the state in two."[2] Northern New Mexico, where the Tewa Pueblos of Santa Clara, Ohkay Owingeh (San Juan), San Ildefonso, Nambé, Pojoaque, and Tesuque are located, is a geologic puzzle of mountainous and volcanic uplift and the earth's crust pulling itself apart along the Rio Grande Rift, through which a river of the same name runs. West of Santa Clara Pueblo a combination of lava, clay, and sedimentary rock slopes downward—sometimes steeply, sometimes gradually—toward the Santa Clara Creek outlet and Rio Grande floodplain, a fertile area where Pueblo Indians established their farms. Extending up from the river basin, flat-topped mesas and mountains rise to the west with exposed layers of accumulated rock. Heading up Santa Clara Cañon, where the Santa Clara Creek flows, toward the mountains west of the Rio Grande vegetation flourishes in semiarid, semi-alpine environments and ranges from low, fragrant sagebrush and grasses suitable for grazing to larger piñon pines, prized for their nuts and timber.

Though Frederic Haskins praised the turquoise blue sky of the territory, land was everything in New Mexico at the turn of the twentieth century. For Pueblo Indians, the land was their origin, their historical record, and an always already living, breathing, continual presence in their lives. For Hispanos, the land became their home, their livelihood, and the place of their history through the twin processes of colonization

*Harvest, Santa Clara Pueblo, New Mexico, ca. 1900. Courtesy of the Palace of the
Governors Photo Archives (NMHM/DCA), #4128.*

and interaction with Pueblo Indian communities, which taught Hispanos of different classes how to live fruitfully upon the New Mexican
land. For Anglos—the newcomers to the area—land was a repository of
natural resources to be admired, harnessed, and often exploited for financial and educational gain. The land was not Anglos' historical record
or their long-lived home, but it became a means for their livelihoods.
Land—the physical geography, the flora and the fauna of a place—is a
full-fledged participant in the story of how Santa Clarans, Hispanos, and
Anglos learned their positions, roles, and strategies in the colonization
of the place called "New Mexico" in the early twentieth century. Each
group had different motives and different temporal orientations to the
land, which grounded their perspectives and their actions during this
period. How Santa Clarans, Hispanos, and Anglos contextualized their
presence along the northern Rio Grande carried the weight of their historical experiences and deeds as well as their beliefs about how they
were supposed to live in the present and the future. Geographer D. W.
Meinig aptly wrote of the region we now call the Southwest: "The term

'Southwest' is of course an ethnocentric one: what is south and west to the Anglo-American was long north of the Hispano-American, and the overlap of the colonizing thrusts of these two continental invaders— the one approaching west from the Atlantic Seaboard, the other north from central Mexico—suggests a first element in the definition of a distinctive cultural border zone."[3] We might add that to the Pueblo Indian, the "Southwest" was a place that had been home for centuries.[4]

The successive waves of colonization by the Spanish, the Mexicans, and the Anglos prompted the people who were already there—the Pueblo Indians—to develop a series of strategies to retain their landholdings. Pursuing land, mineral resources, and glory in the late sixteenth and early seventeenth centuries, Spanish colonial powers, secular and religious, attempted to subordinate Pueblo peoples into slave laborers. By the late seventeenth century, Pueblo Indians had had enough and violently drove the Spanish out of Pueblo Indian communities and Santa Fe in 1680. When the Spanish returned in the early 1690s, Pueblo Indians negotiated land grants to legally establish their landholdings and prevent encroachment by neighboring Spanish settlers. Vigorously protecting their land grants throughout the eighteenth and early nineteenth century, Pueblo Indians adapted their tactics when Mexico and then the United States entered as the new colonial power in 1821 and 1848, respectively. Under the Mexican regime, Pueblo Indians were officially recognized as full citizens of the republic. This meant that land exchanges and acquisitions hinged on the recognition of the right of individuals to participate in such transactions. In some cases, landownership oscillated between the Santa Clara Pueblo and individuals whose self-identification shifted, as will be illustrated with the example of Roque Canjuebe and his descendants. Under the U.S. regime, the federal government surveyed the entirety of the territory and confirmed Pueblo land grants; but the recognition of these grants did not prevent Anglo settlers from attempting to snap up land parcels they found enticing for ranching, mining, archeological, or tourism aspirations. Disagreements over boundaries surfaced, or in some cases resurfaced, and legal actions ensued in the 1890s with Office of Indian Affairs (OIA) attorneys and agents representing Pueblo Indian communities. Hispanos and Anglos, though, were left to defend their claims themselves. By the turn of the twentieth century, leaders of Santa Clara Pueblo were convinced that in order to preserve their landholdings, they would have to convert their land grants into a reservation. This meant giving title of their land to the U.S. government to be held in trust for the use and pleasure of Santa Clarans indefinitely.

Until Santa Clara became a reservation in 1905, the Pueblo's land—like all other Pueblo Indian lands in the region—fell under the terms of the Treaty of Guadalupe Hidalgo, the agreement that ended the U.S. war with Mexico in 1848. Under the terms of the treaty, the United States acquired roughly the northern half of Mexico, or 525,000 square miles, including what is now California, Nevada, Utah, Arizona, New Mexico, western and southern Colorado, southern Wyoming, the southwest corner of Kansas, the panhandle of Oklahoma, and western Texas. Several articles of the treaty were especially pertinent and problematic to landholding in New Mexico under the U.S. regime. Article 8 of the treaty stipulated that the United States was to recognize and respect property belonging to Mexican citizens, Hispano and Native alike; this included both community and private land grants. Article 8 also required that within one year of the ratification of the treaty, residents of the territory had to decide whether they would remain Mexican citizens or become U.S. citizens. Article 11 specified that Indigenous peoples in the territory should not be forced to move off of their lands, nor should open, free trade with Indians exist. In practice, however, the treaty was not self-executing; in order for its provisions to be fully and legally observed, subsequent legislation or executive orders were required.[5] Particularly problematic for Pueblo Indians and Hispanos were community land grants, which were held in common and frequently set aside for particular purposes, such as "community use (*ejidos*) . . . hunting (*caza*), pasture (*pastos*), wood gathering (*leña*), or watering (*abrevederos*)." The U.S. Court of Private Land Claims, which adjudicated land grant claims in the late nineteenth and early twentieth centuries, did not always recognize such grants as they were not labeled with the terms "common," "communal," or "community." Instead, the grants were described by their purpose.[6] Unlike Pueblo Indian communities, which were regarded as corporate entities, U.S. law recognized Hispano communities, which were of Euro-American lineage, by their individuals and their private land grants, rather than those the community shared as a whole.[7] Once the Santa Clara Reservation was created, access to perceived communal land proved volatile. Arguments over lands that had been formerly leased from Santa Clara Pueblo and were still regarded as communal land in practice cropped up repeatedly in the early twentieth century.

Throughout these contests over land, Santa Clarans, Hispanos, and Anglos had to relearn the place of northern New Mexico within changing colonial regimes, shifting land use practices, notions of property, and relationships between each group. Each group's accumulated experiences and learning in different colonial regimes and from different colonial positions played out in their negotiations over land. For Santa Clarans, maintaining their long-standing land practices was paramount. Ironically, they had to give away title to their land in order to preserve its integrity. By creating a reservation, the U.S. government was responsible for enforcing Santa Clara boundaries; this in turn allowed the Pueblo to continue its long-standing land use practices with minimal interference from outsiders. Hispanos, despite their long-lived practices of communal grazing, timber cutting, and irrigation, found that under the U.S. regime, the legal parameters of communal—or community—land shifted in favor of individual landholdings. The creation of Santa Clara Reservation and the adjudication of Hispano land grants in the U.S. Court of Private Land Claims set new rules for land ownership and use in the New Mexico Territory. This court, along with other institutions such as the General Land Office (GLO), the Office of the Surveyor General, and the Office of Indian Affairs, established the U.S. government as a colonizing body and converted the status of the Hispano population from the "colonizer" to the "colonized." For the newcomer Anglos in New Mexico, land was not an instructor or the means through which communities formed and maintained thickly parleyed relationships with one another, as had been the case with Pueblo Indians and Hispanos for centuries. Rather, land for Anglos was generally something to be acquired to expand the holdings of the United States to different ends. Individuals sought to improve their economic possibilities through ranching, businesses sought natural resources through mining, and scholars and politicians attempted to set aside parcels of land as educational and preserved sites through the national parks and monuments system. Beginning with Santa Claran and Tewa history as it is grounded in the land of southern Colorado and northern New Mexico, the accounts presented here proceed chronologically through Spanish and Mexican colonialism to the U.S. colonization of the region.

THE PLACE OF SANTA CLARA (KAH'PO)

The Tewa origin story recounts the geographical origins of this group of Pueblo Indians and describes the process by which Tewa society first split into two moiety groups—the Summer People and the Winter People—and then eventually united.[8] In his 1908 field notes from his years living at Santa Clara Pueblo in the early twentieth century, ethnologist Jean Allard Jeançon recounted a Tewa origin story that Aniceto Swaso,[9] Jeançon's adoptive father at Santa Clara, told him:

> We Tewas came out of the ground at a place in southern Colorado near where now is the town of Blanca, you know where the sand dunes are on the west side of the mountains, well thats [sic] the place, I have heard that there are two lakes in that part of the country, well some of our old men say that the one in the middle of the sand place is the one and others say that the lake is further south and east of the sand place. Anyhow, when the people were coming out of Ci-bobe, thats [sic] the hole in the ground where they came out and is what the Hopi call sipapu, they sent an eagle out first to see what was out there, he flew all around and saw everything how its [sic] seems (condition of the world) and he found that it was all soft and like a swamp. [H]e stayed out 1 day and then went back into the underworld and told them what he had seen. The second day he came out again and found that it was a little drier, the winter priest had been praying and making medicine while he was out the first day. This time he went out the third time and found something kinda [sic] hard on the ground and that it was harder yet. On the fourth day the ground was hard enough for the people to come out so they planted a big spruce tree and as it grew up they used it for a ladder to climb out with. Then all the Indians came out ad [sic] start [sic] to go away from there. They started south, stop at one place and stayed there one day (that means

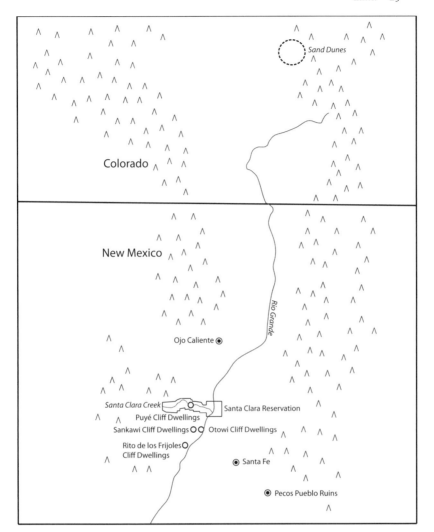

Significant places in Tewa history and the Pajarito National Park effort.
Map by author.

one year) and they went on. There are ruins at that place today; they
kept coming south and finally came to Ojo Caliente, and stop there
two days (2 years). They start to fight there amongst themselves because the Tewas knew more about the prop[h]ecies and medicines,
so the other tribes got jealous and threw rocks at them, they had a
big war and the Tewas drove the other Indians to the east, thats [*sic*]

why they call the Tewas warriors. The other Indians went to Oklahoma and other parts of the country in the east. The Tewas came
down the Rio Grande Valley and went to Pecos, thats [*sic*] as far as
the Tewas went and then they turned around and went back up this
way again. Other Pueblos went further south. The Hopi broke away
from them at Ojo Caliente and went west wi[t]h the Navajos. When
the Tewa turned back from Pecos they had an argument about whose
magic was the strongest the winter or the summer peoples and so
they made two factions the Summer and the Winter people. The
Summer people were like women and the Winter people were like
men. Ever since that time the Winter poeple [*sic*] where ever they
stood never fall back, The [*sic*] Summer people are not so progressive
and draw back easy. But in any ceremonial doings they both took
part. Ever since that time among all the tribes of the Indians they
follow their own religion and customs. When the Tewas turned back
from Pecos they built the other Tewa Pueblos and even Piecuris [*sic*]
and Taos where they are today.[10]

Because of their complementary capacities to grow food and hunt
game, respectively, the Summer People (or Squash People) and Winter
People (or Turquoise People) joined in a dual governance system based
on the seasonal, and eventually agricultural, calendar.[11]

Defined by both Tewa history and the landscape of New Mexico, the
Summer People and the Winter People each filled particular religious,
social, and political roles within Santa Clara Pueblo that harmonized
the community, provided structure for the annual agricultural cycle,
and alternated between the leadership of the Summer and Winter caciques (chiefs). From the vernal equinox in the spring to the autumnal equinox in the fall, the cacique of the Summer People held primary
political authority in the Pueblo. And from the autumnal equinox to
the vernal equinox, the chief of the Winter People maintained the seat
of political power.[12] In his field notes from 1908, Jeançon, who lived at
Santa Clara Pueblo intermittently from 1903 to 1930,[13] wrote that according to Swaso, although the Summer and Winter People had an al-
ternating system of community leadership, there was a long-standing
debate about which cacique had the most powerful spiritual and social

authority. Jeançon wrote that the Summer cacique was responsible for "un[doing] what the winter cacique had done . . . and . . . it is during his [the Summer cacique] term that all plants that feed man grow, and the game animals become fat."[14] The growth and harvest of plants during the summer season was symbolic of femaleness, reproducing the process of gestation and birth. The inverse was true for the Winter cacique; he was responsible for hardening the ground through frost when the Santa Clara migrated to their present site and for encouraging hunting.[15] These processes were primarily male.[16] Both the Summer and Winter caciques held their positions for life or until they were no longer able to serve.[17] The yearly agricultural, religious, and political cycles, then, were complementary, oscillating between growth and movement. Each moiety's ceremonial roles, knowledge, and rituals were specialized and accessible only to its members; one group's knowledge and the power derived from it checked—or balanced—that of the other.

In addition to these Indigenous socioreligious offices, Santa Clara also had a battery of secular political offices that the Spanish Crown had initially imposed in 1620.[18] The Summer and Winter caciques alternately selected men to serve one-year terms in specific offices.[19] The governor, who was the head of this mainly secular group of political officers, served as the liaison between Pueblo socioreligious authorities and outsiders. Diplomatic ability and being conversant in Spanish, and later English, were essential qualifications for the position. The governor's responsibilities entailed maintaining irrigation ditches within the Pueblo, apportioning grazing territory and land leases with neighboring non–Santa Clara people, patrolling Pueblo land for trespassers, resolving land disputes among Pueblo members, and supervising preparations for Pueblo holidays. The governor's primary responsibility, though, was to carry out the directives of the cacique in power.[20] To perform these tasks, the governor had at least one lieutenant governor and a sheriff, in addition to *mayordomos,* who specifically organized the work of maintaining the Pueblo's extensive irrigation ditch network.[21] Dozier notes that once a governor had served his term, he became a *principale,* an advisor to the caciques. The concurrent existence of Tewa socioreligious offices and Spanish political offices underscores the cultural syncretism and embeddedness of the twin system between Pueblo

Indians and their Hispano counterparts by the time the United States annexed the region in 1848. The U.S. government simply acknowledged these offices, though understood very little about how they came to be, and facilitated their continued coexistence. The Spanish offices would become instrumental in the U.S.–Santa Clara relationship regarding issues of land, health care, and citizenship.[22]

From the beginning of their history as a cohesive people, the Santa Clarans—and the Tewa Pueblos—have literally come from and relied upon the land for their sustenance, their socioreligious structure, and their general well-being. Writing about other Indigenous North American peoples, historians, anthropologists, and linguists have demonstrated that place has been and continues to be an active, living participant in Native cultures and histories. Place, as several contemporary Native thinkers describe it, is the particular geographic, plant, animal, and climatic environment in which a people finds itself, to which it adapts, and from which it learns. Place is an orienting tool that simultaneously positions a people in relation to others, grounds its experiences and memories in the physical world, and serves as a normative reminder about how to live and be in that world.[23] Working with the Western Apache in Arizona, anthropologist Keith Basso has demonstrated that specific places hold the stories and memories of past deeds that serve present-day community needs for moral instruction. Once a story is told, its hearers recall it every time they pass by the place where it happened.[24] Laguna Pueblo[25] writer Leslie Marmon Silko's discussion of Pueblo Indian storytelling practices shows them to be analogous to those of the Western Apache: "Location, or 'place,' nearly always plays a central role in the Pueblo oral narratives. Indeed, stories are most frequently recalled as people are passing by a specific geographical feature or the exact place where a story takes place. The precise date of the incident often is less important than the place or location of the happening."[26] Because of their everyday physical proximity to the storyteller (or historian) and the hearer, such places and their stories provide a palpable context that shifts and grows as one experiences the stories' places repeatedly but at different moments in time over the course of one's life. In other words, these stories and their linked places are educative. And these stories, as Swaso demonstrated, go back to the beginning.

SANTA CLARA DITCHING AMID A DEEP
POLITICAL RIFT

Ditching, or the maintenance of communal irrigation ditches by every able Santa Claran man, was an annual spring event organized by the governor to ensure the mutual bounty of fruit, vegetable, and cereal crops over the coming season. In the spring of 1904, two years into Clara True's tenure as the day school teacher at Santa Clara, a conflict over ditching erupted that highlighted the growing dissension between the Summer and Winter People. Through True, the Santa Clara governor, a member of the Summer party, requested C. J. Crandall's assistance in compelling Santa Claran men to work and clean their ditches. Crandall responded,

> The Governor is the recognized mayordomo, and the people should respond to work when he calls for them. As near as I can learn from consulting with the attorney for the Pueblos, the only penalty than [*sic*] can be inflicted on those refusing to work is to shut the water off from them. If Desiderio has no land, there would be no way to punish him under the law. The Governor, who is the mayordo [*sic*], has the distribution of the water, and those who fail to work can and may be given no water.[27]

At first glance, Crandall's response appears to support the governor's—and Summer party's—position. Every able male was to participate in ditching. Crandall's response to the governor likewise suggests a sharp reaction and punishment for those who refused to comply with the governor's order. His letter, however, also implies that the governor should be able to handle such a situation on his own and that internal Pueblo governance was not something that Crandall could or should mediate. But what was going on at Santa Clara that would prompt Desiderio to abstain from clearing and maintaining his family's network of irrigation ditches? To answer this question, it is necessary to understand just how ditching figured into Santa Claran agriculture and power arrangements among the Summer and Winter People.

Lauded by explorers, clergymen, jurists, and anthropologists for their ingenuity in the development of extensive networks of irrigation ditches spreading from the Rio Grande and its tributaries, Tewa Indians developed similarly comprehensive socioreligious systems that served to maintain more practical farming needs. Santa Claran anthropologist Edward P. Dozier argues that a constant water source coupled with a vast irrigation complex required a consolidated governance system that could compel community members to maintain ditches to ensure viable crop yields from year to year.[28] Crops ranged from corn, beans, squash, cotton, and tobacco, which were staples in the pre-Spanish period, to wheat, melons, fruit orchards, chilis, grapes, and alfalfa, which were introduced by the Spanish.[29] These crops, many of which were perennial, required water, and irrigation ditches could deliver water from the Rio Grande and mountain streams to the fields. Ditch work was reinforced by secular officers, namely, the governor and the mayordomos, or ditch bosses, whom the Summer and Winter caciques alternately appointed annually. It is worth underscoring that all secular officers served the cacique in charge; this in turn reinforced the socioreligious structure that was in place before the Spanish entered Pueblo territory in the sixteenth century.[30] As Crandall's response above intimates, the practices associated with the offices of the governor and mayordomo were over 200 years old by the time True and Crandall arrived in the first years of the twentieth century.

Such an extensive irrigation and agricultural system required a committed labor pool to maintain ditches and canals, and it required large swaths of land connected to natural water sources. The Pueblo governor was the primary manager of water and land at Santa Clara before the reservation period began in 1905. In this capacity, he was responsible for organizing the labor needed to maintain the irrigation system. Because of the community's dependence on produce as a food source, Dozier argues, ditching was "the most important" of all communal work at Pueblos along the Rio Grande—community survival depended upon it.[31] While the Santa Clara Pueblo as a whole maintained the larger irrigation canals, each family looked after the ditches on its own plots of land under cultivation.[32] Compulsory labor was not always easy to enforce at Santa Clara, though, particularly in the early twentieth century.

By the time True and Crandall arrived in New Mexico, the balance between the Summer and Winter People at Santa Clara had cracked.

The major rift in the socioreligious and political structures of the Pueblo came in 1894 when the Summer People secured the exclusive right to appoint individuals to Spanish offices.[33] Prior to this break, each new secular officer received a metal-topped cane that the Spanish had given to the Pueblo in the seventeenth century. This tradition continued into the U.S. regime, adding the canes that President Lincoln gave to the Pueblo.[34] Although the details in the literature are vague, the Summer People retained the power to appoint the governor annually by securing and keeping the canes. Anthropologist W. W. Hill surmises that this may have been a reaction to a group of individuals who openly defied the Summer chief's orders. He writes that as Anglos moved into the territory in the late nineteenth century, a dissenter could not simply relocate and form a new Pueblo, as had been done in the past, because by the late 1800s land had become scarce. Instead, dissenters remained at the Pueblo and tensions escalated. In a society that relied on conformity in customary practices and adherence to cacique decisions, dissent was unacceptable. By 1894, the Summer People, "with the connivance of the United States government," took the canes and thus got hold of the authority to appoint the governor every year. Hill adds that a few individuals from the Winter People might have joined the Summer faction, but that no Summer People joined the group who resisted.[35] The Summer People held on to the authority to appoint men to Spanish political offices until 1936, when the Santa Clara constitution was enacted.[36]

Though the secondary literature does not describe what precipitated the political rupture in 1894, scholars trace dissension between the two factions back to 1744, when a man named Roque Canjuebe—a Santa Claran man who wanted to become independent of the Pueblo—petitioned the Spanish Crown for a land grant within the bounds of the Santa Clara land grant. Canjuebe wanted to separate from the Pueblo in order to ranch an individual plot of land adjacent to it and not be obligated to participate in community ceremonials. Governor Cordallos y Rabál agreed to the petition provided that Canjuebe could prove that he had converted to Catholicism. The local priest verified Canjuebe's conversion, and the Spanish governor granted the land. Eventually, leaders within Santa Clara Pueblo determined that this was unacceptable. Under Spanish law, Hispanos, or those who self-identified as Hispano, were not permitted to live or graze stock within at least 1.5 leagues, or 3.9 miles, of an Indian Pueblo. In 1815, the Santa Claran leadership traveled south to Durango to request that the land be returned to the Pueblo since it was technically within its boundaries. The commandant general sided with the Pueblo leadership and in 1817 ordered the land restored to Santa Clara.[37]

This case had several implications for land tenure among Pueblo Indians and non-Indians. Dozier argues that by returning the land to Santa Clara, the commandant general "gave official sanction to the right of an Indian Pueblo to evict members who did not want to conform to tribal customs."[38] This underscored the normative and corporate nature of Pueblo Indian landholding. When the Spanish regime was ousted, however, Mexican law favored individual land ownership. According to legal scholar G. Emlen Hall, individual Pueblo Indians sold land to non-Indians during the twenty-seven-year Mexican regime. When the United States came into the territory under the Treaty of Guadalupe Hidalgo in 1848, Pueblo Indians promptly took their land claims to the U.S. agent.[39] Ethnic identification changed with land tenure. Ethnohistorian Tracy Brown asserts that by attempting to move out of the Pueblo, Canjuebe made the claim that he was no longer an Indian, but a *vecino*, or a Spanish "neighbor."[40]

Through her fieldwork at Santa Clara, anthropologist Barbara Aitken found that a number of families identified as Winter "nonconformists" lived close to Canjuebe and his descendants; those leaders who contested the Canjuebe claim were part of the Summer leadership who did not want to Hispanicize their agricultural and religious customs and beliefs. The Winter "nonconformists" eventually moved back toward the village after Santa Clara recovered the land in question, affirming their Santa Claran ethnicity. Although both groups agreed to carry on longstanding ditching practices, tension between the two parties remained. If Aitken's interpretation of the split between the Summer and Winter groups is accurate, then the tension between the factions percolated for nearly eighty years before it came to a head in 1894. That year, according to Aitken, Francisco Naranjo, the leader of the Winter faction that split away, "announced a definite schism"; but because there was no free land in the immediate area, the faction had to remain within the

Pueblo. Like the Winter "nonconformists" before, members of Naranjo's Winter faction agreed to participate in regular communal ditching efforts, but they would not participate in religious ceremonials as the Summer People performed them. Rather, the Winter faction would follow a "progressive" agenda aimed toward "reform, education, and modernization."[41]

By the time True and Crandall arrived in New Mexico in the first years of the twentieth century, the dissension between the Summer People and Winter "Progressives" seems to have been palpable at times and manifested at different moments.[42] One such manifestation was refusal to do ditch work, as in 1904 when Desiderio Naranjo, a member of the Winter group, abstained from the communal responsibility. True does not appear to have understood the ramifications of the rupture within the Pueblo or in relation to how she wanted to operate as an Office of Indian Affairs representative there. In April 1903, just eight months into her tenure as the day school teacher, True hired a Pueblo man whom she referred to as "the old beggar" to work on her chicken house. Based on Crandall's response to learning of True's new hire, it appears that he understood that if True hired the man, the Santa Clara governor, Diego Naranjo, would require him to work on the community ditches with the rest of the Pueblo's men. On April 13, 1903, Crandall wrote:

> The Governor in all Pueblos is the officer in charge of the communal ditch; each and every man living in the Pueblo should work on the ditch. There is no excuse for his not working on the common acequia. . . . I trust you will see the wisdom in letting the Indians manage their tribal affairs, and in no way influencing Indians not to obey the Pueblo officers, especially when the officers are right as they are in this case.[43]

In his response, Crandall affirmed the authority of the governor, who was a member of the Summer People, and warned True that hiring the man in question would effectively constitute meddling in internal Pueblo matters. Crandall's response likewise suggests that only Santa Clara men in good standing—those who ditched with the rest of the community—were eligible to do intermittent work for Indian Office personnel, or outsiders. The man's status at Santa Clara might have

Governor Diego Naranjo holding a silver-topped cane, 1898. Photograph by F. A. Rinehart. Courtesy of the Denver Public Library, Western History Collection, X-30736.

appeared contradictory to True. While he did not do ditch work as other Santa Clara men did, True learned through other workers that the man often built walls for people when their houses needed repair. The man did not live at the Pueblo, though, implying that he was no longer a part of Santa Claran society. True missed his outsider status, or she did not understand its significance, when she hired him to work on her chicken house. Governor Diego Naranjo presumably informed Crandall that True had hired the man against Crandall's warning before True replied to Crandall's letter two days later.

On April 15, 1903, True wrote to Crandall, explaining that she hired the man upon the recommendation of the singularly named Juanito, who had done work for her in the past. She justified hiring the man in question, stating that there was not any communal work going on at the time when she hired him. She attributed the governor's dissatisfaction to Pedro Baca, who was a member of the Winter party. She claimed that Baca was upset that he did not receive a commission for recommending a man for the work, which True maintained he would have collected if she had hired his brother or cousin. Whether her claim was accurate or true is not known; Governor Naranjo and Baca might well have had a disagreement over something, but it is not at all clear that it was over True's hiring practices. Governor Naranjo approached her to apologize "for interference" and offered to provide her with water for a week. True recounted her reply to Crandall: "I accepted his apology and his proposition for water, and told him I could not promise to please him but good teachers who would were easy to get. He said he didn't want anybody else." True understood this as the governor condoning her actions and her response to him. True's response likewise suggests that at that point in time—early in her tenure as the day school teacher at Santa Clara—she paid little attention to the agricultural calendar and the impending duties it might entail for Santa Claran men who were at the Pueblo. Though she did not yet understand the significance of her actions for Santa Clarans, she wanted to ensure that they and Crandall understood her to be a competent teacher. To demonstrate to Crandall that she was in good accord with the Santa Clara community, True continued her letter with a discussion of how a student she had previously turned away from the day school had spontaneously cut his hair and enrolled in the school. She ended the letter: "I suppose even an angel would have friction if he had to do business with ignorant drunken officials—and I am no [word missing] in temper. This you may have observed."[44] In spite of her self-recognized fiery disposition, True saw herself as competent, and even adept, in working with people whom it is not always clear she respected, such as Governor Naranjo. The governor's apology and offer of compensation suggests that he understood how little True appreciated the internal dynamics of the Pueblo and that he was willing to make concessions to keep the peace with her.

When she asked the governor about the man's history the following day, Naranjo told True that the man had not done communal work at the Pueblo for a number of years. It is not clear whether she knew that by hiring the man to do work within the community that spring, he would then be compelled to do ditch work with the other Santa Clara men. That he had built walls for other people without similar repercussions might have had to do with the timing of the work, the fact that the man was working with a member of the Pueblo, or the possibility that the man volunteered to do the work as a favor rather than for pay. True appears to have tried to correct her mistake by paying Governor Naranjo $1.50 to hire the man; the governor protested. True then offered to "discharge the old man," but Naranjo would not allow her to do so. She recounted that in the same conversation with the governor, she requested to have three men work for her that morning, and the governor sent them. True closed her letter, "Hoping I won't get into any more ditches."[45] True appears to have known that she needed to make amends with the governor for hiring a man who had not lived at Santa Clara for a decade to do work within the Pueblo. She did not, however, appear to understand the nature of her violation or what the appropriate course of reparation was. Although it is not definitively clear whether the man True hired was a member of the Summer or Winter People, it seems plausible that he was a member of the latter, given Aitken's 1910 analysis of the two parties. Paying the governor—a member of the Summer People—to have the man work on her chicken house might have exacerbated tensions between the factions at Santa Clara, and discharging the man would not undo the damage that True had possibly already done. Requesting more laborers when she did not know if they were required for ditch work might have appeared excessively demanding, especially after the tension she had already caused. The apology, the offer of a week's worth of water, and his refusal to let True fire the man all indicate that the governor, as a liaison to outsiders, responded with equanimity and generosity to True's mistakes.

In fact, Governor Naranjo might well have been protecting the Pueblo by keeping True from developing an understanding of how Santa Claran social structure functioned. Indeed, important aspects of community life were often protected through politeness and deflection. Writer David Roberts, who published a book on the Pueblo Revolt of 1680, argues that protecting internal practices and knowledge reflects the belief that "the power of knowledge evaporates when it is too widely spread."[46] If Governor Naranjo's actions did prevent True from understanding the internal dynamics of Santa Clara, she did not appear to be aware of it. Not only does she seem to have missed the significance of spring ditching, she also seems to have missed that the inner workings of the Pueblo might have been shielded from her. Over centuries, Santa Clarans had learned how to cultivate a wide variety of crops in a semi-arid valley, and this learning was deeply intertwined with their socioreligious beliefs and structures. To give that up or give it away might well have jeopardized the whole community. The potential for jeopardizing the community did not, however, stop individuals like Roque Canjuebe from choosing another way of life as a Hispanicized vecino.

HISPANOS AND PUEBLO INDIANS LIVING
NEAR EACH OTHER

When the Spanish colonized the Southwest in the sixteenth and seventeenth centuries, the Crown awarded land grants to both settlers of Spanish descent and Pueblo Indians. Scholars have written that early in the Spanish settlement of the Americas, from the sixteenth century until the Pueblo Revolt of 1680, the Crown gave *encomienda* and *repartimiento* rights along with land grants to elite Spanish settlers. An *encomendero*, or the man who had encomienda rights, could demand labor, or repartimiento, and monetary tribute, or encomienda, from Indigenous people who lived within the grant. In return, the encomenderos were expected to protect the Indigenous workers physically and instruct them in Christianity. Encomienda and repartimiento rights came with land grants that the Crown reserved for elite colonists. After the Pueblo Revolt, the Spanish Crown no longer granted such rights; rather, private and community land grants prevailed, and Spaniards from different socioeconomic classes moved into the area.[47]

The protection of and separation from Indigenous peoples were two codified sides of colonization for Spain, Mexico, and the United States. Be it in the northern frontier of New Spain or Mexico or the western frontier of the United States, however, intercultural interaction was inevitable.[48] Geographer Alvar W. Carlson maintains that after the Spanish resettled in northern New Mexico in 1692, Pueblo Indians and Spanish settlers received separate land grants to keep a distance between the communities to "assure the Indians that they had a place and also to keep them in place."[49] However, as historians Myra Ellen Jenkins and Sandra K. Matthews-Lamb have demonstrated, these distances were not always observed; and if they were, they were not always enforced.[50] Paradoxically, encroachment, along with more cooperative irrigation arrangements between Pueblo Indian and Hispano communities, characterized a type of symbiosis during the Spanish and Mexican regimes. Scholars write that communal land was often used for grazing livestock such as cattle, accessing water, cutting timber, and hunting.[51] Shared land used specifically for such purposes becomes confused in the literature with land grants that were held corporately and individually. Pueblo Indian communities, for example, held their grants corporately, meaning that they, as a group, could make decisions about how the land within their grant was to be used. This included setting aside plots for individual family homes and farming as well as areas where water and timber could be collected and livestock could be grazed. The Spanish Crown made these land grants to Indian Pueblos, however, in the wake of the Pueblo Revolt and the Spanish resettlement of New Mexico in the 1690s; the intent was to keep Pueblo lands intact and protect them against potential Spanish settler encroachment.[52]

Land grants to Spanish settlers—elite and otherwise—and *Genízaros,* or Native non-Pueblo Indians who were Hispanicized, included both individual and community land grants. The literature suggests that community grants were specified by their use, including living areas that contained individual allotments for houses and commons areas for water access, grazing, hunting, and timber collection, and were generally awarded to a village. Within community grants, only individual allotments could be bought or sold; commons areas could not. The assumption with individual grants was that the grantee would build a house, outbuildings, and irrigation ditches to farm on the land. Of course, the grantee could also use his or her land to graze livestock or cut timber. Given the semiarid conditions of northern New Mexico, and the fact that Pueblo Indian communities had some of the best farming lands along the Rio Grande floodplain, Spanish settlers leased and bought land directly from Pueblo Indians and grazed their stock where there was scrub and no official land grant. Grazing on open land that was not "granted" but was adjacent to Pueblo Indian lands frequently led to encroachment.[53] In the United States it has been difficult to track non-Native community land grants over time because the U.S. legal emphasis rested on individual grants during the late nineteenth and early twentieth centuries when the surveyor general and Court of Private Land Claims evaluated and affirmed or rejected land grants. Thus legal title to community land grants among the non-Pueblo Indian population effectively dissipated under U.S. law. Continued shared use of the land, however, did not.[54]

Some of True's earliest letters to Crandall detail livestock trespassing on Santa Clara land. On September 5, 1902, just days after she arrived at Santa Clara, True wrote, "At the request of Pedro Cajete I write to ask your advice as to what shall be done with a stray cow which is

eating up the Indian alfalfa. Pedro is greatly agitated."⁵⁵ That Cajete requested Crandall's support suggests the possibility that he, or perhaps
other Santa Clarans, had done so in the past and that True needed to
be brought up to speed on the recurring encroachment problems Santa
Clara faced. Cajete was, after all, the landlord of the Santa Clara day
school. Crandall responded to Cajete's request through True:

> You may inform Pedro Cajete that the law provides that an estray
> [*sic*] animal may be taken up and held for all damages; that he should
> at once notify the owner of said estray [*sic*], and in case he does not
> know to whom the animal belongs, he should immediately notify
> the nearest Justice of the Peace, who will know the legal steps to take.
> In any event the animal or estray [*sic*] is to be held for all damages
> done.⁵⁶

Neither True's nor Crandall's letter indicates whether the stray cow
belonged to a Hispano neighbor, but because complaints about Pueblo
Indian livestock trespassing into farm fields are nonexistent in the correspondence, it seems probable that this particular stray had a Hispano
owner. Crandall's advice did not help. In fact, Crandall, possibly unwittingly, put Cajete into a bind. By recommending that Cajete request aid
from the local justice of the peace, Crandall was, in effect, recommending that Cajete consult a Hispano to resolve the trespass of livestock
owned by a Hispano.⁵⁷ Subsequent correspondence hints that Cajete
did not consult the justice of the peace.

By November 1902, Santa Clara Pueblo tried to enforce the boundaries of its land grant by putting up a wire fence. Neighboring Hispanos
counteracted the measure by cutting the fence and allowing their stock
to graze freely.⁵⁸ True saw this as criminally taking advantage of the
Santa Clarans. She wrote, "The Mexican depradations [*sic*] are exas-
perating. They cut the wires of the Indian fields and pasture in open
daylight . . . I told the Governor last night to get the names of the trespassers to-day. If he does so I shall send you the list of offenders. They
ought to go to the penitentiary. They feel assured that this old Governor
will not have the nerve to protect the Pueblo."⁵⁹ True thought that some
sort of direct prosecution of those responsible for cutting the fence was
necessary. She was not confident in the governor's ability or willingness
to participate in such an encounter, though. Earlier in the letter, True

remarked on his inability to compel students to attend the day school. But True was new to the community; she did not yet understand the relationships within it, the nuances of specific roles and authority, such as the governor's, or appropriate modes of interaction. Governor Leandro Tafoya, moreover, was so intent on resolving the matter that he submitted a notarized affidavit on November 26, 1902, presumably to a local court, attesting to trespassing cattle the previous month.[60]

Tafoya had to navigate between several different parties at once in trying to resolve the trespassing incidents. True did not seem to understand that what she perceived as his inaction or lack of responsibility might have been part of an unrecognized protocol for working with Hispanos and the U.S. government. As illustrated in the letter above, True thought Tafoya should follow her advice and collect the names of those who cut the fence he and other Santa Clarans had put up. In a postscript to her November 5, 1902, letter to Crandall, True reported that as Hispanos were placing their livestock in Santa Clara fields, the "Governor will not do anything. He *says* he will but he slides out of all responsibility when the crisis comes."[61] The governor might well have attempted to placate True through what he thought was the polite thing to do: simply affirm her wishes to catch and punish the trespassers. Indeed, the governor learned that True unequivocally supported the Pueblo's position on the trespassing issue. But what True did not appear to understand—or to have learned at this point in her tenure—was that the Santa Clarans found themselves in a precarious social situation that had developed over centuries and that required careful, deliberate consideration rather than immediate action. Unlike True, the governor had to consider long-term relationships within the Pueblo and with surrounding Hispano communities.

In fact, Santa Clara had been involved in a land case in the U.S. Court of Private Land Claims against Hispano trespassers since 1892, though the actual dispute had been ongoing since 1758. Santa Clara Cañon, which extends west of the Rio Grande toward the mountains and through which runs Santa Clara Creek, was the seventeen-mile site of contention from 1758, when the Santa Claran leadership challenged the use of a Spanish land grant in the cañon, to 1905, when the cañon, along with the original Santa Clara land grant, became a reservation. In 1724 Spanish governor Juan Domingo de Bustamente awarded a land grant

Jose Leandro Tafoya, governor of Santa Clara Pueblo, near wood ladder and adobe wall, 1899. Photograph by Adam Clark Vroman. Courtesy of the National Anthropological Archives, Smithsonian Institution, NAA INV 06332300.

along Santa Clara Creek to Juan and Antonio Tafoya for grazing cattle.[62] Thirty-four years later, in 1758, the Santa Claran leadership approached Governor Francisco Antonio Marín del Valle for relief when the Tafoyas' livestock damaged Santa Claran crops. Marín del Valle fined the Tafoyas. The remedy did not last long. Five years later, Santa Clara petitioned Governor Tomás Vélez Cachupín. Fray Mariano Rodriguez de la Torre, the Spanish priest at Santa Clara, wrote to the territorial governor on behalf of the Pueblo. In his statement, Rodriguez de la Torre argued that Santa Clara needed more water, as the Tafoyas were consuming more than their share up the creek during a drought year. The Tafoya family had apparently complained about grazing Pueblo livestock in Santa Clara Cañon eating Spanish crops and retaliated by quarantining the offending animals for several days at a time. Santa Clarans claimed that their livestock was not near the seedlings that the Tafoya family had planted, and the Pueblo requested that it be given additional arable land so that it might yield enough produce to survive.[63]

Governor Vélez Cachupín's response was curt and decisive. Not only did he reprimand the Tafoyas for planting crops in an area where only their livestock should have grazed, he revoked their land grant along Santa Clara Creek all together. He then created a new land grant of that particular tract for Santa Clara Pueblo, citing law 20 of the *Recopilación de leyes de las Indias* (book 6, title 3), which stipulated that large herds of livestock should be kept "apart a league and a half from the old bounds of the Indians."[64] The governor ordered that the descendants of Juan and Antonio Tafoya be informed of his decision and that they vacate the area of the new Santa Clara grant. They had lost both the right to graze stock in Santa Clara Cañon and the land itself. Vélez Cachupín did not address the Tafoya descendants' cultivation of the land, a violation of their grant conditions. One might think that transferring the land to Santa Clara Pueblo would have resolved the trespassing issue, but the Tafoya descendants were again investigated by Spanish authorities in 1788. Governor Fernando de la Concha affirmed Vélez Cachupín's decision and ordered the Hispano settlers off the land.

The documentary record then breaks until 1885, well after the Mexican regime had governed New Mexico and lost the territory to the United States. Surveyor General Clarence Pullen revisited the history of the Santa Clara Cañon grant in 1885 after the Pueblo made a claim against the U.S. government for the tract under the Treaty of Guadalupe Hidalgo. In his archival research, Pullen traced the sixty-four-year dispute between Santa Clara Pueblo and the Tafoyas and filed his report in triplicate.[65] But because the surveyor general's office was overburdened during this period by the sheer volume of claims coming through it, the report was apparently set aside.[66] After Congress created the Court of Private Land Claims in 1891, Santa Clara Pueblo again filed a claim for the Santa Clara Cañon grant through the Pueblo's attorneys. Taken up first by D. H. Smith in 1892 and then by G. Hill Howard in 1894, the claim included Pullen's research into the matter as well as a number of records from the Spanish archive.[67] The court confirmed the grant in 1894; however, the Pueblo disagreed with the boundaries set in the survey. G. Hill Howard prodded N. C. Walpole, the U.S. Indian agent for the Pueblos at the time, and was eventually successful in getting Court of Private Land Claims to order a resurvey of the grant in 1898, when Justice H. C. Sluss ordered that Santa Clara Cañon be resurveyed and provided very specific instructions for how to go about it. Howard recommended that the grant be made into a reservation immediately to protect it from Anglo settlers and neighboring Hispanos.[68]

Although there are no archival documents written by Santa Clarans or Hispanos during this time period, their shared history of land tenure suggests that the two groups were well aware of each other's land use practices and the Spanish laws that regulated them. The Santa Clarans quickly learned what their land rights were under the *Recopilación de leyes de las Indias* and sought protection when they needed the laws enforced or when they needed additional lands to support their community. The Tafoyas appear to have learned that the key question in land use was enforcement. Though their land grant specifically stated that the tract was for grazing livestock, they nevertheless cultivated parcels that were arable until Governor Vélez Cachupín permanently took their grant away. Even then, they had to be reminded that the grant was not theirs to use a quarter century later by Governor Fernando de la Concha. For Santa Clarans, their land grants were their homes from time immemorial; the land on the grants was the very origin and foundation of life. For neighboring Hispanos, the land was a colonial outpost that might provide better status and increased wealth and would certainly provide property. Once they had lived on the land for several generations, their interests were vested, and they were loath to give it up. And even though the archival records break near the turn of the nineteenth century, disputes between Santa Clarans and Hispanos continued well into True's and Crandall's tenure in the region as OIA officials one hundred years later. True and Crandall, though, do not appear to have understood the long, disgruntled history of land use among the Pueblo Indians and their Hispano neighbors. Rather, Crandall in particular argued for protecting Santa Clara land from within his role as the acting Indian agent for the Northern Pueblos District.

THE CREATION OF THE SANTA CLARA RESERVATION
AND THE THWARTING OF TRESPASSING

Though Crandall was a school superintendent, his concurrent position as the acting Indian agent for the Northern Pueblos District included gatekeeping and advocacy responsibilities. Crandall argued repeatedly for legal action against neighboring Hispanos who grazed their livestock, cut timber, and lived on Santa Clara Cañon land, and he made a case for the creation of Santa Clara Reservation. The two Santa Clara land grants—the original grant straddling the Rio Grande and the Santa Clara Cañon grant—were converted into a reservation by executive order on July 29, 1905. It appears that Crandall took up Santa Clara's claim two years into his tenure at the Santa Fe Indian School and lobbied particularly vigorously for the reservation when the New Mexico Supreme Court ruled that Pueblo Indians were full legal citizens and were liable for property taxes in 1904. Because Pueblo Indians were by and large subsistence farmers, their incomes were not such that they could pay taxes. This meant that county governments would almost assuredly foreclose on Pueblo Indian landholdings. The antidote to the court ruling was twofold: to lobby Congress for legislation exempting Pueblo Indians from paying taxes and to convert the Santa Clara land grants into a single reservation that would compel federal protection. The full antidote was achieved in the summer of 1905.[69]

On August 29, 1905, Crandall wrote to the Santa Clara governor informing him of the Pueblo's change in status:

> I [sic] affords me great pleasure to announce to you that the reservation asked for, and for which I have diligently worked for more than three years, has been granted. . . . Steps will be immediately taken to protect you in the possession of this reservation. As a reservation, you will understand, that as a Pueblo officer and Governor, you have no jurisdiction over same. The land is for your people; the title is in the Government, and the management rests in the hands of the United States and its officers, the Supt. of the Santa Fe Indian school, being the acting Agent.[70]

Through the creation of the reservation, Santa Clarans would not be able to alienate the land through individual sales or transfer as had been done infrequently during the Spanish and Mexican regimes, and the federal government would be compelled to enforce its boundaries. Crandall—the superintendent of the Santa Fe Indian School—would be in charge of administering the reservation, as he made clear to the Santa Clara governor. Reservation status carried with it changes in authority and relationships between the Santa Clarans, Hispanos, and Anglos living in the area; it likewise marked a lesson in how these groups learned to understand U.S. legal parameters and values regarding land.

The formation of Pueblo Indian reservations contrasted historically with how reservations were formed for other Indigenous groups within the United States. In his 1880 annual report to Congress, Secretary of the Interior Carl Schurz wrote, "When I took charge of this department the opinion seemed to be generally prevailing that it were best for the Indians to be gathered together upon a few large reservations where they could be kept out of contact with the white population, and where their peaceful and orderly conduct might be enforced by a few strong military posts."[71] This was certainly U.S. policy when the Indian Removal Act became law in 1830 and the federal government forcibly relocated southeastern tribes, such as the Cherokee and the Chickasaw, to places far from their traditional homelands. By the mid-nineteenth century, however, reservation policy changed—at least for sedentary Indian Pueblos in New Mexico and Arizona. Instead of relocating tribes, the U.S. government established Pueblo Indian reservations ostensibly to protect Indigenous communities' long-standing homelands, as mandated by article 11 of the Treaty of Guadalupe Hidalgo. Ten years after the ratification of the treaty in 1898, the U.S. government formally recognized the land grants Pueblo Indians held under the Spanish and Mexican regimes even though patents for the land were not issued until 1864, removing land from the public domain.[72] Federal recognition, coupled with land patents, protected Pueblo lands in the U.S. system through legal documentation, and at the time confirmed Pueblo Indian community rights to alienate their property—a hallmark of citizenship—until the land grants were converted into reservations, that is. A reservation contractually compelled the federal government to fight for the land grants the Spanish Crown awarded to Santa Clara Pueblo and at the same time to keep Hispano and Anglo trespassers out. In addition to establishing formal protection, reservations formalized a dependent relationship between the U.S. government and Pueblo Indian communities while simultaneously forcing the Hispano population from the position of colonizer to colonized. Hispanos, in other words, now had to adhere to U.S. law in the paradoxical positions of the subjugated and the full citizen.

Although it is possible that Santa Clara Pueblo had, at some point, leased land to its Hispano neighbors for grazing, timber, and water prior to the U.S. annexation of the Southwest,[73] the fact that Hispanos cut Santa Claran fence in plain view in 1902 suggests that those lands had once been viewed as common grazing fields, particularly in the fall after crops had been harvested. Historian Malcolm Ebright notes that stubble grazing, or allowing livestock to eat the remainder of harvested crops, was expected practice under the Spanish regime. Similarly, anthropologist W. W. Hill writes that unfarmed land or land that did not have a house on it was communally held by the Pueblo. This meant that Santa Clarans could use the land to graze livestock, fish, hunt, collect timber, and collect clay for pottery. At the same time, cutting fence around cultivated land ran contrary to Spanish custom, according to historian Daniel Tyler.[74] Given the fact that Santa Clarans regularly protested Hispano incursions onto Pueblo lands and sought aid from True and Crandall, it seems that Santa Clarans had had enough. They were ready for enforced boundaries, and the prospect of a reservation would ensure just that. The irony, of course, is that in order to protect Santa Clara lands for the Pueblo's use, the federal government would have to take it away. For Hispanos, this meant that their long-standing assumptions about land and natural resources were under fire. U.S. law— and the Santa Clarans' and Anglos' use of it—compelled Hispanos to relearn place. Though the conflict between Santa Clarans and Hispanos was ripe and certainly predated True's and Crandall's entrances into the Rio Grande valley, their willingness to aid Santa Clarans was central to shifting conceptions of land and natural resources in the region.

From 1903 to 1906, Crandall wrote a number of letters to the commissioner of Indian Affairs and the Santa Clara governor regarding Hispanos cutting timber in Santa Clara Cañon. Before Roosevelt's 1905 executive order, Crandall's response to Hispano logging in the area was to recommend creating a reservation for Santa Clara so that the federal government could protect the woodlands.[75] Once the reservation was established late in July 1905, Crandall hired an additional farmer, Samuel Stacher, and two Santa Claran police officers, Anastacio Naranjo and Desidero Naranjo, to enforce the government claim to the land and keep Hispanos outside reservation boundaries.[76] In an October 25, 1905, letter to the commissioner of Indian Affairs, Crandall reported on several Hispano men who had illegally cut timber on the Santa Clara

Reservation and worried how to protect his officers against "very in-
solent" Hispanos who refused to comply with orders. As Stacher had
collected the names of those who did not comply with orders to vacate
the reservation and leave the timber they had cut, Crandall asked the
commissioner of Indian Affairs to prosecute the trespassers through
channels in the Department of Justice.[77] As Crandall made this report,
the additional farmer and police officers who patrolled the reservation
for trespassers were engaged in a confrontation that entangled them
with the local judiciary. Stacher stopped a Hispano man who had a wag-
onload of timber. Stacher told the man to unload the wood; but instead
of obeying, the man left to fetch the justice of the peace, who was also
Hispano. The justice issued a writ of replevin, which legally compelled
Stacher to return the man's wagon, horse, and wood. The justice also
required Stacher to appear before him formally. Crandall was incensed
and complained to the commissioner of Indian Affairs, "As these papers are all in Spanish, and the whole settlement is against the preservation of this timber, we cannot hope to get any justice in a Mexican
court, where the whole proceedings are in Spanish, and the sympathy
all against us."[78] The Hispano man who had cut the timber and retrieved the justice of the peace appears to have been well aware of the
fact that nearly all of the lower court judgeships in New Mexico were
held by Hispanos.[79] Hispanos, in fact, used the local court system and
Spanish language to protect their interests against those of the federal
government. Ironically, only Spanish speakers, including Hispanos and
Santa Clarans, could understand the court documents and proceedings
without interpreters. If Crandall and his superiors in the OIA wanted to
pursue the matter, they would have to appeal the decision of the justice
of the peace and pursue the matter at the district court level, or they
would have to go through exclusively federal channels. The tables were
turned against U.S. government officials in the area, and Crandall felt
this rather acutely. Hispanos, in other words, were schooling Anglos
on what it meant to live in northern New Mexico with limited material
resources.

In late 1905 it seemed as though the Hispano resistance to U.S.
domination around Santa Clara was working, and it escalated as more
Hispano men ignored U.S. government orders to cease cutting timber
on the reservation. On November 30, 1905, Crandall reported that a

number of Hispano men "h[e]ld an indignation meeting" and began to block public roads on the reservation. In turn, he instructed his officers to prevent wood from being hauled off. The tension between the two groups—Hispano and Anglo/Pueblo—must have been palpably intense. Crandall remarked to the commissioner of Indian Affairs that he felt he had acted within his professional limits despite the protest it caused. To garner support from the New Mexico Territory's recently elected congressional delegate in Washington, D.C., Crandall knew that he would have to provide a detailed account of what had occurred, otherwise the representative would not protect the newly created Santa Clara Reservation. In other words, Crandall expected that William Henry Andrews, the New Mexico delegate, would not simply accept Stacher's account of the incident. Andrews, after all, had to ensure that his own alliances in New Mexico and in Congress were solvent in the coming years if he were to accomplish anything of measure. Crandall's recognition that he would need a substantial position in his account of the timber crisis suggests that Andrews, just like previous delegates, had not actively advocated for Pueblo Indians.

The timber-cutting episodes before and after Santa Clara Pueblo became a reservation highlight the relationships between Santa Clarans, Hispanos, and Anglos and how, by legal requirement, they would have to change in the twentieth century. Although Hispano perspectives about these land contests are absent from True's and Crandall's letters, secondary sources help spotlight past practices between Pueblo Indians and Hispanos. Historian Roxanne Dunbar-Ortiz argues that during the Spanish and Mexican periods a class alliance between poor Hispanos and Pueblo Indians surfaced such that the two groups acted in cooperation against the Hispano elite, who had for centuries held political office in the region.[80] Similar alliances resurfaced in the mid-twentieth century to protect Hispano and Pueblo Indian subsistence farmers against outside development.[81] However, at the turn of the twentieth century, when Anglo transplants had staked their claim in the New Mexico Territory and vied for the same resources that Pueblo Indians and Hispanos had bargained for over the previous three hundred years, increased pressures to hold on to limited land and natural resources appear to have fueled conflict between the groups. The fact that Santa Clarans wanted to protect their land grants from encroaching Hispano cattle and timber cutters suggests that the Pueblo might have had to tolerate such incursions before the United States annexed the region. With a new colonial regime, Santa Clarans quickly learned that Indian Office officials might help protect Pueblo boundaries at the expense of Hispano custom. As evidenced through their letters, True and Crandall encouraged Santa Clarans to continue fencing their fields, protecting their natural resources, and reporting neighboring Hispanos who violated reservation boundaries.

Overt encroachment did happen and occurred in tandem with the phasing out of lands that might well have been used for communal grazing purposes. Geographer Alvar W. Carlson argues that Hispanos squatted on Pueblo Indian land in the late 1800s without contest.[82] This practice continued into the early 1900s, but on at least two occasions was challenged by Santa Clara Pueblo. On September 9, 1903, on behalf of Governor Diego Naranjo, a member of the Pueblo wrote directly to Crandall about a Hispano named Sanchez, who claimed land west of Santa Clara as his own. This area was located within the Santa Clara Cañon grant and was significant for the Pueblo as potters retrieved clay from the spot where Sanchez grazed his herd of goats. Naranjo disputed the Hispano's claim after Sanchez forbade Santa Clarans from entering the land in question. The governor wrote that Sanchez had "no deed or title of any kind to prove his ownership to this land." Naranjo requested that Crandall look into the matter and settle the conflict promptly.[83] Crandall wrote back that same day indicating that he would have Robert Bradford, the OIA additional farmer at that time, investigate Sanchez's claim and determine whether it was legitimate. If it was, Crandall could do nothing; if it was not, Crandall would evict the man.[84] There is no further record of Sanchez's claim until two years later, when Crandall had Samuel Stacher, the new additional farmer, investigate squatters' claims on the Santa Clara Reservation. That investigation finally resulted in Sanchez's eviction.

In the intervening year, True reported on a similar case. On November 4, 1904, True wrote to Crandall on behalf of Santiago Naranjo, the second lieutenant governor of Santa Clara. As Sanchez had in 1903, an unnamed Hispano rancher laid claim to land held by the Pueblo. Santa Claran leaders did not dispute his claim, but they did not want him grazing his cattle in Pueblo pastures. Naranjo, following Crandall's

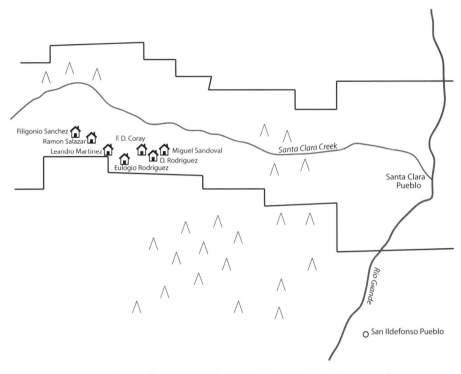

Santa Clara Pueblo land grants and disputed Hispano claims. Map by author.

instructions from the previous year, drove the stock off of Santa Clara land. The Hispano rancher threatened to take Naranjo to court for damages. Naranjo wanted to know if Crandall still recommended "turn[ing] the cattle out" as he was wary that the Pueblo would have to pay for any injury that might occur to the animals in driving them from Santa Clara pastures. Naranjo's apprehension likewise indicates his assumption that a justice of the peace would find in favor of the Hispano man in question. True validated Naranjo's uneasiness, adding, "The Mexicans frequently trump up an old dead cow and ask for damages. This is the annual cattle trouble."[85] This incident affirms Santa Clara Pueblo's position that it did not want Hispano cattle grazing on Pueblo lands, even if crops had been harvested, which would have likely been the case by early November. It also affirms True's support of the Pueblo case in light of the probability that a Hispano justice of the peace would find in favor of the rancher. In writing to Crandall and securing True's support,

Naranjo both gauged the federal position and confirmed the appropriateness of driving the cattle from Pueblo land. Crandall was out of town when True wrote to him on Naranjo's behalf; Crandall's substitute, George Haggett, the assistant superintendent of the Santa Fe Indian School, responded instead. Haggett affirmed Crandall's earlier advice to drive the cattle out of Pueblo pastures: "The fact that the Mexican owns a piece of land within the Indian grant does not give him any special right to pasture his stock on Indian lands against their wishes or consent, is the interpretation given by the attorney."[86] In effect, the U.S. government would support land use practices it recognized as valid under its law, not necessarily what had been customary practice under Mexican or Spanish law. Indeed, U.S. government officials had learned over the nineteenth century that so long as they continued to enforce U.S. laws and federal Indian policy, their position would likely prevail.

After the formation of the Santa Clara Reservation, and in the midst of dealing with Hispanos cutting timber on the reservation, Crandall received a letter from Francis E. Leupp, the commissioner of Indian Affairs, requesting a report on non–Santa Clarans living on the reservation. Even though the timing appears to be coincidental, the commissioner's request required Crandall and his officers to change tactics: instead of focusing on conflicts with local authorities, they would work through federal channels to prevent future trespassing, and they would be more discreet in routing illegal timber cutting as they investigated Hispano squatters' land claims on the reservation.[87] This shift effectively cut out any regulatory power the territorial government—with both Anglo and Hispano officials—might attempt to exercise. Crandall dispatched Stacher to conduct the initial investigation into the squatters' claims. Stacher compiled the data through a survey of the land through Santa Clara Cañon and through interviews with Miguel Sandoval, D. Rodriguez, F. D. Coray, Eulogio Rodriguez, Leandro Martinez, Ramon Salazar, and Filigonio Sanchez, the individuals in question who had ranches and houses along the watercourse. Crandall wrote that very little farming was done on the land; rather, the settlements were established to ensure grazing areas for livestock. The interviews revealed that none of the ranchers complied with the parameters of the Homestead Act of 1862, which stipulated that five years of continuous residence and improvements to the land were necessary to stake a valid claim; nor could the ranchers invoke squatter's rights, as each ranch was settled *after* the land in question—or what became the Santa Clara Cañon grant—was removed from the public domain in 1888. Although three of the seven ranchers said they lived on their settlements with their families "most of the time," all but one said neither they nor their families were living on the ranches when Stacher gathered information for the report. Because of the brevity of their responses and the fact that most of the men interviewed were found living in Española and not on the reservation, Crandall believed the answers to the interview questions were at best incomplete and at worst wholly incorrect. He recommended that the commissioner send an inspector from the OIA to further investigate the matter.[88]

Crandall's letters indicate that the squatters on the reservation were the same individuals who were illegally cutting timber. He wrote that the resistance to federal authorities policing the reservation "ha[s] largely come from these squatters, who under the law, have no valid rights whatever, as this land was virtually withdrawn from entry in 1888." This meant that no one should have been permitted to homestead on those lands and receive patents for them. Five days after Crandall reported on the squatters' claims to Santa Claran land, he informed Commissioner Leupp that even though "there have been many protests and much indignation among the settlers of the Rio Grande valley" in the areas around the Pueblo, illegal timber cutting on the reservation had stopped. With that issue resolved, at least for the time being, Crandall awaited the federal government's decision about the squatters on the reservation.[89] Word came on June 18, 1906. The squatters' claims had been rejected and they were to vacate their reservation properties within thirty days.[90] As the thirty-day mark neared, Crandall wrote to Samuel McKibben, the new additional farmer in charge of protecting the reservation: "None of the settlers will be allowed to remove only [*sic*] their personal property from the Santa Clara Reservation. The houses that they have built with the Indian timber cannot be taken off; it belongs to the reservation."[91] Santa Clara had its reservation lands cleared of the Hispanos, and Crandall and his officers performed the rules of U.S. colonial jurisdiction to the letter. The Hispano ranchers lost natural resources that they would not be able to recover.

The order to vacate their ranches must have galled, and perhaps even humiliated, the Hispano squatters. And there was a curious racial component to the land disputes between Hispanos, Santa Clarans, and the U.S. government, which all three groups had to learn. In evicting the Hispano squatters, the federal government, through its agents, asserted a new pecking order. Crandall's November 8, 1905, letter to Commissioner Leupp suggests the squatters were accustomed to using the land for timber and grazing their livestock, possibly grounding their practices in norms of communal land use established under the Spanish and Mexican regimes. The U.S. government's authority to dictate against the squatter's claims established an effective colonial arm over the New Mexico Territory, transforming the Hispano population from a colonizing majority into a colonized minority. This meant that Hispano orientations toward land and access to natural resources had to shift lest the force of the federal government be necessary to protect the boundaries of Indian reservations. Changes in access to grazing and timberland likewise changed the nature of the relationship between Hispanos and Santa Clarans. While the latter could call on federal officers for protection and boundary enforcement, the former could not, and had to face the U.S. legal system on their own. The role of race in citizenship in New Mexico in the nineteenth and early twentieth centuries, moreover, was ambiguous, leaving Hispanos as a sort of buffer between Indians and Anglos. According to legal scholar Laura E. Gomez, Hispanos—particularly elite Hispanos—could legally identify themselves as racially "White." Gomez argues that this boosted the morale of Hispanos as a colonized group only to the extent that they could distinguish themselves from Indigenous groups, making a claim to racial superiority tenuous.[92] And as Dozier has demonstrated, many of the Hispanos at the turn of the twentieth century were actually Indigenous peoples who left their home communities and became vecinos, or Hispanicized neighbors.[93] For Hispanos living adjacent to Santa Clara Pueblo, their political authority was neutralized when the U.S. government forbade non–Santa Clarans from living, cutting timber, or grazing livestock on Pueblo lands. Despite the ready access Santa Clarans had to their lands, any authority they had to determine how it would be used officially dissolved when the federal government created the reservation;

Crandall—the Santa Fe Indian School superintendent—was in charge. Still, Santa Clarans stayed on their community lands with the support of U.S. authorities. This meant that they could ostensibly continue their long-standing sociocultural practices tied to that place with minimal outside interference. Hispanos who had used Santa Claran lands as a common resource were ousted.

In deciphering U.S. policies on how to deal with Hispanos and their own natural resources, Santa Clarans had to learn the limits of their authority over Pueblo lands once the reservation was created in 1905. As the United States government was reviewing the squatter's claims, True wrote to Crandall on behalf of Governor Leandro Tafoya regarding logging and trespassing cattle belonging to Hispanos. Someone within Santa Clara had accused Tafoya of allowing Hispanos to cut timber in Santa Clara Cañon in order to repair a communal irrigation ditch that Santa Clarans and Hispanos shared. Tafoya maintained that he referred the Hispanos to the additional farmer when they asked if they could cut their timber on Pueblo land. The farmer would not allow this, a decision Tafoya praised.[94] What Tafoya was to do about trespassing cattle, though, was a different concern, which he felt merited immediate attention, and Crandall replied to Tafoya's request promptly. Agreeing with Judge Abbott, the attorney for the northern Pueblos, Crandall recommended that Santa Clarans "take up the stock and turn it over to the nearest Justice of the Peace" without holding the stock themselves.[95] Tafoya was not satisfied with this. Responding on his behalf, True wrote:

The Justice is a Mexican of the village of San Pedro who would merely laugh if asked to serve an Indian. He is the man who insisted on trying Mr. Stacker [sic]. It is the custom of Mexican cattle men to impound trespassing stock and hold it for damages. Leandro cannot see any reason why he cannot do the same thing. . . . He asks for an official notice from you and from Judge Abbott stating what steps you advise the Indians to take and the penalty liable to be inflicted on owners of cattle who continue to allow the stock to run on the Indian alfalfa and wheat fields. He wishes to tack these two "Avisos" up at Pollard's store in Espanola [sic] for the benefit of the Mexicans who will not remove their stock on the request of Leandro. He thinks the typewritten notices will have a good effect as it will convince the Mexicans that the Indians are legally advised.[96]

Tafoya was clearly aware of the nature of the contest between U.S. government officials and local Hispano authorities. He knew full well that Santa Claran fields would continue to be trampled and eaten without the express assistance of federal officials; and, he knew that federal authorities were obligated to aid Santa Clara since it was an Indian reservation. The *avisos*, or notices, advertised this—they were a contractual reminder of both property rights against trespass and the federal government's obligation to protect the land it was supposed to manage. The avisos were also a means of preventing conflict over trespassing in the future.

Crandall disagreed with Tafoya; he did not believe the avisos would help matters. In his response to Tafoya's request, Crandall instructed the governor to follow Judge Abbott's original advice and take the stock to the justice of the peace. He further recommended that Tafoya remind the justice of the peace that he was to follow the law and that the Pueblo had been legally advised on what to do. Crandall added that if the justice did not follow the law, Tafoya was to report it immediately to Crandall, who would then request that the territorial governor remove the justice from office.[97] There was no response from Tafoya, nor is there any record of a Hispano response. It is important to keep in mind that the Hispano squatters' land claims at that time were still under review, and Crandall, though he did not provide direct remedy to Tafoya's predicament, was willing to respond to the justice of the peace indirectly with a coercive reminder of his obligation to follow U.S. law. Crandall's hesitance in resolving Tafoya's problem straightforwardly might be read as a breach of his obligation to manage reservation land, or it might be read as taking a first step in removing an obstacle to his and the U.S. government's authority—a Hispano justice of the peace.

Crandall certainly did not hesitate to clarify where the governor's authority ended and his began. In a letter dated February 28, 1906, Crandall stated that Mr. Stacher reported that Governor Tafoya had, in fact, given permission to the Hispanos in question to cut timber on reservation land. It is not clear in Crandall's letter, though, if these logs were to be used in maintaining the ditch. True had asserted in her February 16, 1906, letter that the Hispanos retrieved timber for the ditch north of the Santa Clara Reservation. The incident that Stacher reported, then, would seem to be a different episode. Crandall delineated the lines of authority on the Santa Clara Reservation to Governor Leandro Tafoya:

> You should understand that as governor of the Santa Clara Pueblo you have no jurisdiction over this reservation, and in attempting to exercise an assumed authority, you are liable to get yourself into trouble. Mr. Stacher's authority does not permit him to allow any Mexican or White people to cut timber on the reservation. This of course does not prevent the Indians from cutting all the timber necessary, but they cannot and must not delegate this authority to Mexicans or others. I trust that there will be no misunderstanding or attempt on your part to assume an authority over the reservation which you do not possess.[98]

In his letter, Crandall does not doubt Stacher's report, and Crandall asserts his own position as the primary authority over Santa Clara land, ignoring the centuries-long role of the governor in liaising with outsiders and managing land and irrigation ditches. Crandall's letter also conveys that Santa Clarans, because they were on a reservation, were physically separate from Hispanos and Anglos. While this confirms the Pueblo's boundaries, it likewise establishes a type of ethnic quarantine. Crandall's letter makes plain his position that he believed he knew what was best for Santa Clarans and for Governor Tafoya. If Tafoya overstepped the bounds of his newly limited authority, he would be in trouble with neighboring Hispanos and with Crandall. Finally, Crandall's response indicates that Santa Clara and its Hispano neighbors would have to adjust whatever long-standing arrangements they had had regarding communal land. If all who used the ditch were still expected to contribute to its maintenance, ways of obtaining materials would have to change. That is, if Hispanos were to continue to use irrigation channels whether or not they lived on reservation land, they would have to travel some distance to obtain logs to fulfill their obligatory contribution to ongoing ditch repair. Santa Clarans, though, could harvest more timber than they needed.

Crandall's gatekeeping role after Santa Clara Pueblo became a reservation was an extension of his role as the acting agent of the Northern Pueblos District and superintendent of the Santa Fe Indian School. From a Santa Claran perspective, it might well have looked like Crandall was usurping authority that had been recognized for centuries. Or it might have been a test to determine the limits of Crandall's willingness to protect Santa Claran resources and boundaries. From a Hispano perspective, Crandall flouted long-standing customs and enforced a new legal order over one that had worked well previously, costing Hispano ranchers valuable resources, land, and status. For Anglos within the OIA, Crandall's actions fulfilled expectations, in spite of resistance lodged by Hispanos or Crandall's misreadings of Santa Claran intent. From each perspective, though, shifting legal authority meant related alterations in each party's relationship to the place of Santa Clara.

SANTA CLARA RESERVATION AND THE
PROSPECT OF PAJARITO NATIONAL PARK

The creation of the Santa Clara Reservation in 1905 occurred in the midst of a movement toward the creation of a network of public national parks, forests, and monuments in the United States. President Theodore Roosevelt enthusiastically supported this movement, facilitating the creation of 5 national parks, 150 national forests, 3 national monuments, 22 American Antiquities reserves, 4 big-game reserves, and 51 bird reserves.[99] In the spirit of preserving and conserving places from utter destruction as populations in the American West grew, Roosevelt, among others, argued that setting aside lands for wildlife and forests as well as public enjoyment and learning was central to the U.S.'s national interests.[100] In New Mexico, particularly in the areas around Pueblo Indian villages along the northern Rio Grande, ancient cliff dwellings became the focus of an effort to create Pajarito National Park. Among these sites were the Puyé cliff dwellings west of Santa Clara Pueblo on the Santa Clara Cañon grant, the Otowi and Rito de los Frijoles cliff dwellings, and the Sankawi ruins near present-day Los Alamos. Attempts to establish the park, however, changed course with political positions. Santa Clarans steadfastly maintained that the Puyé cliffs were the home of their ancestors and their burial grounds. They did not want the cliff dwellings made into a public space, as it would

Ruins of cliff dwellings, Puyé, New Mexico, ca. 1905–1907. Photograph by Edgar L. Hewett. Courtesy of the Palace of the Governors Photo Archives (NMHM/DCA), #42077.

put the site at risk of vandalism. Scholars like anthropologist and archeologist Edgar Lee Hewett shared the Santa Clarans' trepidations. And while researchers were primarily interested in creating national parks to preserve historic and archeological sites in the first years of the twentieth century, others saw such public parks as a means to garner tourist money. Beginning in 1899, advocates for the creation of Pajarito National Park had been successful in removing the proposed park area from the public domain. At this time, too, Santa Clarans were attempting to reaffirm their claim to the Santa Clara Cañon grant west of the Pueblo. For his part, Crandall entered into the debate on the side of the Santa Clarans, working to create a reservation before a national park proposal made it through Congress.

Protecting the land from vandals was the central concern of anthropologists who attempted to create a national park dedicated to the cliff dwellings on the Santa Clara Cañon grant and the surrounding areas. The proposed national park was named after a geologic feature of the area—the Pajarito Plateau on the west side of the Rio Grande Rift—and the main archeological feature of the area—cliffs into which ancient

peoples had carved their houses out of the volcanic tuff. In his brief history of efforts to create the park, historian Thomas Altherr argues that Hewett, who began as the president of the New Mexico Normal School in Las Vegas and later founded the Museum of New Mexico in Santa Fe after earning his doctorate in anthropology, and Representative John F. Lacey from Iowa were instrumental in early efforts to create the park. In 1899, Lacey, who was the chairman of the House Public Lands Committee, prompted the General Land Office (GLO) in New Mexico to conduct surveys of the region. The following year, the GLO withdrew the surveyed land from the public domain, effectively closing it off from settlement under the Homestead Act of 1862. In addition, the office began to examine preliminary archeological and anthropological studies of the area that had already been conducted by the likes of Adolph Bandelier, Charles Lummis, and Hewett. The case for creating Pajarito National Park on the grounds of archeological preservation seemed clear, especially if it would protect the ruins from vandals. But Hewett critiqued the original proposal on grounds that it "made no provision for artifacts from the ruins." Lacey revised the bill, and during 1902 and 1903, several groups criticized the boundaries of the proposed park on grounds that it might encroach on valuable grazing lands.[101]

Crandall, who was well versed in non-Native arguments in favor of grazing land, countered with another concern: the proposed park's encroachment on the Santa Clara Pueblo's lands. The Puyé cliff dwellings, one of the several featured groups of apartment-style houses carved into rock faces that figured in Lacey's proposal, lay within the bounds of the Santa Clara Cañon grant. As in his dealings with Hispanos who squatted or grazed their stock on Pueblo land, Crandall's objective in challenging the park's boundaries was to keep Santa Claran land grants intact for the Pueblo's use and to keep non–Santa Clarans out. Crandall believed the most effective way to do this was to create a reservation. When Crandall took up this charge in January 1903, he discovered that much of the land in question, particularly within the Santa Clara Cañon grant, was the same land on which the Puyé cliff dwellings sat and that had been removed from the public domain in order to create a national park. He wrote to William A. Jones, the commissioner of Indian Affairs, on January 3, 1903, requesting immediate support in pushing through the creation of a Santa Clara reservation that would include both the original land grant around the village and the secondary grant of Santa Clara Cañon. Crandall argued that Santa Clarans needed the Santa Clara Cañon land for timber and that they were the only ones who used the land anyway.[102] Several weeks later, after further investigation into the competing cases for the reservation and the national park, Crandall wrote to True about the status of the land, explaining that he had determined after talking to the commissioner of the General Land Office that the only way to restore the land to the public domain and thereby propose it as part of the Santa Clara Reservation was for Lacey's national park bill to fail in Congress. He was committed to securing the land for Santa Clara use, even if it required an alternate plan:

> In case this Bill becomes law, and the Park is actually created, . . . the management and custody still remains in the hands of the Secretary of the Interior. . . . In this event, the concession in the way of pasturing, farming, cutting of timber, etc. can be secured to the Santa Clara Indians. . . . In case the pending Bill before Congress fails to become law, the land then becomes subject to entry or other disposal, when I shall immediately renew my application to have the reservation created.[103]

Crandall pointed out that the U.S. government would have title to the land regardless of whether it was an Indian reservation or a national park. This, he assumed, allowed the secretary of the interior discretion in how the land would actually be managed and used.

Although Crandall was ready with an alternate plan, he nevertheless continued to push for the creation of the Santa Clara Reservation instead of a national park. In April 1903, he reminded the commissioner of Indian Affairs of his earlier recommendations to convert the land in question to a reservation.[104] The following month Crandall changed tactics—rather than prepare for the failure of Lacey's bill, he made a two-pronged moral argument in favor of the reservation. First, he argued that the Santa Clara Indians had a vested interest in the land and, at the very least, should be consulted about how their grants were to be used. Crandall wrote, "The Cliff Dwellings could and would be protected. It is the burial ground of the ancestors of the present Indians, and why are they to be left out in the consideration of the question?" Second, he built on the claim that the Santa Clarans should be consulted: "The old cliff dwellings would be safer in the hands of the Pueblo Indians, and under such restrictions as your Office might see fit to throw around these ancient ruins, than they would be in a National Park, where vandals are wont and will continue to despoil the old Pueblo graves in the Cliffs of their burial urns, etc."[105] In Crandall's view, not only did the U.S. government have an ethical obligation to discuss the future of the land with Santa Clarans, the Santa Clarans, in conjunction with the Indian Office, could better keep destructive tourists and vandals away from the cliff dwellings than the Park Service. Preservation of the ruins for Crandall meant keeping them from those who had no living or historical connection to them. He was confident that a comprehensive investigation of the land in question would resolve the issue for those interested in the cliff dwellings.

By mid-1903, disagreement between Santa Clarans (communicated via the Indian Office), anthropologists, the Bureau of Forestry, local stockmen, and those pushing for tourism in New Mexico peaked, and Special Agent Stephen J. Holsinger of the GLO was sent to investigate the competing claims to the proposed Pajarito park land.[106] By the end of December, Holsinger had not yet made his survey of the area, and Crandall began a one-man letter-writing campaign beyond the OIA.

He informed Commissioner Jones about the letters he had sent to Representatives Lacey and Bernard Rodey, the territorial delegate in Congress, arguing for Santa Claran land rights in the cañon. Crandall felt the mood in New Mexico was against Indians in general, writing on Christmas Day to Commissioner Jones:

> The people of New Mex. are not in sympathy with the Indian and think that even now the Indian has too much land; they would often be glad to see the Indian become extinct and do not hesitate to say so. Last winter in the Council, the upper branch of the Territorial Legislature, a prominent local statesman remarked that he would vote for a Bill that would assemble all the Indians of New Mex. into a 40-acre lot, give them all the whiskey and guns they wanted, and that the Indians would do the rest.[107]

Against a backdrop of such overt animosity toward Indians, Crandall saw himself as a guardian of their interests. Creating a reservation for the Santa Clarans would both secure the land for the Pueblo's use and make it illegal for outsiders to use reservation land for tourism, archeological research, grazing, and logging without permission from the OIA. Crandall's position can be read as protecting Santa Clarans' most basic need—their lives.

The following day, Crandall wrote to True apprising her of the situation and his efforts to safeguard Santa Claran land rights and create a reservation for the Pueblo. Crandall noted that he had just received word from Holsinger about his imminent arrival in Santa Fe close to the New Year. Crandall further relayed that Representative Lacey did not believe the proposed Pajarito National Park would impinge on the Santa Clara Cañon grant as the boundaries of the park area had already been significantly trimmed. Despite Lacey's assurances, Crandall expressed doubt about the revised proposal, writing, "It is barely possible that the new park does not include Santa Clara Canon [*sic*],—still I believe it does." He also doubted the commissioner's willingness to advocate on behalf of the Santa Clarans: "[I] do not believe the Commissioner cares to interfere in Congressional legislation." Crandall closed by asking True to inform the governor and Pueblo *prinicpales,* or advisory council, of his efforts and Holsinger's upcoming survey; Crandall pinned his hopes for the reservation on Holsinger's inspection and subsequent report.[108] True responded three days later that the Santa Claran leadership appreciated Crandall's interest.[109]

Holsinger's investigation affirmed Crandall's position that the disputed land should become part of a reservation for Santa Clara Pueblo. In his January 7, 1904, report to Commissioner Jones, Crandall detailed Holsinger's examination of the geographic boundaries in question. Curiously, Crandall changed his position about protecting the Puyé cliff dwellings from non–Santa Clarans, noting that he and Holsinger agreed that they could negotiate the boundaries of the proposed national park with Representative Lacey since it was such a small strip of land—only about a mile wide. Crandall also indirectly reiterated his recommendation that the federal government work on behalf of the Santa Clarans since the territorial government, he believed, would attempt to free up the land outlined for the proposed park for settlement and grazing, working against both the Indians and park supporters.[110]

In advocating for Santa Claran rights and land, Crandall bared his paternalism. In discussing the Court of Private Land Claims' rejection of the Santa Clara Cañon grant, he commented, "These Indians, who are much like children, can't understand why this land does not now belong to them; they say they bought it and paid for it, which is true, but as I have stated, the courts did not approve their claim." In describing Santa Clarans as children Crandall implied that they did not have the capacity to understand the processes and decisions of the courts or of policies that were at odds with one another. On the one hand, the Treaty of Guadalupe Hidalgo guaranteed the recognition and protection of legitimate—and provable—land grants; on the other hand, Indians were subject to land policies that were grounded in double standards and did not apply to non-Native peoples. Crandall's paternalism, moreover, reaffirmed his own role as the Santa Claran advisor and protector, which in turn underscored a dependent relationship. Over the course of 1904, though, the push for Pajarito National Park coincided with a delinquent tax case, which would theoretically determine whether or not Pueblo Indians were full citizens of the New Mexico Territory and the United States, or whether they were Indigenous wards of the U.S. government.[111] The outcome of the New Mexico Supreme Court's decision compelled Crandall to redouble his efforts to create a reservation for Santa Clara Pueblo that included both the original land grant and the Santa Clara Cañon grant.

By the time Lacey proposed a revised bill for the national park in Congress in 1905—with the endorsement of Hewett and the writers of the *New Mexican* newspaper—President Theodore Roosevelt had created the Santa Clara Reservation, encompassing both land grants, by executive order. In September of that year, Hewett wrote to Crandall about his intentions to introduce yet another bill for the park. Like the previous bill, its boundaries included the woodlands in Santa Clara Cañon. Crandall rebuffed the proposal, reasserting his position in favor of Santa Clarans' right to use the land.[112] Once the bill was in the House of Representatives in 1906, Crandall again assured Santa Clara governor Leandro Tafoya of his intention to protect the Pueblo's right to the exclusive use of the land.[113] In so doing, Crandall protected land directly under his control and management—the Santa Clara Reservation. And Hewett and Lacey's 1906 attempt to secure a national park failed. Instead, Lacey secured congressional support for the Antiquities Act of 1906, which protected the artifacts that had so concerned Hewett in previous drafts of the Pajarito National Park bill. According to Altherr, Hewett and other anthropologists and archeologists almost immediately lost interest in the national park, simply resuming their scholarly studies of the area. The lucrative potential of tourism and educational trips to bring people and dollars to New Mexico, however, continued to draw supporters, and in 1916, portions of the original Pajarito National Park proposal, including the Otowi, Sankawi, and Rito de los Frijoles cliff dwellings south of Santa Clara Pueblo near Los Alamos, became Bandelier National Monument.[114]

CONCLUSION

The first decade of the twentieth century in the Rio Grande valley marked a period of a crystallized relearning of place for Santa Clarans, Hispanos, and Anglos that called on and challenged the accumulated and remembered experiences of each group over time and space. For Santa Clarans, maintaining the integrity of their landholdings was paramount, and they acted opportunistically to co-opt the colonial and legal apparatus called federal Indian law to ensure the continued viability of their lands and the Pueblo's associated agricultural and ceremonial practices. This meant ceding title to their lands to the U.S. government in order to preserve those lands—an irony in an era of federal Indian policy focused on individual land ownership. The creation of the reservation, however, ensured that Santa Clarans would remain on their ancestral homelands and compelled the federal government to protect the boundaries of Santa Clara from encroaching Anglos and Hispanos. It also disrupted centuries-long practices of common grazing, timber, and watering lands between the Santa Clarans and their Hispano neighbors.

As government agents stepped into the disputes, they found themselves confronting an ethnically divided legal system in New Mexico that held remnants of Spanish and Mexican practices in tension with U.S. law. Hispanos who grazed and farmed in Santa Clara Cañon called on the Hispano echelons of the New Mexican legal system to protect both their lands and their long-standing ranching practices. Crandall, as the OIA official advocating for Pueblo Indians, though, did all he could to thwart Hispano efforts, imposing and reinforcing tenets of federal Indian law. This resulted in the abandonment of several Hispanos ranches in the Santa Clara Cañon. Hispanos, who had lived and worked in the Rio Grande valley since the late seventeenth and early eighteenth centuries, found themselves confronted and sometimes displaced.

For Anglos living in the area, land was the basis of educational and economic opportunity—and in Crandall's case, professional advancement. The cliff dwellings west and south of Santa Clara lured archeologists, who adamantly argued for their preservation on the basis of educational value. Santa Clarans likewise wanted the Puyé cliff dwellings in Santa Clara Cañon to be preserved, but they did not want outsiders to have access to them because the threat of vandalism was simply too great. Other New Mexicans saw the cliff dwellings and the possibility of Pajarito National Park as a means for economic development that would advance the cause of New Mexican statehood. And Crandall mediated it all, lobbying initially for Santa Claran control over the Puyé cliff dwellings, and then conceding that limiting the boundaries of the proposed park was protection enough. Crandall made this decision on his own, arguing in subsequent letters to the commissioner of Indian

Affairs that he acted as a guardian for the Pueblo, comparing Santa Clarans to children, and taking up the fight with anyone who attempted to exceed the parameters of what he deemed appropriate, including Edgar Hewett and Representative Lacey. From each group's orientation, land was the physical site of learning, shifting colonial relationships, legal expectations, and geographic arrangements such that the land itself became a participant in the process.

CHAPTER TWO

Disease; or, The Initiation of
Clara D. True

INTRODUCTION

Within half a year of her arrival at Santa Clara Pueblo, Clara D. True witnessed and was called to account for a diphtheria outbreak among the children of the Pueblo. As the Office of Indian Affairs (OIA) day school teacher—and thus government representative—living in the community, True was responsible for carrying out federal Indian policy. In this case, she was to establish a quarantine, treat the infected children, and report on the course of the disease throughout the community. To do this competently, True had to learn the Pueblo's sociopolitical structure and build relationships with the individuals and groups who lived there in order to nurse the sick and prevent the spread of diphtheria as well as to set the relational cornerstone of her position as day school teacher and U.S. government representative. The diphtheria outbreak of 1903 highlights several interwoven threads of learning that structure a loose fabric of Clara True's education at Santa Clara Pueblo. Most significantly, the diphtheria outbreak at Santa Clara was a liminal event; it changed True and her relationships not only with Santa Clarans but also with C. J. Crandall, her supervisor who was also the superintendent of the Santa Fe Indian School and acting agent for the Northern Pueblos District. In fact, the alliance that True formed with one political faction at Santa Clara endured throughout her tenure as day school teacher and well after her service in the OIA ended.[1]

What happened when True tried to implement federal Indian policy during the diphtheria outbreak of 1903, and what did she learn in the process? How did this event define and shape her relationship with Native communities in the northern Rio Grande valley? How did True and the Santa Clarans adapt federal Indian policy to suit their needs and circumstances during the outbreak? To what extent did True exceed her role as the OIA day school teacher in navigating both the biomedical crisis at hand and the sociocultural terrain at Santa Clara Pueblo?

Bottle of diphtheria antitoxin,
produced by the Hygienic
Laboratory and dated May 8,
1895. Courtesy of the National
Library of Medicine.

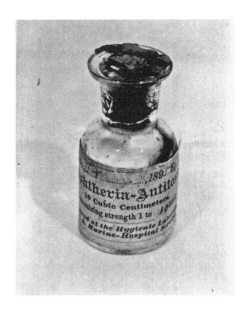

To answer these questions, it is necessary to look at a variety of sources that cast light on the context in which True lived and worked as well as at sources that communicate the experiences that shaped True's biomedical and sociocultural understanding of the diphtheria outbreak of 1903 at Santa Clara. Her written account of events and circumstances throughout the episode, coupled with that of Dr. Holterman, the attending physician, are cataloged in her correspondence with the OIA superintendent's office in Santa Fe. But their correspondence is more than a mere cataloging of what happened because it emphasizes True's and Holterman's experiences and perceptions, conveying their expectations about how people should act in the presence of disease and how they were making sense of the sociopolitical structure and tensions within the Pueblo.

During the diphtheria epidemic at Santa Clara Pueblo in January and February 1903, a number of tensions converged. Not only did True have to negotiate with parents over the treatment of sick children and try to convince people to remain at the Pueblo to contain the disease, she also had to negotiate with officials in Santa Fe for support in enforcing the quarantine. Lines of authority within Santa Clara became blurred as factional conflict came to the surface over how to deal with the disease. Outside of the Pueblo, Crandall felt that True's reports of the outbreak were exaggerated and ultimately challenged his authority as her supervisor and acting Indian agent for the Northern Pueblos District. The diphtheria epidemic also illuminated the fact that the U.S. government did not have a comprehensive health care policy for American Indians. As the actions of True and the Santa Clarans illustrate, policy was, in effect, made on the ground according to circumstance.

DIPHTHERIA HITS SANTA CLARA PUEBLO

On September 5, 1902, just weeks after she arrived at Santa Clara Pueblo to assume her post as day school teacher, True wrote to Superintendent Crandall warning him not to take any students from Santa Clara into the Santa Fe Indian School because the Santa Claran children had been exposed to diphtheria. Crandall responded that same day, telling True to close the day school and contact him immediately if any cases developed at Santa Clara.[2] Three months later, on December 8, 1902, Crandall wrote to True: "Diphtheria has broken out at the San Ildefonso Pueblo, and under no circumstances should any Indian from your Pueblo be allowed to visit there, nor should any Indian from the San Ildefonso Pueblo be allowed to enter Santa Clara. This is important. Only by rigid quarantine can the disease be kept from spreading to other Pueblos."[3]

But True could not maintain a quarantine. With San Ildefonso just six miles south of Santa Clara, True had neither the muscle nor the resources—not to mention Santa Claran authority—to prevent travel between the two Pueblos. Several days before Christmas—less than a month after the initial appearance of the disease at San Ildefonso—she wrote to Crandall noting that even the Santa Clara governor's support of the quarantine was not enough to keep people from San Ildefonso from passing through Santa Clara. By mid-January, Santa Clara experienced a diphtheria outbreak of its own.

Just five months into her tenure at the Santa Clara day school, True found herself in the middle of a health crisis. True and Crandall had feared diphtheria would spread from Pueblo to Pueblo and attempted to take measures to prevent this. Establishing a quarantine around Santa Clara proved impossible, though, and the Pueblo had to contend with a biomedical menace that preyed on its children. But True also found that she had quite literally walked into a community that was in the midst of redefining its sociocultural health. A decade's-old political schism within the Pueblo that disrupted its system of shared governance, as we will see, had begun to play out in the treatment of sick children. True had to quickly learn about the structural questions of authority within the Pueblo as she attempted to treat sick children and rein in the reach of diphtheria bacillus.

True reported the first case of diphtheria at Santa Clara while Crandall happened to be away in Washington, D.C. Francis McCormick, who served as supervisor during Crandall's absence, responded to True on January 13, 1903, indicating that she should close the school and impose a "rigid quarantine" to prevent the spread of the disease. McCormick also notified Mary Dissette and Dr. Holterman, the head teacher and the itinerant physician in the Northern Pueblos District, of the diphtheria case at Santa Clara and the quarantine that True was to impose. In a separate letter that same day, McCormick informed True of what the government would and would not pay for in efforts to eradicate the disease at Santa Clara. He specified that True could count on medicine, antitoxin, and disinfecting chemicals such as formaldehyde, but that the Office of Indian Affairs would not pay compensation for bedding, clothing, and food that had been destroyed to contain the disease, nor would the OIA pay Indians and neighboring Hispanos to clean their quarters.[4] True and whomever she could persuade to cooperate with her in the quarantine were on their own. She was not impressed. She responded to McCormick:

> I beg to say that there will be no expense to the Government for the suppression of contagion, except for disinfectants and antitoxin. I might add that I am daily spending my own money and hourly risking my life in work before me, and it is small encouragement to hear at length "what the Government will not do." I did not, do not, and shall not expect any aid from the Gov't except in supplies herein requested, so there need be no apprehension of outlay at anybody's expense except my own.[5]

McCormick did not acknowledge True's palpable frustration and anger in his subsequent letters. Several days later he informed her that the territorial government of New Mexico did not have the jurisdiction to call out law enforcement officials to compel a quarantine. Instead, McCormick threatened to hold Santa Clara governor Diego Naranjo personally responsible if he did not facilitate the doctor's medical treatment of sick children and enforce the quarantine.[6] McCormick's outlay of payable expenses and his promise to hold the governor liable underscore his assumption that the rules of government jurisdiction mattered in disease treatment and that the Pueblo governor was the primary center of authority within the community. Both of these assumptions proved specious, and McCormick's bid to control the movement of Santa Clarans through the governor failed within a few days.

How was True supposed to establish and enforce a quarantine by herself, especially among people she had known only for four or five months? Clearly, her authority at the Pueblo was limited. According to True, the governor did not make any attempt that she could see to help her enforce the quarantine once diphtheria hit Santa Clara. Whether the governor earnestly supported the quarantine is unclear and might not have really mattered. The governor, after all, was the primary liaison with outsiders, not the ultimate source of authority within the Pueblo. Neither McCormick, True, nor Crandall seemed to understand this at the time. But if the governor's authority was limited, True's authority at Santa Clara might well have been nonexistent. On the same day he ordered True to enforce a rigid quarantine, McCormick attempted to sidestep and delegitimize Pueblo authority altogether when he consulted Judge Abbott, the attorney for the Pueblos, to see if the New Mexico Territorial Board of Health had jurisdiction over the Pueblos. As True put it, "Stripped of a few legal phrases, it is virtually an admission of inability to compel compliance with the doctor's orders."[7]

True's frustration extended from McCormick's hedging to her impotence in dealing with parents and guardians who resisted treatment against diphtheria and vaccination for other diseases. Pueblo members were concerned about the outbreak and met to discuss what course of action should follow. On January 20, 1903, True met a grandmother who fiercely protected the children under her care against the governor.

> Both parties held meetings last night to decide upon measures in case heroic efforts are necessitated by further opposition. I think I have the support of all of the good Indians. The old hag in question owes

allegiance to nobody and she is the mother in law of all the head men apparently. The children she is guarding are orphans.

The old Amazon sent the Governor out of her house yesterday in-stante [*sic*], almost in blue flames. All I could see of his retreat was a striped blanket getting over the ground double quick.

In a previous trouble the same old woman and her household suc-cessfully resisted vaccination when every other family submitted. This victory over small pox [*sic*]—which she had lightly—makes her defiant now.[8]

Seen through True's eyes, the old woman defied the seat of authority—male authority—making her suspect. That True identified the woman in question as related to the male leadership within the Pueblo suggests that grandmother was a member of the Summer People, the party that had officially governed the Pueblo since its political split in 1894. This affiliation would have allowed her to request the Santa Claran medicine societies to treat each of the children under her care. It is not clear from True's and Holterman's letters to Crandall and McCormick that the old woman, in fact, did this, and True might well have not been privy to such information. What seemed to gall True was that a woman took such an overt, strong position against the governor. Perhaps the woman could act in such a way because of her familial relationships with mem-bers of the Santa Claran leadership, or perhaps it was because she held another type of esteemed position within the Pueblo. Regardless, the community as a whole wanted a unified course of action in treating the sick children at Santa Clara, in spite of the internal political struggle be-tween the Summer People and Winter "Progressives." The history and nature of this political struggle was not yet clear to True. In multiple instances, she allied with members of the Winter "Progressives." And during the diphtheria outbreak of 1903 True did not appear to recog-nize that such an alliance might prevent her from effectively interacting with members of the Summer party in the future. By the end of January 1903, she found herself adjusting to Pueblo needs.

On January 26, 1903, True appears to have modified her ideas of what a reasonable quarantine would look like. In a letter to Crandall she wrote,

A number of Indians from Santa Clara went to San Ildefonso. Indians from Pueblos north of here went, taking in Santa Clara en route both ways. It seems impossible to enforce *adequate* measures though we keep up something that passes for quarantine. The chief difficulty is that food is very scarce now and the people cannot be shut off from going to Espanola [*sic*] to trade pottery, work, and beg their daily apology for food. The infected district is under as rigid quarantine as I can get enforced.[9]

What passed for quarantine? True left this unclear, but she acknowledged that whatever they did was not adequate to prevent the spread of the disease. What is most curious in this passage is True's subversion of Crandall's, McCormick's, and, by extension, the Indian Office's authority. Not only did she recognize the Santa Clarans' rejection of the quarantine, she tacitly supported it. What good is a quarantine if people are going to starve to death? In fact, by arguing that the Santa Clarans should be able to go to Española to earn money for food, True might have positioned herself as an ally and advocate for the community. At the same time, by admitting her inability to enforce a strict quarantine and by displacing some of the blame onto the Santa Clara and San Ildefonso Indians, she implicitly called for Crandall's help in dealing with diphtheria at the Pueblo. She could only work with what she knew, and at this point in her tenure at Santa Clara, True did not appear to understand the socioreligious and political organization of the Pueblo nor how to navigate the organization to understand how families were caring for their children and how she might help.[10]

SANTA CLARA SOCIETY

In the 1930s and 1940s, anthropologists Barbara Aitken and Elsie Clews Parsons castigated scholars and others who regarded American Indians as uniformly similar and warned academicians against the silo effect of narrowing the disciplinary lens of inquiry. Aitken called attention to the Euro-American proclivity to assume homogeneity across North American Indigenous groups: "It is a curious fact that English students of religion, who know how the course of European history has been changed by the clash of two diverse religious temperaments, and have lately seen the religious part of their own country struggling with the problem of reconciling these diverse temperaments, are yet willing to believe that religious man outside of Europe can be treated as a unity."[11] Parsons argued that ethnologists and archeologists effectively wore blinders, making them largely ignorant of one another's work, even if their studies were on similar topics. Without intellectual and methodological cross-pollination, scholars made and would continue to make mistakes in cultural interpretation, chronology, social structures, place, and movement. These errors, together with the fallacy of homogeneity, were mistakes an OIA day teacher could not afford to make. If the teacher were to live and work amiably within American Indian communities—and many OIA teachers worked in several—she had to acknowledge the diversity among Native communities and attempt to understand each community's sociocultural and historical worlds. If she did not, day school enrollments would decline. Diversity in Native America was a matter of fact.[12]

Even within small geographies, such as the northern Rio Grande valley of New Mexico, sociopolitical, religious, and linguistic differences characterized Pueblo Indian communities. According to anthropologists Edward P. Dozier, Barbara Aitken, Alfonso Ortiz, Jean Allard Jeançon, and W. W. Hill, Santa Clara's religious and political structures, like those of other Tewa Pueblos, were holistically conceived through a dual leadership, or moiety, system comprised of two groups: the Summer People and the Winter People. As demonstrated in chapter 1, the Summer People and the Winter People served different religious, social, and political roles that were derived from the Tewa emergence in what is now southern Colorado and their journey southward to their present location along the northern Rio Grande. The power-sharing arrangement between the Summer and Winter parties developed over centuries, if not millennia, with the Summer cacique, or chief, governing from the vernal to the autumnal equinox and the Winter cacique governing from the autumnal to the vernal equinox. Each member of Santa Clara Pueblo was affiliated with the Summer or Winter People.[13]

Participation in socioreligious life began early for Pueblo children. Spanning moiety groups, strictly enforced community values, such as conformity, cooperation, respect for elders, politeness, industry, and modesty, permeated and buttressed the dual, shared system of Pueblo governance. When they were old enough to begin learning specific group roles within the community, usually between the ages of six and ten, each young member of the Pueblo joined the Summer or Winter People.[14] There is some ambiguity among anthropologists as to how it was determined which moiety children would join. Jeançon's 1908 field notes from Santa Clara suggest that children followed their mother because "descent was traced through the mother's line."[15] In the 1960s and 1970s, however, Dozier wrote that although there were no hard-and-fast rules regulating which moiety children would join, they most often became members of their father's moiety. But a child could be promised to the other group if he or she was cured of an illness by one of the moiety's members, or a child could be pledged to the other moiety simply to balance the numerical distribution between the two groups.[16] The anthropological literature suggests that the careful balance of moiety responsibilities and power appears to have been maintained at Santa Clara until 1894, when a political rupture occurred, and the Summer People assumed power until the Santa Clara constitution was enacted in 1936.

In order to understand this fracture, an overview of the structure of the socioreligious and political offices of the Pueblo and the relationship between them is necessary. Both before and after the 1894 political break, the Summer and Winter caciques served as the socioreligious and political heads of their respective moiety groups. Specialized religious societies, including the Warrior Association, the Tewa Bear Medicine Society, the Tewa Ké Medicine Society, the Cold Clowns, the Warm Clowns, the Hunt Association, and the Women's Scalp Society also thrived and had members from both the Summer and Winter Peoples. Members of these societies and associations had expert knowledge that they protected and used to promote the well-being of the Pueblo as a whole as well as enforce customs and the ruling cacique's decisions.[17] The secular, political offices came with the Spanish after their reentry into the territory in the 1690s. The governor, whom True initially saw as the primary leader and authority figure at Santa Clara Pueblo, was, in fact, selected annually and alternately by the Summer and Winter caciques. Not only did the governor carry out the directives of the cacique in charge, he was also the primary liaison with outsiders and the de facto head of the other secular, political offices. At the turn of the twentieth century, diplomatic abilities and being conversant in Tewa, Spanish, and English were necessary for the position. As illustrated in chapter 1, "Land," the governor was also responsible for maintaining the community's irrigation ditches, resolving land disputes among members of the Pueblo, allocating shares of grazing and timber land for outsiders, and ensuring that trespassers were dealt with appropriately. (The latter two duties became the responsibility of the superintendent of the Santa Fe Indian School when Santa Clara became a reservation in 1905.) To aid the governor in carrying out his duties were a lieutenant governor, a sheriff, and ditch bosses (mayordomos). After their terms in office, each governor and lieutenant governor became a principale, or a member of a leadership advisory board, which presumably worked closely with the caciques and other political officers.[18]

The major rift in the socioreligious and political structures of the Pueblo came in 1894 when the Summer People secured the exclusive right to appoint individuals to Spanish offices.[19] When the caciques alternately appointed men to Spanish political offices from year to year, they gave each new officer a metal-topped cane that the Spanish had given to the Pueblo in the seventeenth century. This tradition continued into the U.S. regime when President Abraham Lincoln gave similar canes to the Pueblo.[20] Although the details of the split are vague in the literature, it is clear that the Summer People retained the power to appoint the governor annually by securing and keeping the canes. Hill surmises that this may have been a reaction to a group of individuals who openly defied the Summer chief's orders. He writes that as Anglos moved into the territory in the late nineteenth century and land became scarce, dissenters could not simply relocate and form a new Pueblo as had been done in the past. Instead, dissenters remained in the Pueblo and tensions escalated. In a society that relied on conformity in customary practices and adherence to cacique decisions, dissent was unacceptable. By 1894, the Summer People, "with the connivance of the United States government," took the canes and thus got hold of the authority to appoint the governor every year. Hill adds that a few individuals from the Winter People might have joined the Summer faction, but that no Summer People joined the group who resisted.[21] The Summer

People held on to the authority to appoint men to Spanish political offices until 1936, when the Santa Clara constitution was enacted.[22]

The group that split off further, the "Winter Progressives," or simply the "Progressives" according to True and Crandall, refused to participate in traditional religious ceremonies and argued for the separation of political powers. This rift meant, too, that only Summer People would be members of the medicine associations. The reorganization of medicine societies effectively left the health care of Winter People who had separated from the greater Pueblo ceremonial life in the hands of outsiders such as the OIA. Both True and Crandall register the Winter Progressives' agreement with U.S. government efforts to modernize the Pueblo through biomedical treatment and disease prevention as well as through formal schooling in their letters. By the time True arrived at Santa Clara in the fall of 1902, Francisco Naranjo appears to have been the primary leader of the Progressives, joined by Pedro Cajete, José Domingo Gutierrez, and Vidal Gutierrez, among others.[23]

AFFLICTIONS AND MEDICINE AMONG THE TEWA AND IN THE INDIAN OFFICE

Beliefs and practices about health, medicine, and illness differed between Pueblo Indian communities and the Office of Indian Affairs. For the Tewa, "medicine" invoked a complex, protected body of knowledge about the network of relationships between people and the world around them as well as specific powers and unknowns that individual humans, plants, and animals possessed.[24] "Medicine" for the Tewa, in other words, had both sociocultural and biomedical manifestations and implications. For Indian Office personnel, "medicine" was simply a biomedical treatment for physical illness. The differences in Tewa and OIA understandings of medicine, disease, and health laid the groundwork for points of conflict and cooperation in the actions of and interactions between Santa Clara Indians and OIA personnel during the 1903 diphtheria outbreak. Medical treatment sponsored and conducted by the Indian Office simultaneously became an expression of the U.S. government's colonial reach, a necessary means for the treatment and prevention of illness, and a target of Native resistance.

Prior to the passage of the Snyder Act of 1921 (Public Law 109-224), which legislated a systematic federal approach to health care and schooling, the U.S. government intermittently appropriated funding for Indian health and education services. In addition to treaties with individual tribes, the federal government also set out a series of provisions in the antebellum period to protect "against the further decline and final extinction of the Indian tribes" along the edges of U.S. settlement.[25] This would in turn protect U.S. settlers and military personnel from diseases such as smallpox.[26] In her brief institutional history of the Indian Health Services agency, Ruth M. Raup traced the precedent for federally sponsored health care for American Indian tribes to the 1819 *Civilization Fund Act*, through which Congress appropriated $10,000 annually for schooling, agricultural training, and other activities that accorded with "the habits and arts of [Euro-American] civilization."[27] Until 1871, when the U.S. government stopped making treaties with individual tribes, provisions for schooling and health services were frequent elements of such treaties. As blanket policies soon after became the norm, the Office of Indian Affairs began centralizing its efforts with the creation of the Division of Education and Medicine.[28] By 1874, about half of the Indian agencies in the United States had a physician, but that did not come close to meeting the needs of American Indians, in spite of the push for the creation of hospitals attached to Indian schools.[29] Raup suggests that low physician salaries explain part of the lag; but, if we consider Meriam et al.'s 1928 report, it appears that competent, committed physicians—even if they were itinerant—were not the only people difficult to attract to the Indian Service. The government also had a hard time attracting effective teachers and school administrators, even after professionalization efforts, including the 1878 provision that required physicians to have a medical degree and the 1891 civil service law that required teachers and administrators to pass the civil service exam.[30] The extent to which students could be considered healthy at on- or off-reservation schools varied according to the administrative, medical, and teaching personnel the OIA could attract and retain.

Children's health at OIA boarding schools first became precarious under W. A. Jones's tenure as commissioner of Indian Affairs (1897–1905). Shortly after his appointment to the post, Jones instigated a campaign to dramatically increase the number of students at OIA-run schools.

Historians Brenda Child and Diane T. Putney write that OIA agents and superintendents often disregarded the age of students they enrolled, the wishes of students' parents, and the health of students who were placed in schools. A result of Jones's headstrong push to boost enrollments was that sick children went to school and lived with healthy children in close quarters, facilitating the spread of diseases such as tuberculosis, a highly contagious respiratory illness called "the great Indian killer,"[31] and trachoma, a painful bacterial eye infection for which there was no cure at the time.[32] The Indian Office noticed the proliferation of disease and in 1902 "prioritized student health."[33] The following year, the OIA began to systematically study student health through data collected by teachers, matrons, nurses, doctors, and superintendents.[34] In her recent study of the Sherman Institute, an off-reservation OIA boarding school, and its attached hospital, Jean Keller documents how Harwood Hill, the superintendent of Sherman, learned from the data collected and practices at other boarding schools. He created and maintained a physically healthful and beautiful institution for Native students for a number of years.[35] Keller argues, in fact, that "medical observation equaled education" in the OIA in the early twentieth century,[36] not only advancing health within the Indian School Service, but providing object lessons for public health more generally as it developed into a full-fledged field of its own.[37]

Because of day schools' locations within Native communities, the patterns of health and disease at school mirrored those of the reservation.[38] During True's tenure at Santa Clara Pueblo, trachoma and diphtheria were the ailments she and Crandall most frequently discussed. Trachoma, or "sore eyes," is a painful bacterial eye infection caused by *Chlamydia trachomatis.* Trachoma begins as conjunctivitis, or pink eye, with the swelling of the eyelid lining. As the inflammation intensifies, the infected eyes may become itchy or irritated, develop granular follicles, be sensitive to light, and discharge mucus or pus. At these early stages, the disease is very contagious and can be spread through direct contact with infected eyes or by touching items, such as towels, clothing, or bedding, that have touched infected eyes.[39] Dr. Julius Boldt, who published a book on trachoma in 1904, wrote that treatment at this stage of the disease consisted of washing the infected eye with "chlorine water, solutions of lead acetate, zinc sulphate, or silver nitrate," rubbing the inner eyelid with a copper stick, and ensuring that the sufferer got plenty of fresh air and rested the eyes.[40] If this treatment was ineffective, scarring of the inner eyelid, ingrown eyelashes, and eventually the clouding of the cornea could occur.[41]

Trachoma appears to have affected each Indian tribe differently; the populations of some tribes, such as the Hopi in Arizona, suffered in large numbers while others seem to have been relatively unaffected.[42] The 1901 *Course of Study for the Indian Schools of the United States* noted that sore eyes were common in OIA schools and recommended that teachers instruct students "always to bathe in hot water. Boric acid, one-half level teaspoon to the pint, added is good. Apply to the eyes and bandage. Caution against rubbing the eyes. Isolate the sore-eye patients. Guard against infection."[43] As late as 1928, Meriam et al. recognized that doctors did not know if trachoma was a contagious disease or developed from dietary deficiencies. They thus argued that the Indian Service should provide robust diets and improve sanitary conditions to prevent the spread of the disease in Indian schools and on reservations.[44] Ten years later, in the midst of the Great Depression, doctors found that sulfanilamide cured trachoma.[45]

Along with trachoma, Santa Clarans experienced diphtheria and smallpox at different times. In comparison to other Native groups, Meriam et al. observed, the design of Pueblo villages and homes contributed to the overall health of the community since houses, in general, were well kept and well ventilated. However, sewage in the streets and the practice of corralling livestock next to houses were problematic and likely fueled the spread of contagions and contaminated well water— conditions school personnel were expected to remedy through instruction.[46] Without adequate sanitary measures, such as frequent laundering and the individual use of bedding, clothing, and towels, communicable diseases could proliferate rapidly in any population. Diet was likewise a significant factor in thwarting or advancing the spread of the disease; and this, too, became problematic when OIA officials limited nutritious food resources at schools.

Diphtheria was of special concern in the early twentieth century because it was life-threatening, particularly among children and the elderly. Those who were undernourished, did not have immunizations, had a weak immune system, or lived in crowded spaces were also at risk. Since the late nineteenth century, physicians have understood that *Corynebacterium diphtheriae,* or the rod-shaped diphtheria bacillus, is transferred from an infected person to others through the coughing or sneezing of airborne droplets.[47] The disease attacks the respiratory and glandular systems; those afflicted—including cows, dogs, and cats—experience inflamed airways and lymph nodes as well as a fever, a hacking cough, and a grayish film on the back of the throat.[48] Antitoxin was, and still is, the recommended course of treatment in the early stages of diphtheria. If not treated promptly, the disease can spread to the liver, heart, kidneys, and nervous system—if the patient does not die first.[49] Physicians writing in the late nineteenth and early twentieth centuries recommended that infected children be isolated from other members of their families and communities and that sickrooms be disinfected with carbolic acid and formaldehyde gas.[50] In fact, Dr. W. Gilman Thompson argued in 1893 that infected children be isolated from one another because "crowding them together in wards greatly increases the virulence of the disease."[51] This became a problem in the home of the grandmother who refused OIA treatment for the children at her house.

Health practices among the Tewa, though, appear to foreground their sociocultural understandings of people's roles and intentions within the community and to background the biomedical causes and effects of illness. Anthropologist Richard I. Ford, who did fieldwork among the Tewa in the 1970s, traced their health practices to their origin stories and the beliefs that the Tewa derived and cultivated from them. In particular, the belief in the dual existence of order and chaos and the belief in the capacity of humans to variously do good, make mistakes, and do harm are central to understanding how sickness was regarded and treated among the Tewa. The tension between wellness and illness was expected and held in check by the orthogonal forces of medicine people and witches. Early on, the Tewa created medicine societies to counteract disorder and illness within Pueblo communities. This meant, in effect, that the intention or message underlying the illness was central to its cure, along with other factors such as the sex of the patient. Healers carefully developed and administered highly individualized treatments that simultaneously observed proper practice and systematically eliminated the affliction.[52] The protocols for developing such treatments and the treatments themselves were forms of knowledge that were protected, and thus not shared with nonhealers or with outsiders. The relationship between the afflicted and the particular sickness sometimes had larger community origins and implications, making health a sociocultural concern with biomedical manifestations. For example, historians Malcolm Ebright and Rick Hendricks analyze such cases in Abiquiu between 1756 and 1766, when the Genízaro, or Native non-Puebloan, population and the Spanish clergy there experienced a series of health crises in relation to the supposed practice of witchcraft.[53] Preventing illness was thus theoretically possible if one maintained balance through appropriate relationships, actions, and intentions within the community.

The extent to which Santa Clarans held to their historical understandings of health and sickness is not entirely clear in the written record from the early twentieth century. (By the late twentieth century, when he did his fieldwork, Ford notes that traditional Tewa medicinal practices and knowledge were diminishing.)[54] What is clear, however, is that there was a dispute within the Pueblo between the Summer People and the Winter Progressives over political authority and ceremonial observances. True was not fully aware of the rift between the two factions. She, along with the doctor, was charged with maintaining a quarantine and treating the sick. Her training and the curriculum laid out by the Office of Indian Affairs emphasized establishing a hygienic environment that was biomedically sound at the expense of any sociocultural implications such a strategy might have. The five years True lived and worked as the day school teacher at Santa Clara were enveloped in the OIA's nationwide expansion of medical services. And although the Santa Fe Indian School and the Laguna Sanatorium were nearby, the Northern Pueblos District also employed an itinerant physician when hospital care was not necessary or would be impossible. True, as the day school teacher, was responsible for routine vaccinations and nursing Pueblo members in cases that were not urgent. Historian Richard M. Frost notes that day school teachers were proficient in household nursing at the time, which included "using iodine, carbolic acid, mustard, ipecac, Curitcura salve, 'croton oil,' laudanum, and other such remedies."[55] But True's observations, however informative or accurate they might be, were second to those of the itinerant Indian Office physician,

Dr. Holterman. He was responsible for documenting the movement of disease and his treatment of it. Holterman's reporting of the diphtheria outbreak was strictly biomedical, and Crandall preferred this to True's lucid descriptions of sociocultural affiliations and their possible relationship to the resistance of OIA medical treatment.

The 1901 *Course of Study for the Indian Schools of the United States* blurred the boundary between the biomedical and sociocultural aspects of OIA schooling within Native communities, but its emphasis was on cleanliness and building up Indian children to persevere in the non-Native world. Estelle Reel, the superintendent of the Indian schools from 1898 to 1910 and author of the *Course of Study*, stressed the importance of sanitation around food: "The question of bacteria should be emphasized, their enemy being cleanliness. Wash all cooking utensils, garbage cans, milk pails, pots and pans of all kinds, with boiling water, which destroys many germs. Filth is the surest breeding place of disease. All food needs to be protected from germs and dust. . . . The health and happiness of the family depends largely upon the cooking."[56] In shielding food from germs, one protected people from illness, and teachers were to use as much time as necessary to drive this point home. Cleanliness and food preparation within OIA schools fell under the purview of women and girls, whom teachers were to train as viable homemakers. Knowing how to keep a pristine house and prepare a nutritious meal were elements of the industrial and domestic curriculum. Students were also supposed to learn about the importance of pure water and how it could be contaminated by proximity to cemeteries and corrals as well as how to treat sore eyes, fevers, and other medical emergencies. This was preservationist knowledge, in fact, that would attend to the physical bodies of Indian children and infuse their brains with "vigor." Reel viewed this as essential if Indian students were "to bear the strain that competition in business and earning a living [would] impose."[57] According to the Indian Office, physical health preceded sociocultural health.

PRECEDENT AND RESISTANCE

In November 1902, a Santa Clara medicine society member was ailing; he submitted to and praised Dr. Holterman's treatment. This endorsement, two months before the 1903 diphtheria outbreak, might well have contributed to the doctor's relative success in treating affected Santa Clara children. However, not everyone at the Pueblo agreed that the doctor's treatments for diphtheria and measures to disinfect homes were acceptable or even safe. Treatment involved injecting infected children with antitoxin, closely monitoring their condition, providing them with nourishing food, and making sure that other people did not touch or use items they had used. Disinfection involved fumigating the school and houses where infected children lived and sometimes died with formaldehyde gas. Fumigation was not a foreign concept among Santa Clarans. In fact, fumigation with juniper, which has disinfecting properties, was something that the Tewa would have done to protect the house from witches and the spirits of those who died.[58] Burning the clothing, bedding, and linens used by sick children was another option, although, as McCormick unequivocally stated, the government would not reimburse True or other individuals for incinerated items. The regular cleaning of houses, dishes, and cloth items with soap and water would have certainly aided in the containment of the disease, as would separating sick children from one another and from healthy children. Several people did not tolerate either the doctor's treatment or his measures to disinfect the homes of sick children, but resistance did not appear to be widespread. Even so, the resistance that did exist bothered True, McCormick, and Crandall.

The first instance of resistance appears to have occurred one week after the first case of diphtheria at the Pueblo surfaced. On January 20, 1903, True reported to McCormick that an elderly woman who cared for several orphaned children refused to let Dr. Holterman into her house to treat the children for the disease. According to True, the woman was related to the male leaders within the community, and she had enough authority to defy the Pueblo leaders' orders and repel what True perceived as the governor's efforts to make the children in her household submit to the doctor's treatment.[59]

The elderly woman's actions suggest that women had multifaceted power within the Pueblo. Their authority at Santa Clara is somewhat unclear in the literature because the anthropologists who have written most extensively about the Pueblo—Dozier, Jeançon, and Hill—did not write extensively about gender roles, perhaps because they were male. Dozier mentions the Women's Society as a religious group within the Pueblo; Jeançon notes that Santa Clara in the first decade of the twentieth century was matrilineal; and Hill claims by the 1940s that "women were considered second-class citizens at Santa Clara Pueblo." Hill argues that because women did not hold positions in religious societies that used and transmitted protected knowledge specific to that particular association, women's knowledge of taboos was nonexistent, making them susceptible to inadvertently breaking them. Hill's claim is problematic in part because he acknowledges that he did not (or could not) obtain "detail[ed] information on the rites" of the Women's Society and thus could not comment definitively. In contrast, he explains, women were midwives and healers of the same caliber as men.[60] The specialized knowledge needed to perform healing acts and produce traditional arts, such as pottery, would certainly have given women some clout within the Pueblo, but this might not have accorded them the political status that outsiders would recognize as significant.

According to Ortiz, women did not hold offices, such as the cacique or the governor, but they were part of all the socioreligious societies with the exception of the Hunt Society. Women held ranked leadership positions only within the Women's Society. They served as advisory members without rank in all other religious societies as well as advisors to the caciques. If the socioreligious and political structure Ortiz has outlined accurately represents Santa Clara, then Hill has made an error; women were part of the highest-ranking religious societies at the Pueblo—the medicine societies. This did not necessarily translate into political equality across gender lines, though. There is evidence that the Santa Clarans did not believe women and men had the same capacities to know and exist in the world. Ortiz writes that while women could only be female, men could be both female and male, meaning that men possessed both male and female qualities and could assume female ceremonial roles. Women, however, only had female qualities and were not permitted to take on male ceremonial roles.[61] While being only female did not preclude socioreligious rank, particularly in the Women's Society, it may support to some extent Hill's contention that women were considered unknowledgeable in certain areas. This might have been enough to create gendered power disparities in day-to-day activities within the Pueblo. Then again, the old woman's resistance to

Dr. Holterman's treatment might have had more to do with the deep undercurrent of contention between the Summer and Winter People than with gender.

On January 21, 1903, True sent a letter to McCormick reporting that the group led by Francisco Naranjo, a member of the Winter People, was the only group explicitly endorsing Dr. Holterman's treatments against diphtheria at Santa Clara. In fact, members of this group requested that True identify them as supporters in her correspondence with the superintendent's office. The head of the other faction, according to True, was Governor Diego Naranjo, a member of the Summer People and Francisco Naranjo's brother. True noted that Diego Naranjo's group, which included the Pueblo's medicine societies, had not yet reported to her whether it would back the doctor's treatments and disinfection efforts. She commented that she "tried to act with tact, yet with firmness" in working with both factions; True also wrote that she intended to "have the suspects examined when the doctor comes."[62] The "suspects" were the children who lived with the elderly woman.

Especially troubling for True in this health crisis were the actions of Mr. Thomas Dozier, an Anglo man who married into the Pueblo after having been the day school teacher.[63] True suspected him of encouraging Pueblo members to avoid submitting their children to the doctor's vaccine and antitoxin treatments. True believed that he visited the old woman who had turned away the governor and was refusing to allow the doctor to visit the children who lived with her. The possibility that Dozier, an Anglo, had relinquished allegiance to his race seemed unthinkable to True. She called him "a freak who should have been put into an insane asylum in infancy."[64] While insanity might have been the most acceptable reason True could find for Dozier's alliance with the Pueblo, his actions likely carry more nuance than she could recognize at the time. Dozier exploded True's assumption that another educated Anglo would be a strong advocate for modern medical treatment and that he would remain outside the Pueblo's familial network once he had married into it. That Dozier visited the grandmother whom True viewed as an obstacle is not surprising if, through marriage, Dozier was related to her. Indeed, he might well have been expected to visit the grandmother for reasons not apparent to True or anyone else deemed an outsider. True likewise might not have known that Thomas Dozier was the OIA day school teacher at Santa Clara during a massive small-pox outbreak at neighboring Pueblos in 1898–1899.

Although the epidemic missed Santa Clara Pueblo, it hit Indian Pueblos in the Rio Grande valley, at Zuni in western New Mexico, and at Hopi in Arizona.[65] The disease killed one person at San Ildefonso immediately to the south of Santa Clara and infected another person at San Juan to the north. To the south and west, the disease struck Isleta, Acoma, Laguna, Jemez, Cochiti, Santo Domingo, San Felipe, and Zuni Pueblos especially hard, killing a total of 601 individuals.[66] And smallpox devastated the Hopi living on Second Mesa, killing 74 percent of those who were infected. As a result of an ineffective quarantine on First Mesa, they had contracted the disease from their Hopi neighbors who attended the Shaloko ceremony at Zuni Pueblo. According to historian Robert A. Trennert, the Second Mesa Hopi rejected the treatment of OIA doctors, teachers, and field matrons because U.S. government agents forcibly removed their children and sent them to OIA schools.[67] The Hopi on First Mesa, who accepted OIA treatment and nursing, fared better, because they were treated for secondary ailments such as dehydration and other infections.[68] Compared to the Mandan, Cherokee, and Huron, who did not receive nursing and had mortality rates of between 50 percent and 90 percent, the Zuni mortality rate of 14 percent during the 1898–1899 smallpox epidemic demonstrates that illnesses secondary to smallpox were often lethal and treating those illnesses dramatically improved the survival rate of those who suffered from smallpox.

The importance of treating secondary illnesses may well have been something that Santa Clarans had already learned. Repeated exposure to smallpox since the initial Spanish invasion in the sixteenth century and the syncretic agricultural and religious practices that Pueblo Indians and their Genízaro and Hispano neighbors cultivated because of their proximity in the Rio Grande valley in the eighteenth century suggest that they developed ways of dealing with the disease. In fact, according to an 1878 newspaper article from the *Daily Evening Bulletin* in San Francisco, smallpox swept through Rio Arriba and Taos counties, infecting scores of Natives, Hispanos, and Anglos. Although no Pueblos are named in the article, we can speculate that Santa Clara and San Juan Pueblos in Rio Arriba County and Picuris and Taos Pueblos in Taos County were affected by the outbreak. According to a doctor interviewed for the article, mortality averaged between 10 percent and 12 percent, suggesting that communities had established ways to attend to the secondary effects of the disease or were already immune to the disease.[69] By the time smallpox hit the Rio Grande valley again in 1898–1899, Santa Clara Pueblo appeared to be prepared. Historian Richard H. Frost writes that during the 1898–1899 epidemic, Dozier administered the smallpox vaccination to Santa Clarans, who "understood its use and did not need to be instructed" as to its benefit.[70] True's correspondence makes it clear that she did not know of Dozier's actions several years before diphtheria hit Santa Clara. And when Dozier visited the grandmother, True saw collusion in what might have been comfort. She unmistakably did not want to be held responsible for others' actions that she perceived to be oppositional.

True's frustration with her lack of control over Santa Clara extended beyond quarantine and treatment efforts. In her letters, she seems to have realized that she was only one person vying for authority. She had recognized that the power structure within the Pueblo seemed to be in the process of deteriorating. On November 28, 1902, she noted:

> Santa Clara is so divided against itself that there is no head to appeal to. Nearly half the people acknowledge no tribal regulations and wholly ignore the gubernatorial proclamations. These, however, are the better class of Indians, really held together by Francisco Naranjo. They will not participate in the secret dances, of which the present governor is a strong advocate. I have succeeded in getting both parties into school as well as a class of independents who are the hard drinkers of the Pueblo.[71]

True acknowledged at least two factions and a group of independents, but it is not clear that she understood the nature of those factions.

Although neither the Summer nor the Winter faction at Santa Clara had explicitly called for the people to resist the doctor's treatment, more than one parent refused to let the doctor near his child. True reported, "In the case now suspected, the father stations himself by his little one and substantively says that he will fight to the limit to prevent any interfering whatever. The Grandmother is an old tigress whose house is a den of iniquity resorted to by low class Indians and Mexicans."[72] One wonders if the father's and grandmother's responses were informed by the taking of children from Hopi towns a decade before. By actively resisting the OIA doctor's treatment, the grandmother and the father, José Volupez Naranjo, acted in a way they thought would protect the child from government officials. In a very real sense, this is a response to colonization—the grandmother, the father, and to some degree the Summer faction were reacting to interference by outsiders. After all, they would not even have experienced diphtheria had Europeans not settled in the area.

Federal government officials assumed they knew more than Indians. In the case of biomedically containing and treating diphtheria, this assumption might have had merit. However, imposing this treatment on a group of people who were already in disagreement among themselves ignored the specific historical roles of individuals and groups within the Pueblo and its ongoing adjustments to ensure the community's well-being. Some Santa Clarans might have perceived the OIA position as arrogant and offensive, particularly if True insisted that parents and guardians obey her directives. We might speculate that the grandmother and the father resisted because they disliked True, because they had heard about or witnessed unsavory OIA actions toward children, because they fundamentally disagreed with the Winter Progressives' alliance with the OIA health policy, or because they believed they could better squelch yet another epidemic. Indeed, the rumor of smallpox one year later in 1904 prompted many Santa Clara families to line up for vaccinations.[73]

Smallpox was different from diphtheria, however, and on January 28, 1903, True reported, "The doctor tried faithfully to be permitted to try his powers, but what can a doctor do in the presence of three guns, a frenzied old woman and several desparate [*sic*] men?"[74] Diphtheria is a bacterial infection that can be successfully treated if antitoxin injections begin early enough and are coupled with diligent nursing care. Smallpox, on the other hand, is a viral infection that cannot be cured and often results in death. Both diseases, though, were evidence of colonization, and each infection was a reminder of this fact.

True, Crandall, and McCormick carried the accretion of colonization through in their pronounced assumption that they knew what was right and best for Indians; they represented the U.S. government, after all. At the turn of the twentieth century, this might have seemed quite logical from an Anglo perspective. Not only had the United States colonized many groups of Indians across North America, there was also a pervasive hope that Indians would become civilized through schooling and land ownership.[75] This line of thinking only makes sense it if is coupled with the tandem belief that Indians would recognize the superiority of Euro-American culture and want to conform to such a model. This model of civilization occurred in conjunction with the rapid technological advancement of the twentieth century, and many reformers mistakenly conflated technological innovation with social progress.[76] Technological advances such as the railroad, telegraphs, and the antitoxin for diphtheria, however, were not enough to change the minds of the father or the grandmother.

The old woman continued to resist intervention even after children began to die. On February 9, 1903, True reported that the son whom José Volupez Naranjo had protected from the doctor had died. True speculated that the dead boy had stayed at his grandmother's house during his illness. After the boy's death, his father allowed the doctor to fumigate his house. True added that four of the six children living with the grandmother had died in the previous three weeks, and one boy still living at her house was sick. True wrote that although she could not verify that the dead and sick boys had contracted diphtheria, "common sense forbids any other supposition." According to True's observations, ten children had been ill in the last month, six of whom had died. Of those six, four had lived at the old woman's house. True ended the letter, "In only one case has the doctor been called—He was not really called but 'permitted' there. The patient died after antitoxin was administered. This created an opposition sentiment hard to meet."[77] Another child died in the same house the following day.[78]

When Dr. Holterman submitted his report on the diphtheria outbreak to Crandall in late February, he confirmed True's reports. He wrote that the only way he and True learned which children were sick was by witnessing their burials. After the children died, and if he was invited to fumigate the house and the family's effects after the funeral rites, Dr. Holterman found that the house was usually completely emptied. The items most needed for disinfection, those that might still harbor the bacteria and spread the infection—clothing, bedding, dishes,

and furniture—were gone. He further noted that the unsanitary practices of dumping refuse into the open spaces between houses and in the
middle of plazas likely facilitated the spread of diphtheria.[79]

Funeral customs might have exacerbated the diphtheria infections
at the grandmother's house. Despite this, True and the doctor observed
Santa Clara custom. True wrote in one of her letters, "The Indians of
the suspected house promise that they will permit disinfection in four
days, this being the time they think required for a departed spirit to
leave its accustomed haunts. The doctor will return in four days to use
the Formaldehyde Generator."[80] Dozier, Jeançon, Hill, and Ortiz corroborate True's account, stating that death rituals had a four-day cycle,
during which a living person was required to stay in the house where
the deceased had lived to prevent his or her spirit from returning when
it should be departing to find the afterworld.[81] After this four-day period, the house would have been fumigated anyway with juniper.[82] During that four-day period, though, the grandmother's house would have
been a diphtheria incubator for the children who lived there. But had
True or Holterman tried to disinfect the house before the funeral cycle
was completed, the old woman and her supporters might well have
resisted.

Until Dr. Holterman verified True's reports, Crandall appears to have
suspected her of exaggerating the scope and severity of the diphtheria
outbreak at Santa Clara, indicating that he privileged both Holterman's
biomedical assessment and *his* observation of what had happened.
Upon his return from Washington, D.C., in late January, Crandall read
True's letters and probably listened to McCormick's account of the situation. Crandall took the threat of an imminent epidemic seriously and
was prepared to bend federal and territorial jurisdictional rules in order
to enforce a strict quarantine. He wired Dr. Holterman for an update
and then composed a letter to True on January 29, 1903:

> The Doctor's reply is to the effect that he has visited all the houses
> in Santa Clara, that there is *one case of diphtheria* and that only one
> house refused to admit him. . . . The condition of affairs at Santa
> Clara does not warrant, it would seem, the position I have taken, as
> I have interested the Governor of New Mexico, the U.S. District At-
> torney and Inspector Nessler. To-day has been spent wholly in the

interest of this matter, and the question has largely rested on [*illegible*] shall troops be sent to Santa Clara, or shall the principal offenders be arrested and taken into the U.S. District Court. The Secretary of the Interior has awaited the result of your telegram as well as that of Dr. Halterman [*sic*]. . . . It seems that there is no reason for alarm, and that Dr. Halterman [*sic*] can handle any cases that may arise, there are none now, so he says, and the [*illegible*] would not be justified in sending out troops to subdue one old woman. I feel that I have acted too promptly or quickly in this matter and without sufficient grounds basing my information on telegrams and letters from you. I am, at least open to censure, and feeled [*sic*] constrained to instruct you hereafter to be careful to report only facts and reliable information unembellished with a narrative and from which I can draw proper conclusions.[83]

Crandall demanded that the people who worked for him follow his orders and comply with the proper rules and procedures customary in the Indian Office. Had he not wired the doctor, troops might well have been sent to Santa Clara. What had become concern over a serious diphtheria epidemic transformed by the end of January 1903 into an incident over the superintendent's authority and the proper role of a day school teacher—at least for True and Crandall. Crandall had in essence charged True with exceeding her position and compromising his through misinformation.

But True was not a source of misinformation. Although her letters conveyed her frustrations and anger lucidly, at the end of January, she reported only one confirmed case of diphtheria and its fatal outcome.[84] She reported at least two other sick children and one death at that time, but she said she did not know if those cases were due to diphtheria. What she had described extensively in her letters up until that point were two cases of family resistance and her inability to enforce a quarantine. She also shared her suspicions that the old woman's house was the epicenter of the disease. Such a full discussion of her concerns, perhaps in addition to McCormick's report, might in a quick reading have led Crandall to believe that there was a full-blown epidemic under way. Crandall did not trust the conclusions he thought True drew.

But Crandall's experience of the diphtheria outbreak occurred from a distance. His sense of professional efficacy, unlike True's, was not on the line; he was not deeply enmeshed in personal confrontations with Pueblo members who refused to have their children treated.

True's response to Crandall's admonition is startling. She began her six-page report: "There is practically nothing new to relate this morning," and then launched into what seems to be a very detailed account of the goings-on within the Pueblo. She stated that she declined an invitation to attend a community meeting the night before to explain again Crandall's decision that there would be no law enforcement involved in the quarantine; she silenced the discussion of plans the Summer People made to resist her actions as a U.S. government representative; she found the supposedly secret house where the medicine men met; she stated that medicine men had treated Leandro Tafoya, the former governor, for sore eyes as he had "decided to discontinue civilized treatment"; and she mentioned she might have a lead on an old murder case. After this exhaustive discussion, she thanked Crandall and complimented him for getting to the bottom of the diphtheria matter before, quite literally, calling out the guard. "I gave you every opportunity in a previous letter to place the blame and responsibility of this Diphtheria affair upon me by saying that I have made blunders from ignorance. Many men would have taken me at my word, scolded me and let themselves out. I was sure you were not of this category but you didn't wish to smooth over a rough place without going to the bottom was like Mr. Crandall."[85]

True reiterated her lack of knowledge in how to enforce a quarantine and appealed to Crandall's honesty and integrity in dealing with her stated mistakes at Santa Clara. In so doing, she underscored her subordinate position and attempted to charm him. In other words, she had met her foe and strategically opted to play the woman. True's response is consistent with Patricia A. Carter's reading of other women who worked for the Indian Office during this time period. In an examination of teachers' diaries from 1900 to 1910, Carter found that all of the women she studied openly resisted or covertly subverted the OIA authority structure, which operated on assumed gender and racial hierarchies. The teachers' resistance was performed at an individual level, however, as most of them taught in isolated areas under supervisors who could make their own rules about teacher dress, conduct, and leisure.[86] This appears to align with True's experience.

True's negotiation for power through charm turned to subversion when she suspected that several students attending the day school on February 9, 1903, were infected because of the "'brassy,' offensive smell" of their clothing. Her solution was to send all of the students home to give them "a fighting chance."[87] She argued that she believed this was what Crandall would have wanted her to do. She ended by saying that her attempts to coerce families into treating their children all had failed, and that sending healthy children home in order to keep them away from infected children might be a better course of action to take. This is the same letter in which True reported that six children had died since the first case of diphtheria surfaced at Santa Clara in early January.

On February 10, 1903, Crandall sent letters to both True and the doctor. In each letter he stated that only the doctor could make recommendations about closing the school. He also refuted True's claim that there were ten cases of diphtheria (she said "sick children"), as the doctor had reported that there was not even one case at Santa Clara.[88] Nine days later, Crandall apparently changed his mind about the extent of diphtheria at the Pueblo, and he used True's reports to coerce the governor into making people allow the doctor to disinfect their homes. He wrote to the Santa Clara governor:

> You will see that parents leave all blankets and clothing in the house after a death and that the Doctor is notified, that he may disinfect the quarters effectually.
>
> This is given to you as an order, and should you disobey my request in this matter, I fear that as the head officer of the Pueblo you will be held responsible and lay yourself liable to arrest. You will therefore see that Dr. Holterman is notified of each and every death, and that he is permitted to properly disinfect the house.[89]

In this mandate, Crandall made two mistakes that could potentially have escalated Pueblo resistance to the doctor: he assumed (1) that the governor had ultimate decision-making authority in the Pueblo, and (2) that the governor could force families to submit all of their blankets and clothing to fumigation. Whether Governor Diego Naranjo attempted to follow Crandall's orders, or at least present them to the cacique, is not known, as the outbreak appears to have ceased by the end of February 1903.

The day after Crandall demanded compliance from Diego Naranjo, Dr. Holterman's report on diphtheria at Santa Clara confirmed True's account that most of the sick children lived in one house. As mentioned earlier, Holterman was able to identify cases of diphtheria only by witnessing the burials of children who had died of the disease. Based on his observations that diphtheria had been the cause of death in these cases, he made several recommendations. First, he though that the school should remain open as it was the safest place for uninfected children to be. Second, he advised that children who lived in the house that had had so many of the sick not be permitted to attend school. Third, he recommended that the school be fumigated and thoroughly cleaned every weekend. Fourth, he argued that children should receive a daily lunch at school that consisted of vegetable soup with meat. Finally, he advised that children wash their hands at least two times a day with antiseptic soap.[90] Crandall implemented all of the doctor's recommendations except one—lunches of vegetable soup with meat. In a letter to Mary Dissette, the supervising teacher for the Northern Pueblos District, he justified his decision, writing that "it will be impossible to get the necessary authority by April 1st [to purchase foodstuffs] . . . [and] I do not feel justified in recommending same." He added that he felt Santa Clara had "plenty of corn and wheat, and as Pueblos go, they have sufficient subsistence supplies."[91] The doctor's authority had its limits.

CONCLUSION

The diphtheria outbreak of 1903 at Santa Clara Pueblo demonstrates the collision of specific cultural frames of reference in the midst of a crisis that potentially threatened an entire generation of Santa Clarans. Improvisation and specific learnings grounded in past experience and relationships on the ground, however, mediated the health crisis and demonstrate that at least two types of health were in play: biomedical health, which focused exclusively on the well-being of the physical body, and sociocultural health, which emphasized the well-being of relationships between individuals and groups within the community. As a direct result of the proliferation of tuberculosis and trachoma at federal Indian boarding schools in the late nineteenth century, the Office of Indian Affairs began paying close attention to the biomedical movement and prevention of disease in its schools, in spite of the absence of a comprehensive federal Indian health care policy. The OIA even embedded aspects of early medical studies into the 1901 *Uniform Course of Study*, featuring specific lessons on hygiene. Santa Clarans necessarily attended to both the biomedical and sociocultural forms of health during the diphtheria outbreak of 1903, at a time when the Pueblo was also in the middle of a significant political shift that would not be resolved until the Santa Clara constitution was enacted in the mid-1930s. Clara D. True, the day school teacher at Santa Clara, was caught between Indian Office policy and her supervisor's interpretation of it within a gendered, hierarchical bureaucracy; she was also caught between internal debates taking place at the Pueblo.

When True arrived at Santa Clara in August 1902, she knew very little about Santa Clarans in particular or about Pueblo peoples in general. Her learning curve was steep as she attempted to operate simultaneously as the eyes and ears of the OIA, the day school teacher, the de facto public health official, and the primary U.S. government liaison to the Pueblo—all while diphtheria wreaked havoc upon the children of Santa Clara. In her attempts to treat sick children, True found that her lack of understanding about what epidemics the Pueblo had experienced in the past and how the Pueblo experienced them produced seemingly natural alliances and hostile relationships between her and different Santa Clarans. Most pronounced in True's letters are the frustration she felt and her disdain for the grandmother who refused treatment for several children under her care. True's reaction to the grandmother's actions reflected both how little she comprehended about the power relationships within the Pueblo and how the grandmother's position as a woman made her suspect in True's eyes. To be sure, the grandmother and True each acted from their own culturally specific understandings of what women, and women of a certain social position, could and should do. When Crandall confronted True for exaggerating the urgency and direness of the situation at Santa Clara, True strategically played the woman, appearing to acquiesce to Crandall's judgment. She did not, however, give any appearance of regret in her subversion of the

Indian Office's quarantine policy. In fact, it is quite possible that True tested Crandall's perceived boundaries of authority within the hierarchical OIA so that she might skirt them at a future time.

True likewise learned that the sociocultural harmony (or strife) between the Summer and Winter People affected her attempts at biomedical interventions in the treatment of children infected with diphtheria. She found that the Santa Clara governor did not have ultimate authority within the Pueblo and that she would not be given free rein to do as she thought right. This lesson was especially confounding as the incident with Thomas Dozier brought out True's racial assumptions about the positions Anglos should take, even if they had married into a Native community. Though her subsequent letters do not indicate whether she ever changed her mind about Dozier, she did form long-standing tight alliances with Santa Clarans that extended well into the 1930s, and she frequently spoke out against Anglo ethnographers and anthropologists, such as Matilda Coxe Stevenson.[92] True's learning during the diphtheria outbreak of 1903 rattled her and forced her to cross a liminal threshold—she was initiated, at least obliquely, into the inner workings of the Pueblo and the limitations of Crandall's jurisdiction in the Northern Pueblos District.

In this health crisis, Santa Clarans learned at least two important lessons: that True would meddle in internal Pueblo affairs in order to do what she thought was right and that outsiders might have viable treatments for illness that were worth considering. While it is not clear if Santa Clarans realized what True wrote in her letters to Crandall and McCormick or the tone she took in writing about the Pueblo, it is clear that they treated her, and perhaps the doctor, with caution and sometimes defiance. This had more to do with how she approached members of the Pueblo than with her medical competence, however. Those who resisted treatment served as reminders that detrimental colonization experiences at Indian Pueblos were alive in the memories of Santa Claran community members. Even so, without Santa Clarans' cooperation in 1903, True and Holterman would have had no chance to treat the sick or curb the spread of disease. That a member of one of the Bear Societies endorsed Holterman likely affected the decision of a number of parents to let Holterman and True treat their children.

The primary record, as detailed by the various policy actors in this episode, as well as secondary sources on Santa Clara and Tewa Pueblo social organization, reveals uncharted historical possibilities. Because True and Crandall appear to have believed that the governor was the highest source of authority at Santa Clara, it seems that the Pueblo community was quite adept at concealing its extended social, political, and religious hierarchy from outsiders. This gave Santa Clarans a degree of insularity, or protection, that would have allowed them to maintain their customs. The Pueblos' long experience with colonization strategically informed their dealings with U.S. government representatives like True, Crandall, and Dr. Holterman. Second, True and Crandall may not have bothered to ask about the authority structure within Santa Clara, though True certainly had to learn the sociopolitical terrain of the Pueblo quickly. By the end of her tenure at Santa Clara and after her return in 1910, she appears to have understood the complex socioreligious hierarchy, as evidenced in her correspondence in the 1920s, interviews she participated in with folklorists, and her enduring connections with members of the Winter party.[93] Third, we see that women had household authority that has not been recognized or methodically explored by anthropologists. True's reports about the grandmother and her capacity to openly defy Santa Clara officials, such as the governor, without retribution suggest that women, perhaps of a particular age or social rank, carried more authority than previously realized. In all, with the diphtheria outbreak of 1903, we see that issues of power, including resistance, coercion, and subversion, as well as normative expectations about how people should care for children and remembered experiences of the past, converged at Santa Clara.

CHAPTER THREE

Citizen; or, The Legal Education of Clinton J. Crandall

INTRODUCTION

As Crandall began his tenure as the superintendent of the Santa Fe Indian School and Northern Pueblos District, he walked into a legal conundrum that perplexed the local, territorial, and federal courts: were Pueblo Indians in fact "Indians," and thus wards of the federal government, or were they citizens of New Mexico and the United States? Pueblo Indians, after all, manifested many of the hallmarks of "civilization." They built permanent, multistoried houses, they were sedentary farmers, and they were practicing Catholics; yet, they looked and acted like other Indians whom the U.S. government did not deem "civilized," wearing handmade regalia, producing and using Native arts such as pottery, and infusing local Indigenous beliefs and ceremonies into their daily and holiday practices. These conflicting appearances of "civilization" and "Indianness" stymied U.S. government agents who were supposed to train individuals within Native communities to become "citizens" through the two-pronged "civilizing" assimilation policy of land allotment and schooling; but in the process, many of these agents treated Indians as childlike wards of the federal government and missed several important lessons.[1]

Clinton J. Crandall was one of these agents. As Crandall carried out his mission to "civilize" Indians as superintendent of the Santa Fe Indian School, he also fashioned his own form of legal education in two ways: (1) by probing the nuances and contradictions of federal Indian case law and congressional legislation; and (2) by learning how to use the apparatus of federal Indian law to carve out colonial jurisdictions among Pueblo Indian communities. His legal education was paradoxical and characterized by glaring blind spots regarding long-standing customary practices between Pueblo Indians and their Jicarilla Apache and Hispano neighbors around issues of land use and alcohol consumption. Santa Clarans, through their long experience with colonial regimes,

Two white girls posing during ceremonial at Santa Clara Pueblo, 1910. Photograph by H. S. Poley. Courtesy of the Denver Public Library, Western History Collection, P-1507.

quickly learned and worked federalism to their advantage in order to protect their lands with Crandall's advice and aid, but they often did so in direct contrast to his "civilizing" mission and his authority. But the fruits of Crandall's legal education showed in the spring of 1904 with a tax case brought forward by authorities in Bernalillo County, New Mexico. Countering both the county and the New Mexico territorial courts, Crandall lobbied the commissioner of Indian Affairs to urge Congress to pass a law that simultaneously recognized Pueblo Indians' claim to their lands, exempted Pueblo Indians from paying property taxes, and prohibited Pueblo Indians from selling their lands. The tax case, coupled with established yet murky rights around land tenure and alcohol consumption, explicitly distinguished Pueblo Indians from other American Indians in the United States.

In the late nineteenth and early twentieth centuries, the Pueblo peoples of New Mexico were not like other Indigenous groups with which the U.S. government had dealt, in that they did not move from wards of the federal government to U.S. citizens: the territorial and federal governments initially regarded the Santa Clarans and other Pueblo Indians as full citizens under the Treaty of Guadalupe Hidalgo, which ended the U.S. war with Mexico in 1848. As such, Pueblo Indians could buy and sell land, and the U.S. government recognized Pueblo Indians as sovereign entities. Over the last half of the nineteenth century, Pueblo Indian citizenship was tested in the courts, with no clear ruling that might unequivocally guide the New Mexico territorial court and U.S. Supreme Court in the early twentieth century. Rather, ambiguity prevailed, and that was the legal milieu that Crandall entered when he became the superintendent of the Santa Fe Indian School and acting agent of the Northern Pueblos District in 1900. Crandall was quite active in lobbying the courts, Congress, and the president of the United States on his own and through the commissioner of Indian Affairs. In fact, Crandall's recommendations in conjunction with a series of court cases and statutory provisions dealing with Pueblo Indian landholding, tax paying, and rights to buy and sell alcohol influenced judges and lawmakers. They responded in the first decade or so of the twentieth century by pruning back Pueblo Indians' full-citizen status to that of partial citizen and eventually to ward of the government.

U.S. citizenship for American Indians had long depended on individual, fee simple landownership. Owning land, by extension, implied that Native landowners could alienate their property through sale or transfer, and that they would pay property taxes. While landownership and taxation were two qualifications for citizenship for everyone in the early years of the Republic, unlike other ethnic and racial groups, American Indians faced another qualification: the legal right to buy and sell alcohol. This third qualification proved to be a legal double standard that surfaced periodically in the courts over the nineteenth and early twentieth centuries. Though Indigenous peoples' legal status was important for the U.S. and territorial governments, members of the Santa Clara Pueblo appear to have been more interested in maintaining their centuries-old equilibrium with their Native and Hispano neighbors, which had, over the previous 200 years, allowed Pueblo Indians to protect their customary practices. As the citizenship cases in the first decade of the twentieth century illustrate, Pueblo Indians were rightly concerned about the unforeseen consequences of accepting new rights and responsibilities structured by the new territorial and federal governments. To the Santa Clarans, legal citizenship status mattered only to the extent to which it changed their customary sociocultural practices, including leasing land, routing trespassers, and sharing alcoholic drinks with neighbors. Substantive changes in U.S. law, however, shifted the relationships between the Santa Clarans and groups outside the Pueblo. Land, liquor, and taxes were interlocking litmus tests for American Indian citizenship.

LAND

New Mexico v. Persons on the Delinquent Tax List illustrates how Pueblo Indians' legal citizenship status hinged on landownership. And indeed, land—owning it, being able to alienate it, and paying taxes on it—was a hallmark for Pueblo Indian citizenship in New Mexico as it had been for Euro-American men in the early republican period of the United States. One of the steps taken in the 1904 tax case was establishing whether Pueblo Indian landholdings were recognized by Spain and Mexico. In a series of court proceedings after the U.S. Civil War, Pueblo Indian land grants were confirmed, and these served as precedents for the delinquent tax case. The property rights to the original Santa Clara land grant can be traced through the documentary record to 1689, when the Spanish Crown awarded the Pueblo land straddling the Rio Grande. Seventy-four years later, Don Tomás Vélez Cachupín, the Spanish governor and commander general of New Mexico, made a second land grant to the Pueblo that extended up the Santa Clara valley to the source of the creek that flowed down it.[2]

In 1856, eight years after the ratification of the Treaty of Guadalupe Hidalgo, the U.S. government formally recognized the land grants Pueblo Indians had held under the Spanish and Mexican regimes, although the federal government did not begin issuing patents for those lands until 1864. This had the twin effect of protecting Pueblo Indian lands through legal documentation, which was used in land courts later, and affirming Pueblos' right to sell and transfer their property, a hallmark of citizenship. In surveying and confirming the land grants for Pueblos, the United States acted in a protective capacity—something it appears to have done only for sedentary Indians in the Southwest.[3] This suggests that federal officials believed they were dealing with a population that adhered to Euro-American standards of "civilization," marking a possible break with the accumulated body of learning about how "Indians" were supposed to be. The survey of Pueblo Indian lands would seem to have implicitly recognized Pueblos' U.S. citizenship.

In 1861, the U.S. surveyor general's office affirmed the 1856 U.S. survey based on Santa Clara's original Spanish land grant. President Abraham Lincoln declared:

> The United States . . . have given and granted and by the present do give and grant the said Pueblo of Santa Clara in the County of Rio Arriba aforesaid and to the successors and assigns of the said Pueblo of Santa Clara the tract of land above described as entraced [*sic*] in said survey . . . that this continuation shall only be construed as a relinquishment of all title and claim of the United States to any of said lands, and shall not affect any adverse valid rights should such exist.[4]

Santa Clara Pueblo Indians thus corporately owned their land by fee simple title, a status that conveyed with the Treaty of Guadalupe Hidalgo. Ironically, President Lincoln's affirmation of Pueblo Indian status marked the beginning point of the reverse trajectory of legal citizenship New Mexico Pueblo Indians experienced. And this became the paradox for Crandall and the courts: because landownership has such a prominent place in the historical definitions of citizenship and civilization in the United States, then Pueblo Indians, who had already owned land under two previous colonial regimes, must thus be "civilized."

Indian Civilization through Land Tenure

The conclusion that Pueblo Indians were "citizens" and "civilized" disrupted federal programs created to transform Indigenous populations in the United States to a Euro-American values system through land allotment and government-run schools. The hope of those who supported allotment was that Indians would earn their citizenship, in part, through farming practices that resembled those of their Anglo neighbors. Modeled after allotment provisions in treaties between the U.S. government and individual tribes, the concept underlying the General Allotment Act of 1887, or the Dawes Act, received widespread support from non-Indians. Carl Schurz, the secretary of the interior from 1877 to 1881, argued for an allotment policy in his 1880 annual report, and the "Friends of the Indians" similarly lobbied for such a policy.[5] As a policy, the Dawes Act laid out several provisions to transform American Indians into yeoman farmers. Most fundamentally, Native nuclear families were to learn the ideals of U.S. citizens by cultivating a 160-acre plot over a twenty-five-year probationary period. During that time, the U.S. government held the land in trust, which prohibited alienation of that land and allowed OIA agents to monitor the Indians' cultivation efforts. At the end of the twenty-five-year trust phase—if the secretary of the interior deemed it appropriate—a given householder would receive a patent to the land, which transferred ownership of the land to its holder, ceded tribal control of the land, and made the patent holder a full citizen of the United States and the state or territory in which she or he lived.[6] In 1906, Congress amended the Dawes Act with the Burke Act, which stipulated that if an allottee died before the twenty-five-year trust period was over, the lands would become the property of the United States and the secretary of the interior had to decide what to do with those lands. He had two primary options: (1) issue a patent for the land to the heirs of the deceased; or (2) sell the land, issue a patent to the purchaser, and give the proceeds from the sale to the heirs of the deceased. With either option, the secretary of the interior could forgo the twenty-five-year trust period, and the patented lands would be taxable.[7] Both the Dawes Act and the Burke Act legislated individual landholdings and stripped out the common, shared ownership of lands that had previously been the practice of many tribes. By carving up reservations into 160-acre allotments, the federal government frequently sold unallotted plots to non-Natives and physically broke up reservations,[8] drawing attention to the missed lesson that Native America was diverse and that multiple notions of "citizenship" within distinct societies were in play.

Through the General Allotment Act, many Indigenous peoples' legal citizenship status progressed from that of ward of the federal government to full citizen.[9] This was not the case for Pueblo Indians in New Mexico—their lands were not allotted. Instead, Indian Pueblos owned their lands communally and outright; they were first legal citizens and fully entitled landholders, and then wards of the federal government. In understanding Pueblo Indian citizenship within the context of American Indian citizenship more generally, then, it is important to keep two sets of relationships in mind. First, in relationships between the United States and American Indian tribes, the federal government assumed a dominant-subordinate, superior-inferior relationship with Indian tribes beginning in the early nineteenth century. This dependant relationship was codified and hardened through several court cases, having the corollary effect of legally regarding disparate Indian groups as fundamentally the same. Distinctions among different Indigenous cultures are rarely apparent in federal case and statutory law, and the reliance on precedents perpetuated pan-Indian policies regardless of whether Indians wanted or recognized them.

Perhaps the most often-cited legal precedents in federal Indian case law are *Johnson v. M'Intosh* (1823), *Cherokee Nation v. Georgia* (1831), and *Worcester v. Georgia* (1832).[10] In *Johnson v. M'Intosh*, the Marshall Court defined the scope of the colonial doctrine of discovery in terms of the unquestionable right of Euro-Americans to be on the North American continent and for them to hold title to all lands they had "discovered" in spite of the Indigenous peoples who already lived there and considered the lands part of their own nations.[11] Legal scholars Vine Deloria Jr. and Clifford M. Lytle argue that the ruling in *Johnson* established a "landlord-tenant relationship between the government and the Indian tribes . . . in which a judicially recognized federal responsibility over Indian affairs was articulated."[12] The U.S. Supreme Court's subsequent ruling in *Cherokee Nation v. Georgia* expanded the *Johnson* ruling by identifying Indian communities as "domestic dependent nations" whose members were effectively wards of the U.S. government.[13] The following year in *Worcester v. Georgia*, the same Court rendered that the United States had a trust relationship with Native tribes. Each of the decisions tendered by the Marshall Court reinforced the colonialist project, first of the Europeans and then of the United States, by relying on the rights of discovery and treaty-making authority that conveyed from the British after the U.S. Revolution. As the federal government made individual treaties with sovereign tribes, it undertook obligations to provide negotiated services, protections, and monetary compensation, often in exchange for land. Tribes with treaties became, in effect, protectorate nations.

The second set of relationships to bear in mind is that between the federal government and state governments; jurisdictional boundaries were unclear. In the nineteenth and very early twentieth centuries, states and territories enacted laws and their courts ruled on cases with American Indians as plaintiffs and defendants. At the same time, both Congress and the U.S. Supreme Court regularly exercised their supremacy over the state and territorial legislatures and courts, as when the Court ruled in *Worcester v. Georgia* that federal law trumped state law when it came to regulating movement and trade with Indian tribes. This ruling was not always or automatically applied when each state legislated rules of conduct with Indigenous peoples. In effect, federal, state, and territorial authorities had to navigate their own interactions with American Indians as well as the jurisdictional lines that separated different governmental branches when dealing with the tribes themselves. Not surprisingly, the implementation of various laws and rulings across jurisdictions was often idiosyncratic, as is evident in cases dealing with Pueblo Indians' legal status on the basis of landholding.

The first test of Pueblo Indian citizenship in New Mexico came with *U.S. v. Lucero* in 1869, twenty-one years after the territory became part of the United States. The case materialized when José Juan Lucero, a Hispano, entered Cochiti Pueblo and settled there in 1867. The Pueblo viewed this as trespassing and sued Lucero for damages. Upholding the federal Trade and Intercourse Act of 1834, which outlawed non-Native settlement on Indian lands, the New Mexico Supreme Court ruled in favor of Cochiti Pueblo. Tracing the history of Pueblo peoples in the area, the court relied on past Pueblo behavior and Spanish and Mexican precedent in its decision. By dating Pueblo Indians' sedentary, agricultural way of life to time immemorial, the court argued that Pueblo Indians practiced a form of civilization that was readily apparent to Anglo newcomers to the area. The court compared Pueblo Indians to Hispanos living in the region:

> This court has known the conduct and habits of these Indians for eighteen or twenty years, and we say, without the fear of successful contradiction, that you may pick out one thousand of the best Mexicans in New Mexico, and one thousand of the worst Pueblo Indians, and there will be found less, vastly less, murder, robbery, theft, or other crimes among the thousand of the worst Pueblo Indians than among the thousand of the best Mexicans or Americans in New Mexico.[14]

In the court's view, Pueblo Indians were fundamentally distinct from other Native groups in New Mexico or the United States—they lived peacefully in established, corporate communities with permanent housing; they farmed land; and they practiced Catholicism. These cultural elements were enough for the court to regard Pueblo Indians as "civilized Indians" and reduce all others to "savage Indians," those who lived as nomadic or seminomadic hunter-gatherers and traders. Laws made for "savage Indians" were "wholly inapplicable to the Pueblo Indians of New Mexico."[15] Since the U.S. acquisition of the New Mexico Territory, Pueblo Indians had uniquely possessed two sets of rights: the natural rights of the individual and the corporate rights of the community. In an 1847 statute, the territory of New Mexico declared that Indian Pueblos were corporate entities with particular rights, including the right to hold and use land in common; the right to pass on land to descendents; the right to "sue and be sued, plead and be impleaded" in courts in order to project their lands, their collective and individual rights, and the right to bring legal action against those who encroached or trespassed on their lands.[16] Citing this statute in the *Lucero* opinion, the New Mexico Supreme Court referred to Cochiti Pueblo as "a corporate body," which was entitled to protect its boundaries and lands from encroachers, such as José Juan Lucero.[17] The court, moreover, ruled that the Cochiti Pueblo had held fee simple title to its lands since 1689 and because Indians were considered citizens of Mexico under the Plan of Iguala, which granted full citizenship to its inhabitants regardless of race, Pueblo Indians were also full legal citizens of New Mexico and the United States under the terms of the Treaty of Guadalupe Hidalgo. The emphasis on Pueblo Indians' individual and corporate rights in the *Lucero* case both protected Cochiti Pueblo's action to preserve its boundaries and opened up the possibility for New Mexico counties to sue Pueblo Indians for past-due taxes. Ultimately, in *Lucero*, the court reasoned that it did not make sense, after all, to regress from the status of citizen to that of ward of the federal government.[18] Pueblo Indians, then, were exceptional and civilized; they were not wholly subject to other federal laws regulating the rights of other American Indians.

Several years later, the U.S. Supreme Court upheld the *Lucero* ruling in *U.S. v. Joseph* (1876), a trespassing case at Taos Pueblo. As in the *Lucero* case, the Court compared Pueblo Indians to other communities in the

United States: "If Pueblo [*sic*] Indians differ from the other inhabitants of New Mexico in holding lands in common, and in a certain patriarchal form of domestic life, they only resemble this in regard to the Shakers and other communistic societies in the country, and cannot for that reason be classed with the Indian tribes of whom we have been speaking."[19] The Court reiterated that Pueblo communities had held title to their lands long before the United States acquired the surrounding area. Like the New Mexico Supreme Court, the U.S. Supreme Court reasoned that since Mexico had recognized Pueblo land grants given by the Spanish Crown, the United States should do the same under the Treaty of Guadalupe Hidalgo. The recognition of exclusive Pueblo Indian land rights—and, by extension, citizenship rights—held for nearly another thirty years, through the delinquent tax case in 1904. The *Lucero* and *Joseph* cases, it would seem, served as a corrective lesson to the federal government.

Indeed, by the time *New Mexico v. Persons on the Delinquent Tax List of 1899* reached the New Mexico Supreme Court, case law had established that Pueblo Indians were legal citizens of the territory and the United States, but whether Pueblo Indians were "Indians" and therefore not taxed under a proviso of the U.S. Constitution remained an ambiguous question for Congress and for Crandall.[20] In 1905, one year after the New Mexico Supreme Court's ruling that Pueblo Indians were Indians who could be taxed, Congress effectively upended the court's decision and created a legislative property tax exemption for Pueblo Indians, largely through the efforts of the All Pueblos Council and C. J. Crandall. This congressional move can simultaneously be read as (1) a legislative response to judicial action; (2) an assertion of federal supremacy over states in cases dealing with American Indians; and (3) an exercise of exclusive plenary power, or the authority to govern—in theory—completely.[21] In their discussion of plenary power within the context of American Indian sovereignty and federal law, David E. Wilkins and K. Tsianina Lomawaima, as well as Vine Deloria Jr. and Clifford M. Lytle, note that the supposed authority that comes with plenary power coexists in contradiction with Indian sovereignty. Although this congressional power is not constitutionally delegated, the U.S. Supreme Court has supported it, most notably in *U.S. v. Kagama* (1886) and *Lone Wolf v. Hitchcock* (1903). In spite of the muddled logic that required each court to recognize federal jurisdiction in Indian Territory for capital crimes and to abrogate treaties with Indians, respectively, both courts acknowledged congressional plenary power.[22] By the time Crandall was superintendent of the Santa Fe Indian School, he had learned that Congress had such power, and he leveraged it to protect Pueblo Indian lands.

Creating a Reservation

In relieving Pueblo Indians from their tax burden, Congress paradoxically protected Pueblo lands from confiscation and pruned Pueblo Indians' legal citizenship status. If no tax exemption had been applied, Pueblo Indians would have almost certainly lost their lands to the territorial government, since, as Crandall insisted, their incomes were not large enough to cover the assessed taxes. Because Pueblo communities had existed for centuries in the same place, the threat of displacement and the potential physical disintegration of their societies must have been terrifying for Pueblo Indians. While the congressional tax exemption resolved this, the option of creating a reservation by transferring title of the land grant to the federal government likewise made it possible for Pueblo Indians to remain on their traditional homelands, and it created a buffer to further protect each Pueblo community's culture. This option, though, deepened the land-citizen conundrum: to preserve their customary ways of living as civilized societies, Pueblo Indians would no longer be distinguished from other Indigenous groups—they would become "Indians not taxed" and Indians living on a federally run reservation. But this did not appear to be a problem for Pueblo Indians; they had refuted their territorial and U.S. citizenship in the delinquent tax case, and in the first decade of the twentieth century, becoming wards of the federal government meant protection. In fact, Santa Clarans and Crandall worked simultaneously on the tax exemption legislation and the conversion of the Santa Clara land grants to a reservation. Santa Clarans learned how to navigate the U.S. colonial system, and Crandall learned that in spite of their differences with other American Indian groups, Pueblo Indians were nevertheless "Indians" who did not toe the assimilationist line.

Although there are no letters from Santa Claran members themselves, Crandall's letters to the commissioner of Indian Affairs and the Santa Clara governor regarding the creation of the Santa Clara Reservation suggest that the Pueblo leadership wanted to convert the land grants into a reservation.[23] President Theodore Roosevelt felt amenable to this prospect. Just four months after Congress exempted Pueblo Indians from paying property taxes, the president issued an executive order on July 29, 1905, creating the Santa Clara Reservation.[24] One month later, Crandall wrote to the Santa Clara governor:

> I [sic] affords me great pleasure to announce to you that the reservation asked for, and for which I have diligently worked for more than three years, has been granted, and created by an executive order, which was duly signed by the President at the White House, July 29, 1905. I shall have maps made showing the boundaries of this reservation; it embraces some 33,000 acres; it is from three to four miles wide, not less than three miles at any place, and extends from your eastern line of the Santa Clara Pueblo grant west to the mountains, or the grant known as Location, NO. One.[25]

Crandall was pleased by the executive order. Even though the order further eroded Pueblo Indians' citizenship status and directly breached Crandall's conclusion that Pueblo Indians were citizens, the order opened up the possibility for Crandall to set Santa Clarans on the accepted OIA path toward civilization, moving from federal ward to full citizen. Crandall became a federal "guardian" of Pueblo Indian interests and lands, which, as historian Frederick E. Hoxie writes, was a justifiable, protective "intervention that did not compromise Indian citizenship,"[26] or at least the future prospect of it. Crandall, as the acting agent for the Northern Pueblos District, would manage Santa Clara lands and would "teach" the Pueblo sanctioned land use—and thus citizenship—practices.

Crandall continued his announcement to the governor: "Steps will be immediately taken to protect you in the possession of this reservation. As a reservation, you will understand, that as a Pueblo officer and Governor, you have no jurisdiction over same. The land is for your people; the title is in the Government, and the management rests in the hands of the United States and its officers, the Supt. of the Santa Fe Indian school, being the acting Agent."[27] Under U.S. law, authority to manage land followed the title to the land. This meant that Crandall, as the superintendent of the Santa Fe Indian School and acting agent

for the Northern Pueblos District, had jurisdictional authority in granting grazing permits, timber-cutting permits, and permits for passage
through Pueblo Indian reservations to outsiders. The creation of the
reservation, too, shifted the relationship between Santa Clara Pueblo
and the federal government. Santa Clara Pueblo, from the vantage point
of Crandall, Congress, and the courts, became dependent on the United
States. Santa Clarans did not necessarily view the creation of the reservation in the same way, though.

Despite the New Mexico statutory provision recognizing Indian
Pueblos as corporations, with their attendant rights, Santa Clara continually had to deal with Anglo and Hispano encroachment and trespassing
as well as the possibility that the U.S. government would appropriate
part of its land for a national park. These threats would be quashed if
Santa Clara Pueblo became a reservation—the OIA, then, would be legally compelled to protect Santa Clara boundaries, rout trespassers and
encroachers, and block efforts to make tribal land into a national park.
Such protection, however, would further erode the legal citizenship status of the Santa Clarans, making them functional wards of the U.S. government. While this might seem an uncomfortable backtracking from
independent landownership to dependency, the Santa Clarans did not
seem to view landownership and citizenship in the legalistic way the
federal government did. Rather, they seemed to focus on the long-term
viability of their sociocultural practices. This orientation allowed the
Santa Clarans to accede the management of their lands to the federal
government when it appeared that Pueblo ways of living were threatened. The creation of the Santa Clara Reservation represents a fundamental paradox of landownership, residency, and control for Pueblo
Indians: in order to protect Santa Clara land for the Pueblo's use, it had
to be relinquished to the federal government.

Crandall closed the August 29 letter, "Again I congratulate you; you
now have land sufficient for all time, and if your people will work in
harmony, may become wealthy and the most prosperous of all the Pueblos."[28] Crandall saw the new reservation as an advancement toward the
Pueblo's future economic well-being as well as an opportunity to unify
the factions that had divided Santa Clara since 1894; he learned little,
however, about the Pueblo's motives. The Pueblo, though, had quietly
subverted the assimilationist goals of the OIA, and had the president of

the United States create a place that would be safeguarded from Hispano and Anglo encroachers; the Santa Clarans had learned how to work the U.S. colonial system. The United States had, in effect, created a colonial protectorate wherein Santa Clarans could attend to their daily business with apparently minimal interference.

TAXES

Just two months before Clinton J. Crandall's arrival at the Santa Fe Indian School in February 1900, the district attorney for Bernalillo County in Albuquerque sued Pueblo Indian communities for delinquent property taxes over the previous decade. This case, *New Mexico v. Persons on the Delinquent Tax List of 1899*, together with legal disputes over land and liquor were the litmus tests for Pueblo Indian citizenship in New Mexico. The fundamental question at hand was: were Pueblo Indians "Indians," or were they citizens of New Mexico and the United States? Since the conclusion of the U.S. war with Mexico in 1848, local, state, and federal courts indecisively ruled on this question through the triangular frame of land, liquor, and taxes, with land as the linchpin.

From 1889 to 1898, a number of Pueblo Indian people living in Bernalillo County close to Albuquerque did not pay property taxes on their landholdings because they had never done so previously, and they did not regard themselves as citizens of the New Mexico Territory or the United States. *New Mexico v. Persons on the Delinquent Tax List of 1899* (1904) was the first attempt to enforce the tax obligations of citizenship on Pueblo Indians, and thereby exclude them from the U.S. constitutional provision "Indians not taxed."[29] The case began in 1899, when T. A. Finical, the district attorney for Bernalillo County, sued Indian Pueblos on behalf of the territorial government. In the claim Finical attempted to establish the legitimacy of the suit, and he outlined the ramifications for those individuals who did not pay their property taxes during that nine-year period. As with other tax claims that might have resulted in litigation, this claim's authority hinged on both the accuracy and the process of evaluating annual tax assessments. To establish this, Finical stated that county officials assessed taxed property every year. Those assessments were then verified and endorsed by the Board of Equalization. When assessed taxes were not paid, they accrued a

5 percent penalty, and the tax collector, who was also the county treasurer, published the delinquent tax list in the *Albuquerque Weekly Citizen* for five consecutive weeks.

In the 1899 delinquent tax case against Pueblo Indians, the public advertisement of who owed past-due taxes did not have the desired effect; the taxes went unpaid, producing a series of ramifications for both the county and the individuals on the delinquent tax list. First, a decline in tax revenue hampered the city and county budgets for public schools and programs for other "special purposes." Second, because the property taxes were in arrears and costing the county money, Finical underscored the necessity of the 5 percent tax penalty, and he requested that individuals on the list pay the court costs of the case. Finally, he recommended that the tax collector advertise and sell the land in question to pay the back taxes.[30] The attorney for the Pueblo Indians, G. Hill Howard, requested that two copies of all pertinent documents be sent to him, one for his use as legal counsel and the other for the commissioner of Indian Affairs, who was responsible for assigning representation to the Pueblo Indians sued.[31] The document trail then stops until 1904, when the New Mexico Supreme Court ruled in favor of Bernalillo County. It is at this point that Crandall figures prominently in the legal debate.

On March 12, 1904, just nine days after the court ruled on the tax case, Crandall wrote to the commissioner of Indian Affairs informing him of the Pueblo Indians' legal status:

> The [Supreme Court] of [New Mexico] finds, as I have for along [*sic*] time held, that these Pueblo Indians are citizens in the full sense of the Territory of New Mex., and as citizens, are entitled to all of the rights and benefits of citizenship; that they can and may hold office, as the Court cites they have heretofore done in some instances under Mexican or Spanish regime; that being citizens, means also that they must bear their share of the burden of maintaining the Territory, and that they may be taxed on both real and personal property.[32]

It would seem from this that Crandall was in agreement with the territorial court; but Crandall's position ended up being ultimately quite different from that of the court. The legal question under review in this case was "Are the lands of the Pueblo Indians in New Mexico taxable?"[33] In order for the New Mexico Supreme Court to answer this, it first had to determine if Pueblo peoples were Indians without title to their land, or if they actually had the full rights of land alienability as citizens of the territory and the United States. The court used the Treaty of Guadalupe Hidalgo to ascertain the arrangements the federal government had with different groups—including Pueblo Indians and other Indigenous groups—who lived in the area annexed by the United States. In its opinion, the territorial court cited article 7 of the treaty, reasoning that since the Spanish Crown had given Pueblo Indian communities land grants, which both the Spanish and Mexican regimes recognized, the U.S. government likewise had to recognize Pueblo land claims, as well as those of former Mexican citizens.[34] The court added that because the U.S. government did not hold title to Pueblo lands, and because each Pueblo had a form of self-government, "the Pueblo Indians of New Mexico are citizens of New Mexico and of the United States, [they] hold their lands with full power of alienation, and are, as such, subject to taxation."[35] Because Pueblo Indians owned land and had a history of legitimate landownership sanctioned by colonial governments, the court held that they were "civilized" peoples and should be legally recognized and treated as such. In other words, all Pueblo Indians—not just those on the delinquent tax list—were indeed full citizens of the territory and were thus responsible for paying their share of taxes.

The ruling prompted quick action from both Crandall and the All Pueblos Council. Crandall, in fact, found himself in a bit of a logical conundrum. Although he viewed Pueblo Indians as citizens like the court, he knew that the decision would likely result in significant land loss for the Pueblos. In the same March 12 letter to the commissioner of Indian Affairs in which he expressed his accord with the court on the issue of Pueblo Indian citizenship, Crandall disagreed on their tax responsibility, remarking, "I fear that it means that they will be unable to pay the taxes assessed against them, and that their lands will fast pass into the hands of the Mexican element."[36] In Crandall's view, the U.S. government had to protect Pueblo Indian lands from neighboring Hispanos, even if this meant lost revenue for county coffers. Over the next two weeks, Crandall, the commissioner, and likely the All Pueblos Council

hatched a plan to protect Pueblo Indian landholdings: they would simply ask the U.S. Congress to pass a law that exempted Pueblo Indians
from paying taxes and prevented them from selling their lands.

The All Pueblos Council added further nuance to the plan. As Crandall describes it, the Northern Pueblos Council held a "junta" in Santa
Fe on March 24, 1904, in which the Pueblo representatives agreed that
they opposed the court's decision, that they had never exercised citizenship rights, and that did they did not desire to act as or become citizens.[37] Members of this delegation agreed to meet with delegates from
the Southern Pueblos District two weeks later. When the All Pueblos
Council met on April 6, 1904, the representatives drafted a letter to
the president of the United States, the Department of the Interior, and
Congress. They began by stating what their relationship was to their
individual home Pueblos and the greater Pueblo Indian community in
New Mexico. They continued, "We wish to ask that the President and
the authorities at Washington, and Congress shall hear us in our protest against the taxation of our lands and other property which we pos-
sess." In their protest, the All Pueblos Council—like the New Mexico
Supreme Court—established the Pueblo Indians' distinct and legally
valid land claims, dating to the pre-Spanish period. The council then
argued that since the "President and Congress, the Secretary of the Interior and the Indian Department" were Pueblo Indians' "friends" and
wanted to see their friends treated well in turn, U.S. government officials would surely be willing to listen to the Pueblo request for a tax
exemption in order to protect their lands. The council also argued that
Pueblo Indians were not prepared for citizenship because they did not
have the appropriate education or understanding of the "intelligence"
in play under the U.S. regime. The council wrote, "To tax our people
when we are not by education and otherwise competent to discharge
the duties of citizens is to do us an injustice." To learn these duties,
the council recognized that formal education was necessary and it expressed appreciation for the schools the U.S. government provided and
the expectation that Pueblo Indians would eventually learn the duties
of citizenship. The letter concluded:

> We, therefore, pray that the Indian Department, the Department of
> the Interior, the President of the United States and Congress will act

together in our behalf in this matter to the end that our lands shall be by law exempted from taxation, and to the end that the right of alienation shall be so restricted that our lands may not be sold or disposed of except by the consent of the Pueblo acting as a community through its officers, and of the Secretary of the Interior.[38]

For Pueblo Indians in New Mexico, the core of the tax issue was protecting their lands from the territorial government and those who would buy up property that had been foreclosed upon or sold by individuals living within a Pueblo Indian community. The council's letter would also seem to set them on the expected trajectory for Indian citizenship—from that of ward of the government to full citizen via OIA schooling.

In addition to requesting tax relief, the All Pueblos Council's letter subtly expresses confrontations within communities that undoubtedly stemmed directly from U.S. annexation of the region and subsequent colonial efforts. That the council requested individual sales of Pueblo land be prohibited without the consent of the community and the secretary of the interior suggests that such sales, as discussed earlier in chapter 1, "Land," had occurred in enough communities to warrant a comprehensive ban on them. This further suggests dissension within communities over what appropriate "citizenship" looked like. Did it entail performing the regular collective ditching efforts and ceremonial performances unique to each Indian Pueblo? Or did it mean learning and adapting to the expectations and obligations of citizenship under U.S. law? What the All Pueblos Council letter did not confront was Bernalillo County's claim that public schools were being deprived of tax revenue and the issue of voting. Pueblo Indian children attended OIA or Catholic mission schools, and Pueblo Indians typically did not vote in elections outside of their communities. If True and Crandall's correspondence is any indication, most Native, Hispano, and Anglo people in New Mexico knew this. Even if it were part of the larger idealized social contract inherent in U.S. citizenship, Bernalillo County attempted to tax Pueblo Indians for services and procedures they would not use. Perhaps these points were moot. Regardless, they would have to wait several generations as Pueblo children continued to attend OIA and Catholic schools and presumably learned the rights and responsibilities of U.S. citizenship.

In the meantime, Pueblo Indians in the northern district had declared that they did not want to be citizens of New Mexico, nor had they ever been active citizens under the Spanish and Mexican regimes. Even though the New Mexico Supreme Court had found that both Spain and Mexico regarded Pueblo Indians as "civilized" because they had title to and could sell land, both regimes recognized Pueblo Indians as having an unusual status. The Spanish Crown, for example, afforded certain protections, such as tax exemption and providing legal counsel to Pueblo Indian communities, and accorded Pueblo Indian communities corporate rights.[39] And the Mexican regime, while fully recognizing Pueblo Indians' right to buy and sell land, nevertheless required government approval.[40] Legal scholar Felix S. Cohen writes that although the Mexican government awarded full citizenship status to Pueblo Indians, the practice of treating Pueblo Indians as wards of the government carried through the Mexican Revolution and until 1848, when the United States annexed the northern half of Mexico.[41] In part, the Mexican government viewed the status of "citizen" as a type of reward for the Pueblo peoples who fought alongside Mexican revolutionaries in their bid for independence from Spain. According to the courts and legal scholar Laura E. Gomez, the newly independent Mexican government enacted the Plan of Iguala, which granted full citizenship to its inhabitants regardless of race.[42] The extent to which the Plan of Iguala was enacted, though, appears to have been limited, as evidenced by Pueblo Indians' repeated claims that they never were practicing citizens in Mexico or New Mexico. Additionally, citing historian Herbert O. Brayer, Cohen writes that Mexican authorities were lax in their enforcement of land laws, and many non-Natives acquired Pueblo Indian land.[43] This suggests that the recognition of Pueblo Indian citizenship was very likely in name only, gaining little traction in practice.

The New Mexico Supreme Court's argument that full citizenship for Pueblo Indians conveyed with the negotiation and ratification of the Treaty of Guadalupe Hidalgo, then, seems to rest on tenuous ground, at least as it was lived by Pueblo Indian and Hispano residents. Problematic, too, is the court's assumption that Pueblo Indians had chosen to become citizens of the United States. Under article 6 of the treaty, Pueblo peoples could move to Mexico and retain their Mexican citizenship, or, under article 9, they could remain in their home communities and automatically become U.S. citizens.[44] That the court imagined Pueblo Indians elected to become U.S. citizens by staying put rests on the twin assumptions that Pueblo Indians were informed of and understood the terms of the treaty and that the options in the treaty were reasonable, if not fair. In fact, what Pueblo Indian had chosen was not to become Mexican citizens. This distinction is a subtle point but an important one. For the courts and the U.S. government, this meant that Pueblo Indians became U.S. citizens by default. For Pueblo Indians, this meant they maintained fidelity to their own communities, not a colonizing regime. As the members of the Northern Pueblos Council announced on March 24, 1904, that they never had been nor did they want to be citizens of the territory and United States, Crandall realized their interest in holding to their own communities, and this caught him off guard. In both cases, the learning reflected was based on centuries of dealing with the Other.

Crandall's March 28, 1904, letter expresses his sense of urgency about protecting Pueblo lands through congressional legislation; but it also clearly establishes his own sense of what he thought Pueblo Indians needed in order to make them good U.S. citizens. After arguing that Congress pass legislation exempting Pueblo Indians from property taxes before New Mexico became a state, Crandall concluded his letter: "I would suggest . . . that a clause be inserted giving the United States Government at least one acre in each Pueblo for school purposes . . . it will remove the many obstacles that now present themselves to acquiring school-house sites."[45] Even though the Northern Pueblos Council announced on March 24, 1904, that its people never were and did not want to be citizens of the territory and United States, Crandall recommended a federal, statutory provision carving out space on Indian land for the U.S. school. Leaving Pueblo peoples to their own devices simply was not an option for him because of his position as the superintendent of the Santa Fe Indian School and his belief in the U.S. colonial project. In either case, he was tightly wedded to the idea that Pueblo Indians would be schooled and eventually become U.S. citizens in the fullest sense of the term.

In the meantime, Congress granted Pueblo Indians a reprieve in paying taxes. Crandall wrote to the Santa Clara governor quoting the full clause of the exemption provision:

The lands now held by the various villages or Pueblos of Pueblo Indians, or by Individual members thereof, within Pueblo reservations or lands, in the Territory of New Mexico, and all personal property furnished said Indians by the United States, or used in cultivating said lands, and any cattle and sheep now possessed or that may hereafter be acquired by said Indians shall be free and exempt from taxation of any sort whatsoever, including taxes heretofore levied, if any, until Congress shall otherwise provide.[46]

The legislation not only protected Pueblo Indians from the territorial government, it also ensured that "the Mexican element" would not acquire the lands, as Crandall had wanted.[47] Historian Reginald Horsman writes that as the United States annexed the northern half of Mexico, Hispanos, or former Mexican nationals, were typically depicted by Anglo-Americans as a bastardized, slothful race of people.[48] Gomez argues that racial categorization was different in New Mexico than it was in other territories and states because the Native and Hispano populations were very large in comparison to their Anglo counterpart. The opposite was true for territories such as Texas and California, which had sizable Anglo populations. According to Gomez, this meant that the U.S. government had to co-opt the Hispano population in colonizing New Mexico if it were to make the region "American." One way to do this was to allow Hispanos to identify themselves legally and racially as white. This likened Hispanos to Anglos and excluded Indigenous groups—including Pueblo Indians—altogether; this may or may not have been what Hispanos wanted, as all of the attendant responsibilities, such as paying property taxes, came with "white" citizenship.[49] Historians John Nieto-Phillips, Manuel G. Gonzales, Mario T. García and autobiographer Frances Equibel Tywoniak refer to Mexican elites as Hispanos, or those who took pride in their Spanish heritage and denied any American Indian lineage.[50] This is not necessarily an adoption of whiteness; rather, it is an expression of European descent. The distinction is slight but significant. Calling oneself Hispano recognizes what may be characterized as a racially elite or pure status without claiming the whole of U.S. history as one's own.

Although Hispanos in New Mexico were considered full citizens under U.S. law, neither their legal status nor their identification as white proved tantamount to equality within the territory. Racial assumptions factored into how the law was applied to different groups, despite the courts' charge to follow the laws of the United States. In fact, the composition of the courts in New Mexico was racialized. Gomez writes that in the twenty years after the Treaty of Guadalupe Hidalgo was ratified, justices of the peace in New Mexico were typically Hispanos; district judges and territorial supreme court justices were Anglo.[51] Crandall's letters corroborate this. As illustrated in chapter 1, a Hispano justice of the peace conducted proceedings and issued court orders in Spanish against Samuel Stacher, the additional farmer who tried to enforce Santa Clara Reservation boundaries by preventing Hispanos from cutting timber there. The Hispano justice of the peace found in favor of the Hispano claimant, contesting U.S. governmental authority in the region. The reverse was true with the New Mexico Supreme Court's ruling in the delinquent tax case, which can be seen as an affirmation of Anglo authority in making decisions about land use and ownership.

The reconfiguration of Santa Claran, Hispano, and Anglo relationships came to a head with the 1904 delinquent tax case and the 1905 executive order making Santa Clara Pueblo a reservation. U.S. law conferred jurisdictional authority to manage Santa Claran land on C. J. Crandall, the superintendent of the Santa Fe Indian School and acting agent for the Northern Pueblos District. In turn, this muted previous Santa Claran–Hispano customs on grazing and timber cutting. Crandall—and, by extension, Santa Clarans—had learned how to use U.S. federalism to the Pueblo Indians' benefit. For Crandall, it meant protecting Pueblo Indian lands from those who would encroach upon or simply take them in the name of grazing or past-due taxes. For Santa Clarans, this meant preserving their lands and establishing a regularly patrolled and enforced boundary so that they might go about their internal business with minimal interference from the outside.

LIQUOR

Since the sixteenth century, controlling Indian access to alcohol had been a feature of the European colonization of North America and in the United States; in fact, being able to buy and sell alcohol was a marker of legal U.S. citizenship among American Indians. This was not true of other ethnic groups in the United States, but as historians Izumi Ishii and Peter C. Mancall argue, Euro-American colonists' fears about Indian drinking were the basis of the policies against alcohol consumption and its attendant commerce.[52] The restrictive policies that emerged, though, did not recognize long-standing cultural practices involving alcohol by Indigenous peoples and their neighbors, nor did they serve any original educative role for Native peoples. Rather, liquor policies in New Spain and the United States taught both Native and non-Native peoples how to subvert and co-opt legal regulations. For Santa Clarans and their neighbors, this meant conducting annual fiestas much as they had always done. For Crandall, this meant futile attempts to curtail Pueblo Indian drinking and allegedly joining in the clandestine liquor trade. Whether under the U.S. government or the Spanish Crown, buying and selling alcohol in Indian Country was an illicit activity in spite of a long history of Pueblo Indian and Hispano wine production in New Mexico.

Attempts at colonial control over Indian drinking began roughly fifty years after European arrival. In 1575, in the early period of the Spanish regime, King Philip II of Spain ordered that "no liquor was to be sold to Indians."[53] In the United States, Thomas Jefferson wrote letters to state governors in 1808 asking them to persuade their legislatures to pass laws against selling alcohol to Indians.[54] And in 1834, the federal Trade and Intercourse Act made enforceable the constitutional clause that only the U.S. government could engage in trade and treaty making with American Indian tribes. The act stipulated that only individuals licensed by the U.S. government could buy from and sell goods to Indians, and it banned licensed traders from selling liquor to Indians under penalty of losing trading privileges altogether.[55] The penalties for selling, giving, or bartering liquor with Indigenous populations stiffened at the turn of the twentieth century, at the same time widespread temperance efforts were under way in the United States. Under the law called the Intoxicating Drinks to Indians Act of 1897, the minimum sentence for the first offense of selling liquor to Indians was sixty days in jail and a $100 fine; the fine for subsequent offenses increased to $200.[56] Congress extended the federal reach of the prohibition to the New Mexico Territory with the New Mexico Enabling Act of 1910. This statute required the prospective state to ban the sale of liquor in Indian Country, which included Pueblo Indian communities.[57] Before this act, however, it was unclear whether or not Pueblo peoples were considered Indians.

For Crandall, Indians were Indians, and this included Pueblo peoples. From his perspective, being an Indian meant being subordinate to Anglos and relying on OIA officials for legal assistance. To Crandall, drinking to the point of drunkenness was one of the primary markers that Pueblo Indians were "Indians" and were thus not ready for full citizenship. Both Crandall and True were alarmed and repulsed by the drinking practices of the Santa Clara Indians and their neighbors, particularly on festival days. Other markers, such as the lack of formal schooling, abstaining from participating in U.S. institutions, and practicing traditional tribal customs, were also important, but drinking conveyed a lack of the moral clarity needed for citizenship. While True eventually extended this view to include non-Natives and Natives alike when she became an active member of the Women's Christian Temperance Union, Crandall appears to have maintained different standards for the two groups. The fact that Pueblo Indians requested his assistance and service in tax and land matters reinforced his view that Pueblo peoples were subordinate to and dependent on the federal government. They were, in his eyes, functional wards for whom he had to care, never mind the fact that Pueblo Indians' socialization, with or without alcohol, hinged on relationships developed over centuries.

Pueblo Indian Festivals and Drinking

Pueblo Indian exceptionalities highlighted in the land and tax cases appear to have lost their political grip for Crandall when it came to liquor consumption. For Crandall and True, alcohol use was one of the most despicable and dangerous indicators of Indians' "need" for outside help. Alcohol use or abstention was a type of morality gauge that informed OIA officials of Indians' readiness to become part of mainstream U.S. society. When Pueblo Indians, Jicarilla Apaches from northern New Mexico, and Hispanos celebrated together at annual Pueblo festivals or informal get-togethers along the Rio Grande, long-standing sociocultural practices, such as drinking and gambling, came to the fore. In Crandall's eyes, these practices served as evidence that Jicarilla Apaches and Hispanos corrupted Pueblo Indians, and that the U.S. and New Mexican governments should step in to curb such vices.

After his experience at the 1902 Santa Clara festival, Crandall wrote to the commissioner of Indian Affairs describing what had happened; he also requested that the OIA provide law enforcement officers to check drinking and fighting at other Pueblos on their festival days. According to Crandall's account, N. S. Walpole, the OIA agent for the Jicarilla Apache Reservation, forewarned Crandall that he could not prevent people from attending the Santa Clara festival. When the "50 to 100 Jicarilla Apaches" arrived, they were armed and had liquor, behavior that Crandall might not have seen as unusual for Anglos. Crandall wrote that "a few of the worst element from the Pueblos joined with the Apaches in drinking," which led to fighting. Men and women alike took part in the drinking and brawling, but nobody was seriously injured. The drinking and fighting at the festival unnerved Crandall, though. He recommended "that some steps should be taken to convict the parties who are constantly furnishing these Indians with liquor," and he urged Commissioner Jones to dispatch law enforcement to the upcoming festival at Taos to prevent similar carousing.[58]

Crandall was especially pointed about keeping Jicarilla Apaches out of the Northern Pueblos District. Elaborating on his initial report on the 1902 Santa Clara festival, Crandall wrote a week later:

> On the 12th inst. I reported the state of affairs at the annual feast at Santa Clara Pueblo when one hundred or more Jicarill[a] Apaches came into the Pueblo, got beastly drunk, fought and made it unsafe for all present. I should have stated that nearly all of these Apaches were armed. In view of the fact that it seems impossible for the Agent to keep these Indians at home on their own reservation, and also that there will be another and larger fiesta at Taos Pueblo September 30th, I desire to employ special police for the protection of the Pueblos and the public. I also desire to arrest and hold any of these renegade Apaches that may come to Taos on that date, as they are sure to get drunk and become very offensive and dangerous.[59]

Crandall considered the Jicarilla Apaches to be outsiders who had a corrosive influence on Pueblo Indians' safety and goodness. Neither of Crandall's letters—the August 12 or August 20, 1902—suggest what Santa Clarans thought about the Jicarilla Apaches coming to the festival and drinking, nor do the letters provide much if any clue as to what

festival practices, drinking or otherwise, might have been well established between the two groups. But his letters clearly express what he
did not learn about the two groups—that they had a long-standing relationship with attendant customary practices.

Although little has been written about American Indians' historic
use of alcohol, several studies offer speculative glances that established
practices among Indigenous peoples in northern New Mexico did exist. Anthropologist Edward P. Dozier writes that alcohol consumption
among ceremonial participants at Indian Pueblos was forbidden; how
far this sanction reaches back in time, however, is not clear.[60] But his observation is corroborated by Crandall's observation that only a few of
the Pueblo Indians engaged in drinking, implying that the non-Pueblo
Indians were involved in the ceremonials. The record is similarly scant
for Jicarilla Apaches. Writing about the 1851 extension of the Trade and
Intercourse Act of 1834 into New Mexico Territory, historian Michael
D. Heaston argues that the Mexican government first used alcohol to
undermine Apaches' raiding efforts.[61] After the Treaty of Guadalupe Hidalgo, Jicarilla Apaches continued to drink, and in at least one case, it
resulted in a fight that ended with a Jicarilla chief being killed. In his
comprehensive survey of drinking practices among American Indians,
historian Peter C. Mancall writes that Apache and Navajo peoples used
liquor to reaffirm and strengthen social bonds.[62] It thus seems possible
that the Jicarilla Apaches who attended the Santa Clara festival were
fortifying relationships either among themselves or with their Santa
Clara neighbors.

Crandall either did not or could not recognize this possibility,
though, and he interpreted the behavior he witnessed as singularly destructive and a threat to his authority as the acting Indian agent in the
Northern Pueblos District. Alone, neither he nor Agent Walpole could
compel the Apache and Pueblo Indians to stop drinking at community
celebrations. And if Crandall was to arrest the drinking, he was going
to need the help of law enforcement officers. Apparently, the commissioner of Indian Affairs did not feel the need to contain Jicarilla Apaches
as acutely as Crandall. By mid-September 1902, the commissioner still
had not guaranteed law enforcement for the Taos Fiesta of San Geronimo, and Crandall wrote again urging that Jicarilla Apaches be kept out
of Taos. Crandall warned that without law enforcement, he would "be

helpless against these vagabonds, who in addition to getting drunk, will camp among the Taos Indians and live off from them . . . [until they] are on the verge of starvation owing to the destruction of their crops by grasshoppers."[63] Crandall's implication is clear: if the Jicarilla Apaches were not contained, they would exploit the hospitality of the Taos Indians to the point of breaking, and the appearance of an OIA hold over the Jicarilla Apaches would be shattered.

In marking distinctions between Jicarilla Apaches and Pueblo Indians, Crandall highlights signs of what he believed constituted "civilization," such as farming and having permanently established towns. But what he failed to recognize was that Pueblos along the northern Rio Grande, particularly Taos and Picuris, had centuries-old relationships with the Jicarilla Apaches that had endured throughout the Spanish and Mexican colonial episodes. Historians note that in the early eighteenth century, Pueblo Indians along the northern Rio Grande and northern Apaches had a "symbiotic" relationship that hinged on the exchange of goods and military alliances against common enemies such as the Comanches. Pueblo Indians traded portions of their agricultural yields of corn, beans, and cotton for the Apaches' meat, hides, and salt. These trade networks were natural extensions of already cemented relationships. During the mid- to late seventeenth century, Spanish demands for labor and tribute among the Pueblo Indians became unbearable, provoking the Pueblo Revolt of 1680. In the decades leading up to the rebellion, a number of Pueblo Indians fled their towns and joined the Apaches in what is now northeastern New Mexico. According to Anderson, this conglomerate group became the "Jicarilla" Apaches. As the Pueblo Indians and Apaches lived together, they learned from one another and eventually created a settlement called El Cuartelejo, located in southwestern Kansas, which had irrigated crops, single-story houses, and pottery. The Comanches and Pawnees to the south and the east, however, raided the Jicarilla Apache villages. After nearly a century of syncretic living, the Jicarilla Apaches moved west to the mountains to escape the raids of their Plains neighbors.[64] This history, though, did not register as context or as a concern for Crandall.

What was important to Crandall was controlling the impending situation and ensuring his efficacy as an Indian agent. Throughout 1903 and 1904, Crandall repeatedly requested law enforcement support from the commissioner of Indian Affairs, but was disappointed to learn that he would need to file a specific complaint with the Department of Justice—after the fact—to have a U.S. marshal at his disposal. After the Santa Clara festival of 1903, Crandall lamented, "The Pueblos are usually sober and industrious, but on occasions of this sort it seems they are about as bad as any other Indians."[65] Drinking to excess, then, did not mark a holiday for Crandall, as it appeared to for the Santa Clarans; rather, it signified a weakness of will and "Indianness." It also marked his own inability to curb Indian drinking, something he disdained in other Indian agents.

Even as he struggled to maintain control over his own jurisdiction, Crandall expected other agents to control "their" Indians. On August 7, 1907, Crandall wrote to the commissioner of Indian Affairs about Superintendent H. H. Johnson, the new agent in charge of the Jicarilla Apache Reservation. Apparently, Johnson had written to Crandall, claiming that three Pueblo Indians from the Northern Pueblos District were responsible for providing alcohol to Jicarilla Apaches. Johnson requested that Crandall track down the accused so that they would face charges for distributing liquor to Indians. Crandall responded with ambivalence: "I stand ready to assist in meting out punishment to the guilty—and especially whisky peddlers—but am not sure that we ought to hound the ignorant Indians into the Penitentiary." He also subtly questioned Johnson's effectiveness as an Indian agent: "I feel that the Jicarilla Apache should be protected and not debauched with whisky, and to this end would suggest that he be kept closer on his reservation, and not be allowed to make frequent visits to the Pueblo villages, thus escaping temptation and saving myself and others lots of trouble in dealing with them."[66] Crandall clearly wanted to keep Pueblo and Jicarilla Apache Indians separate from one another, and he expected Johnson to act as a gatekeeper and enforcer. Crandall's response does concede a point Johnson made—that Pueblo Indians and Jicarilla Apaches drank when they socialized at holiday celebrations. Johnson's request that the Pueblo Indians who brought liquor to the Jicarilla Apache Reservation be punished signaled not only that Crandall should hold Indians under his jurisdiction responsible for their actions, but it implied that Pueblo Indians were subject to the law in ways that Jicarilla Apaches were not, drawing attention to the ongoing ambiguity of Pueblo Indians' legal status.

Crandall was also frustrated by Santa Clarans' drinking and gambling with their Hispano neighbors. On December 20, 1906, Crandall wrote to Commissioner Leupp:

> Complaints have come to me repeatedly from the Pueblo of Santa Clara that the Indians from this Pueblo are in the habit of inviting Mexicans to their village and gambling, drinking, and carousing at night. The old governor, Leandro Tafoya, has earnestly tried to break up this debauchery but as his Indians do not obey him he has been helpless to do anything, and has called upon me to use the two police stationed at Santa Clara to assist him in this matter. I have refused to authorize the police to act with the governor believing that as the Pueblo is not [*sic*] an Indian reservation they had no jurisdiction. I have notified some seven heads of families in Santa Clara, however, where gambling and drinking are carried on frequently, that unless this practice is stopped at once I shall file complaints against them before a Justice of the Peace or in the District Court and ask that they be punished according to sections 1305-6-7-8- of the compiled laws of New Mexico, 1897, which provides a heavy fine and imprisonment for gambling. The governor and better men of the Pueblo are acting with me in this matter, and it is the only way that I see in which to break up this state of affairs which has resulted recently in the death of one of their number and the serious injury of another.[67]

That Santa Clarans socialized with neighboring Hispanos is not surprising; but it is surprising that Crandall saw Governor Tafoya's situation as beyond the purview of the OIA and the superintendent's office. Crandall mistakenly claimed that Santa Clara was not a reservation in 1906, perhaps as the result of a typographical error, and he deflected responsibility for managing disagreement over drinking and socializing practices between Santa Clarans and Hispanos; he argued that the territory should prosecute Hispanos for gambling at Santa Clara Pueblo. Crandall's statement that Santa Clarans paid no mind to Governor Tafoya's efforts to stop drinking and gambling at the Pueblo might suggest another manifestation of the ongoing dissension between the Summer and Winter People. This might have been the case to some degree in 1906, but members from both parties later in the decade appear to have united on the liquor question and issues of Crandall's land management. They worked with Father Haelterman, the Catholic priest at the nearby Hispano village of Santa Cruz, Clara D. True, who had returned from her superintendency in California, and William E. Johnson, a special investigator for the OIA, to have Crandall removed from his position as the superintendent of the Santa Fe Indian School and acting agent for the Northern Pueblos District.[68] Just why Crandall abdicated responsibility for intervening on Tafoya's behalf remains unclear, and little secondary literature exists describing alcohol practices between Pueblo Indians and Hispanos in New Mexico.

Drinking Policies

The issue of Indian drinking was not only vexing for OIA officials; it was also problematic for territorial officials in New Mexico who wanted to limit liquor traffic. Pueblo Indians' indeterminate status as full citizens and wards of the federal government was a troublesome obstacle in legislating provisions for the liquor trade in the territory. The rulings in *U.S. v. Lucero* (1869), *U.S. v. Joseph* (1876), and *New Mexico v. Persons on the Delinquent Tax List of 1899* (1904)—all land and tax cases— maintained that Pueblo Indians were not like other Indians and should not be treated as such with regard to property rights. The issue of alcohol use among Pueblo Indians would seem to diverge from the issue of property and taxes; however, like land taxes, the legal ability to buy and sell alcohol was a litmus test of citizenship. During the first decade of the twentieth century, two cases dealing with the distribution of liquor to Indians came before the U.S. and New Mexico supreme courts.

In the 1905 case *Matter of Heff*, the U.S. Supreme Court ruled that Indians who obtained state and U.S. citizenship by going through the land-allotment process possessed all the rights, responsibilities, and privileges of citizenship, including buying and drinking liquor. At issue in the case were three questions: (1) When do land allottee's citizenship rights and responsibilities begin? (2) Do states or the federal government have jurisdiction in instances where Indians buy or sell liquor? and (3) Does federal guardianship over Indians continue after they have become U.S. citizens? In addressing the first question, the

Court noted that the ambiguous wording in the Dawes Act and its subsequent amendments did not clearly delineate when American Indians who have allotments actually have U.S. citizenship rights—when they began cultivating the 160-acre plot of land, or when the federal government issued a patent to the land to the allottee at the end of the twenty-five-year probationary period. The Court found that allottees, not patentees, were considered citizens. The second question over jurisdiction was similarly murky. Tracing the authority of the Trade and Intercourse Act of 1834, which reserved the federal right to regulate the liquor trade with Indians, and the 1897 Intoxicating Drinks to Indians Act, which stiffened the penalties for selling liquor to Indians, back to article I, section 8 of the U.S. Constitution, the Court argued that although states typically have the right to police infringements of the law, the federal government had jurisdiction in cases involving the buying and selling of alcohol to Indians because the Constitution gives Congress the right to regulate *all* trade with Indians. In attending to the final question of whether the federal government continued its role as guardian over Indian tribes, the Court wrote, "Can it be that because one has Indian, and only Indian blood in his veins, he is to be forever one of a special class over whom the General Government may in its discretion assume the rights of guardianship which it has once abandoned, and this whether the State or the individual himself consents? We think the reach to which this argument goes demonstrates that it is unsound."[69] Federal guardianship, then, did not necessarily continue when the U.S. government awarded a final land patent to an allottee, but the Court declined to argue the question fully. Ultimately, neither the states, territories, nor federal government could legally prohibit the sale and consumption of alcohol by Indians who had become full citizens through the allotment process.

But Santa Clarans did not go through the allotment process. Not only did they live on a reservation as of 1905, but they also had tax-exempt status. Pueblo Indian drinking, then, was another legal contest over citizenship rights, responsibilities, and control. In 1907, the New Mexico Supreme Court heard and ruled on *U.S. v. Mares,* a case focused on the distribution of liquor outside of Taos Pueblo. The territorial court found that Pueblo Indians were "citizens" rather than "Indians," arguing that Pueblo Indians were not wards of the government, that they could alienate their land, that they were subject to property taxes, and that they were not beholden to an Indian agent. Citing the 1897 law regarding the distribution of liquor to Indians, *Heff, New Mexico v. Persons on the Delinquent Tax List of 1899,* and *U.S. v. Joseph,* the attorney for Mares argued that Pueblo Indians were not, in fact, "Indians"; they were full legal citizens. The court agreed and provided an explanation as to why the U.S. government provided Pueblo Indians with services similar to other Indian tribes who were considered wards of the federal government: "While Congress has as a mere gratuity from time to time provided agents and special attorneys for them, it has never attempted thereby to reduce them to a state of tutelage or to put either them or their property under the charge or control of the government or its agents."[70] The court's ruling left out significant developments since the delinquent tax case. Notably, the court did not recognize the 1905 federal legislation that exempted Pueblo Indians from paying taxes; the court also overlooked the fact that Santa Clara had become a reservation, making Santa Clarans unable to alienate their land and C. J. Crandall the Indian agent in charge of managing it.

Upon hearing the territorial court's ruling in the *Mares* case, Crandall immediately reengaged the tactic he had used in the delinquent tax case—he recommended to the commissioner of Indian Affairs that bills prohibiting the sale of alcohol to Indians be drafted by both the U.S. and territorial legislatures. With the help of the special attorney for the Pueblos, Crandall felt confident that he could get such a bill passed in New Mexico. He argued that without such measures, the Pueblo Indian would surely destroy himself with liquor and "lose what little property he now has and be an object of pity."[71] Within three months, the New Mexico legislature had passed a law banning the sale of alcohol to Pueblo Indians.[72] This legislation, coupled with the property tax exemption and the creation of the Santa Clara Reservation, moved Pueblo Indians' legal status closer to that of ward than citizen. Crandall's strategy proved successful again—he was able to override a judicial decision through legislation. At the same time, as the Indian agent for the Northern Pueblos District, he carved out jurisdictional authority to enforce an alcohol ban at Indian Pueblos, power he abdicated in 1906 when Governor Tafoya sought Crandall's aid. Why Crandall reversed his position is unclear.

Pueblo Indians' legal status, however, would remain blurry until the U.S. Supreme Court overturned both *Mares* and *Joseph* in the 1913 case *U.S. v. Sandoval*. In evaluating whether Pueblo Indians were citizens or Indian wards of the federal government, the Court found that Pueblo peoples were wards. The Court held that Pueblo Indians were not entitled to the rights and privileges guaranteed to full citizens for several reasons: (1) Pueblo Indians were exempt from paying property taxes; (2) Pueblo Indians could vote only in elections pertaining to ditch work; and (3) a number of Pueblos were reservations under the control of the U.S. government. Quoting Crandall's annual reports to the commissioner of Indian Affairs extensively, the Court argued that Pueblo Indians were economically poor, they still practiced pagan rituals (albeit in tandem with Catholicism), they had not and did not want to integrate into U.S. society, and they had an antiquated sociopolitical system that was not democratic.[73] *Sandoval* resolved the ambiguity of Pueblo Indians' legal status for the time being—they were not citizens.[74] Rather, they were "Indians" like all other Indians, and this signified the Court's missed lesson in the diversity of possible citizenships in Native America.

Battling Saloons in Indian Wine Country

Crandall's apparent protectionism of Pueblo Indians manifested in his attempt to rout saloons in Española, a town just a couple of miles northeast of Santa Clara and San Ildefonso Pueblos and a couple of miles south of San Juan Pueblo (Ohkay Owingeh). In 1903, one year before the New Mexico Supreme Court held that Pueblo Indians were indeed citizens in the delinquent tax case, Crandall wrote a strongly worded letter to the owners and managers of saloons in Española letting them know that he was watching them sell liquor to Pueblo Indians living nearby. He considered "this prima facia [*sic*] evidence or sufficient grounds upon which to institute proceedings against those liquor dealers who allow and permit Indians to enter their place of business, or to loaf and loiter at their doors."[75] Crandall then threatened to bring charges against the saloon keepers using federal law if they did not desist. Presumably, Crandall referenced the 1897 Intoxicating Drinks to Indians Act, which hardened the penalties for selling liquor to Natives. But Pueblo peoples in 1903 were not considered to be like other Indians under the law, making Crandall's threat only that. His letter to the saloon keepers does underscore his position: he was the Indian agent in charge of looking after Pueblo Indians along the northern Rio Grande, and in order to do this with distinction, clearly delineating the boundaries between Indians and non-Indians and invoking the law when appropriate were necessary. And on this issue, Crandall had True's support.

Working through the Santa Clarans she befriended and collecting her own observations, True served as an informant for Crandall, surveilling the flow of liquor and its consumption in the region. In the fall of 1904, she wrote: "There appears to be no secret over the source of the supply—the American saloon in Espanola [sic]. Since the Pueblo citizenship situation has been discussed, the Indians and some other people are under the impression that a citizen Indian is a legal victim for the saloon keeper. Responsible Indians tell me that very little liquor comes to Santa Clara that is not bought from the American dealer."[76] Preceding the liquor cases *Matter of Heff* and *U.S. v. Mares,* True's report reveals that she believed Pueblo Indians to be in a disadvantaged position, preyed upon by non-Native barkeeps in spite of the then-recent 1904 New Mexico Supreme Court decision in the delinquent tax case. Like Crandall, she did not view Pueblo Indians as citizens. While protection might well have been the motive in tracking liquor and threatening reprisal, Crandall and True had to distinguish themselves from both the Pueblo Indians and the saloon keepers. Pueblo Indians were the OIA officials' charges, not their equals, and saloon keepers were simply morally inferior to those trying to teach "Indians" how to live as "Americans." Temperance, after all, was an attribute of responsible citizenship; however, it was myopic in scope and a double standard in practice that neglected the histories of Indian Pueblos and their Spanish neighbors.

Neither Crandall's reports and correspondence nor the opinions of the courts acknowledged that Pueblo Indians had been winemakers for centuries. Although practically no historical research has been done in this area, primary source evidence from the eighteenth century suggests that the relationship Pueblo Indians and neighboring Hispanos had to alcohol was significantly more complex and long-standing than Anglo newcomers recognized in the written record. In a pamphlet published by the Ponderosa Valley Vineyards and Winery, Henry K. Street traces wine growing in New Mexico to 1629 when Spaniards, against Spanish law, brought grapevines to their northern colonies in the Americas. Despite the Crown's prohibition on winemaking in the Americas to protect the interests of Spanish vintners in Europe, the demand for wine among Spanish colonists and the church in New Mexico was great enough to flout the law. Wine production in New Mexico began south of Albuquerque at Senecú Pueblo and spread north to Santa Cruz de la Cañada, a Spanish town just east of Española, by 1775. Grapevines fared better further south, but they were certainly not unknown north of Albuquerque.[77] Much of what Street found for his pamphlet relies on Fray Francisco Atanasio Domínguez's inspection report of the Spanish missions in New Mexico. Beginning his tour in 1775, Fray Domínguez noted the agricultural practices and crops grown at each mission and Pueblo as well as the local church's amenities and the local priest's efforts to convert Pueblo Indians to Catholicism. In addition to noting vine stocks at Albuquerque, Isleta Pueblo, and Santa Cruz, Domínguez found numerous fruit orchards and melon crops at Indian Pueblos throughout the northern Rio Grande valley. These yields would almost certainly have been traded in the northern Pueblos with their Jicarilla Apache neighbors for hides, meat, and salt. Domínguez also described the rivers near communities and how irrigation systems had been constructed. Though each of the agricultural entries is brief, as a whole they reveal well-established, extensive, and productive agricultural systems that included grape vineyards.[78] In fact, in 1852 John Greiner, one of the first U.S. Indian agents in New Mexico, remarked that Pueblo Indians made "moonshine."[79] Greiner might not have recognized that the "moonshine" was wine.

Just who used the wine from these vineyards and for what purposes is somewhat of a mystery, though we might speculate that hospitality and Catholicism figured prominently. Mancall writes that drinking served a variety of functions depending on the community, including "to enhance hospitality, to appease deities, to bring temporary respite from quotidian troubles, to create or solidify alliances, to facilitate bouts of spirit possession, to lower inhibitions and allow freer communications."[80] If Dozier's assertion that Pueblo Indians who participated in Indigenous ceremonials did not drink is true and traces back to the turn of the twentieth century, then alcohol consumption would not have necessarily been considered a sacred act, as it is with the taking of Communion in the Catholic Church. Pueblo Indians might well have consumed wine during Communion at their mission church, possibly signifying that a relationship between the community and the church—and its priest—existed and was worth renewing. Outside of the church, Pueblo Indians might have shared alcohol with their Native and non-Native neighbors to affirm their bonds, as with the Jicarilla Apaches or with Hispanos who socialized with Indian Pueblos. This possibility is speculative, as Crandall's and True's observations were accompanied by damning judgments against liquor consumption.

Historians Peter C. Mancall and Kathryn A. Abbott argue that U.S. government officials often did not understand the role alcohol played in different Native communities. Mancall argues that federal policy makers integrated the temperance movement's charge into its "civilizing" mission for American Indians, as seen with the Trade and Intercourse Act of 1834, while Native religious revivalists adopted temperance as a form of resistance against Euro-American encroachment.[81] Both Mancall and Abbott point out that Anglos who observed and commented on Indian drinking, most of whom were Indian Office employees, did not seem to notice Euro-American drinking, which surpassed that of Indians. Abbott attributes observers' comments to their own cultural biases about alcohol and Indians as well as their limited access to the full range of social spaces and circumstances in which Indians drank.[82] Crandall's and True's commentary on Pueblo Indian drinking at festivals and at Española saloons certainly corroborates Abbott's and Mancall's argument. The limited view of the possibilities for why Indians drank and its resulting skewed generalization that all Indian drinking was to excess perpetuated the "firewater myth," or the claim that Native peoples were biologically more prone to drunkenness and alcoholism than any other racial or ethnic group. Although researchers have debunked this myth with clinical tests, Crandall and True appear to have taken the firewater myth as fact.[83] For example, in the fall of 1904 he wrote to True, "These Indians have drank all their lives, as near as I can determine, and I fear we will be unable to reform them. Many people are under the impression that citizenship for the Indian changes his status so far as buying liquor goes; I have corrected many, and we should try to inform the public on this."[84] Crandall appears to have believed that Pueblo Indians—like all Indians—were innate drinkers whose access to liquor needed to be cut off if they were to become viable citizens.

Drinking also carried certain gender expectations. For Euro-Americans in the nineteenth and early twentieth centuries, respectable women did not drink in public. According to Mancall and Abbott, though, many Native women did. Mancall argues that Indian women in the Great Lakes region in the early nineteenth century were responsible for maintaining and running local trade networks. Thus, women were often the ones engaged in distributing alcohol. In the early twentieth century, Abbott writes, Anishinaabe women drank in saloons. She argues that non-Natives used this fact to undermine Native cultural practices and claim Euro-American superiority. Women drinking was beyond the bounds of moral acceptability for those set on assimilating American Indians to Anglo-American ideals of behavior.[85] These norms manifested in Crandall's and True's commentaries. After his 1902 experience at the Santa Clara festival, Crandall remarked, "The [Apache] women are little better than the men."[86] Two years later, True wrote to Crandall complaining of drunken brawls at Santa Clara: "This morning I found two of my little school girls trying to take care of a drunk father, a drunk mother and two crying babies."[87] Both Crandall and True scorned women drinking, implying that even if no Indians should drink, gendered differences should exist, or else violence and family neglect were sure to result. These were certainly troubling outcomes of drinking, and they would be for any community. But Santa Clara was not any community; it was an Indian Pueblo being watched and judged by OIA officials who had their own moral views about liquor and its gendered use.

Those Pueblo Indians who demonstrated some desire to change their drinking practices found friends in the Indian Office. In one case, True lobbied for two young women who wanted to enroll in the Santa Fe Indian School. One was divorced and her baby had died, prompting her to drink herself into muteness at the 1904 Santa Clara festival. True wrote to Crandall that she believed the woman to be earnest in her effort, and that with the support of her friend, she would do well under Crandall's care. "She is improving in speaking and appears perfectly well [in] every other way. She and the first girl I mentioned are great friends and I have an idea that one would not go without the other. The grass widow speaks English as she was a Santa Fe pupil some years ago. Both girls are better behaved than average and are good workers at home."[88] True believed the young women to be "good" and capable of succeeding in school. She respected their efforts to change themselves, particularly since their efforts aligned with Crandall's and True's shared ideals of Indian betterment. True's letter convinced Crandall of the merit in the young women's efforts, and he enrolled them in the Santa Fe Indian School.[89]

True also observed and reported on those who did not move to reform their practices. In late 1903, she reported that two Santa Clara men—Benjamin and Severiano—obtained alcohol from employees at the Santa Fe Indian School for a year-end festival at the Pueblo. True implied that Crandall should have had control over the employees at his school, stating, "I cannot make affidavit to this but I am told it is true and I don't doubt it."[90] Crandall deflected suspicion away from the Santa Fe Indian School and stated that the two men who allegedly supplied the liquor denied doing so. Crandall said he believed them, but added that they might have contributed money to purchase it. Crandall added, "They are both fairly good boys, and I have as much confidence in what they tell me as any information that you could get in the Pueblo."[91] While this exchange might reflect different views Crandall and True had about these two young men, it also signals Crandall's lack of trust in True's information and True's lack of confidence in Crandall's administration.[92] Their mutual distrust does not appear to have ever been remedied, nor their views of Pueblo Indian drinking modified.

CONCLUSION

The issue of legal citizenship for Santa Clarans and other Pueblo Indians in the late nineteenth and early twentieth centuries is complex and often contradictory, bouncing back and forth between judiciaries and legislatures as well as territorial and federal authorities. Each case that landed in the courts on the issue of citizenship illustrated how Anglo judges and lawmakers regarded Pueblo Indians as distinct from other American Indian groups. In part, this had to do with Pueblo Indian communities' long-standing sedentary, agricultural lifestyle and their practice of Catholicism. Too, the U.S. government and its officials paid close attention to the fact that the previous colonial regimes—the Spanish and the Mexican—regarded Pueblo Indians as unique, meriting special provisions such as community land grants. When instances of encroachment, property taxes, or the sale and consumption of alcohol became issues of public debate and legal discussion in the U.S. colonial regime, the exceptionality of Pueblo Indians and their official legal standing were tested.

Perhaps unexpectedly, Clinton J. Crandall, the superintendent of the Santa Fe Indian School and acting agent for the Northern Pueblos District, became a force that federal authorities took seriously. His legal education, including a deep understanding of federalism and discrete OIA policies and territorial laws, enabled him to advise Santa Clarans and other Pueblo Indian communities in ways that officially protected their land base and other property holdings. Crandall was instrumental in obtaining tax exemptions and a reservation for the Santa Clarans; at the same time, he was also influential in passing a territorial law banning the sale of alcohol to Pueblo Indians. Each of Crandall's actions through his reporting and lobbying efforts in cases of land, liquor, and taxes amplified the federal government's role—and thus Crandall's—as a guardian of Pueblo Indian peoples as it chipped away at individual Pueblo Indians' citizenship rights and responsibilities. What emerges is a picture of Crandall as an agent who sought exceptions to carrying out certain federal and territorial citizenship policies in a paradoxical attempt to control the bounds of Pueblo citizenship, all the while positioning himself as an advocate for the Pueblos as Indian communities. In each of the negotiations in which Crandall served as a Pueblo Indian advocate or critic, he neglected their histories as sovereign communities and peoples who had cultivated long-standing relationships with Hispano and other Native groups, simultaneously developing attendant social practices.

Crandall missed the lesson that had served Pueblo Indians so well over the centuries: learning the policies and systems of a new colonial regime was necessary for survival. Pueblo Indians used Crandall's education to build their own, learning U.S. federalism and strategies they might employ to protect their homelands and social practices. Crandall missed Santa Clarans' underlying intention to convert the Santa Clara land grants into an Indian reservation so that its boundaries might be protected from encroachment so that they could live on their own terms. Crandall similarly missed the All Pueblos Council's rationale for apparently conceding ignorance in U.S. custom and citizenship policy. There is certainly a degree of truth to its claim, but it is worth underscoring that the council paradoxically requested tax relief while simultaneously refusing to participate in the U.S. system. At first glance, it would seem that U.S. government officials would be pleased with this move and that Santa Clarans and other Pueblo Indians reduced themselves and their status without a fight. It might appear as though they acknowledged their Indianness and acquiesced to normative expectations about how Natives should assimilate to U.S. society. This interpretation breaks down, however, when we consider that living on a reservation and becoming wards of the U.S. government offered more protection than living as landowners and full citizens of New Mexico and the United States. In this way, the Santa Clarans and other Pueblo Indians radically subverted federal Indian policy.

CHAPTER FOUR

Institutions; or, Getting Schooled by the U.S. Colonial System

INTRODUCTION

By the turn of the twentieth century, Natives and non-Natives found themselves in colonial relationships that had been entrenched and re-iterated over the previous century. And as these colonial relationships became more ensconced in the national zeitgeist of the nineteenth century with the rapid expansion of non-Natives into Native territory, institutions such as schools and the Office of Indian Affairs (OIA) became corporeal bodies that simultaneously symbolized colonial relationships and reproduced them discretely over an expansive geographic area. The concurrent expansion of formal Indian schools and the Indian Office in the late nineteenth and early twentieth centuries occurred in an era of reform in the United States. Not only did the Progressive agenda emerge, working to curb such things as child labor and excessively long workdays, but growing too was an increasingly pervasive orientation toward the scientific streamlining of production and management processes. Both would be hallmarks and evidence of "progress" in technology and in social development. The institutional development of the Indian Office and its schooling project, though, substituted protective regulations for an industrial model in which students at boarding schools maintained the school and its grounds, with only a portion of their day dedicated to academic learning. And the OIA accounted for student activity, as well as that of teachers, superintendents, matrons, and disciplinarians, through a highly bureaucratic and hierarchical system of policy and procedure.

The institutional aspect of the U.S. colonization project has been well documented in histories of schools—particularly on- and off-reservation boarding schools—established to transform American Indian children into U.S. citizens and converts. Much of the scholarly attention in this vein has illuminated both the OIA's Indian School Service structures and curricula as well as students' and their families'

Santa Fe Indian School, ca. 1902. Courtesy of Gordon Crandall, Family Collection.

experiences in and with boarding schools. Little has been written, though, about on-reservation day schools established for Indigenous children under the age of twelve or the Indian Office as a singular institution. But much of what went on inside the day school at Santa Clara, among others, remains a mystery to be uncovered. In part, this can be attributed to teachers like Clara D. True, who did not account for their adaptations (or subversions) of the OIA's *Uniform Course of Study*, the comprehensive curriculum for Indian Office boarding and day schools, nor did they document their pedagogical practices or save their students' work. Instead, for True at least, issues that permeated the Santa Clara community in which she lived and worked comprised the subject matter of her correspondence with Crandall. We are left with only glimpses of what went on inside the walls of the Santa Clara day school during her watch. In addition to a limited documentary record of pedagogy, little scholarly attention has been paid to day schools, leaving much of the archival material not yet explored and oral histories not yet recorded. Presumably, though, the *Uniform Course of Study* governed action within a given school, and certainly expected protocols reflecting OIA hierarchy and procedure were enforced.

The compulsory aspect and structure of schooling, its curriculum, and the organization of the Office of Indian Affairs reflected how Euro-Americans' perceived relationships with Indigenous populations. Looking at these relationships through the institutional lens of the school and the OIA, we see gross imbalances of power, with the U.S. government and its representatives—the colonizers—defining policy and shaping narratives about American Indians—the colonized—that would be echoed and replayed throughout the nineteenth and twentieth centuries. This does not mean that Indigenous groups subscribed to outsiders' characterizations; but it does imply that Indigenous groups were institutionally caught in those characterizations and the relationships that emerged from them. Little in the correspondence between True and Crandall reflects what students and their families felt or thought about the Santa Clara day school or the Santa Fe Indian School. Approaching the correspondence obliquely, and corroborating it with other regulatory documents, does offer glances at how True and Crandall interpreted the curriculum and "civilizing" policies they were expected to carry out and suggests how they learned to work the institutions of the school and the OIA to their advantage in locations remote from headquarters in Washington, D.C.

SCHOOLING NATIVES

Speaking at the 1888 annual Friends of the Indian meeting at Lake Mohonk, New York, reformer Lyman Abbott declared, "Adequate, continuous, systematic education of fifty thousand pupils for less than half a century would solve the Indian problem. It would not be costly. Schools are less expensive than war. It costs less to educate an Indian than it does to shoot him. A long and costly experience has demonstrated that fact."[1] If education was cheaper than the comprehensive extermination of various tribes, and if predominantly Anglo policy makers still believed in their superiority to Indigenous peoples, the government's schooling of American Indian children would be a hard-line experiment of controlled cultural conversion in the name of civilization. The "Indian problem" was a racialized cultural predicament for Anglo reformers, policy makers, and—by association—American Indians. The "Indian problem" was, in fact, a profound colonization problem for non-Native reformers. Seth Low, a prominent New York City leader and member of the Friends of the Indian society, framed it this way: "The Indian problem, in its fundamental aspect, is, then, Must the red man disappear with his civilization?"[2] By displacing the problem of cultural conversion in U.S. colonization efforts onto American Indians, both Abbott and Low presuppose the ultimate victory of Euro-American civilization over Native cultures and the North American landscape. Francis Leupp, the commissioner of Indian Affairs from 1905 to 1909, saw it a bit differently. Writing in his annual report to Congress in 1905, he commented that Anglos made two common mistakes in thinking about and dealing with Indians: (1) that the Indian "is a white man with red skin"; and (2) "that because he is a non-Caucasian he is to be classed indiscriminately with other non-Caucasians." Leupp argued instead that American Indians were part of a distinct racial group with unique cultural standards and ways of living that Anglos needed to understand if they were to grasp the nature of "the Indian."[3] In making this statement, though, Leupp made an analogous error—he lumped all Indian groups together. While there may be striking similarities across a number of North American Indigenous societies, there are distinguishing characteristics between them. And as has become apparent, Pueblo Indians did not fit many of the cultural or legal generalizations made about American Indians. Regardless of this error, reformers did not consider American Indians and Anglos to be the same or equivalent; they believed that Native peoples needed to be "civilized" by Anglo agents and institutions.

The idea that Indians could become "civilized" through schooling rests on several assumptions. Broadly, the process of civilization was tantamount to the assimilation of the ideals and practices held by members of the dominant culture, including individual land ownership, Christianity, compliance with the law, and schooling the young. Fundamental to assimilation was a strong belief that people change in an evolutionary manner and that schools can hasten the development of peoples from savage to civilized. As Abbott implied with his assertion that "schools are less expensive than war," reformers believed that changing the way children thought and interacted with each other, their home societies, and the dominant society was the best way to reshape entire minority cultures. Not only were children malleable, particularly when removed from their families, but, reformers also believed, children, as agents of civilization, would sustain the cultural transformation of their tribes by becoming members of the dominant society.[4] The motivating belief underlying assimilationist programs was reformers' deeply held conviction that Anglos were meant to dominate the North American continent. Technological innovation as well as the rapid expansion of domestic and foreign markets was seen as evidence of divine favor.[5] The foundational elements of mainstream U.S. culture—capitalism, Christianity, and technological advancement—did not operate independently; they were mutually reinforcing. Thus, every acre gained by an Anglo settler and every Indian who became a Christian was validation of the American experiment and God's approval of it. Such a circular validation eliminated the need to atone for the removal of non-Christian Indians from their land and reflected a profound lack of consideration for Native ways of knowing and living in the world.

Educating Indians for productive citizenship in U.S. society was supposed to be an experience of wholesale intellectual, social, cultural, and religious conversion, or the complete relinquishment of one sociocultural system for another. Thomas J. Morgan, the commissioner of Indian Affairs from 1889 to 1893, wrote that through education, Indians were to become like whites: "When we speak of the education of Indians, we mean that comprehensive system of training and instruction which will convert them into American citizens, put within their reach the blessings which the rest of us enjoy, and enable them to compete successfully with the white man on his own ground and with his own methods."[6] The ways of "American citizens," then, were the measuring stick by which success in society was to be determined. Elliott West, a historian of western U.S. history, and James D. Anderson, a historian of education, argue that in colonizing what we now know as the continental United States, Anglo policy makers assumed their sociocultural superiority and never seriously considered having to find ways of living amicably and equally with people of other racial groups. Anglos were, after all, the people making policy from positions within the U.S. government. By the 1870s, a pungent belief in social Darwinism had taken hold in the United States. At the end of the nineteenth century, this expanded to include the idea that although different races might be at unequal stages of development, they all followed the same evolutionary

trajectory. Believing that they were at the leading edge of this multieth-
nic evolutionary trajectory toward cultural homogeneity, Anglo policy
makers postulated that schooling could accelerate "lower" races' progress. This, in turn, marked policy makers' shift in how they addressed
the so-called Indian problem from extermination to assimilation. The
Office of Indian Affairs' educational system for Natives reinforced the
goal of assimilation through an evolutionary schooling trajectory that
included compulsory provisions, a uniform curriculum, and several levels of "progressive" schooling.[7]

In carrying out a program of assimilation, which stipulated that
American Indians should become self-sufficient U.S. citizens, the federal government assumed guardianship over Native students, including
Pueblo Indians. As the U.S. government negotiated treaties with various Indigenous tribes throughout the nineteenth century, it established
a series of trust relationships that provided a variety of services to those
tribes, often in exchange for land. One such service was schooling for
Native children. Even though treaties had not been concluded with each
Pueblo community, the federal government acted on learned colonization precedent—it assumed a trust relationship existed and formed Indian agencies for Pueblo Indians and other Indigenous groups that lived
within the region the United States had acquired under the Treaty of
Guadalupe Hidalgo in 1848. Regardless of formal agreements, the federal government expected Indians to assimilate to Anglo-defined norms,
values, and social practices.[8] In 1889, Commissioner Morgan argued:

> They must stand or fall as men and women, not as Indians. Society
> will recognize in them whatever is good and true, and they have no
> right to ask for more. If they persist in remaining savages the world
> will treat them as such, and justly so. Their only hope of good treat-
> ment is in deserving it. They must win their way in life just as other
> people do, by hard work, virtuous conduct, and thrift.[9]

If American Indians failed to meet the standards set by white reformers, Indians had failed; Anglos had not. This was to be a one-directional
transformation: Indians were to become like Whites, not the other way
around.

For Pueblo Indians, the assumed trust relationship of the U.S. government was problematic in terms of their citizenship, as illustrated in

the previous chapter. Between 1869 and 1913, the courts, Congress, and the office of the president diminished Pueblo Indians' legal citizenship status. When the U.S. Supreme Court definitively ruled that Pueblo Indians were wards of the federal government, the Court recognized that a trust relationship had been in place for a number of years. The Court quoted extensively from C. J. Crandall's annual reports to the commissioner of Indian Affairs in its opinion to illuminate the dependency Pueblo Indians had on the U.S. government as well as their inferiority as distinct cultures. In this way, Crandall, the schoolmaster of Pueblo Indian students and the agent-implementer of federal Indian policy, ended up being a policy maker.

Compulsory Schooling

The push for compulsory schooling was a significant and problematic detail for the Indian Office. While those who ran Indian schools believed they helped assimilate and prepare Native children for their lives beyond the tribe, Indian schools were dependent on the attendance of Native children, as historians of Indian education have pointed out. In spite of—and perhaps because of—this dependence, many school administrators thought the solution was compulsory education. In 1888, Lyman Abbott argued that only compulsory education would lead Native children from barbarism to civilization and that Indian parents had no moral grounds for keeping their children out of schools. No comprehensive federal law was passed to compel Indian students to attend government-run schools, however; this was left to state and territorial legislatures.[10] One strategy for compelling Native families to send their children to school came in 1893, on the heels of Thomas Jefferson Morgan's term as the commissioner of Indian Affairs. In its appropriations bill for the Indian Office, Congress tied families' rations and stipends to their children's school attendance. If parents living in areas where there were adequate schooling facilities refused to send their children there, the secretary of the interior could withhold treaty-stipulated rations. In the following year's appropriations bill, Congress mandated that Indian agents obtain voluntary consent from parents to send their children to school and specified that Indian agents could not withhold rations from Native families if they did not agree to send their children to school. That was at the discretion of the secretary of the interior.[11] In

1896, though, Commissioner of Indian Affairs Daniel Browning frankly stated that Indian parents did not have a right to decide where—or whether—their children would go to school. The Browning Ruling was a hard-line position that officially lost support under William A. Jones's tenure as commissioner of Indian Affairs, but that remained the policy in practice into the mid-twentieth century. Both Jones and Leupp specified that parents could decide where to send their children to school, but they could not keep their children out of school. These strategies, coupled with the addition of a number of new schools in western territories and states, appear to have worked on a large scale. As historian David Wallace Adams notes, the total number of Indian children in federal schools quadrupled between 1880 and 1900.[12]

The increase in attendance at Indian schools across the country did not appear to ameliorate Crandall's unease about student enrollment in schools within the Northern Pueblos District, likely because appropriations for each school were based on its enrollment.[13] Crandall began advocating for a territorial compulsory education law before True's arrival in the Española valley. In fact, Crandall wanted to make sure that students remained at the government school in which they initially enrolled to prevent student transfers to Catholic schools in the area. This not only protected his enrollments at the Santa Fe Indian School and at day schools within the district, it "require[d] Indians to take advantage of the free schools which have been established."[14] Crandall wanted this "advantage" to be compulsory for Pueblo Indians. He drafted and attempted to get a compulsory education law passed in the New Mexico Territory in the fall and winter of 1902, requesting information about the Idaho compulsory school law from the office of Estelle Reel, the superintendent of Indian Schools. Though her office did not have a copy of the law, Crandall persisted in his efforts.[15] He thought that it would pass within a year, "tak[ing] the school question out of the hands of parents and Pueblo officers."[16] Crandall found support for his bill with William A. Jones, the commissioner of Indian Affairs, and the editor of the Santa Fe daily newspaper, the *New Mexican*, who stated that he thought the bill was "a step in the right direction."[17] The territorial legislature, however, concluded that compelling Indian students to attend school was beyond its jurisdiction since Indians—including Pueblo Indians—were quasi wards of the federal government.[18]

Pueblo Indian parents did not always agree with Crandall regarding the "advantages" of schooling. In 1906, Julius Seligman, the owner of the Bernalillo Mercantile Company situated between Santa Fe and Albuquerque, wrote to Crandall, reporting that the governor and principales of Santo Domingo Pueblo had opted not to send children to school after their initial five-year enrollment. Seligman wrote:

> They say, that none of the Principals know anything about the agreement which you mention, only, that they were supposed to send 52 children to school for 5 years, and that, when their time expired they were not supposed to put other children in their places. They say, that they know of no agreement to put other children in their places. They wish to know, who, was the Indian, who made an agreement, such as you mention, also, who was Governor at the time, and who acted as interpreter.[19]

The Santo Domingo leadership had understood their students' enrollment in the Santa Fe Indian School to be a onetime negotiated contract, not a perpetual requirement. Their questioning of Crandall about the Santo Domingoan who made the deal with Crandall and the interpreter who translated the negotiation suggests that the sentiment within the community had changed. Though the 1906 Pueblo leadership was willing to return to the Santa Fe Indian School students who had not finished their five-year stint, they were not keen on sending an additional group of students to the school.

By 1907, New Mexico still did not have a compulsory education law for American Indian students. Though the territorial legislature considered such a law in 1905, it did not pass, and the only compulsory education law on the books applied exclusively to students whose parents were citizens. For Crandall, this left Pueblo Indian children in an uncertain position given their parents' indeterminate status as quasi citizens. And, according to Crandall, the law was not enforced. Unlike other states that had passed compulsory education laws for Native students, such as Idaho and South Dakota, New Mexico lagged behind in carrying out—or smoothing the way for Crandall to carry out—its colonial mission of schooling Indigenous youth. Crandall steadfastly believed that Pueblo Indians needed a law that compelled them to send their children to school. He remarked, "Indian parents are often prevented from sending their children to school through the whimsical notion of some old grandmother, and there are many obstacles in the way of a superintendent in getting children into school."[20] Crandall's comment supports the argument that government-run schools were dependent on Indian families' agreement to send students.[21] More pointedly, Crandall's comment suggests that women, particularly older women, in Pueblo Indian communities had significant say over what children in their households did. This certainly echoes True's frustration with one grandmother during the diphtheria outbreak of 1903. It also suggests that Hill's understanding of household authority was undeveloped and that his assertion that Santa Claran women did not have powerful roles in the community might well have been flatly wrong or at least misunderstood. Indeed, Jeançon's field notes from the early twentieth century indicate that grandparents were the primary caretakers of children during the day, and that men moved to where their spouses lived.[22]

Generally speaking, and perhaps in contrast to other Pueblo Indian communities, the Santa Claran response to U.S. government schooling appears to have been enthusiastic. Not only did True report early on in her tenure that the governor and principales urged children to attend the day school, they also said they would enforce their recommendation. The governor told True that he would "compel the regular attendance of all pupils," and one of the principales instructed True to "flog his own boy in the presence of the school for truancy."[23] The governor's and principales' apparently fervent enthusiasm for the government-run school is arresting in light of the abundant literature on American Indian boarding school education. Scholars recount numerous instances of government officials stealing children away from their home to make them attend boarding schools distant from their families. At the same time, there are numerous examples of parents and students willingly acceding to the necessity of school and of students forming lasting and profound relationships with each other at boarding schools.[24] The physical location of the day school on Santa Clara land, however, coupled with the normative expectations of social behaviors at the Pueblo, may have been a factor in the governor's and principales' response to True. According to anthropologists, conformity, or the expectation that community members would adhere to rules of behavior and abide by decisions Pueblo leaders made, was a central tenet of Tewa societies, including Santa Clara Pueblo. The Santa Claran governor, principales, and Summer cacique might have tactically decided to compel attendance at the day school for several reasons: (1) to observe True as an OIA agent; (2) to demonstrate trust in or willingness to work amicably with True in her new role at the Pueblo; (3) to garner Crandall's support for other causes, knowing that True would have to report her enrollment numbers to him; (4) to direct attention toward something government agents wanted to see in order to draw attention away from other practices the U.S. government frowned upon, such as customary dances and rituals; (5) to ensure that the government upheld its end of a contractual relationship; or (6) to learn from Anglos about non-Native U.S. society in order to navigate relationships that would foreseeably continue into the future. Given the other events that were developing at the time, such as the push to create a reservation, some combination of these options is likely.

Santa Claran support for schooling was limited, though, when it came to sending their children—particularly their girls—away to boarding school. Crandall commented on the Pueblos' reluctance to send girls to the Santa Fe Indian School in his annual reports to the commissioner of Indian Affairs. In 1905 he wrote to Commissioner Leupp:

> The Pueblos send the younger children to school and keep the larger and older ones at home to work; the Pueblo girls seldom remain in school after they reach the age of thirteen or fourteen; in some of the the [*sic*] Pueblos, the most of them for that matter, there is strong objection to education for the girls. They will permit the boys to attend school possibly five years, but they can see no reason for sending the girls to school; they say that the girls must keep the house, grind the meal, carry the water, etc., and that education does them little or no good. It is therefore hard to get girls into the school, and when we do they are generally young.[25]

Two years later, Crandall again reported on the small number of girls enrolled at the Santa Fe Indian School, attributing it to girls marrying at an early age. It would seem that the Indian Pueblos were not convinced that the practical, domestic curriculum for girls was worth the labor and expense of having them away from home for so long, especially if they were supposedly learning skills they already had. Even if the Santa

Fe Indian School had offered a curriculum that extended the possibilities for girls to do something beyond household management, Indian
Pueblos might not have sent girls to school if they were likely to reject
their home communities' social customs upon their return or leave the
home communities all together. Indeed, Crandall remarked that those
students—male and female—who continued at the Santa Fe Indian
School had a very difficult time reintegrating into Pueblo life when they
had finished their schooling.[26]

When older Santa Claran girls were interested in attending the Santa
Fe Indian School, Crandall enthusiastically admitted them, and there
were several such during True's tenure as day school teacher. In the fall
of 1904, following True's recommendation to enroll two young women
from Santa Clara Pueblo who spoke English and had been in school
when they were much younger, Crandall admitted the women the day
after receiving True's letter. Notably, one of the young women was divorced and had a child who had died.[27] The following year, two more
girls from Santa Clara requested to be enrolled at the Santa Fe Indian
School; Crandall likewise admitted them immediately.[28] And throughout True's term at Santa Clara, both Clara Naranjo and Brigida Swaso
attended the Santa Fe Indian School. When Naranjo and Swaso eventually left the school, they worked for the Indian School Service as laundresses at day schools in the Northern Pueblos District.[29]

The seemingly anomalous enrollment of each of the girls True sent
to Santa Fe is curious and begs the question of why they were permitted to go away to school for extended periods of time. In the case of
the divorcée, it is possible that she had lost her place in the Santa Clara
community and might have seen the Santa Fe Indian School as a type of
refuge. Anthropologist W. W. Hill writes that divorce was uncommon
and socially undesirable at Santa Clara. True's regular community reports support this. In her letters, she noted there were not any divorces
during the five years she spent at Santa Clara. As for Swaso, her father
was a member of the Winter party. While True and Crandall character-
ize this faction as supportive of the schooling and medical treatment
provided by the U.S. government, it is also possible that the daughters
of Winter party members had nothing to lose by going to school for a
longer period than was customary.[30]

There is a certain irony in compulsory schooling for American

Indians. One of the primary motivations of the government in providing schooling for Native peoples was to make them individually self-sufficient, a quality many nineteenth- and early twentieth-century reformers and policy makers thought most Indigenous peoples lacked. Yet, the dependent relationships in which Indians found themselves were reminders that the means by which they had been tribally self-sustaining had been largely removed. Rather than see this irony, many reformers saw Indians as culturally deficient and pushed for individualism and self-sufficiency. In his annual report to Congress in 1901, William A. Jones, the commissioner of Indian Affairs, wrote, "Born a savage and raised in an atmosphere of superstition and ignorance, he [the Indian] lacks at the outset those advantages which are inherited by his white brother and enjoyed from the cradle."[31] One way that reformers thought they could ameliorate such "deficiencies" was through a uniform curriculum and a comprehensive system of schools.

In 1889, Thomas J. Morgan, the commissioner of Indian Affairs, began a public campaign among reformers to systematize the network of Indian schools and their curriculum. His crusade came to fruition when Estelle Reel became the national superintendent of Indian Schools in 1898. Morgan advocated for a standardized academic and vocational curriculum, and Reel produced just that in 1901. The *Course of Study for the Indian Schools of the United States, Industrial and Literary* emphasized industrial instruction, or manual training and the domestic arts along gender lines, followed by a rudimentary academic program for all students. The manual training curriculum, as it was called, included agriculture, blacksmithing, carpentry, dairying, engineering, gardening, harness making, painting, printing, shoemaking, and upholstering, while the domestic arts curriculum included baking, cooking, housekeeping, laundry, sewing, and tailoring. The academic and arts program included coursework in arithmetic, basketry, geography, history, music, physiology, reading, English, spelling, and writing. Reel's comprehensive *Uniform Course of Study* was detailed and prescriptive, inciting school superintendents and teachers "to advance the pupils as speedily as possible to usefulness and citizenship."[32] To this end, historian K. Tsianina Lomawaima argues, Reel stressed practical training based on Booker T. Washington's experiences at two industrial schools: the Hampton Institute, which served both African American and American

Indian students, and Tuskegee. Reformers who supported an industrial curriculum hoped that graduates would return to their home communities to model and spread what they had learned. Initially, American Indian graduates of off-reservation industrial boarding schools did find work with the Indian Office on their tribal homelands or in other American Indian communities. But once Estelle Reel and Francis E. Leupp assumed their posts as the superintendent of Indian Schools and the commissioner of Indian Affairs, respectively, in the first decade of the twentieth century, the rate at which Hampton alumni secured employment in the Indian Office declined sharply. Reel apparently wanted her *Uniform Course* to extend only as far as training, not actual service for pay in the OIA.[33]

The Curriculum

Reel's emphasis on manual training and the domestic arts over academics reflected her belief in the inherently inferior evolutionary position of American Indians and her conviction that an overeducated Indian was not desirable. Domestic arts, with their focus on tribal basketry, sewing, pottery, and weaving, might at first seem contrary to the overarching goals of Indian schools to culturally and linguistically transform Native peoples into likenesses of their Anglo counterparts. However, as scholars Lomawaima and McCarty argue, these crafts in and of themselves were "safe"; they did not threaten the social and racial rankings already in place in the United States, and they served as benchmarks for American Indians' evolutionary progress.[34] In fact, Reel recommended that schools find and utilize Native teachers in these arts so as to prevent modernization and maintain the "old methods" of production. Reel warned,

> Modern designs, suggested by the modern articles on sale at the agency stores, cheapen the wares of the Indian, and his individuality does not assert itself as it should and as it does in all the work of the old Indians of generations past. The importance of preserving the Indian designs and shapes can not [*sic*] be overestimated. The object must be to weave the history and traditions of the tribe in all distinctively Indian work, thus making it historical, typical, and of value.[35]

Reel, like a number of ethnologists during the same time period, argued for preservation and perpetuated a static representation of American Indians. And, as will be illustrated in the next chapter, Santa Clarans used characterizations of "Indianness" to their economic advantage at the 1904 Louisiana Purchase Exposition in St. Louis, subverting Reel's justification and co-opting market principles to their own advantage. Conveniently, the domestic skills described, illustrated, and explained in the *Uniform Course of Study* reinforced the Office of Indian Affairs' goal of Native self-sufficiency.

The extent to which Reel's curriculum was used at the Santa Clara day school and at the Santa Fe Indian School is somewhat unclear. Crandall confirmed receipt of the *Uniform Course of Study* in a letter to Commissioner Jones in late 1901, adding that teachers under his supervision at the Santa Fe Indian School and in the Northern Pueblos District were required to use it. Apart from that brief mention, little evidence in the documentary record elucidates how teachers interpreted and utilized the curriculum nor how students experienced it. There is, however, some evidence that True carried out part of the curriculum by teaching girls at the day school how to embroider. Hill writes that Jeançon, the ethnologist who lived at Santa Clara during True's tenure there, recorded in his field notes—possibly in 1906—that girls at the Pueblo embroidered "with colored yarn on coarse commercial cotton fabrics." Jeançon believed they had learned how to do this at school.[36] If Jeançon was correct, it means that True or her mother, who was the school's housekeeper, taught the girls this skill and provided them with materials. It also means that if True followed the scope and sequence of the sewing curriculum Reel laid out, Jeançon would have observed fourth-year students, girls who had persisted at the school, likely with their parents' approval. Those students who attended the Santa Fe Indian School appear to have followed a practical, vocational program of learning, too. In his annual reports to the commissioner of Indian Affairs, Crandall detailed how his school embodied the industrial model—it was fully self-sustaining as students worked in the garden, the dairy, the blacksmith's shop, and the carpentry shop as outlined in Reel's *Uniform Course of Study*. Crandall also relayed the gendered nature of the curriculum: boys were trained as tailors and cobblers while girls honed their domestic skills in housekeeping, cooking, sewing, and weaving. At the very least, Crandall implemented the major provisions of Reel's syllabus.[37]

The outing system, through which Native children worked on Anglo farms and within Anglo households, was likewise part of their practical education beyond the schoolroom. Before the publication of Reel's *Uniform Course of Study,* which included the outing system as part of its comprehensive program, Commissioner Morgan promoted the benefits of the system at the Carlisle Indian School and Hampton Institute. Writing in 1889, Morgan wanted other Indian schools to adopt the outing system in order to bring Native students "into intimate relationship with the highest type of American rural life" and complement the manual and academic aspects of their curriculum at school.[38] Crandall instituted the outing system for a number of students at the Santa Fe Indian School. Each summer he sent between forty and seventy boys to Rocky Ford, Colorado, to work in the sugar beet fields. At the same time, Crandall sent girls to work as domestic servants in Anglo households in Santa Fe.[39] In his annual reports to the commissioner of Indian Affairs, Crandall emphasized the money male students made while working in Colorado, suggesting that he saw the outing system as a way to instill the desire to accumulate wealth within individual students. Indeed, he found that "while it is an easy matter to teach the boy and girls to earn money, it becomes a greater problem to teach them to save it."[40] What students spent their money on or whom they gave their money to is uncertain, but if they spent it only on themselves, they would contradict the Santa Clara value against acquisitiveness. If, on the other hand, they gave the money to their families, parents might have seen their formal, vocational education as fiscally advantageous.[41]

Students also were instructed in a more classic academic curriculum that included the three Rs—reading, writing, and arithmetic—as well as geography, history, physiology, and music. Like its vocational counterpart, the academic curriculum was rhetorically geared toward the assimilation process, underscoring reformers' belief that learning to read, write, and converse in English while simultaneously abandoning Indigenous languages was crucial to the Americanization of Native students. By 1880, the Indian Office required that all instruction in missionary and government-run Indian schools be in English. The rationale for the policy was twofold: to ensure that Indigenous children could interact and engage in business with anyone in the United States and to break down tribal affiliations. Coupled with school celebrations of U.S. holidays, the anniversary of the Dawes Act, and the commemoration of Columbus's arrival in the Americas, the OIA's English-only policy was supposed to instill a sense of patriotism among American Indian students.[42] Added to this were military drills for boys at the Santa Fe Indian School. Off-reservation boarding schools were already characterized as militaristic because of their adherence to a rigid schedule, with bells and whistles punctuating shifts in student activities. Boarding schools also enforced a disciplinary hierarchy that included military drills for boys and a punishment system based on the U.S. military's court-martial process. In 1902, A. C. Tonner, the acting commissioner of Indian Affairs, wrote to B. S. Rodey, New Mexico's territorial representative in Congress, discussing the War Department's response to Crandall's request to furnish the Santa Fe Indian School with 200 Krag-Jorgenson rifles. The War Department stated that it had no jurisdiction to transfer guns from the New Mexico Territorial Guards to OIA schools and thereby furnish Native students with guns for military drills. Crandall would have to go through the territorial government itself.[43] In 1906, Crandall was still seeking guns for his male students at the Santa Fe Indian School. Frank D. Baldwin, a brigadier general in the U.S. Army, responded to Crandall's request with reluctance, not wanting to place live guns in the hands of Indians. He recommended that Crandall consult the territorial arsenal for defunct guns.[44] Crandall's records do not indicate if he followed Baldwin's advice or whether drills without guns were adequate to cultivate a sense of patriotism among his male students.

While English and patriotism were certainly taught, and quite possibly emphasized, at the Santa Clara day school and the Santa Fe Indian School, True and Crandall, out of necessity, did not take a hard-line English-only approach to interacting with adult Pueblo community members. To Commissioner Leupp, Crandall highlighted the efforts at the Santa Fe Indian School to teach children how to speak, read, and write in English, adopting at the very least the appearance of promoting and implementing OIA directives. To True, Crandall made a point to commend her Memorial Day celebration at Santa Clara and what he thought would be its lasting effect on students in understanding their roles as U.S. citizens.[45] Day-to-day interaction with Pueblo members, though, required flexibility that a comprehensive English-only policy would not allow. True relied on interpreters in communicating with Santa Clarans in her capacity as a liaison between Pueblo leadership, Crandall, and Judge Abbott, the Pueblo's attorney. Presumably, Santa Claran interpreters translated between Tewa and English.[46] Crandall's letters also indicate that Spanish, like English, was a primary language used in formal communications. Given his complaints about the justice of the peace using only Spanish in legal proceedings, Crandall, too, relied on an interpreter. Without language accommodations in talking with Pueblo members, neither True nor Crandall would have been a very effective government employee. Such compromises in the way school programs were structured, however, were not favored by the Indian Office.[47]

The Schools

Driving the proliferation of OIA schools were the agency's leaders' complementary beliefs in social evolution and the possibility that schools could hasten the development of peoples from "savage" to "civilized." These twin beliefs fueled curricular uniformity, English-only instruction, and vocational training in on-reservation day schools for younger children who lived with their families and the on- and off-reservation boarding schools, both of which followed an industrial model wherein half the day was spent on academic training and the other half on vocational, or manual, training. Policy makers and reformers at the end of the nineteenth and beginning of the early twentieth centuries expressed a preference for off-reservation boarding schools because they believed Indigenous sociocultural practices and beliefs could more easily be stripped away from students if they were isolated from their home communities.[48] Featured in the 1884 program of the annual Friends of the Indian meeting at Lake Mohonk, New York, was the position that Indian students should be taken "from the reservation to be trained in industrial schools [and] placed among communities of white citizens."[49] Distance from family coupled with an industrial model of schooling, reformers believed, would leave students with only one option—that of learning how to become viable U.S. citizens. In practice, however, day schools were the most numerous. Adams writes that in 1900 there were "147 reservation day schools, 81 reservation boarding schools, and 25 off-reservation boarding schools."[50] In roughly the last decade of the nineteenth century, student enrollments in OIA schools grew sevenfold, with 3,598 students in 1877 and 21,568 students in 1900.[51] In spite of the national attention off-reservation boarding schools received, it was the local, on-reservation schools that affected the greatest number of students, and these required OIA officials to directly engage with Native parents and families not only about the schools their children attended, but a myriad of other issues ranging from land tenure to citizenship to public health.

In addition to government-run schools, missionary schools for American Indian children were established by different religious denominations throughout the colonization of the Americas. Within the first thirty years of permanent European colonial settlements in North America in the sixteenth and seventeenth centuries, Catholic and Protestant missionaries founded schools for Native children. Missionary schools continued to operate throughout the eighteenth and nineteenth centuries, often receiving U.S. government subsidies to assist in the effort to "civilize" American Indian children. As government subsidies grew, Congress and the Indian Office likewise increasingly expected missionary schools to abide by federal policies, such as English-only instruction. Missionary schools also represented competition for OIA schools. Crandall, in fact, was adamant in his recommendation that students be required to remain with the course of study—and school—in which they had initially enrolled. The tension Crandall projected was nationwide and had been percolating for some time. Twenty years earlier, reformer Lyman Abbott argued that the federal government should assume full responsibility for Indian schooling. The competition over students, however, did not change the fact that the underlying motives of both OIA and missionary schools were the same: to make Native students into "civilized" participants in mainstream U.S. society.[52]

Although Crandall agreed with Commissioner Morgan's earlier position that Indian children had to spend at least part of their schooling away from their home communities in order to become assimilated, both men commented separately that parents needed to be able to visit their children and to be informed of how they were doing physically and academically.[53] In his 1907 report to Commissioner Leupp, Crandall wrote of the Santa Fe Indian School:

> Our school is located so near the different Pueblos that the Indian parents visit their children once or twice during the school year. This in itself did not appeal to me at first, but I have come to believe that it is a benefit rather than a hindrance. In this way parents and children keep in close touch; when the child leaves the school he goes to his home and is thus prepared for his home life, and has not become estranged, forgotten his mother tongue, and does not feel that he is neither an Indian nor a white man.[54]

This statement could be read as flouting the general sentiment of the time—assimilation meant giving up one's Native culture and social ties. Then again, Crandall's statement might not have been perceived as insubordinate; Pueblo Indians, after all, were considered to be "civilized Indians." This premise would seem to undermine the assimilative purpose of the government's presence among the Pueblos, however. Why bother schooling people who are already civilized? If the U.S. government did not see Pueblo Indians as threatening because of their perceived civilized or quasi-civilized ways of life, keeping children away from parents might not have been so terribly important. In any case, Crandall revealed his learned preference for allowing family relations to persist and even develop in Indian schools. Just as there was a sentiment that Indians could change, Anglo government agents, too, adapted to their situations.

OFFICE OF INDIAN AFFAIRS

In developing a system of comprehensive schooling for American Indian children, the Office of Indian Affairs grew into a highly centralized bureaucracy whose rules, norms, and mandates filtered from the commissioner of Indian Affairs down to the lowest-ranking echelons of the Indian Service by the first decade of the twentieth century. In other words, the OIA grew as the United States expanded westward, engulfing Indigenous tribes along the way. Historians Paul Stuart and David Wallace Adams argue that the increased bureaucratization and centralization of the Indian Office grew out of civil service reforms in the second half of the nineteenth century. Stuart adds that administrative reforms were just as important as policy reforms for the Friends of the Indian society. The increased bureaucratization, with its centralized authority in Washington, D.C., facilitated localized leadership and governance that depended largely on procedure and the clout of the district superintendent and agent.[55]

The hierarchical structure of the Office of Indian Affairs began before Congress created the organization. As early as 1818, Congress appointed Indian agents on behalf of the U.S. government to work with individual tribes. Six years later, in 1824, Congress created the Bureau of Indian Affairs (most often called the Office of Indian Affairs) and located it in the War Department under the premise that Indian tribes were foreign to the United States, not part of it. And in 1832, Congress introduced the formal, hierarchical structure of the Indian Office when it legislated the position of the commissioner of Indian Affairs, who answered directly to the secretary of war. Individual Indian agents, who were typically non-Native, reported to the commissioner, whose job it was not only to report to the secretary of war but also to liaise with other U.S. government departments and agencies in carrying out federal Indian policies. Two years later, Congress expanded the OIA with the creation of superintendency positions for OIA schools. Like Indian agents, superintendents reported directly to the commissioner of Indian Affairs, and both sets of positions were presidential appointments, as were the positions of the commissioner of Indian Affairs and the secretary of war. By 1849, one year after the United States ratified the Treaty of Guadalupe Hidalgo, the congressional stance toward American Indian tribes had shifted such that the OIA was transferred from the War Department to the Department of the Interior. Finally, by 1851, Congress added Indian agencies throughout the newly acquired Southwest.[56] By this time, not only had the landmark Supreme Court cases *Cherokee Nation v. Georgia* (1831) and *Worcester v. Georgia* (1832) rendered American Indian tribes "domestic dependents" who had some sovereign authority, but U.S. government officials had conducted a host of treaty negotiations with individual tribes throughout the East and Midwest, facilitating the movement of Indigenous peoples to contained reservation areas and non-Native peoples into former Native homelands.

Thus the policy of Manifest Destiny was well under way, and through a series of subsequent land, trade, and citizenship policies, Congress aided the geographic and cultural reach of Euro-Americans, and later African Americans, across the American West. The expansion of non-Native settlement and the growing bureaucracy of the Indian Office required a modicum of proficiency—or at least the appearance of it—among its employees.

By the time True and Crandall landed their OIA positions in New Mexico at the turn of the twentieth century, civil service reforms had been in place for nearly a decade. Beginning in 1891, President Benjamin Harrison amended the civil service classifications in the Indian Office, specifying that the positions of physician, school superintendent and assistant superintendent, teacher, and matron were all civil service positions with specific hiring criteria and examinations. The following year, under the umbrella of civil service reform, the OIA began converting the position of Indian agent into that of school superintendent and fusing the duties of each. And in 1896, President Grover Cleveland expanded the list of classified positions to include all of the clerical positions at Indian schools and on Indian reservations.[57] Both Crandall and True were vetted under the 1891 hiring criteria and exams. When Crandall became superintendent of the Santa Fe Indian School in 1900, he was not only responsible for running the school, he was also the acting Indian agent for the Northern Pueblos District, which meant he had authority over all of the day school teachers, housekeepers, and additional farmers, among others, in the area.

The Indian Office's organizational hierarchy had clear chains of command and also provided agents and superintendents with significant power over their subordinates. Even with the scrutiny of the civil service exams and the comprehensive efforts to standardize practices within the OIA, superintendents often ran their schools idiosyncratically and according to whim. As superintendents changed their minds, or as they left and transferred to new schools, teachers, teachers' assistants, and matrons lived in wakes of uncertainty. Inconsistency also came from the central office in Washington, D.C. In her examination of autobiographies penned by women teachers in the OIA between 1900 and 1910, historian Patricia A. Carter found that school supplies and paychecks were frequently late in coming. These systematic instances of unreliability occurred despite Thomas J. Morgan's 1889 call for professional teachers who would be paid salaries that corresponded to those of teachers in public schools. Many OIA teachers could not rely on regular, substantive professional development, nor could they assume that they would stay at the same place for a long period of time.[58] By the end of the nineteenth century, this perhaps had something to do with gender.

Working in the OIA

As the OIA moved into the twentieth century, its teaching force—including teachers and teachers' assistants—was comprised overwhelmingly of women. Just a decade earlier, barely a majority of OIA teachers were women. Historian David Wallace Adams attributes this increase in the female teaching force to the feminization of teaching in the United States fifty years earlier. Adams notes that most of the women who joined the Indian Office as teachers came from west of the Appalachians; Carter adds that most of these women were Anglo. Following the argument of Catharine Beecher, an advocate for women teachers and sister of Harriet Beecher Stowe, women were not only less expensive to hire than men, since they earned less than men and often quit when they married, people also believed that women were morally superior to men and were uniquely suited to nurture children, particularly young children. But the preference for women teachers on economic and moral grounds at the policy level does not explain why so many women became OIA teachers. Adams offers several reasons for women's interest in teaching at Indian schools. In line with policy advocates, women often felt it was their moral duty to serve as custodians of American Indian children, teaching them Christian tenets and aiding their assimilation into mainstream U.S. society. At the same time, these women could create a career for themselves and be economically independent. Furthermore, OIA teaching service offered more autonomy and adventure than other teaching opportunities. Women teachers quickly learned, though, that working for the Indian Office placed them in positions that were unfamiliar, isolated, and physically exhausting. Within the OIA system, most women were not able to advance their careers beyond the position of principal, and many faced sexual harassment from male colleagues. The threat of such harassment and abuse

amplified if the female teacher was Native.[59] For True, the most significant factors in her job experiences within the OIA had to do with prescriptive regulations governing reporting and accounting procedures
and Crandall's observance of them.

Crandall seems to have differed from other superintendents in that
he tended to administer his district by OIA rules. In fact, he can be
characterized as the consummate bureaucrat in that he strictly adhered
to Indian Office rules and expected his employees to do the same. Only
once did True complain of not having enough supplies for the number
of students she was to enroll.[60] If True requested specific supplies and
Crandall could not provide them, he simply noted that he did not have
the provisions, and True left it at that.[61] These instances were very rare,
though. Similarly, Crandall reliably sent out paychecks every month;
the salaries might have been inadequate to support a comfortable standard of living, but teachers were paid. It seems likely that Crandall's
reliability in following protocol could well have earned him the respect
of teachers in his jurisdiction. Whether True faced sexual harassment
from Crandall or any man working for Crandall is not known.

Crandall frequently reprimanded True for failing to follow proper
OIA policy and procedure in issues ranging from whom she could and
could not enroll at the day school to revising forms that were filled out
incorrectly or incompletely to obtaining specific permissions she should
have sought to lend out or give away OIA property. Throughout 1902
and 1903, Crandall reminded True of the policy not to enroll students
at the day school who were over twelve years old or who had attended
either St. Catherine's Catholic school for Indians or the Santa Fe Indian
School. Each time Crandall reiterated the policy, True had asked about
specific cases in which she was not sure if an exception would apply,
such as when she was uncertain of a student's age or when a chronically
ill student over the age of twelve wanted to attend the day school. Crandall responded to every query by referring True back to the policy.[62]
True made all these queries in her first two years at Santa Clara, suggesting that she evaluated Crandall's response to each circumstance she
presented to test his commitment to the strict execution of the policy
as he interpreted it. True learned that in the case of rules regarding student enrollment, Crandall held fast to policy.

Crandall could be persnickety when people in his charge breeched proper procedures or lines of authority. Every fall, shortly after the school year began, Crandall wrote to True about Santa Claran students who had not yet shown up at the Santa Fe Indian School. In 1902, Crandall warned True about enrolling students at the day school who should have already arrived at his school in Santa Fe.[63] The following year, when only one out of ten of the Santa Claran students arrived on time, Crandall tried to get True to entice the students and their parents by saying that his school would be at capacity if they did not hurry up and take their places. At the same time, Crandall threatened to withhold farming equipment from the Pueblo if the returning students did not get to school immediately. He wrote, "Hope you can get some of the Santa Fe children started soon; I expect to have plows, hoes, shovels etc. to issue to good Indians this fall, and should like to include Santa Clara."[64] If True did not do her part in urging families to send their children to Santa Fe, then, she would be responsible for their not receiving necessary farming equipment. Crandall expected True to influence "good" Indians—those who sent their children to school—by using the relationships she had formed in the year she had lived at the Pueblo.

In 1904, Santa Claran students were again late arriving at the Santa Fe Indian School. Crandall appears to have anticipated that this would happen and sent his clerk (and sister), Miss Ferris, to the Pueblo in mid-August "to make a canvass of Santa Clara Pueblo and try to get a prompt return of all pupils."[65] This canvass was unsuccessful. In mid-September, Crandall requested that True "commence a crusade on the parents" and start sending students to Santa Fe by train. He added that if they did not get to school immediately, they would not finish the school year in time to go home for the summer.[66] True responded with equanimity. She wrote that the students were needed for a late corn harvest due to late rains, making it impossible for students to leave Santa Clara before the end of September. She added, "I feel provoked at the delay but have done my utmost to hasten the matters."[67] Whom she felt provoked by is not explicit, but she assured Crandall that she had not neglected her duties. At the same time, she clearly was not going to make Crandall's students abandon their communal responsibilities and deprive the Pueblo of needed labor, nor disrupt her relationships with Santa Claran families. Her negotiation of Crandall's coercive attempt to get his students to school became an act of subversion as she tactfully refused to send the children to Santa Fe before the harvest was done. True demonstrated her learning of the Santa Claran calendar and the importance of having the whole community present at a time when its survival depended on it.

Enrollment at the Santa Fe Indian School depended not only on parents' willingness to send their children to school and students' willingness to go but also on teachers' initiative in convincing parents and students that school had fixed starting and ending dates every year. The late harvest and subsequent tardiness of Santa Clara students in 1904 prompted Crandall to issue attendance contracts to Santa Claran students and parents in June 1905. Perhaps these contracts helped Crandall achieve his goal, as there are no letters in the collections from Crandall requesting that tardy students be brought to school in the fall of 1905 or 1906. Too, the timing of the spring and summer rains may have been more amenable with the commencement of the academic year in the autumn. In the fall of 1907, however, Crandall again appealed to True to persuade late students to make their way to school in Santa Fe. His requests in 1904 and 1907 illustrate just how dependent he was on Santa Clarans' belief in the importance of schooling and the day school teacher's influence on and relationships with local families. Crandall's assumption, as his 1904 letter illustrates, was that school attendance should trump all community needs, even if the need was for something crucial to the Pueblo's survival like the annual harvest.[68]

Crandall's desire to inculcate the value of schooling was so great that he made a point of publicly commending former Indian students who worked for him at the Santa Fe Indian School. In his 1907 annual report to Commissioner Leupp, which he submitted before the 1907 school year began, Crandall wrote, "The returned students among the different tribes are a great help to this school. [Those who] have been here are now in turn sending their children to us, and a spirit favorable to schools and especially Santa Fe seems to be growing."[69] Crandall was impressed—and even heartened—that Pueblo Indians who had attended the Santa Fe Indian School would send their own children there. His tone conveys both a sense of accomplishment in his and his staff's efforts at the school and a recognition that Pueblo Indian parents could well have sent their children to St. Catherine's, the local Catholic school for Native students. Crandall's report would seem to be the fruition of reformer Lyman Abbott's desire, expressed in 1888, that Indians should become teachers so that they could "become the educators of their own people."[70] Crandall's commendation of returning students also suggests a contradiction to the overall decline of Indian employees in the OIA under Estelle Reel's tenure as the superintendent of Indian Schools during the first decade of the twentieth century. Reel's belief that American Indians were inherently inferior to Anglos shaped both her *Uniform Course of Study* and her hiring practices. Scholar Anne Ruggles Gere's study on Native teachers in Indian schools supports Lomawaima's and Ahern's earlier findings that racial disparities permeated the hiring, firing, and compensation practices of the Indian Office. Writing that American Indians who worked in Indian schools were often cultural arbiters, translators, and sources of comfort for Indigenous students, Ahern argues that Anglos who worked with Indians often found Native employees' insider status with students to be culturally and politically threatening.[71] That Crandall openly supported some of the Indigenous employees at the Santa Fe Indian School suggests not only that he was confident in his relations and those of his Anglo teachers with Indian colleagues, but that he ran the school in ways that he and some Natives found meaningful.

Although Crandall seems to have felt comfortable recommending practices that were not in vogue at the Indian Office, he did not seem to like his subordinates to make such recommendations to him. This point was particularly illuminated when True recommended her friend Sallie B. Neal for the position of day school teacher at San Juan Pueblo. Before True wrote to Crandall on Neal's behalf, Harwood Hall, Neal's supervisor at the Riverside School in California, wrote to Crandall in June 1903 inquiring about openings in the Northern Pueblos District. After Neal apparently contacted True two weeks later, True lobbied enthusiastically for Neal's appointment to the San Juan Pueblo day school. True made two attempts to persuade Crandall to recommend Neal for the day school teacher position at San Juan. The first was on June 18, 1903, after Neal initially contacted True about changing positions within the OIA. True began her letter to Crandall by discussing Neal's teaching ability and noting other school superintendents' desire to hire her in the past. True cited the example of her former supervisor's attempts to employ Neal as a teacher at the Ft. Spokane School in

Washington State. True ended the letter by commenting on Neal's roots in Kentucky, which she shared with True, and on Neal's son, who was in law school there. Several days later, in a letter to Charles H. Dickson, an Indian Office supervisor based in Indiana, Crandall evaluated each of the day school teachers in his district, indicating that he intended to recommend Roy D. Stabler for the day school teacher position at San Juan Pueblo since Stabler's current school at Santo Domingo Pueblo was soon to close. Crandall apparently told True something similar, or that there would not be an opening for Neal at San Juan, as True wrote to Crandall several days later expressing her regret.[72]

Crandall did not follow through on his intention, however; the position at the San Juan day school remained unfilled at the beginning of the 1903 school year. In early October, True again attempted to persuade Crandall to hire Neal as the teacher and Lizzie Randall, True's sister, as the housekeeper at San Juan. True's letter fetched no response from Crandall. Later that month, True wrote to Crandall again, announcing that Neal had made a surprise visit to Santa Clara on her way home to Kentucky from California, presenting Crandall with the opportunity to recommend hiring her immediately. True explained that she had asked Neal to inform the Indian Office that she was at Santa Clara and would be willing to fill the day school teacher position. In doing this, True—and Neal—had gone around Crandall and violated the sacred hierarchy on which the institution depended.[73] But Crandall was partially at fault. In a letter he wrote to Commissioner Jones, he explained, "Without considering the danger and impropriety, I inadvertently informed the day school teacher at Santa Clara day school, recently while on a visit to Santa Clara, that a change would possibly [be] made at San Juan in the near future."[74] He believed that True had conspired with Mary Dissette, the itinerant head teacher for the Northern Pueblos District. Crandall continued with a protest against Neal's application for the position—he did not approve of the way in which she tried to secure the job through True. He did not tell True his real reason for not wanting Neal at San Juan, though, simply informing True that the Indian Office would hire a male teacher and his wife for the positions.[75] True responded with a telegram: "For her own sake, I hope she will *not* get San Juan or any other similar school as she is too good to be 'wasted on the desert air'—but she wants to stay and thinks she knows her business but being an old maid, *I* know what is best for her."[76] Neal did not get the post and True felt that Crandall had lost an excellent candidate.

Power with Position

Though Crandall was a stickler for procedure, he was not immune to enjoying the power he wielded in the Northern Pueblos District. An extensive list of Crandall's strong-arm tactics appears in the documentary record after True left Santa Clara for the Potrero School in California in 1907. Pedro Baca, a leader in the Winter party at the Pueblo and sometime employee of the OIA, wrote a thirteen-page letter to Father William Ketcham, the head of the Bureau of Catholic Indian Missions, detailing how Crandall exploited Pueblo Indians, Pueblo Indian lands, and OIA teachers.

> The conditions prevalent in the villages are getting to be the common remarks of all who pass through them. A traveller [*sic*] from Oxford University within a week remarked that were such a maladministration of affairs to be found in a district of Indians, half a dozen men would be "broken" for it. The schools are deteriorating under the present regime. The teachers say they cannot help themselves. In San Ildefonso, for example, the government has erected splendidly equipped buildings for settlement work of the widest scope, yet there the teacher sits, unable to secure anything with which to work except as she buys it out of her salary, and unable to get an attention to the crying needs of the Indians.[77]

Though True's letters in the OIA collection do not corroborate Baca's account, it is possible that she could not have written such complaints without retaliation by Crandall or other Indian Office officials. Mary E. Dissette, the itinerant head teacher in the Northern Pueblos District, did just that. Two years into Crandall's tenure as superintendent, Dissette wrote to William H. Pope, the attorney for the Pueblos, describing complaints against her for "lack[ing] tact" and detailing a cover-up Crandall allegedly perpetrated. When Crandall went to the carnival at Taos, he brought the Santa Fe Indian School band. According to Dissette, members of the band got drunk at the day school, which Crandall knew. He then proceeded to quiet "the matter up in his school, though the Indian who procured the liquor was one of his teachers and he could easily have made him tell where he got it." Dissette had no patience for this and she requested "to be made independent" of Crandall.[78] Dissette's allegations support Baca's assertion that Crandall created a small fiefdom for himself; they also suggest that Crandall acted with the knowledge that day school teachers in his charge could do little to refute his actions directly. Without more documentary evidence, however, it is difficult to determine satisfactorily if Crandall was like other superintendents described in Carter's work.

Crandall stringently followed the rules when it came to carrying out employment and enrollment policies, and this was also the case in accounting for and disposing of government property. In October 1904, True submitted a list of property to be disposed of, which included several books, a blackboard, and a lamp. Crandall rejected her request, stating that library books could not be disposed of or given to students, nor could True get rid of the blackboard and lamp until replacements arrived.[79] True replied: "I am sorry I did not know of the distinction in books. Those I cannot use myself nor give to the children I have been putting on the magazine and newspaper table I have kept for returned students, hence the wearing out of the so called 'Library' books, or most of them. 'Indian Boyhood' and 'Middle Five' were enjoyed."[80] True's brief statement is striking for two reasons. First, she was clearly engaged with students who had moved away from the Pueblo to complete their schooling and then returned. This is the only piece of correspondence reviewed that indicates True actively forged relationships with students whom she did not teach. Second, the "worn-out" books that True wanted to strike from the government property list were new autobiographies of two prominent American Indian men who lived and worked in both Anglo and Native societies. Charles A. Eastman (Santee Sioux), also known as Ohíye S'a, published *Indian Boyhood* in 1902. Eastman was an OIA physician famous for treating Lakota victims of the 1890 Wounded Knee Massacre in South Dakota. Francis La Flesche (Omaha), who published *The Middle Five* in 1900, was a well-known anthropologist who was trained by Alice Fletcher and worked for the Smithsonian's Bureau of Ethnology. In one sense, True had succeeded in one of the government's missions—reinforcing Indian students' practice in reading English. In another sense, True facilitated a form of pan-Indian identity. That returned students were reading about other

Indians' experiences in Indian schools suggests that Native experiences, to some degree, transcended specific school sites and that Santa Claran students could empathize with others' experiences.

True continued her response to Crandall:

> I expend a lot of property I know, but I try to get the intended good out of it and get rid of it as I have not room enough to turn around in anyway. If I put discarded stuff outside the house I seldom see it again. I kept a variety of junk on the roof until I found it was causing leaks by interfering with the running off of rain water. To keep from sitting up at night with stove legs and desk irons I have buried them in the chicken yard where they await the final resurrection.[81]

Keeping these other materials, as dictated by policy, seems absurd, especially when True had to go to such lengths to keep other people from salvaging what they could of worn-out items. There might not have been enough supplies in working order for OIA teachers, but there appears to have been quite a lot of waste.

True similarly violated property usage rules in May 1905 when she lent out old desks to a school in Española. Crandall was angry:

> You have done this without the knowledge of this office, and your action is not approved. It is therefore imperative that this Gov't property be returned at once, as [*illegible*] be kept at the day-school at Santa Clara, and not elsewhere. [*illegible*] a full explanation is desired. The board of survey which was recently convened at the Santa Clara Day-school was authorized to act on any property worthless or worn out, or unfit for Gov't use, and could issue to Indians where they thought best. If this property was subject to the action of this board, why was it not at school? If it was and is new property, why was it loaned?[82]

Not only did True act without the proper authority, she flouted government policy by lending out the property at her school, an Indian school, to another school, the public school in Española. While she was responsible for maintaining the desks and retaining them if they were worn out, she was not the one to determine if they were unusable, nor could she allow others to use them. Crandall saw this as the final act necessary to recommend her transfer to another school. Citing the incident with the desks, her attempts to dispose of other government property, and her irregular school hours, Crandall recommended to Commissioner Leupp that True be placed in a boarding school where she would be under close supervision. At the same time, Crandall recognized her as an excellent teacher. Exercising initiative was apparently grounds for removal when one was expected to follow the rules without deviation, even if they did not make much practical sense. Crandall, however, could not transfer True himself; that was a task only the Indian Office could carry out, and they saw fit to keep True at Santa Clara until the end of 1907. Only then was she transferred and promoted to the position of superintendent of the Potrero School on the Morongo Reservation in southern California.

CONCLUSION

The institutions of the Office of Indian Affairs and the OIA school—with their "civilizing" and managerial missions—were colonial bodies that sought to transform Native peoples from "Indians" to "Americans." The development of these institutions depended on a foundational conception of racial hierarchy and a set of rules and regulations that governed both the American Indian peoples who fell under their purview as well as the Indian Office officials who administered day and boarding schools. Among those who worked for the OIA, as typified by Clara D. True and Clinton J. Crandall, disagreements over how specific policies were to be interpreted and then carried out produced power struggles that were only, and only partially, resolved by rank. Differing interpretations also produced subversive acts that split with particular OIA regulations and procedure, and quite possibly the *Uniform Course of Study*. This official curriculum proved to be a unidirectional guide to converting, or "progressing," Native children into economically viable "American" citizens. At local school sites, however, such as the Santa Clara day school, strict adherence to the curriculum and OIA policy and procedure softened and faded into the background of the day-to-day needs of the day school teacher and the community.

In spite of the one-directional "civilizing" orientation of the Indian Office curriculum and policies, day and boarding schools depended on the widespread acceptance of Indian Office practices among its employees and Native parents. Crandall's repeated requests for True to send Santa Claran children who were late for the start of the school year demonstrate just how reliant he was not only on parental permission but also on True's relationships with Santa Claran families. Though he tried to frame requests for parents to send their children to the Santa Fe Indian School as the necessary consequence of a compulsory school law for Indian children in the territory, he was unsuccessful and resorted to writing contracts with individual parents and threatening to withhold farming equipment. True's actions in response to Crandall's appeals to send children to Santa Fe reflect her growing understanding of the Santa Clara agricultural cycle, the Pueblo's dependency on it, and her need to maintain an amicable rapport with both parents and students. Some regulations, like the start date of the boarding school, were just not worth enforcing if they compromised important aspects of local community life.

Yet, enforcing OIA policy and procedure was a source of power and authority for Indian Office officials in positions of middle management like Crandall. He allowed little leeway for exceptions to the regulations governing student enrollments at the Santa Clara day school and the Santa Fe Indian School. Nor did he permit exceptions to proper procedure in True's hiring recommendations or in the disposal and lending of OIA property, even when the circumstances appeared absurd, as with her storing worn-out goods on her roof or burying them in her chicken yard. Crandall's strict understanding of OIA rules and regulations as well as federal Indian law might have, in fact, facilitated his own corruption, even as he carried on with the appearance of perfect propriety. If Pedro Baca's allegations against Crandall's management of resources that were to be allocated to Indian Pueblos are correct, then Crandall most certainly did use his position for personal gain and aggrandizement. If not, Crandall was the consummate bureaucrat. Becoming a corporeal part of the OIA and its colonizing mission was part of the job description for True and Crandall, even if they did not always agree on how it should be carried out.

CHAPTER FIVE *Education; or, Learning within a Colonial Regime*

INTRODUCTION

When the Office of Indian Affairs posted True and Crandall at the Santa Clara day school and Santa Fe Indian School, respectively, both were charged with the task of keeping school. Indeed, their stated purpose for being at Indian schools in northern New Mexico was to teach children how to speak, read, and write English; basic math skills; practical vocational and domestic skills; patriotism; and citizenship. But, as the previous chapters have demonstrated, education at Santa Clara Pueblo and its environs extended well beyond the walls of the Santa Clara day school and the Santa Fe Indian School. What went on in the classrooms of each school is not the subject of True and Crandall's correspondence; rather, their letters reveal that schooling was only one component of American Indian, Hispano, and Anglo education in New Mexico.

As OIA school keepers, True and Crandall found that their duties exceeded the institutional bounds of their classrooms. They were responsible for mediating a wide range of federal Indian policies that affected and were appropriated by the Pueblo Indians they served. Issues of and responses to land tenure, public health, citizenship, and the institutional placement of children are the subjects of the bulk of True and Crandall's correspondence. Their letters, notwithstanding their official nature and the circumstance of their having been written within the organization of the Indian Office, are the residue of what Pueblo Indians, Hispanos, and OIA officials saw as important in that particular place—northern New Mexico—and at that particular time—the first decade of the twentieth century. True's and Crandall's letters likewise reveal what happened to federal directives as they traveled from Washington, D.C., and landed at specific locales. When True and Crandall wrote about matters pertaining to schooling, they almost always centered on administrative concerns, such as student enrollment, supply requests

In the village of Santa Clara, ca. 1900. Photograph by Edward Curtis. Courtesy of the Library of Congress, Prints & Photographs Division, Edward S. Curtis Collection, LC-USZ62-112218.

and receipts, following the proper channels of authority, and reporting procedures. That their letters do not address curricular and pedagogical issues as they arose in their respective schools is telling: teaching and administering official curricula was but one part of their duties.

Schooling, learning, and education take on distinctly different yet related hues when examined through the issues that Pueblo Indians, Hispanos, and Anglos deemed central to their day-to-day and future lives. Schooling, or the transmission of knowledge and skills from teacher to student through formal institutions, has been the most studied manifestation of education among historians, sociologists, and policy scholars, in spite of very pointed calls to broaden the scope of inquiry. To be sure, schools and schooling have become increasingly significant in U.S. society since the Industrial Revolution transformed its technological and economic capacities and, in turn, reshaped family life. The school took on many of the roles previously filled by parents, making schooling not just about academic preparation but also about the socialization of the child in the greater U.S. society. As David Labaree has illustrated in his provocative work *How to Succeed in School without Really Learning*, schools and their curricula became consumables that individuals used to obtain credentials to advance their economic, social, and political possibilities. Considered in contrast to schooling, learning becomes the internal, individual process that shapes and reshapes how one sees and understands the world by connecting experiences with new knowledge, skills, and attitudes. Learning is thus relational and is a liminal middle ground that has the potential to transform the individual intellectually, socially, and culturally, though its effects may not always be seen by others or be perceived by the learner until much later. While learning within and learning outside of the context of schooling have become two aspects of education popularly studied by historians of education over the last half century, the study of learning and education beyond the institution of the school has remained a largely untapped vein of inquiry.[1]

The task of studying learning beyond the institution of the school has proven daunting for scholars in part because there is no shared definition of "education," and methodological difficulties arise when looking at an elusive phenomenon that has no set boundaries. What does one study? And how does one recognize that what one is studying might be considered "education"? In his 1960 treatise against the focus on school as the primary means of studying the history of education in the United States, Bernard Bailyn wrote that early historians of education had effectively donned blinders by exclusively studying the school, missing entirely the larger social "transformation that had overtaken education in America." Education, Bailyn wrote, is "the entire process by which a culture transmits itself across the generations." Historian Lawrence Cremin countered that education typically required some element of intentionality, or "the deliberate, systematic, and sustained effort to transmit, evoke, or acquire knowledge, attitudes, values, skills, or sensibilities, as well as any outcomes of that effort," but recognized that learning often transpired without a target in mind. Richard Storr took another tack. Rather than attempting to define education before studying it and its processes and thus risk producing an account that was "teleology in reverse creep," he argued for an inductive approach, "examining the whole record of human experience in an effort to discover an ingredient of it that can sensibly be described as educational."[2] This approach, however, would seem to open up too wide a field of study, and indeed, very few histories of education have followed this lead.

This history does, though. In the spirit of Bailyn and under Storr's advisement, the education studied here is delimited temporally, albeit somewhat arbitrarily, by Clara D. True's tenure as the day school teacher at Santa Clara Pueblo, and spatially by the Pueblo and its environs along the northern Rio Grande. Focusing on what occurred in the Santa Clara day school and the Santa Fe Indian School was simply not tenable because when True and Crandall wrote specifically about their schools, the detail and descriptions were primarily administrative, not pedagogic. But learning was going on all around them, and True and Crandall described it in their letters. The subjects of education in the northern Rio Grande valley from 1902 to 1907, then, encompass issues of land, disease, citizenship, and navigating U.S. institutions. The learnings that occurred and that True and Crandall document are instructive in understanding (1) how True, Crandall, Santa Clarans, and Hispanos appropriated federal directives within the context of their past experiences as well as their differing organizational and authority structures; and (2) how each group's "educations" developed over multiple generations. The learnings also describe something about education for these groups: it was social and communicative; it was structured through individuals' and groups' interactive experiences and the meaning they created around them; and it was historical and cumulative, ranging at least over the course of a single life and often over the span of multiple generations. Philosopher John Dewey calls the processes by which learnings become education "educative."[3] The educative process, writes Dewey, "is a continuous process of growth, having as its aim at every stage an added capacity of growth" or "further education" and the capacity to determine just how previously learned lessons should play out in current or future situations.[4] Evidence of these educative processes, as well as of missed lessons, has been the substance of this study.

This chapter proceeds with the unreserved view of education that Bailyn, Storr, and Dewey had in mind. Beginning with examples of cultural tourism, the experience of travel and of learning about the "Other" play out as Santa Clarans travel to St. Louis to participate in the 1904 Louisiana Purchase Exposition and as Anglos travel to New Mexico in the late nineteenth and early twentieth centuries to see sites and peoples that were so unfamiliar to them. The remainder of the chapter is a synthetic analysis of the educative processes and missed lessons documented in previous chapters. As will become clear, Bailyn's observation resonates: "Education not only reflects and adjusts to society; once formed, it turns back upon it and acts upon it."[5]

THE 1904 ST. LOUIS EXPO

The 1904 Louisiana Purchase Exposition in St. Louis, Missouri, was a forum for learning the norms of Anglo-Native relations. Billed as an event that highlighted the vast territory acquired by the Louisiana Purchase, the 1904 World's Fair featured exhibits and peoples from the far west of the North American continent and included technological innovations that dazzled visitors. Newspaper and magazine writers at the time argued that the fair was an "educative force," displaying explicit classroom learning with Native populations and structuring exhibits to teach visitors something new. Writing for *Outlook* magazine on Independence Day 1903, Ernest Hamlin Abbott remarked, "The chief question that concerns thoughtful men as they think of the Expositions at St. Louis is, What will it tell concerning the character of America? what [*sic*] will it reveal of the soul of the Nation?"[6] One answer, according to historians Nancy J. Parezo and Don D. Fowler, is that the St. Louis Expo showcased the so-called March of Progress that advanced westward across North America with Anglo settlers. Indigenous peoples from the Americas and other parts of the world were invited to juxtapose their customary ways with the ways of "progress." The presentation of American Indians at world's fairs was nothing new by 1904, though. Historian Robert A. Trennert Jr. writes that Thomas Jefferson Morgan, the commissioner of Indian Affairs from 1889 to 1893, began to promote the U.S. government's Indian education system through displays at various exhibitions around the country in the 1890s. The idea then, as it was in 1904, was to demonstrate the "civilization" process of Native students through live classroom demonstrations. Organizers found, however, that the people who attended the exhibits were much more interested in seeing American Indians perform their customary practices or play Indians in Buffalo Bill's Wild West Show than in seeing Native children practice reading drills in familiar classrooms.[7] Although neither Parezo and Fowler's nor Trennert's studies discuss Native motivations for participating in such fairs and expositions, True's and Crandall's letters offer a glimpse into Pueblo Indian participation in the 1904 St. Louis Expo.

Recruitment for the Indian exhibits at the fair began in the spring of 1903. Samuel McCowan, the superintendent of the Chilocco Indian School in Oklahoma, was in charge of the Office of Indian Affairs–sponsored exhibits: the classroom at the model Indian school and members of various tribes producing arts unique to their cultures. McCowan contacted OIA officials to identify and enlist Native individuals to participate in the fair.[8] On May 14, 1903, McCowan wrote to C. J. Crandall describing an overview of what he hoped to create and requesting Crandall's best male students to participate in an Indian band:

> I have been appointed "Charge Des Affairs" of the Indian exhibit at St. Louis next year. It is our purpose to maintain a model school there. I hope to have not less than one hundred pupils in attendance taken from the various schools in the Louisiana Purchase Territory. This brings you in. I want to have with us an Indian school band of not less than forty pieces. This band will not be a Chilocco band, a Haskell band or a Santa Fe band but an Indian school band, and I want to collect for this aggregation a few of the best players from the best bands at the various Indian schools. What can you furnish us from you [sic] band? Please give me the names of the boys, their ages, and band experience. I desire to have as many full-bloods as possible.[9]

McCowan's band, as he envisioned it, was to continue the success he had had four years earlier at the Greater American Exposition, or "The White Man's Burden" exhibit, in Omaha, Nebraska. After a shaky start with his Chilocco band in St. Louis, McCowan hired a new director, sent many of the band members back to Oklahoma, and began recruiting resourceful and fully Native yet acculturated students from across the country through their school superintendents. McCowan's band would display its members through a seeming paradox: world-class musicians who did not have the phenotype music aficionados might expect—or trust. The band would demonstrate the extent to which those who were the most "biologically Indian" could excel in certain aspects of the dominant culture. It is not clear from True's and Crandall's letters if any male students from the Santa Fe Indian School left to join McCowan's band, but Crandall did send artists from Indian Pueblos in his district to participate in the St. Louis Expo.[10]

In early 1904, Crandall wrote to True asking her to recruit skilled potters for the fair. True replied on January 20, 1904, "The best potter in Santa Clara Pueblo is willing to go to the St. Louis Exposition."[11] True added that she believed the woman wanted to attend because her husband would be joining the Cliff Dwellers exhibit, a demonstration not sanctioned by the Indian Office. Whether or not True's speculation was true, the potter was so skilled that she was able to negotiate with Crandall. She asked that she be permitted to take her daughter to St. Louis or, if that was not possible, that the girl be enrolled in the Santa Fe Indian School so that she could be with her older sister. Crandall responded that the potter could do what she preferred. He also recommended that she begin collecting enough pottery materials to last several months in St. Louis. Throughout January, February, and March, Crandall regularly inquired about the potter's interest in going to the fair; she responded in kind, asking about updates to their travel plans and other necessary preparations. The woman's presence at the St. Louis Expo—as a Pueblo representative of his district—meant something to Crandall. Her work and presumably her demeanor made her a person worth showcasing. The potter was none other than the renowned artist Maria Martinez from the adjacent San Ildefonso Pueblo.[12]

Despite the interest Santa Clarans expressed in attending the St. Louis Expo, Crandall nearly rescinded his agreement to send Pueblo Indians from the Northern Pueblos District because of McCowan's treatment of Indians in St. Louis. Writing to True on February 29, 1904, Crandall protested, "Mr [sic] McCowan expects to secure Indians without money and without price,—that they will construct their own habitations when reaching St. Louis, and live like savages rather than progressive citizens in decent habitations, like most of our Pueblos do live." Crandall declared that he would not send people from his district to St. Louis unless McCowan provided minimally for the participants.[13] What McCowan might not have fully disclosed in his initial request for skilled artists was that his budget was quite limited; he had

Maria Martinez, 1912. Photograph by H. S. Poley. Courtesy of the Denver Public Library, Western History Collection, P-2144.

Black lustrous ware from Santa Clara and San Juan Pueblos, ca. 1890–1900.
Courtesy of the Denver Public Library, Western History Collection, X-30149.

only $65,000 for the construction and maintenance of the entire Indian school and its array of exhibits and Native exhibitors. Industrial schooling—something McCowan and his students knew well—proved to be one solution among several, and students completed the construction of the Indian school, the landscaping, and the setting up of individual exhibits.[14] Even with these constraints, Crandall must have come to some sort of agreement with McCowan, as Martinez and several other Santa Clarans attended the St. Louis Expo.

That Santa Clarans participated in the fair did not mean that Crandall was comfortable with the portrayal of Pueblo peoples as somehow barbaric. At the time the arrangements for the expo were coming together, Crandall was embroiled in the delinquent tax case and the creation of the Santa Clara Reservation. The two cases underscored the dynamic perception and representation of Pueblo peoples and confounded state and federal officials' understandings of Pueblo Indians as legal citizens or as Indian wards. McCowan's plan for the model Indian school did not leave much room for interpretation. The juxtaposition of "old" (savage) and "new" (civilized) Indian ways was to be a demonstration showing two sides of the same Indian coin. On one side was the fixed representation of American Indians practicing "old" arts in a static fog of nostalgia, positioning Native participants as exotic and uncultivated; on the other side was the dynamic representation of American Indian children as Americanized individuals who had become experts in various musical, culinary, vocational, academic, and comportment skills.[15] Even though the legal status of Pueblo Indians was under scrutiny at the time, Crandall maintained that the old-new, savage-civilized binary simply did not apply to Pueblo Indians because of their extant civilized practices of farming, Catholicism, and permanent villages. Pueblo Indians were—and had always been—civilized Indians.

Selecting Pueblo Indians to participate in the St. Louis Expo required careful attention to individuals' skills, demeanor, and ingenuity. True's and Crandall's letters emphasize their recruitment of "good" Indians. Not only did McCowan want to present the "best players from the best bands," True and Crandall wanted to ensure that individuals whom they deemed worthy of epitomizing Pueblo Indians attended the fair. True and Crandall, then, were gatekeepers, deciding who could and could not attend the event. In her letter to Crandall evaluating potential potters from Santa Clara, True wrote, "There are plenty of women who would go but they are not needed here nor elsewhere, as they are idle, dirty loafers who wouldn't make pottery worth the name."[16] True's assessment of the women's skills and moral character implies that one's work reflected the quality of one's character. True's statement likewise reflects her own standard of worth: in order to be considered "good," one had to be industrious. If True's evaluation of the women she described to Crandall is accurate, Santa Clarans might not have recognized them as ideal representatives. According to anthropologist W. W. Hill, industry was one of the central values in Santa Claran society: "Exemplification of this virtue was usually present at home, and the child could not fail to be impressed by constant example. This was fortified by direct reference and encouragement to emulate persons in the family or village who possessed this trait in high degree."[17] Though Hill does not indicate whether children were instructed (formally or informally) in skills like pottery by their families or other Santa Clarans, it seems doubtful that the women True described would have taught pottery to children.

True lobbied vigorously on behalf of those Santa Clarans whom she liked and respected. After Crandall visited Santa Clara in mid-April

Pedro Cajete and son-in-law, ca. 1908–1910. Photograph by H. S. Poley. Courtesy of the Denver Public Library, Western History Collection, P-333.

1903, Pedro Cajete, a Winter party member and landlord for the day school property, asked Crandall—through True—if he and his daughter Genevieve might attend the St. Louis Expo. Before approaching True, Pedro Cajete planned his strategy for approval. First, he obtained permission from St. Catherine's boarding school in Santa Fe for Genevieve to attend the fair. Second, he garnered information about the Indian Office exhibit and the Cliff Dwellers exhibit and expressed to True his preference to participate in the OIA program. Third, he demonstrated to True how both he and Genevieve would appear and comport themselves. When True wrote to Crandall advocating for the Cajetes, she was convinced that they would be exemplary representatives: "Genevieve is rather nice looking and makes passable pottery. She has any amount of handsome Indian clothing which she would expect to wear exclusively. Her father showed me the wardrobe today. It is very nice from an Indian point of view. Pedro has numerous warlike garments. He will lay in a supply of native products, silver jewelry and all sorts of similar articles."[18] Pedro Cajete, and by extension Genevieve, demonstrated to True that they were "good" Indians, successfully navigating True's charge and expectations. Cajete understood that appearing "Indian" was a fundamental qualification for attending the St. Louis Expo. He proved his capacity to do this by showing True the clothing he and Genevieve intended to wear and the jewelry he intended to sell. In doing this, Cajete was extremely courteous, which seemed to further endear him to True, who referred to Cajete by his first name—something she did only with individuals with whom she was on friendly or familiar terms. In the opening of this particular letter, True amplified their familiarity by calling him "Pedro Chiquito Cajete." At the end of her letter, she argued that the Cajetes would complement the work of the Swasos, whose plans to attend the expo were already confirmed. True closed the letter, "If you don't let him go, I'll have him to bury and he is so shrewd he will beat me out of his funeral expenses."[19] True saw Cajete not only as a "good" Indian but also as an intelligent man with diplomatic and negotiating skills.

Pedro Cajete did not face resistance from Crandall; he faced it from José Jesus Naranjo, the Santa Clara governor. Cajete lobbied to go to the expo in the midst of community ditching efforts. Before he could pick up Genevieve from St. Catherine's in Santa Fe, Governor Naranjo

Pedro Cajete's daughter (possibly Genevieve), ca. 1908–1910. Photograph by H. S. Poley. Courtesy of the Denver Public Library, Western History Collection, P-328.

required Cajete to repair an irrigation ditch six miles away from the Pueblo. When Cajete offered to pay for a substitute, the governor refused. True attributed the governor's action to jealousy and thought it was a move to humiliate Cajete. Despite her obvious sympathy for Cajete, True could not help that Governor Naranjo was the primary overseer of ditch labor for the Pueblo and had the right to call able-bodied men to work. It is also possible that the apparent tension between Cajete and Naranjo stemmed in part from the rift between the Summer and Winter parties, or that Cajete was simply standing out too much. According to anthropologist W. W. Hill, standing out as an individual at the Pueblo was contrary to the values of conformity, anonymity, and modesty. Being selected to attend the St. Louis Expo as part of the government exhibit by soliciting True's and Crandall's favor might well have been perceived as an affront to other Santa Clarans, exacerbating the sociopolitical friction that already pervaded the Pueblo. Pedro Cajete worked on the ditch, though, without apparent complaint, fulfilling his community duties. It was a concession that allowed him to go to St. Louis and return to Santa Clara to live afterward. Cajete had demonstrated a type of double consciousness: he understood both Pueblo Indian and Anglo worlds. Not only did he know when to be "Indian" and when to be "civilized" for Anglos, he knew when he had to meet his duties as a Santa Claran.[20]

Understanding how to appear as both "good" and "exotic" Indians according to True's and Crandall's expectations was a basic prerequisite for Santa Clarans who wished to attend the St. Louis Expo. As Indian Office employees, True and Crandall served as gatekeepers not only for Pueblo Indians but also for Pueblo Indians' audiences at the fair. As such, True and Crandall delineated what it meant to appear "Indian" in the early 1900s; they were also responsible for dispelling myths and assumptions about Indigenous North Americans being dirty, lazy, or inherently violent. And in some ways, the government Indian exhibit at the expo did just that. Parezo and Fowler write that the government's Indian exhibit at the expo was a successful draw, with the average daily attendance of 30,000 visitors. They note, however, that daily attendance often surpassed 50,000 visitors. People found the exhibit fascinating and frequently commented on Native students' expertise and industry in manual training classes, the laundry, and the coffee shop, all of which featured or were run by students. Some, though, felt that students had become too Americanized and were virtually indistinguishable from their Anglo counterparts.[21] That was simply one of the many costs of acculturation. In the case of Santa Clarans who participated in the fair, possessing and using a double consciousness as Cajete displayed is evidence not only of their perceptive understanding in interacting with Anglos but also of their long-term education rooted in multiple waves of colonization. Santa Clarans and other Pueblo peoples had to learn how to navigate multiple cultures well in order to maintain their own.

In fact, the St. Louis Exposition was a display of fraught, contradictory ideas about what it meant to be "civilized" and "exotic." The Indian Office had a decade-long history of presenting American Indians in sometimes "civilized" and sometimes "exotic" ways. Trennert argues that exhibition pamphlets and letters from government officials from fairs dating back to 1893 show that visitors were drawn to exhibits that depicted American Indians as exotic. Side-by-side exhibits of Indians in their customary regalia performing tribal tasks and rituals and Indians dressed as Anglos performing computational drills in classroom settings did not appear to convince the attendees of prior fairs that Anglo social values and practices would or should displace those of Native cultures. Shows of being "Indian"—appearing Indian and acting Indian—were the well-attended curiosities of previous fairs.[22] Anglo visitors, after all, likely knew something of what it meant and felt like to attend school; but many did not know much about distinct Native societies, and visiting exhibitions in which traditional arts and practices were demonstrated by Indigenous peoples was a learning experience. Anglos were learning about Indians from Indians.

Recruiting American Indians who still practiced tribal arts proved difficult for McCowan. Several OIA superintendents responded that assimilation efforts at the reservations where they worked were simply too successful—tribal arts and skills had been bypassed for those promoted by Euro-Americans. Whether these superintendents saw what they wanted to see or what they were meant so see is unclear. But their assumption that Native peoples were interested in going to the St. Louis Expo to perform exclusively authentic, traditional "Indian" roles for non-Natives, rather than attend the fair as a business venture, just did not hold. In a letter to *Outlook* magazine, one Indian agent quoted from the catalog of an American Indian farmer who produced traditional handicrafts:

> All goods quoted are genuine Indian design and made by them in the old way. We allow no thread to be used by them in the construction, but insist on sinew being used exclusively, as that was the only thread known before the white man came and is much more lasting. With very few exceptions, all the articles quoted are practical. Take, for instance, the golf-belts; they are original and beautiful, practical and durable; combined with the purse there is no more practical article in the market. So it is with moccasins and card-cases, music-rolls, book-covers, etc.[23]

Those Indians who created such items for non-Natives were clearly responsive to the market demands of buyers who likely lived beyond the tribe's reservation. Santa Clarans who attended the St. Louis Expo were a case in point.

Those who participated in the fair had the opportunity to make money, travel, and interact with people from around the world. Before opportunities opened up with the government's exhibit, Santa Clarans like Julian Martinez, who was married to Maria Martinez, and Pedro Cajete made plans to participate in the Cliff Dwellers exhibit. Organized by promoter W. Maurice Tobin, the Cliff Dwellers exhibit was created to attract crowds and their cash. It conflated distinct Puebloan tribes, such as the Zuni, the Hopi, and the Rio Grande Pueblos, as well as several tribes from different geographic regions, including the Arapaho, the Santee Sioux, and the Nez Perce. The Cliff Dwellers exhibit included an Indian Congress, and it staged tribal dances with dancers from various tribes wearing Plains Indian clothing. Parezo and Fowler note that many of the dances performed were parodies of proper dances or were proper dances given different names to invoke popular lore among non-Native attendees. In contrast, the OIA exhibit of the model Indian school was not driven by profit. Although it was entrepreneurial, and participants could sell the goods they produced, the spirit was meant to be informative. Crandall confirmed this in one of his early recruitment letters to True, and Cajete prepared for such sales by gathering a variety of handicrafts that he could sell at the fair. The St. Louis Expo, in other words, presented an occasion for Santa Clarans to earn money quickly by selling goods to people who might have never seen Puebloan pottery, jewelry, beadwork, or blankets. The expo, too, was a way for Santa Clarans to meet people with whom they might otherwise never have come into contact.[24]

By the end of April 1904, travel arrangements were solidified for Pedro and Genevieve Cajete as well as the Swaso family. After their arrival in St. Louis in mid-May, True wrote to Crandall forwarding Swaso's request to expedite the shipment of the missing equipment he needed for the government exhibition. True added that Pedro Cajete said he was "having the time of his life." Genevieve captured the attention of many at the fair because of her looks and her ability to carry a ceramic pot on the top of her head, as was customary among Pueblo Indian women. Pedro Cajete was doing so well that he made fast friends with McCowan and actively began recruiting students for the Chilocco Indian School.[25] While this might have delighted McCowan, Crandall was not pleased. Crandall wrote to Cajete that summer:

I have no objection to your soliciting pupils in the Pueblos [for Chilocco], provided that you do not entice any of my pupils who are spending the summer vacation at home, to go with you. You are further told that you must take no Pueblos from Santa Clara or any of the other Pueblos without first bringing them to this office for my approval and the doctor's examination. If you should diobey [*sic*] this order i [*sic*] you will get your self [*sic*] in trouble with this office.[26]

In his enthusiasm for the Chilocco Indian School, Cajete stepped onto turf over which OIA superintendents fought. Contests for student enrollments among Indian Office superintendents were part and parcel of the federal Indian schooling system. Crandall certainly did not want to lose his students to McCowan, and Crandall did not want Cajete to appropriate federal Indian schooling for his own purposes. That jurisdiction was supposed to be Crandall's alone. Rules were rules, and following proper procedure was a hallmark of a superintendent's competence within the OIA.

TRAVELS TO THE LAND OF THE TURQUOISE SKY

As people attended the St. Louis Expo to learn about other people, so too did people travel to New Mexico for its exotic and simultaneously new and ancient flair. In fact, the Pueblo Indians and Hispanos of New Mexico were so different from what Anglo-Americans were accustomed to that they wrote detailed newspaper and magazine articles of their travels to the territory. A number of these accounts were anthropological in nature. Adolph Bandelier, the well-known anthropologist who wrote extensively about Pueblo Indians and the cliff dwellers, published articles on the Pueblo Revolt of 1680 as well as ethnological accounts of Pueblo Indians in the 1890s. Other accounts were travelogues of tourists and those sent out to explore possible settlement sites. Still other writers lobbied Congress and its constituents for New Mexico statehood. Regardless of the intent underlying publishing the articles, each author described New Mexico and typified its inhabitants in particular ways, some laudatory, some castigating. And many of the authors provided very detailed descriptions of geography, architecture, and fauna such that readers might visualize what the author recounted.

Most the articles examined here, published in the 1890s, provided prospective travelers and those interested in the exotic the means to imagine what New Mexico was like without having been there. We might speculate that by the time large numbers of tourists began arriving in the early twentieth century, they knew what they expected to see when they met Pueblo Indians and Hispanos in their home environments, when they glimpsed the distinctive architecture, or when they tasted the local cuisine.[27]

Many of the early articles published convey words of wonder, expressing the authors' fascination with the sheer difference of the place. Most such accounts are anthropological in orientation even if they were not written by people who had been on archeological digs at Pueblo ruins. For those who visited the cliff dwellings in Santa Clara Cañon or Rito de los Frijoles, the ancient ones who had lived in the cliffs ranked in interest comparable to those who had lived in ancient Egypt or Mexico. Most curious to many authors was the nature of the captivating people who had built and lived in the elaborate cave apartments.[28] One anonymous author wrote, "The houses vary greatly in size, some being very small, and others extending several hundred feet in length. The walls are often thirty to forty feet high. Windows or doors afford light and access to nearly all the rooms. It seems almost uncanny to see human workmanship in such wild and strange surroundings." The writer compared the stonework in the cliff apartments to that of "old farmhouses in Eastern States" and then went on to note, "The mortar often shows the marks of small finger-tips, which indicates that in construction, women's hands had been used instead of trowels."[29] Another author likened the dramatic apartments to that of other curious dwellings found in nature: "Those cliffs ranged usually in narrow terraces, are honeycombed with the adobes of human beings, looking at a distance of miles like the nests of bank swallows."[30] The cliff dwellings were exquisitely mysterious to the authors who visited them, surely peopled, as the writers speculated, by a brilliant yet lost civilization. The cliff apartments and their previous inhabitants were ripe for study.

Bandelier and his counterparts, like anthropologist Edgar Lee Hewett, argued for extensive archeological research in the area. In 1890 Bandelier wrote, "New Mexico is a most valuable yet hardly explored field for archaeological studies."[31] Nine years later another writer who visited the ruins in Santa Clara Cañon called the area "a rich field for research that is comparatively little known."[32] This was just the argument Hewett made in his public support for creating Pajarito National Park in 1902, so long as artifacts were preserved. In fact, looting was a key concern among anthropologists and Pueblo Indians alike. Accounts from the early and mid-1890s document how visitors not only excavated but also took objects from the cliff dwellings. One author wrote that those who visited the apartments were "rewarded by a fine collection of stone implements, pottery, skeletons, etc." Another wrote that "to dig for relics is fascinating, there is a charm in being the first to handle anything after the original owners dropped it untold centuries ago" but added that "it seems like desecration when . . . you resurrect the form of a little child, perchance a small jug, a stone knife, or a bone needle, all placed along side, and which undoubtedly had been put there by loving hands."[33] Given the accounts, Hewett's concern about tourists taking artifacts from the cliff dwellings was warranted. For Pueblo Indians, protecting the apartments was more akin to preventing such a violation from ever happening. Santa Clarans, for one, did not want the Puyé Cliff Dwellings on their land grant in Santa Clara Cañon open for visitors; they wanted the site to be included within the Santa Clara Reservation to ensure that the U.S. government would protect it. That did not stop people from visiting Puyé or the other cliff dwellings in the region, however. In 1910 Charles S. Rawles, the Indian Office additional farmer at Santa Clara, requested that Crandall send him placards to post throughout Santa Clara Cañon so that travelers would know "that they are crossing a government reservation" where particular rules applied. In the mid-1890s, though, tourists were taking relics at such a rate that there would be little left for anthropologists to research.[34]

One source of possible information about the cliff dwellings and their inhabitants, as Hewett and anthropologist Jean Allard Jeançon found out, was their contemporary Pueblo Indian neighbors. Both anthropologists worked with Native guides in their excavations of the cliff apartments. Others who visited the ruins placed little credence in the idea that the Pueblo peoples of the late nineteenth and early twentieth centuries might well know something about their ancestors who had lived in the cliffs. Frederick Schwatka stated that Pueblo Indians who lived in villages in 1890, when he wrote his article, had forgotten the cliff dwellers' traditions. Contemporary Pueblo Indians were backward people who "tilled the soil in a rude way" and committed themselves to being "permanent savages." And Schwatka seemed to find little allure in turning over the responsibility to learn about the cliff dwellers to professional anthropologists, recounting what another had written: "The descriptions of them seem more suitable to form parts of the most romantic works of fiction than of sober and scientific memoirs from the pens of Government explorers."[35] Official studies were simply not as sexy or exciting as actually visiting the cliff apartments oneself—or having the right to study the sites as a matter of course. This sentiment did not appear to have bothered Santa Clarans as they pushed for a reservation that would encompass the Puyé cliffs; rather, it marked a lesson quickly learned: mediating outsiders' access to important sites was a way of protecting both what was physically there and extant knowledge about a place and its history.

Many visitors seemed to miss this perspective entirely, opting for descriptions and evaluations of contemporary Pueblo Indians and Hispanos that emphasized their differences from Anglos. In some cases, this meant that authors idealized Pueblo Indians and Hispanos; in others it meant that they were chastised. Charles Lummis, a journalist who lived in New Mexico and explored contemporary Indian Pueblos and cliff dwellings, recorded a number of Indigenous stories (and likely histories), which he then published in children's magazines. Lummis characterized Pueblo Indians as "gentle" and "industrious," the latter reflected by their extensive farming and irrigation networks up and down the Rio Grande valley. He also noted that Pueblo healers safeguarded their knowledge by not allowing outsiders to witness health treatments.[36] Others similarly typified the Pueblo Indians they met as "quiet" and "industrious," though wedded to old ways of doing things. One visitor, F. S. Dellenbaugh, was especially admiring of Pueblo peoples, drawing parallels to their colonization under the Spanish to that of the American colonies under the British. He called Pueblo Indians "native patriots" who instigated a "mighty uprising" against their oppressors. Dellenbaugh also discussed their prominent qualities as farmers, their preferences for turquoise, coral, and silver in jewelry, and their manners, which were reflective of civilized societies.[37] George Thomas Dowling quoted a Mr. Fiske at length in arguing that Pueblo

Indians were a "peaceful and self-respecting people, and in true refinement of behavior are superior to ourselves. We still have much to learn from them concerning ancient society, and we ought not to be in too great a hurry to civilize them, especially if they do not demand it of us." Mr. Fiske's position was unusual, even though many writers lauded Puebloan calmness, irrigation farming, and artistic proclivities.[38]

Two anonymous writers commented on the distinctive pottery of contemporary Puebloans and their cliff-dwelling ancestors. One wrote, "The pottery produced is very beautiful, but is also very fragile, and cannot be shipped without the greatest care in packaging." A visitor to a group of cliff dwellings described the pottery found as "generally symmetrical. The decoration is frequently attractive, and most all of it is in black color on an unpainted background. Some samples are finished to a degree that almost equals modern glazing."[39] The latter account describes the black-on-black ware that Maria Martinez, the renowned potter from San Ildefonso Pueblo who traveled to the 1904 St. Louis Expo, re-created after working with the ancient pots and shards found in archeological excavations. Indeed, pottery in the late nineteenth and early twentieth century was a form of art for which Pueblo Indian artists were well known. For others, the artistic lens was not enough or was wholly absent.

Many of the travelogues denigrated Pueblo peoples' cultural traits and practices. At the mildest, writers characterized Pueblo Indians as static or antiquated. William E. Curtis saw Pueblo Indians through a progressive lens, noting a strong preference for "ancient customs" and the tendency for children to "resume their ancestral habits" upon their return to their home communities after they had been away at boarding school.[40] While some writers commented on the ingenuity in Pueblo Indian irrigation systems and farming practices, others noted the continued use of apparently outdated methods: "Threshing is done on the threshing floor in precisely the same manner as among the people of 3,000 years ago by driving animals over it until the grain is threshed out of the straw."[41] No mention was made of the advanced corn, or maize, agriculture and the corresponding scientific knowledge that had dominated the Rio Grande valley since well before the Spanish incursion in the sixteenth century. In 1905 New Mexican territorial governor Miguel Otero attributed Pueblo Indians' adherence to long-standing customs

*Potters demonstration for the School of American Research with Dr. Hewett, 1912.
Photograph by H. S. Poley. Courtesy of the Denver Public Library, Western History
Collection, P-1488.*

to a death wish, noting decreasing census numbers and a general lack
of intelligence. He remarked, "The children at the various schools are
generally found to be gentle, docile and tractable. They are none too
bright, and it takes many years to drill an average school education into
them."[42] Clearly, Otero missed the savvy negotiations of the All Pueblos
Council in the delinquent tax case and Santa Clarans' rationale in pushing for a reservation.

At the extreme end of non-Native evaluations of Pueblo Indians are
those who were repulsed by their experiences in New Mexico. R. W.
Shufelt, representing himself as an army physician who had traveled
extensively and lived among a variety of Native tribes, wrote an article
called "Beauty from an Indian's Point of View." The article was anything but that, however. Shufelt systematically commented negatively
on the appearance of women in southwestern tribes. Beginning his article with a description of the racial hierarchy from which he drew his
assumptions, Shufelt wrote: "It will almost invariably be found that the

lower the race in the scale of civilization the more fixed and restricted are their ideas [of beauty]." He then proceeded to describe the facial features of women, the ways in which they wore their hair, their jewelry, and how women aged. Describing a Zuni woman, he deemed her "nose lacking in fine chiseling" and found her "mouth devoid of much character." Shufelt continued, "After the birth of their first child, Zuñian women seem to part forever with all the beauty they ever possessed, and in old age they become very ugly and exceedingly masculine in their features." In nearly every case, with the exception of a woman from Laguna Pueblo, Shufelt thought the women unsavory because of their work outdoors, their lack of character, and their distinctive jewelry, which he considered "heavy" and "barbaric."[43] Tourist and playwright Edith Sessions Tupper had a similar reaction to Pueblo Indians upon her visit to New Mexico. She focused on what she perceived to be a loose morality that manifested in hygiene, physical appearance, and Pueblo Indians' reluctance to sell treasured possessions to her. Tupper thought Puebloan pottery to be "rude" and their everyday dress to be "primitive" and "gaudy." The nudity of children repulsed her, and she found Pueblo homes to be decorated in a "tawdry" manner. Tupper concluded her article, "When you leave an Indian Pueblo, with its filth, smells, mangy curs, screeching papposes [sic], and bald nudity, you are very ready to acquiesce to the general Western article of faith that 'there is no good Indian but a dead one.' The noble Red Man is a pleasing fiction of the East."[44] Both Shufelt and Tupper held a figurative measuring stick of what they found to be familiar and admirable against the Indigenous peoples they met, not considering that they, too, might be judged by their Native counterparts. Ironically, Shufelt wrote that one of the shortcomings of Indian peoples was that they had inflexible views of beauty, "fail[ing] to recognize any beauty in the members of other tribes . . . at least of the Indo-European races."[45]

Tourists made analogous characterizations of Hispanos living in New Mexico as both dreadful and laudable. Tupper's views of Hispanos paralleled her views of Pueblo Indians; she wrote, "This [placita] is the family garden, and here the various members squat—lazy, shiftless, smiling, sunny, dirty, picturesque—the people of the land of tomorrow; the tomorrow that never brings work." Other writers likewise identified Hispanos as "shiftless" or exotic.[46] Virginia Conser Shaffer was fascinated by the Penitentes that she and her traveling companions spotted from their train car. She described the religious procession,

> Although the ground was very rough and stony, these men were clad simply in white cotton trousers and their feet were bare. Their naked backs—horrible sight—were red with blood from neck to waist! Each man carried in his right hand a plaited whip, and at every step forward he lashed his back first right, then left, rivulets of blood starting at every stroke. Following this ghastly group [of six or seven] came two men, each staggering under an immense wooden cross, three or four times his own weight, the end of the cross dragging the ground behind.[47]

The image Shaffer invokes with her description is graphic and underscores the novelty and foreignness of the people she and her companions witnessed. Unlike Shaffer, Tupper believed the Penitentes to be incorrigible villains, at least when the ceremonies were complete and they returned to their daily lives. Edward Coale also remarked on the exotic feel of New Mexico, particularly its architecture, "All the buildings in these old places are *adobe,* with massive walls from three to four feet thick . . . which with the prevailing Mexican color, language, appearance, and habit makes one feel like a stranger in a strange land." Indeed, the Otherness Anglos felt in New Mexico extended from ceremonies to architecture to food; one tourist believed that enchiladas were a type of disease akin to measles. She was relieved to find otherwise.[48]

National impressions of the territory were important to those who sought statehood for the region and who wanted to exploit economic opportunities. Joseph E. Wing, a tourist from Pennsylvania, thought Hispanos "patient" and "gentle," though "not too energetic." Quoting Colonel Thomas Catron, a politician in New Mexico and an early advocate for statehood, a traveler recorded in 1881 that Hispanos were "not only the most law-abiding people in the Territory, but in the world." Territorial governor Miguel Otero echoed this sentiment fourteen years later, stating to William E. Curtis, "The Mexican, as you call him, is a first-rate citizen" who is honest in financial dealings and "dignified but courteous, hospitable to the extreme and very anxious to learn."[49] Despite tourists' contrary characterizations of Hispanos, at least two prominent politicians extolled their virtues. But the temperament of

Penitent[e]s "crucifying" one of their own, 1888. Photograph by Charles F. Lummis. Courtesy of the Library of Congress, LC-USZ62-48453.

territorial residents was not enough; there had to be some form of economic promise for Anglos looking to relocate to the area.

Agricultural potential and mineral prospecting seemed to fit the bill. In 1890 tourist Ellenore Dutcher wrote of the fruit she sampled in the territory, noting that the mission grapes "brought to the country from Spain" were "the finest, sweetest grapes one could wish for." So too were the fruits from local orchards. Dutcher raved that the "peaches . . . weigh half a pound each and [are] of delicious flavor, and both egg and blue plums and fine apples grown in the valleys." Frederic J. Haskins also noted the size of the grain and produce New Mexican farmers cultivated, writing of "barley that stands seven feet high, oats whose heads measure 30 inches, pears weighing 19 ounces each, peaches that will balance a pound of gold, water-melons that weigh 40 pounds each and cabbage heads that tip the beam at 42 pounds."[50] To be sure, the agricultural networks along river valleys were extensive, but as Pueblo Indians and Hispanos who had lived in the region for centuries knew, water was essential, and not all land in New Mexico was tillable. One alternative economic venture was mining. A particularly rich mineral vein was found near Cochiti Pueblo, and speculators began constructing a new town called Bland. An anonymous reporter wrote, "Mr. James Kernahan has located a number of claims beyond the head of Santa Clara canon [*sic*], twenty miles north of Cochiti canon [*sic*]." Reporter "Old Rustler" noted, "At present a man can hardly hear what another says for the noise made by the carpenters building houses on all sides."[51] As with other mineral rushes in the mountain states and the great land grab during and after the Civil War, non-Natives continued to be interested in pursuing their economic enterprises. Their history, after all, told them this was possible so long as there was territory left to grab.

EDUCATIVE PROCESSES AND MISSED LESSONS

Of the learnings that occurred in relation to land, disease, citizenship, and navigating OIA institutions, four major educative processes and four missed lessons emerge. As Dewey posits, educative processes are lessons that produce subsequent learning; this in turn expands the capacity for individual and group learning at that moment and in the future. In applying Dewey's notion of "educative" processes to the learnings that occurred in the Rio Grande valley in the first decade of the twentieth century, we see that the relationships among Santa Clarans, Hispanos, and Anglos and the memories of all three groups undergird their dynamic "educations," which occurred not only during the period of True's tenure as the Santa Clara day school teacher, but also over centuries past. But not all episodes of learning for one group were passed on to another; there were missed lessons, and those are just as instructive in drawing out how colonialism and the process of colonization were learned.

Educative Processes

One of the most striking educative processes that emerges from the Santa Claran, Hispano, and Anglo responses to land use and management in the Rio Grande valley is the multigenerational construction of an educational toolkit dealing specifically with colonization and its various policies. Actions taken and responses made to circumstances and events regarding land tenure, grazing, and citizenship serve as the evidence for this particular educative process. At its core, the multigenerational learning displayed in the context of land and citizenship is simultaneously the effect of each group's learning over the previous centuries and its deliberate actions in the early twentieth century based on that learning. In other words, each of the situations described in the land and citizen chapters were educative moments in which the past became superimposed on the present (or vice versa), creating the possibility for further learning.

For the Santa Clarans, evidence of their multigenerational learning around issues of land, law, and citizenship manifests in their efforts to protect both their original land grant created by the Spanish regime and their secondary land grant in Santa Clara Cañon. The documentary evidence for this educative process begins in the mid-eighteenth century with two cases: the Tafoya case and the Canjuebe case. In 1724 Antonio Tafoya, a Hispano, received a land grant from the Spanish colonial government to graze livestock in Santa Clara Cañon, just west of the Pueblo. By the mid-eighteenth century, Santa Clarans argued that the Tafoyas' livestock damaged their crops, that the Tafoyas were growing crops of their own, and that they were using too much water from Santa Clara Creek, which ran the length of the cañon; the Pueblo leadership petitioned two Spanish governors for relief. In 1763, Spanish governor Vélez Cachupín rescinded the Tafoya grant and transferred it to Santa Clara Pueblo. In the second case, Roque Canjuebe attempted to renounce his Santa Claran identity and remake himself into a Spanish citizen. He successfully petitioned the Spanish governor for a parcel of land adjacent to the Pueblo. By the early 1800s, though, the Santa Claran leadership called out this arrangement as illegal, which it was under Spanish law. The Canjuebe grant was within 1.5 leagues of the Pueblo, which was to be reserved as a type of buffer zone between Pueblo Indian communities and Hispano ranchers. A delegation from Santa Clara traveled south to Durango requesting the return of the Canjuebe grant to the Pueblo. It succeeded, and the land reverted to Santa Clara in 1817. These cases demonstrate that Santa Clarans had effectively learned the provisions of Spanish law that were issued to protect Pueblo Indian land, and they learned the processes by which to execute those provisions in order to protect and enforce the boundaries of the Pueblo. Working through the local Spanish governor or traveling to the Spanish seat of power in Durango both proved effective. The Santa Claran leaders in each case had fruitfully advocated for themselves, and they distinguished themselves from their Hispano neighbors as Pueblo Indians who were entitled to unique protections.

Although there is a break in the documentary record during the tenure of the Mexican regime (1821–1848), the fact that Santa Clarans and Hispanos actively pursued land claims during the early years of the U.S. regime suggests that contention over land use persisted during the Mexican and early U.S. colonial periods. As the surveyor general measured and documented land grants in New Mexico, Santa Clarans and Hispanos alike acted to ensure that their claims were valid under U.S. law. Most litigious was the Santa Clara Cañon grant, which Vélez Cachupín awarded to the Pueblo in 1763. As the documentary record makes clear, Antonio Tafoya's descendants had to be reminded that the land in Santa Clara Cañon was no longer theirs to use. Disagreement over who had the right to graze livestock, plant crops, collect timber, and use water in the cañon continued into the early twentieth century. Presumably, Hispano ranchers were able to prevail over their Pueblo Indian counterparts to an extent during the Mexican regime, as repeated Hispano attempts to use land and collect resources continued into the U.S. administration. Santa Clarans attempted to thwart Hispano efforts by working closely with C. J. Crandall to create a reservation whose boundaries federal officers would patrol and protect. The creation of the Santa Clara Reservation by executive order in 1905 signaled an end to the Hispano agricultural presence on Santa Claran land.

Shortly after the establishment of the Santa Clara Reservation, Hispanos who lived, harvested, or worked their livestock on Santa Claran land found that they could no longer make special arrangements with the Pueblo governor. That did not prevent Hispanos from attempting to assert their perceived rights through the customary channels they had used regularly during the previous two colonial regimes. For example, when Samuel Stacher, the OIA additional farmer, found a Hispano man with a cartload of timber cut in Santa Clara Cañon, he demanded that the man leave the timber and not approach the reservation again. The man, however, sought remedy through the Hispano justice of the peace, who in turn demanded that Stacher return the timber to the Hispano who had harvested it and that Stacher appear before the justice formally. All proceedings, of course, were conducted in Spanish. This remedy appears to have been effective. Both Stacher and Crandall were aggravated by this, and Crandall no doubt took measures to ensure that Hispanos who had settlements in Santa Clara Cañon were permanently removed from the reservation. Using the U.S. court and OIA system, Crandall worked to have the ranchers' claims investigated; they were evicted from Santa Clara Cañon in 1906, roughly one year after the Pueblo became a reservation.

The cases of Hispano timber-cutting and ranching claims in Santa Clara Cañon suggest three significant learnings developed among Hispanos throughout the Spanish and Mexican colonial periods. First, Hispanos assumed that they would have access to Santa Clara Cañon lands, whether it was a matter of negotiating an arrangement with the Pueblo governor, going through formal Spanish channels as Antonio Tafoya did, or simply laying claim to the land and using it at will. Second, Hispanos had learned—likely during the Mexican regime—that working through the justice of the peace was favorable to them. Previous avenues under the Spanish regime, such as going through the Spanish governor, ended in favor of the Santa Clarans; this made alternate means of protecting Hispano claims necessary, even if they were not legal. Third, Hispanos learned that the actual enforcement of land decisions was key. The Tafoya land grant in Santa Clara Cañon illustrates this point: the Spanish governor had the authority to issue verdicts in contested land claims, but the rapid succession of Spanish governors was likely to result in inconsistent enforcement of gubernatorial decisions. Hispanos tested this learning repeatedly during the first half century of the U.S. regime, but it dissolved as Crandall and the OIA began rigidly implementing federal obligations in managing the new Indian reservation of Santa Clara Pueblo.

For their part, Crandall and the OIA learned through their actions in sorting out and enforcing Santa Claran and Hispano land claims that so long as they believed in and actively persisted in carrying out legally binding obligations in federal Indian law, their authority would eventually prevail. This was a difficult lesson, though. To start, when the United States annexed the New Mexico Territory, the country increased its land size, but it had to figure out how to deal with the peoples who already lived there. Santa Clarans and other Pueblo Indians were unlike other Native peoples the U.S. government had encountered and colonized. They were "civilized" Indians who held their land grants as corporate entities, making the breaking up of Pueblo Indian lands under the General Allotment Act unnecessary. At the same time,

Pueblo Indians needed to be excepted from certain laws of citizenship, like property taxes, to maintain their holdings. Too, federal agents like Crandall sought to protect Pueblo Indian lands from non-Native encroachers, particularly Hispano residents. To do this, Crandall invoked a series of federal laws and proceeded to work the U.S. federalist system to exempt Pueblo Indians from taxes and create a federally protected Indian reservation for Santa Clara Pueblo. Hispanos were left to their own devices in navigating the U.S. legal system as they resisted yet were transformed from the colonizer to the colonized.

The educative process of constructing a multigenerational toolkit within a colonial context relates closely to the second major educative process: learning one's relationship to other groups based on one's relationship to specific places. Much of this educative process was based on the degree to which each group—Santa Clarans, Hispanos, and Anglos—moved physically from place to place in its history. Santa Clarans had lived where Santa Clara Creek meets the Rio Grande from time immemorial, as their history, conveyed through oral tradition, details. Santa Clarans and other Pueblo peoples became so knowledgeable about the places along the Rio Grande and their attributes that societies were able to construct not only an extensive irrigation ditch network to grow a variety of fruits and vegetables but also a sociopolitical system that fused cultural practices to the land. In fact, Santa Claran agricultural and sociocultural practices were so tightly interwoven with the surrounding land that the place itself became a participant in the community's life. Moreover, the historical record of the Pueblo was inscribed in the landscape, with different land features being sites of historical memory that reminded Santa Clarans from where they had come. As Spaniards moved into the region in the sixteenth and seventeenth centuries, they, too, formed settled groups that became intimately familiar with the land and its features along the northern Rio Grande over the 250 years or so that Hispanos lived adjacent to Pueblo Indians. But these parallel Spanish understandings of the land came at the price of being evicted by a united Pueblo front in 1680 and being allowed to live near to Pueblo Indian communities only after the Spanish Crown issued protective guarantees such as formal, codified land grants. While these measures did not always prevent disputes over resources, both Pueblo Indians and Hispanos understood their dependence upon the land for their internally valued ways of life. By the time U.S. Anglos moved into the region in the mid-nineteenth century, Pueblo Indians and Hispanos had formed distinct but lasting ties with the places in which they lived and worked. In so doing, the two groups had developed relationships with one another that were often fraught, sometimes amiable, but always based on centuries of experience and negotiation as well as long-standing memories of each other's actions. Unique places, in other words, produced unique peoples.[52]

Anglos who moved into the area, it seems, did not understand Pueblo Indian and Hispano relationships to specific places in the Rio Grande valley or their significance. Rather, Anglos' relationships to particular places and particular peoples were not premised on staying still; their relationships were premised on movement and on acquisition. In his widely cited and debated 1893 speech, "The Significance of the Frontier in American History," Frederick Jackson Turner characterizes the Euro-American movement westward as a "perennial rebirth" that continually reshaped the "American" identity by its persistent colonial repositioning across the North American continent.[53] What came with this rebirth was a type of blindness toward differences among diverse peoples such that the U.S. courts, legislatures, and Indian Office were confounded when they met Pueblo Indians, who in many respects appeared to be "civilized" by Euro-American standards. That Hispanos—whom the federal government legally considered "White" but whom Anglos treated as subordinate in practice—lived alongside Pueblo Indians in New Mexico further complicated the colonial Anglo-Indian binary that had so long been part of the U.S. social memory of westward expansion. Instead of dismantling the binary, though, U.S. officials living and working in New Mexico shifted it. A new Anglo–non-Anglo binary prevailed, which allowed the relative newcomers to persist in their efforts to sweep through and acquire the territory and its resources. The new binary also allowed Anglos to maintain a clear colonialist orientation that did not require a sharp understanding of long-standing relationships in the region. In fact, Crandall's letters suggest that neither he nor his colleagues in the Indian Office had any interest in understanding the bonds Santa Clarans and Hispanos had with the land or the connections they had with one another. Because of the then constant movement that had characterized the Euro-American settlement of North

America, specific places were not as important in cultivating relationships as was marking them temporally through policy shifts that incorporated newly colonized peoples.

Santa Clarans and Clara D. True realized the third educative process, learning to read the Other. As illustrated by the delinquent tax case and efforts to create a reservation, Santa Clarans clearly learned the parameters of U.S. colonial policies (or federal Indian policies) as they had learned Spanish and Mexican policies before. Santa Clarans also learned how to read and exploit the desires of tourists by the time they reached the St. Louis Expo. Not only did they "play Indian" to the tourists' delight and expectations, they also taught tourists about their culture and their art forms. Pueblo Indians' previous experiences with tourists in the Rio Grande valley likely informed their performances as "Indians" and as "civilized" people at the fair, knowing that outsider views could flutter between the connotations of those two perceived extremes. Learning to read the Other—the non-Native tourists—ended up being an economic move by Indigenous peoples at the expo and later by Puebloans who relied on tourist dollars in New Mexico.

True learned to read Santa Clarans by living in their community, and she learned to read Crandall by working in his jurisdiction. Shortly after her arrival at Santa Clara Pueblo in the fall of 1902, True faced a diphtheria crisis in which she not only had to identify and treat sick children, she also had to quickly learn the sociopolitical structure of the Pueblo. Perhaps unwittingly, True aligned herself with members of the Winter party, who agreed outright to allow True and Dr. Holterman, the itinerant OIA physician, to treat children affected by the disease. The division between the Summer and Winter People over the treatment of children who contracted diphtheria proved difficult for True to navigate at the time because of her nascent understanding of the Santa Claran social structure and her own sense of right and wrong. Indeed, her connections to members of the Winter party continued well after she left the Pueblo in 1907 and returned to the valley in 1910 to settle permanently.[54] By the time Crandall asked her to canvass the Pueblo and send tardy Santa Claran children to the Santa Fe Indian School in the fall of 1904, True—with equanimity—refused to send them until the harvest was complete. She had learned the agricultural cycle of the Pueblo and its fundamental importance to Santa Claran survival. True likewise learned that the relationships she had developed with families at the Pueblo were significant for both her own work at Santa Clara Pueblo and Crandall's enrollments in Santa Fe. In fact, Crandall depended on her relationships, and this offered her leverage in negotiating with him on the Pueblo's behalf. This did not always make True's dealings with Crandall easy or collegial. During the diphtheria outbreak, she quickly discovered that he trusted Indian Office procedures and the physician's observations of what was happening at the Pueblo more than he trusted her reports. True responded to Crandall's admonitions by subverting his orders to enforce a rigid quarantine and by playing the subordinate woman in order to dismiss her "errors" and restore her competency as the eyes and ears of the Indian Office at Santa Clara.

Crandall's adherence to the OIA's processes, procedures, and hierarchy reflects the fourth educative process that emerges from the learning in the previous chapters: learning the system. Clearly, Santa Clarans proved themselves adept at learning the parameters of the governmental and legal systems of each colonial regime they experienced. And they built this knowledge over many generations. By the early twentieth century, they understood enough to co-opt U.S. policies distinguishing American Indians from the rest of the population as well as to work the federal system of government. In cooperation with Crandall, the All Pueblos Council was successful in petitioning Congress to pass an exemption freeing the Pueblo Indians from paying local property taxes, overriding the New Mexico Territorial Supreme Court's ruling that Pueblo Indians were full citizens with all attendant rights and responsibilities. Similarly, Santa Claran leadership worked with Crandall to have the Pueblo's land grants converted into a formal Indian reservation via executive order. Crandall's letters suggest, however, that the Santa Claran motives for wanting a reservation were different than his own. While he saw reservation life as a step toward U.S. civilization and citizenship, Santa Clarans viewed the reservation as a means to ensure the protection of their lands and the privacy they desired to live their day-to-day lives with minimal disturbance from outsiders. While these tax and land provisions meant shelter from external forces for Santa Clarans and other Pueblo Indians, they paradoxically also meant a regression along the path to full citizenship as it was conceived in federal Indian policy and law.

In order to intelligently advise Santa Clarans and other Pueblo Indians in navigating court decisions in the early twentieth century, Crandall had to learn the details of U.S. federalism and federal Indian law. He also had to learn the internal bureaucracy of the OIA in order to function effectively and with authority as superintendent of the Santa Fe Indian School and acting Indian agent of the Northern Pueblos District. Not only did Crandall work the federal system at the national level, helping Pueblo Indians protect their property from foreclosure and encroachment, he also attempted to work the territorial legislature to pass a compulsory education law for Native children. Though he was unsuccessful in this bid, Crandall was able to work the Indian Office system well. He demanded that his employees follow correct procedure, be it through enrolling students at day schools, working to have friends and family hired, or accounting for government property. Crandall's by-the-book disposition, at least as it manifested in his correspondence, lent him a reputation for consistency; it also reinforced his position of authority over OIA employees in the Northern Pueblos District, which subsequently enforced the hierarchical structure of the Indian Office.

True responded to Crandall's implementation of OIA rules and regulations with charm, subversion and, it is likely, by withholding information. As the day school teacher at Santa Clara Pueblo, True served as the eyes and ears of the Indian Office, a public health official, a gatekeeper, and a primary liaison between Santa Clarans and Crandall's office. In this capacity, True first had to learn the extent to which Crandall allowed exceptions to the rules, and conversely, how faithful he was to the literal interpretation and enforcement of those rules. The 1903 diphtheria outbreak proved instructive, as did repeated queries about possible student enrollments at the Santa Clara day school. In some cases, Crandall's strict adherence to government policy proved untenable, as with maintaining a rigid quarantine during the diphtheria episode or sending children to Santa Fe during harvest times. In these cases, True subverted policy. In other instances, such as when Crandall accused True of inflating the scope of the diphtheria outbreak, or when he scolded her for giving away and lending out government property regardless of the circumstances, True responded with charm or parody, underscoring the absurdity of the given policy in place and his adherence to it. Tellingly, True did not describe her pedagogic practices or her thoughts on the *Uniform Course of Study*. It might well be that it was not her custom or the custom of other day school teachers at the time to report on classroom experiences. Or it might be that she chose not to write about her practice to avoid further confrontation with Crandall. In either case, True understood her role in the OIA system and her professional relationship to Crandall in part as a result of her experiences as the day school teacher at Santa Clara Pueblo.

Missed Lessons

As educative processes emerge from True and Crandall's correspondence and the related source material, so too do missed lessons, or lost opportunities to learn from the circumstances, events, and situations at hand. A year and a half after she left her post as the Santa Clara day school teacher for a superintendency at the Potrero School in southern California, Clara D. True wrote in *Outlook* magazine:

> It is to be regretted that in dealing with the Indian we have not regarded him worth while [*sic*] until it is too late to enrich our literature and traditions with the contribution he could so easily have made. We have regarded him as a thing to be robbed and converted rather than as a being with intellect, sensibilities, and will, all highly developed, the development being on different lines than our own only as necessity dictated. The continent was his college. The slothful student was expelled from it by President Nature. Physically, mentally, and morally, the North American Indian before his degradation at our hands was a man whom his descendants need not despise.[55]

True's statement is striking. Not only does she summarize the intention underlying many U.S. policies created to Americanize Native peoples, she also conceives of learning broadly and in a way that varies by culture and geographic position. In a way, True's lament reflects missed lessons as well as potential missed educative gifts. The U.S. approach to Indian policy and the bureaucracy of the Indian Office effectively furnished many U.S. government officials with blinders such that they would not necessarily have recognized a potential educative moment if it was right in front of them. True, however, appears to have figured out how to take off those blinders, if only for a moment, to see what she and other non-Native peoples had missed.

True's initial months at Santa Clara Pueblo reflect her struggle to learn the sociopolitical structure of the community and its normative expectations. Her first scrape was with the 1903 diphtheria outbreak at Santa Clara. In pushing Santa Clarans to allow her and Dr. Holterman to treat sick children, True aligned herself with "Winter Progressives" who had split with the long-standing governance structure of the Pueblo. Whether or not True realized it at the time, she had allied with a dissenting group, at least for the short term. Subsequent literature suggests that her Santa Claran friendships from her early days at the Pueblo endured over decades, though it is not very clear if she was subsequently able to form friendships with members of the Summer party. True again crossed a Santa Claran line of which she did not appear to be entirely aware when she hired an old man to do work on her chicken house. The Santa Claran man no longer lived at the Pueblo and did not engage in community ditching activities, but True did not realize this when she hired him. After two separate discussions with the Pueblo governor, Diego Naranjo, over the propriety of the old man doing work for True, the man was permitted to work on her chicken house, but True's letters indicate that she never made this mistake again. By the time Crandall tried to coerce Santa Clarans to send their children to the Santa Fe Indian School during the fall harvest of 1904, True politely refused to strong-arm families. She had learned from her mistakes and recognized missed lessons early in her tenure. Her blinders seem to have come off.[56]

This was not the case with other U.S. government officials. Instead, an abstract vision of the "civilization process" directed federal Indian policy, the creation of organizational positions, and the courts. In failing to account for differences among American Indian tribes and Hispanos, the law's definition of the Other ensured that Anglos in governmental positions—and perhaps many more people from outside New Mexico—would have a difficult time reconciling the characteristics of Pueblo Indians with other American Indian groups in North America. U.S. law during the nineteenth century increasingly defined the Other abstractly. This, in turn, produced ambiguous interpretations of the law at the local, state, and federal levels, interpretations that were not necessarily attentive to circumstances on the ground. For example, Hispano ranchers who had set up settlements in Santa Clara Cañon found their property claims rejected by the U.S. system. Part of this had to do with Hispanos settling on the land without discrete, individual land grants under the Spanish or Mexican regimes; it also had to do with where the Hispanos in question settled: on one of Santa Clara Pueblo's two corporate land grants. But significantly, U.S. law did not recognize customary uses of land and customary land management practices under the previous two colonial governments. As the 2001 and 2004 U.S. General Accountability Office reports on the Treaty of Guadalupe Hidalgo suggest, U.S. courts primarily focused on vetting individual land grants, with the exception of corporate land grants held by Pueblo Indian communities. Other communally held or used parcels of land were often entered into the public domain, leaving Hispano individuals and communities to come up with alternate solutions to their grazing area and natural resource shortages. Unlike the case of Pueblo Indians, there was no U.S. government office or agency that specifically advocated on Hispanos' behalf.

U.S. law and the interpretation of it in the courts and among OIA officials likewise conflated American Indians legally, with limited attention devoted to the very basic fact that Indigenous peoples had unique cultures, resources bases, and ways of making sense of the world around them. Indeed, the definition of "Indian" hardened during the first decade and a half of the twentieth century. Beginning in 1869 with *U.S. v. Lucero,* the courts tested whether Pueblo Indians were "Indians" or "citizens" under the law. Initially, the New Mexico Supreme Court found that Pueblo Indians were full legal citizens of the territory and the United States, which allowed them to buy, sell, and give their land at will and obligated them to pay taxes on their property. The U.S. Supreme Court affirmed this ruling in 1876 in *U.S. v. Joseph,* in which it likened Pueblo Indians to insular religious communities. This determination held through the 1904 delinquent tax case. But Pueblo Indians did not consider themselves, nor did they want to be, citizens of New Mexico and the United States. Crandall agreed, arguing that while Pueblo Indians were indeed "civilized" in many of their practices, they were nevertheless "Indians" in need of protection. The U.S. Congress and President Theodore Roosevelt likewise concurred, exempting Pueblo Indians from property taxes and converting Santa Clara Pueblo land grants into a reservation, respectively. Thus began the slide of the

Pueblo Indians' legal status from full citizen to ward of the federal government. Their legal status, however, remained ambiguous after the 1907 *U.S. v. Mares* case, in which the New Mexico Supreme Court held to its 1904 ruling—Pueblo Indians were full citizens. But in this particular case, it meant that Pueblo Indians could buy, sell, and drink alcohol legally. The New Mexico Territorial Legislature rendered this ruling null and void, however, with the passage of a law that banned the sale and distribution of liquor to Pueblo Indians, identifying them as noncitizens. The transition from citizen to ward was further solidified in 1913 with *U.S. v. Sandoval,* in which the U.S. Supreme Court overturned *U.S. v. Joseph* and *U.S. v. Mares,* ruling that Pueblo Indians were Indian wards under the law. In each of these cases, the courts relied heavily on Indian Office reports and evidence given as to the history of Pueblo Indian status during the previous two colonial regimes. And in each case, the courts defined citizenship as a form of status for the individual rather than the group. American Indians, like Hispanos, under the law became an abstract Other. In so doing, the courts and other U.S. government officials missed learning about these groups as they lived together in New Mexico at the turn of the twentieth century.

Reliance on U.S. law and the federal system during those years subsequently blacked out the histories of the peoples who lived in New Mexico—another missed lesson. This became especially apparent through Crandall's letters after President Roosevelt created the Santa Clara Reservation by executive order in 1905. At that point, Crandall became the Indian Office agent responsible for managing land on the reservation, and he enforced the jurisdictional boundaries strictly. This meant that Hispano ranchers could no longer lease grazing land from the Pueblo via the Santa Claran governor, nor could they go onto the reservation to cut timber or pasture their livestock without Crandall's express written permission. This change in policy and procedure transformed centuries-long practices and drew a fixed line between Pueblo Indian and Hispano communities. In taking a hard line against Hispanos Crandall found little reason to pay attention to the history between the different groups living in the Rio Grande valley. His dismissal of their shared past came to confound and aggravate him later, not only with the encroachment of Hispanos' livestock on reservation land but also with drinking practices among Pueblo Indians, Hispanos, and Jicarilla

Apaches. Crandall's expressed anger in dealing with drinking practices clearly identified him as an outsider who would continue to remain beyond the pale of local custom; it also reflected his commitment to the one-directional "civilization" program the U.S. government constructed for American Indians.

Indeed, the unidirectional nature of the "civilization" program also functioned as a set of blinders, preventing many Anglo officials from learning with any depth about Native cultures and communities. The standardized *Uniform Course of Study* and the hierarchical organization of the Office of Indian Affairs structured a top-down approach to aligning American Indians to the dominant social, political, and economic arrangements in place in U.S. society. Because of its focus on manual training with minimal academic preparation, the curriculum offered in OIA schools slotted Native students into particular socioeconomic outcomes. Though it provided students with technical skills they might otherwise not have acquired and dispelled many non-Natives' perceptions of how Indians were supposed to be, as with the St. Louis Expo, the curriculum also limited Indigenous children's social and professional opportunities within and outside their home communities. The standardization of the curriculum and of the Indian Office itself similarly ignored the contributions of distinct tribal groups, making all of its students simply "Indian." The hierarchical structure of the OIA made its lower echelons—its day school teachers, in particular—invisible. If Clara D. True's experience and learning are minimally representative, then the day school teacher was a significant arbiter and liaison between Native communities and the U.S. government. Because of their physical positioning on Indian reservations, often isolated from other OIA employees, day school teachers had unique opportunities to learn about Indigenous people—and it would seem that day school teachers could relatively easily subvert OIA policies and curriculum with little interference. But the reports of OIA superintendents, who appear to have been more willing to toe the Indian Office line, were far more important to the organization. This emphasis on hierarchy and on the standardized one-directional program of the OIA formally prevented Indian Office officials from "extraneous" learning about Native peoples.

Epilogue

Office of Indian Affairs day schools are untapped settings for studying not only colonization in the history of North America but also the attendant educative processes and missed lessons that various groups and individuals experienced in Native communities. This particular study inductively follows school keepers' accounts of circumstances and events in order to understand learning within broader social, political, and colonial contexts. Through their descriptive reports, their normative asides, and their regular patterns, True's and Crandall's letters reveal that learning largely took place outside of the schoolhouse walls. The school, in fact, transforms from a site where formally mandated instruction occurred to a prism through which we might witness larger social, political, and economic incidents. Santa Clarans, Hispanos, and Anglos each had different stakes in the outcomes of these incidents, and each group's experience with one another and the "Other" shaped their responses to different events such as the 1903 diphtheria outbreak at Santa Clara Pueblo, the 1899 delinquent tax case, and the creation of the Santa Clara Reservation. And in spite of directives handed down from the Indian Office, the courts, Congress, and the president of the United States, federal Indian policy was not carried out in a neat, uniform method; rather, different individuals and groups co-opted diverse policies to suit their own ends in ways that reflected their learning and their education over time. In other words, place, the histories of the people in that place, and the relationships that different peoples have with one another in that place matter.

This study would seem to challenge the very notion of generalizability in academic scholarship and perhaps within the field of the history of education. Indeed, this study calls attention to the dangers of overgeneralization most directly through court cases that question the degree of "civilization" among Pueblo Indian peoples. Federal policies and law did not have a tidy way to deal with Native groups who appeared to be exceptions to the rules about how Indians should live, look, and behave. That Pueblo Indians lived in permanent villages with

Pueblo of Santa Clara, New Mexico, ca. 1881. Photograph by William H. Jackson.
Courtesy of the Palace of the Governors Photos Archives (NMHM/DCA), #4226.

multistoried houses, farmed extensively, and practiced Catholicism
was evidence enough in the nineteenth century that they were "civilized" and thus "citizens" of the New Mexico Territory and the United
States. For agents like Crandall, though, this was not an accurate representation of Pueblo Indians, and simply being "civilized" should not be
tantamount to being a citizen. Regardless of their appearances of "civilization," Pueblo Indians maintained their pre-Spanish social, political,
and religious beliefs and practices. Pueblo Indians, in other words, presented a colonization problem for Anglos—they offered an alternative
form of civilized living, which met European-derived definitions and
criteria, but Pueblo Indians were still very much indigenous to North
America. Pueblo communities defied the social and racial evolutionary
scale by which they were measured. They had syncretic cultures, and
they made it clear in many circumstances that they did not want to relinquish what they had known and practiced for centuries in favor of
lifestyles and beliefs advocated by Anglos. Crandall repeatedly stated in
his annual reports to the commissioner of Indian Affairs that Pueblo Indian communities just wanted to be left alone to live as they saw fit. For
their part, Pueblo Indians refused citizenship and took on the label of

"Indian" to ensure their protection from encroachers onto their lands and from local tax authorities. Neither Crandall nor the U.S. Supreme Court could make sense of this. The Court made Pueblo Indians wards of the federal government in order to set them on the right trajectory toward U.S. citizenship.

In living among and working with Santa Clarans, Clara D. True was an OIA employee and a community teacher. Much of the learning she facilitated occurred outside the schoolroom. True's previous posts in the Indian School Service, coupled with her role as a communication conduit for Santa Clarans, allowed her to voice her interpretation of various federal directives and at times work in tandem with the Pueblo to subvert them, as with the quarantine order during the diphtheria outbreak. Although True wrote about many of the activities at the Pueblo and frequently advocated for individual Santa Clarans, much of her documented teaching and learning within the Pueblo no longer exists, as the number of letters in the National Archives collection sharply drops off in 1905. It is clear that True continued to write letters to Crandall, as he copied his responses into press copybooks. Why most of True's letters were apparently discarded, though, is mysterious. It was in 1905 that Crandall first recommended that True be transferred to a boarding school, where she would be closely supervised; this was also the year Crandall's sister, Miss Ferris, became his clerk. She typed most of his letters and might have done his filing as well, throwing out what she thought was unimportant. Consulting the letters of other day school teachers in the Northern Pueblos District might solve this small mystery.

Studying how True, Crandall, Santa Clarans, and Hispanos co-opted territorial and federal laws and OIA directives demonstrates the need to contextualize American Indian education within the more general spheres of borderlands history and education policy. As historian David Weber has noted, scholarship on the Spanish borderlands history in North America has been uneven since Herbert Bolton first argued its significance in the early 1920s.[1] Weber's own work as well as more recent scholarship on children and citizenship in the Southwest are foundational and orienting studies for this book because they are attentive to the competing cultural claims that are particular to specific places. It is worth noting that the rugged geography and harsh climatic conditions in the Rio Grande valley likely aided Pueblo Indians' physical survival. Scarce resources, especially water, deterred a large number of Spanish, Mexican, and U.S. settlers from moving to the region. Those non-Natives who did come to live in the area had to physically and culturally adapt to the place, inducing competing cultural claims that opposed colonialism as a binary construct.

These competing claims are carried out within the day school context through the appropriation of federal policies. Yet the general literature on formal education policy—particularly policy implementation—typically does not include sections on American Indian education or schooling. This is a significant gap. The system of government-run schools for Native children operated in fundamentally different ways than regular public schools in the United States: tribes and the schools on their reservations had direct relationships with the federal government, bypassing state education agencies. Not studying this history and more current trends in American Indian schooling as part of a holistic education policy environment could be seen as an abdication of an ethical obligation to understand critically the institutions that have perpetuated a colonial mind-set.[2]

In addition to (re)considering how American Indian education might be contextualized, it is worth considering the substantive directions future research might take in light of the study presented here. First, most of the secondary literature about American Indian education to date has focused on Native experiences in missionary and government-run boarding schools. Without a doubt, these studies have served as the instructional foundation for this project; yet very little has been written about day schools and their influence on learning within and on the borders of Indigenous communities.[3] This area of research is noteworthy because day schools were sites through which Native communities actively appropriated policies handed down through the Indian Office or other U.S. government agencies or branches. If we want to understand the multifaceted processes and effects of colonization and racialization on American Indians and Anglos, among others, day schools offer rich, substantive terrain.

Second, day schools illuminate that the professional roles their teachers were expected to fill often came into conflict with both traditional Anglo-American and American Indian gender roles at the cusp of the twentieth century. Generally, little research has been done on the women who worked for the OIA or about American Indians who graduated from and went on to work in OIA schools. Szasz's edited collection, Coleman's in-depth study of American Indian autobiographies, and Lomawaima's history of the Chilocco boarding school figure most prominently as book-length studies of gender and OIA schools.[4] Since the early 1990s, though, this scholarship has waned. Given the central position of day school and boarding school teachers as cultural arbiters within the greater U.S. and Native contexts, further study is warranted.

Third, limited scholarship exists on Indian health care policy and practice before the passage of the Snyder Act in 1921, when Congress officially established systematic funding for Indian health services. The pre–Snyder Act period is important to research because Indian health care was a significant arm of federal interventions in Native lives and because federal Indian health care policy efforts were early attempts at public health initiatives in the United States. Jean Keller's recent work on health care at the Sherman Institute in California is one of the few examples of deep scholarship in this area, demonstrating how at least one OIA school was at the cutting edge of public health policy and practice at the time.[5] More can and should be done. Teachers were, after all, often the default public health officials in Native communities, and they, like many of us today, understood little about Indigenous medical treatments and their community roles.

Methodologically, this study's inductive and microhistorical approach seemingly challenges the notion of generalizability in research and leaves out large-scale survey approaches to studying American Indian education and its relationship with colonization and racialization processes. This is not necessarily a problem when one regards the school as a prism for seemingly disparate forms of learning that go beyond the boundaries of the schoolhouse. One can follow leads inductively and trace the processes and experiences that were educative for individuals and groups. While following learning inductively is liberating, it requires that one set aside—or perhaps even relinquish—concrete definitions of education. For once "education" is pinned down and fixed in the mind, recognizing other viable and possibly infinite forms of "education" becomes increasingly difficult, if not exponentially so. Yet, some researchers have conducted remarkable studies of education through an inductive approach, even if they did not frame their studies as such. In particular, those studying the history of the Atlantic world and the history of slavery offer compelling examples of inductive histories of education; and there are several recent studies within the field of the history of education that offer similar examples.[6] Their substantive and methodological innovations are instructive and can push the field of the history of education in insightful and fruitful new directions. There is much work to be done.

Chronology

1540–1542	Francisco Vázquez de Coronado encounters Rio Grande Pueblo Indians
1595–1598	Don Juan de Oñate recruits colonists to colonize Pueblos
1598	Oñate's expedition leaves central Mexico and establishes headquarters in San Juan
1680	Pueblo Revolt
1690	Spanish land grant awarded to Santa Clara Pueblo
1724	Governor Domingo de Bustemente awards land grant to Tafoya brothers
1744	Roque Canjuebe defects from Santa Clara and obtains Spanish land grant
1763	Governor Vélez Cachupín transfers Tafoya grant back to Santa Clara; awards Santa Clara whole cañon grant
1788	Governor Fernando de la Concha investigates Tafoyas for trespassing, affirms Vélez Cachupín's decisions, and orders Tafoyas off of land
1810–1821	Mexican war for independence from Spain
1815	Santa Claran leadership travels to Durango to contest Canjuebe grant
1817	Spanish commandant general returns Canjuebe land grant to Santa Clara Pueblo
1819	Civilization Fund Act passed
1824	Congress creates Bureau of Indian Affairs within War Department
1832	Congress creates commissioner of Indian Affairs position; commissioner reports to the secretary of war
1846–1848	U.S. war with Mexico
1848	Treaty of Guadalupe Hidalgo ratified
1849	Congress transfers Bureau of Indian Affairs to Department of the Interior
1864	U.S. government issues patents for Pueblo Indian land grants
1880	English-only policy instituted in federally run Indian schools
1885–1888	J. D. C. Atkins's tenure as commissioner of Indian Affairs
1887	General Allotment Act passed

1889–1893	Thomas J. Morgan's tenure as commissioner of Indian Affairs
1891	Civil Service Act passed
1893–1897	Daniel M. Browning's tenure as commissioner of Indian Affairs
1893–1898	William Hailmann's tenure as superintendent of Indian School Service
1894	Pueblo attorney G. Hill Howard petitions to have Santa Clara Cañon grant affirmed by U.S. government or converted into a reservation
1894	Political rift between Summer and Winter people at Santa Clara Pueblo
1894	Dr. Anna Wessels develops antitoxin for diphtheria
1897–1904	W. A. Jones's tenure as commissioner of Indian Affairs
1898–1899	Smallpox hits San Ildefonso, San Juan, Isleta, Acoma, Laguna, Jemez, Cochiti, Santo Domingo, San Felipe, Zuni, and Hopi (First and Second Mesas) Pueblos
1899	Land for Pajarito National Park removed from entry; the slated park land can no longer be settled under the Homestead Act of 1862 or bought or sold through other means
1899–1910	Estelle Reel's tenure as superintendent of Indian School Service
1901	*Uniform Course of Study* published
1902	Leandro Tafoya becomes governor of Santa Clara
1902	Crandall drafts compulsory education law for Territory of New Mexico; it fails
1902	Diphtheria at San Ildefonso Pueblo
1903	Diego Naranjo becomes governor of Santa Clara
1903	Diphtheria outbreak at Santa Clara Pueblo
1904	José Jesus Naranjo becomes governor of Santa Clara
1904	*New Mexico v. Persons on the Delinquent Tax List of 1899:* New Mexico Supreme Court rules Pueblo Indians are citizens
1904	Louisiana Purchase Exposition in St. Louis
1904–1930	Jean Allard Jeançon collects field notes at Santa Clara Pueblo, which W. W. Hill uses in his seminal book, *An Ethnography of Santa Clara Pueblo, New Mexico*

1905	San Juan Naranjo or José Jesus Naranjo governor of Santa Clara
1905	Santa Clara becomes a reservation
1905–1909	Francis Leupp's tenure as commissioner of Indian Affairs
1906	Leandro Tafoya becomes governor of Santa Clara
1906	Jemez Forest Reserve created
1906	Antiquities Act passed
1906	Squatter's claims rejected
1907	Avalino Chevarria becomes governor of Santa Clara
1907	*U.S. v. Mares*: New Mexico Supreme Court rules that Pueblo Indians, as citizens, can buy and sell alcohol
1912	New Mexico achieves statehood
1913	*U.S. v. Sandoval:* U.S. Supreme Court rules that Pueblo Indians are wards of the federal government, not citizens
1916	Bandelier National Monument created
1921	Snyder Act passed; comprehensively ensures health care and schooling for American Indians
1936	Santa Clara Constitution enacted

Notes

INTRODUCTION

1. I use "American Indian," "Indian," "Indigenous," and "Native" inter-changeably when referring generally to the Indigenous or aboriginal peoples in the Americas. Likewise, I use "Pueblo Indian" and "Pueblo" when refer-ring to Indigenous Pueblo peoples living in what is now New Mexico and Arizona. When possible, I use a tribe's own name.

2. Today, the Office of Indian Affairs is called the Bureau of Indian Affairs (BIA). In the National Archives and Records Administration inventory of Pueblo Indian records, Robert Svenningsen, the author, notes that although the bill that created the organization within the Department of War in 1824 uses the term Bureau of Indian Affairs, people called the organization the Office of Indian Affairs. The federal government formally adopted the name Bureau of Indian Affairs in 1847. Before that, the Office of Indian Affairs was also called the Indian Office. I use "Office of Indian Affairs" and "Indian Office" interchangeably. R. Svenningsen, *Preliminary Inventory of the Pueblo Records Created by Field Offices of the Bureau of Indian Affairs, Record Group 75* (General Services Administration, National Archives and Records Adminis-tration, Washington, D.C., 1980), 1.

3. True and Crandall used the term "Mexican" when referring to people of Spanish descent in New Mexico with no class distinction. Other schol-ars have written that "Hispano" or "Spanish" was the preferred term among those descended from Spanish ancestors. I use "Hispano" throughout this book. See Manuel G. Gonzales, *Mexicanos: A History of Mexicans in the United States* (Bloomington: Indiana University Press, 1999); John Nieto-Phillips, "Mexican Yankees and American Jibaros: The Americanization of School-children in New Mexico and Puerto Rico" (lecture, Indiana University, Bloomington, November 19, 2004), and *The Language of Blood: The Making of Spanish-American Identity in New Mexico, 1880s–1930s,* illustrated ed. (Albu-querque: University of New Mexico Press, 2004).

4. Elsie Clews Parsons, *Tewa Tales* (Tucson and London: University of Arizona Press, 1994), 112–113.

5. Ibid., 113.

6. Clara Kern Bayliss, "A Tewa Sun Myth," *Journal of American Folklore* 22, no. 85 (September 1909): 334.

7. Ibid.

8. Ibid., 335.

9. For an extended discussion of the language relationships and group-ings among Pueblo Indian communities, see Edward P. Dozier, *The Pueblo Indians of North America* (New York: Holt, Rinehart & Winston, 1970), 37. Prior to the Spanish *entrada,* more than three dozen Indian Pueblos existed in New Mexico and Arizona; this changed, however, with Spanish colonization. See Joe S. Sando, *Pueblo Nations: Eight Centuries of Pueblo Indian History* (Santa Fe, N.Mex.: Clear Light, 1992), 20.

10. Sando, *Pueblo Nations,* 20; Edward P. Dozier, *Hano: A Tewa Indian Community in Arizona* (New York: Holt, Rinehart & Winston, 1966), 4; Robert C. Galgano, *Feast of Souls: Indians and Spaniards in the Seventeenth-Century Missions of Florida and New Mexico* (Albuquerque: University of New Mexico Press, 2005), 2. See also Dozier, *The Pueblo Indians of North America,* 43–45; and Sando, *Pueblo Nations,* 52–54.

11. Dozier, *Hano,* 4; Dozier, *The Pueblo Indians of North America,* 44–45; W. W. Hill, *An Ethnography of Santa Clara Pueblo, New Mexico* (Albuquerque: University of New Mexico Press, 1982), 6; Sando, *Pueblo Nations,* 54, 59–63; David Roberts, *The Pueblo Revolt: The Secret Rebellion That Drove the Spaniards out of the Southwest* (New York: Simon & Schuster, 2004), 72, 78–90; Galgano, *Feast of Souls,* 9, 39–40, 45, 132–136.

12. Dozier, *The Pueblo Indians of North America,* 55–60; Galgano, *Feast of Souls,* 136–141; Roberts, *The Pueblo Revolt,* 9–27; Sando, *Pueblo Nations,* 63–69.

13. Alvar W. Carlson, "Spanish-American Acquisition of Cropland within the Northern Pueblo Indian Grants, New Mexico," *Ethnohistory* 22, no. 2 (Spring 1975): 96. Spanish settlers were not permitted to be within 1.5 leagues of Pueblo towns. One league is equivalent to 2.6 miles. Dozier, *The Pueblo Indians of North America,* 67–68, 189–191; Hill, *An Ethnography of Santa Clara Pueblo,* 189, 191; Barbara Aitken, "Temperament in Native American Religion," *Journal of the Royal Anthropological Institute* 60 (1930): 385. See also Dozier, *Hano,* 12; Edward P. Dozier, "The Pueblo Indians of the Southwest: A Survey of the Anthropological Literature and a Review of Theory, Method, and Results," *Current Anthropology* 5, no. 2 (April 1964): 90.

14. Vine Deloria Jr. and Clifford M. Lytle, *American Indians, American Justice* (Austin: University of Texas Press, 1983), 72; Dozier, *The Pueblo Indians of*

North America, 107; Dozier, "The Pueblo Indians of the Southwest," 85; David Lavender, *The Southwest* (Albuquerque: University of New Mexico Press, 1980), 141.

15. "White" generally refers to people of northern European and British, or Anglo-Saxon, descent. This term becomes problematic when used in the New Mexico context as Hispanos were sometimes categorized as White. Whites living in New Mexico referred to themselves as "White" or "American" and they referred to former non-Native former Mexican citizens as "Mexican." In order to alleviate confusion, when "Whites" are discussed within the New Mexico context, I will refer to them as Anglo.

16. Christine A. Klein, "Treaties of Conquest: Property Rights, Indian Treaties, and the Treaty of Guadalupe Hidalgo," *New Mexico Law Review* 26 (1996): 201.

17. Alexis de Tocqueville, *Democracy in America* (Chicago: University of Chicago Press, 2000), 302–325; David Wallace Adams, "Fundamental Considerations: The Deep Meaning of Native American Schooling, 1880–1900," *Harvard Educational Review* 58, no. 1 (February 1988): 2; David Wallace Adams, *Education for Extinction: American Indians and the Boarding School Experience, 1875–1928* (Lawrence: University Press of Kansas, 1997), 5–27; Helen M. Bannan, "The Idea of Civilization and American Indian Policy Reformers in the 1880s," *Journal of American Culture* 1, no. 4 (1978): 787–799; Edgar L. Hewett, "Ethnic Factors in Education," *American Anthropologist*, n.s., 7, no. 1 (March 1905): 1–16.

18. Henry L. Dawes, "Solving the Indian Problem, 1883," in *Americanizing the American Indians: Writings by the "Friends of the Indian," 1880–1900*, ed. Francis Paul Prucha (Cambridge, Mass.: Harvard University Press, 1973), 28. Carl Schurz served as a senator from 1869 to 1875. He also served as secretary of the interior from 1877 to 1881. Carl Schurz, "Present Aspects of the Indian Problem, 1881," in Prucha, *Americanizing the American Indians*, 14; Adams, "Fundamental Considerations"; Adams, *Education for Extinction*, 5–27; Wilbert H. Ahern, "An Experiment Aborted: Returned Indian Students in the Indian School Service, 1881–1908," *Ethnohistory* 44, no. 2 (Spring 1997): 263–304; Bannan, "The Idea of Civilization and American Indian Policy Reformers in the 1880s"; Michael C. Coleman, "The Responses of American Indian Children to Presbyterian Schooling in the Nineteenth Century: An Analysis through Missionary Sources," *History of Education Quarterly* 27, no. 4 (Winter 1987): 473–497; Irving G. Hendrick, "Federal Policy Affecting the Education

of Indians in California, 1849–1934," *History of Education Quarterly* 16, no. 2 (Summer 1976): 163–185; K. Tsianina Lomawaima and Teresa L. McCarty, *"To Remain an Indian": Lessons in Democracy from a Century of Native American Education* (New York: Teachers College Press, 2006), 4–6; Jon Allan Reyhner and Jeanne M. Oyawin Eder, *American Indian Education: A History* (Norman: University of Oklahoma Press, 2006), 4, 6–7.

19. U.S. Bureau of the Census, "1880 United States Census, Fulton, Callaway, Missouri," 1880, http://www.familysearch.org/Eng/search/frameset _search.asp?PAGE=ancestorsearchresults.asp.

20. Clara D. True Employment File, National Archives and Records Administration, National Personnel Records Center, St. Louis, Mo. (hereafter cited as NARA—NPRC); Edgar A. Allen to F. H. Abbot, "Letter regarding Clara D. True's Behavior at Chilocco Indian School," July 21, 1911, NARA—NPRC; Benjamin S. Coppock to Edgar A. Allen, "Letter regarding Clara D. True's Behavior at Chilocco Indian School," August 10, 1911, NARA—NPRC.

21. C. J. Crandall to William A. Jones, "Letter regarding Clara D. True's Arrival at the Santa Clara Day School," September 4, 1902, vol. 3, p. 94, Press Copies of Letters Sent to the Commissioner of Indian Affairs, February 1900–November 1913, Records of the Bureau of Indian Affairs, RG 75, entry 34, National Archives and Records Administration, Rocky Mountain Region, Denver, Colo. (hereafter cited as NARA—Commissioner); C. J. Crandall to William A. Jones, "Letter regarding the Resignation of W. C. B. Biddle and Transfer of Clara D. True," June 24, 1902, vol. 2, p. 427, NARA—Commissioner; C. J. Crandall to William A. Jones, "Letter regarding the Transfer of Clara D. True to One of the Pueblo Day Schools," June 21, 1902, vol. 2, p. 420, NARA—Commissioner; Clara D. True to C. J. Crandall, "Letter to Superintendent Discussing Personnel," October 15, 1902, Letters Received from Day School Teacher Clara D. True, 1902–1907, Records of the Bureau of Indian Affairs, RG 75, entry 38, National Archives and Records Administration, Rocky Mountain Region, Denver, Colo. (hereafter cited as NARA—True); C. J. Crandall to Lizzie M. Randall, "Letter to Lizzie M. Randall regarding a Journalist in the Area," July 17, 1907, vol. 27, p. 180, Press Copies of Letters Sent ("Miscellaneous Letters"), June 1890–December 1913, Records of the Bureau of Indian Affairs, RG 75, entry 32, National Archives and Records Administration, Rocky Mountain Region, Denver, Colo.; Clara D. True to C. J. Crandall, "Letter to the Superintendent Recommending a Housekeeper for Sallie Neal at the San Juan Day School," October 8, 1903, NARA—True; Ruth Burke, "Devil

of the Rio Grande," *True West* 48, no. 1 (January 2001): 37–38; C. J. Crandall to Clara D. True, "Letter to Clara D. True Granting Her Permission to Temporarily Reside at Her New Ranch," October 3, 1907, roll 28, Press Copies of Letters Sent concerning Pueblo Day Schools, March 1900–June 1911, Records of the Bureau of Indian Affairs, RG 75, M1473, National Archives and Records Administration, Washington, D.C.; Cheryl J. Foote, *Women of the New Mexico Frontier, 1846–1912* (Albuquerque: University of New Mexico Press, 2005), 140; Frances D. True to C. J. Crandall, "Leave of Absence for Submitted to Crandall," October 1, 1907, vol. 8, p. 481, NARA—Commissioner; Clara D. True, "No Place Like Home," *Independent Woman*, December 1914.

22. Svenningsen, *Preliminary Inventory of the Pueblo Records*, 6–7; U.S. Bureau of the Census, "1870 United States Census, Rockford, Wright, Minnesota," 1870, http://search.ancestrylibrary.com/cgi-bin/sse.dll?db=1870usfed cen%2c&gsfn=Clinton&gsl . . . ; U.S. Bureau of the Census, "1900 United States Census, Santa Fe Ward 1, U.S. Indian Industrial School, Santa Fe, New Mexico,"1900,http://search.ancestrylibrary.com/cgi-bin/sse.dll?db=1900us fedcen%2c&gsfn=Clinton&gsl. . . .

23. Richard J. Storr, "The Education of History: Some Impressions," *Harvard Educational Review* 31, no. 2 (Spring 1961): 124–135; Richard J. Storr, "The Role of Education in American History: A Memorandum for the Committee Advising the Fund for the Advancement of Education in Regard to This Subject," *Harvard Educational Review* 46, no. 3 (August 1976): 334.

24. Bernard Bailyn, *Education in the Forming of American Society: Needs and Opportunities for Study* (New York: Vintage Books, 1960); Storr, "The Education of History"; Storr, "The Role of Education in American History"; Donald Warren, "History of Education in a Future Tense," in *Handbook of Research in the Social Foundations of Education*, ed. Steven Tozer, Bernardo P. Gallegos, and Annette M. Henry (New York: Routledge, 2010), 41–60.

25. Bailyn, *Education in the Forming of American Society*, 48.

CHAPTER ONE. LAND; OR, RELEARNING PLACE IN A NEW COLONIAL ERA

1. Frederic J. Haskins, "New Mexico," *Duluth News-Tribune*, February 2, 1910.

2. Halka Chronic, *Roadside Geology of New Mexico* (Missoula, Mont.: Mountain Press, 1987), vii.

3. D. W. Meinig, *The Southwest: Three Peoples in Geographical Change, 1600–1970* (New York: Oxford University Press, 1971), 3.

4. For a groundbreaking study on different perceptions and uses of land among American Indian and European groups, see William Cronon, *Changes in the Land: Indians, Colonists, and the Ecology of New England*, rev. ed. (New York: Hill & Wang, 2003).

5. "Treaty of Guadalupe Hidalgo and Protocol of Querétaro," May 30, 1848, in *1873 Treaties and Conventions Concluded between the United States of America and Other Powers* (1873), 566, 567; Laura E. Gomez, "Off-White in an Age of White Supremacy: Mexican Elites and the Rights of Whites and Blacks in Nineteenth-Century New Mexico," *Chicano-Latin Law Review* 25 (Spring 2005): 16; Christine A. Klein, "Treaties of Conquest: Property Rights, Indian Treaties, and the Treaty of Guadalupe Hidalgo," *New Mexico Law Review* 26 (1996): 217, 218; Susan D. Sawtelle, Alan R. Kasdan, and Jeffrey D. Malcolm, *Treaty of Guadalupe Hidalgo: Findings and Possibly Options regarding Longstanding Community Land Grant Claims in New Mexico* (Washington, D.C.: U.S. General Accountability Office, June 2004), 10.

6. Susan A. Poling and Alan R. Kasdan, *Treaty of Guadalupe Hidalgo: Definition and List of Community Land Grants in New Mexico, Exposure Draft* (Washington, D.C.: U.S. General Accountability Office, January 2001), 6, 10. Daniel Tyler defines *ejidos* as "unplanted, unenclosed areas used for grazing, recreation, a place for stray animals, and a garbage dump." "Ejido Lands in New Mexico," in *Spanish and Mexican Land Grants and the Law*, ed. Malcolm Ebright (Manhattan, Kans: Sunflower University Press, 1989), 24.

7. Roxanne Dunbar-Ortiz, *Roots of Resistance: A History of Land Tenure in New Mexico* (Norman: University of Oklahoma Press, 2007), 114; Klein, "Treaties of Conquest," 236.

8. Tewa is a distinct language within the Tanoan language group spoken at Santa Clara, Ohkay Owingeh (San Juan), San Ildefonso, Pojoaque, Nambé, and Tesuque Pueblos. See the map in the introduction.

9. Swaso's last name has several different spellings in the sources used. True wrote "Sousea" in her correspondence with Crandall, and anthropologist W. W. Hill wrote "Swazo" in his ethnography of Santa Clara. "Suazo" also appears in other sources consulted. Here and in subsequent pages, the spelling used by the source author will be employed with a note clarifying who the person in question was, if necessary. Although it is not entirely clear in the record, Swaso might have originally been from Tesuque, another Tewa Pueblo in northern New Mexico. Apparently, he married into Santa Clara.

10. Jean Allard Jeançon Papers, n.d., folder 11, Western History and

Genealogy 196, box 1, range 9A, section 14, shelf 4, Denver Public Library, Denver, Colo. A number of other variations of this origin story exist in print. See also Alfonso Ortiz, *The Tewa World: Space, Time, Being, and Becoming in a Pueblo Society* (Chicago: University of Chicago Press, 1969), 13–16; Elsie Clews Parsons, *Tewa Tales* (Tucson and London: University of Arizona Press, 1994), 9–15.

11. Edgar L. Hewett and Bertha P. Dutton, *The Pueblo Indian World,* Handbooks of Archaeological History (Albuquerque: University of New Mexico Press, 1945), 34.

12. Ortiz, *The Tewa World,* 103–106.

13. Even though Jeançon lived at Santa Clara during True's tenure as day school teacher, neither appears to have written about the other in their notes or correspondence.

14. Jeançon Papers, folder 11.

15. Ibid.; Edward P. Dozier, "Factionalism at Santa Clara Pueblo," *Ethnology* 5, no. 2 (April 1966): 173.

16. Edward P. Dozier, *The Pueblo Indians of North America* (New York: Holt, Rinehart & Winston, 1970), 207; Ortiz, *The Tewa World,* 36, 82–83.

17. Joe S. Sando, *Pueblo Nations: Eight Centuries of Pueblo Indian History* (Santa Fe, N.Mex.: Clear Light, 1992), 13.

18. Dozier, *The Pueblo Indians of North America,* 189–191; Edward P. Dozier, *Hano: A Tewa Indian Community in Arizona* (New York: Holt, Rinehart & Winston, 1966), 12; Ortiz, *The Tewa World,* 61; Sando, *Pueblo Nations,* 14–15, 172; Edward P. Dozier, "The Pueblos of the South-western United States," *Journal of the Royal Anthropological Institute of Great Britain and Ireland* 90, no. 1 (June 1960): 153.

19. The Santa Clara constitution of 1935 modified the selection of these positions when it took effect in 1936. W. W. Hill, *An Ethnography of Santa Clara Pueblo, New Mexico* (Albuquerque: University of New Mexico Press, 1982), 97; Ortiz, *The Tewa World,* 64.

20. Hill, *An Ethnography of Santa Clara Pueblo,* 188–189; Ortiz, *The Tewa World,* 60, 69, 71, 72; Dozier, "The Pueblos of the South-western United States," 153.

21. There is some discrepancy between the sources on the number of lieutenant governors. Ortiz and Pritzker write that there are two, while Hill and Dozier state that there is one. True's and Crandall's letters do not resolve this discrepancy as there is no mention of this position. Hill, *An Ethnography*

of Santa Clara Pueblo, 189; B. M. Pritzker, *A Native American Encyclopedia: History, Culture, and Peoples* (Oxford: Oxford University Press, 2000), 86; Ortiz, *The Tewa World,* 62; Edward P. Dozier, "The Pueblo Indians of the Southwest: A Survey of the Anthropological Literature and a Review of Theory, Method, and Results," *Current Anthropology* 5, no. 2 (April 1964): 153; Dozier, *The Pueblo Indians of North America,* 189.

22. Dozier, "The Pueblos of the South-western United States," 154; Hill, *An Ethnography of Santa Clara Pueblo,* 196; Ortiz, *The Tewa World,* 66–67.

23. Vine Deloria Jr. and Daniel R. Wildcat, *Power and Place: Indian Education in America* (Golden, Colo.: Fulcrum, 2001), 23; Vine Deloria Jr., *God Is Red: A Native View of Religion,* 2nd ed. (Golden, Colo.: Fulcrum, 1992), 72–73, 122, 272–275; Donald Lee Fixico, *The American Indian Mind in a Linear World: American Indian Studies and Traditional Knowledge* (New York: Routledge, 2003), 70–71; Manuali Aluli Meyer, "Indigenous and Authentic," in *Handbook of Critical and Indigenous Methodologies* (Thousand Oaks, Calif: Sage, 2008), 219.

24. Keith H. Basso, "Wisdom Sits in Places: Notes on a Western Apache Landscape," in *Senses of Place,* School of American Research Advanced Seminar Series (Santa Fe, N.Mex.: School of American Research Press, 1996), 53–90; Keith H. Basso, "Stalking with Stories," in *Schooling the Symbolic Animal: Social and Cultural Dimensions of Education,* ed. Bradley A. U. Levinson (Lanham, Md.: Rowman & Littlefield, 2000).

25. Laguna Pueblo is part of the Keres language group. See the map in the introduction.

26. Leslie Marmon Silko, "Landscape, History, and the Pueblo Imagination," in *The Ecocriticism Reader: Landmarks in Literary Ecology,* ed. Cheryll Glotfelty and Harold Fromm (Athens: University of Georgia Press, 1996), 269.

27. C. J. Crandall to Clara D. True, "Letter to Clara D. True regarding Refusals of Some Santa Clarans to Work on the Ditches," March 24, 1905, roll 27, Press Copies of Letters Sent concerning Pueblo Day Schools, March 1900–June 1911, Records of the Bureau of Indian Affairs, RG 75, M1473, National Archives and Records Administration, Washington, D.C. (hereafter cited as NARA—Pueblo Day Schools).

28. Dozier, *The Pueblo Indians of North America,* 131–132.

29. Ibid., 127; Francisco Atanasio Domínguez, *The Missions of New Mexico, 1776: A Description, with Other Contemporary Documents* (Albuquerque:

University of New Mexico Press, 1956), 50–51, 59, 71, 89–90, 119, 151, 207; Edgar L. Hewett, "Notes on the Primitive Agriculture of the Indians," Edgar Lee Hewett Collection, 89ELH.048, box 4, Museum of Indian Arts and Culture, Santa Fe, N.Mex.; Sando, *Pueblo Nations,* 43. Sando and Dozier disagree about when Pueblo Indians began to farm chilis. Dozier claims the Spanish brought chilis from Central America, and Sando argues that chilis were indigenous to Pueblo territory.

30. Barbara Aitken, "Temperament in Native American Religion," *Journal of the Royal Anthropological Institute* 60 (1930): 385–387; Dozier, "The Pueblos of the South-western United States," 153; Dozier, *The Pueblo Indians of North America,* 189; Hill, *An Ethnography of Santa Clara Pueblo,* 188–189; Ortiz, *The Tewa World,* 60, 69, 71, 72.

31. Dozier, "The Pueblos of the South-western United States," 150.

32. Ibid., 150–151; Hill, *An Ethnography of Santa Clara Pueblo,* 26.

33. Aitken, "Temperament in Native American Religion," 385–387; Dozier, "The Pueblos of the South-western United States," 154; Dozier, "Factionalism at Santa Clara Pueblo," 177; Hill, *An Ethnography of Santa Clara Pueblo,* 195–196.

34. Dozier, "Factionalism at Santa Clara Pueblo"; Hill, *An Ethnography of Santa Clara Pueblo,* 196; Ortiz, *The Tewa World,* 66–67.

35. Hill, *An Ethnography of Santa Clara Pueblo,* 195–196.

36. Dozier, "Factionalism at Santa Clara Pueblo"; Hill, *An Ethnography of Santa Clara Pueblo,* 196; Pritzker, *A Native American Encyclopedia,* 86.

37. Aitken, "Temperament in Native American Religion," 385; Tracy Brown, "Tradition and Change in Eighteenth-Century Pueblo Indian Communities," *Journal of the Southwest* 46, no. 3 (Autumn 2004): 472; Dozier, *The Pueblo Indians of North America,* 82; G. Emlen Hall, "Land Litigation and the Idea of New Mexico Progress," *Journal of the West* 27, no. 3 (1988): 50–51. The extent to which league boundaries applied varied by time, by Pueblo, and by Spanish governor. See Myra Ellen Jenkins, "Spanish Land Grants in the Tewa Area," *New Mexico Historical Review* 47, no. 2 (1972): 113–134.

38. Dozier, *The Pueblo Indians of North America,* 83.

39. Hall, "Land Litigation," 52.

40. Brown, "Tradition and Change," 473.

41. Aitken, "Temperament in Native American Religion," 385–387.

42. True called the Winter faction the "Progressives" in all of her correspondence.

43. C. J. Crandall to Clara D. True, "Letter to Clara D. True regarding Indian Labor," April 13, 1903, roll 25, NARA—Pueblo Day Schools.

44. Clara D. True to C. J. Crandall, "Letter to Superintendent Recording the Problems with the Governor over Laborers and Delivery of Water," April 15, 1903, Letters Received from Day School Teacher Clara D. True, 1902–1907, Records of the Bureau of Indian Affairs, RG 75, entry 38, National Archives and Records Administration, Rocky Mountain Region, Denver, Colo. (hereafter cited as NARA—True).

45. Clara D. True to C. J. Crandall, "Letter to Superintendent Reporting on Problems with Laborers on the Construction of a Chicken House, a Well, and a Ditch," April 16, 1903, NARA—True.

46. David Roberts, *The Pueblo Revolt: The Secret Rebellion That Drove the Spaniards out of the Southwest* (New York: Simon & Schuster, 2004), 158.

47. Dunbar-Ortiz, *Roots of Resistance*, 36–39; Robert C. Galgano, *Feast of Souls: Indians and Spaniards in the Seventeenth-Century Missions of Florida and New Mexico* (Albuquerque: University of New Mexico Press, 2005), 37, 91; Manuel G. Gonzales, *Mexicanos: A History of Mexicans in the United States* (Bloomington: Indiana University Press, 1999), 33; Jenkins, "Spanish Land Grants in the Tewa Area," 113; David Lavender, *The Southwest* (Albuquerque: University of New Mexico Press, 1980), 47, 54, 61; Sawtelle, Kasdan, and Malcolm, *Treaty of Guadalupe Hidalgo*, 16; Malcolm Ebright, *Land Grants and Lawsuits in Northern New Mexico* (Santa Fe, N.Mex.: Center for Land Grant Studies, 2008), 14–15.

48. For an extended discussion, see J. Adelman and S. Aron, "From Borderlands to Borders: Empires, Nation-States, and the Peoples in between in North American History," *American Historical Review* 104, no. 3 (1999): 814–841.

49. Alvar W. Carlson, "Spanish-American Acquisition of Cropland within the Northern Pueblo Indian Grants, New Mexico," *Ethnohistory* 22, no. 2 (Spring 1975): 96.

50. Jenkins, "Spanish Land Grants in the Tewa Area"; Sandra K. Matthews-Lamb, "'Designing and Mischievous Individuals': The Cruzate Grants and the Office of the Surveyor General," *New Mexico Historical Review* 71, no. 4 (October 1996): 341–359.

51. Carlson, "Spanish-American Acquisition of Cropland," 96; Klein, "Treaties of Conquest," 236; Jenkins, "Spanish Land Grants in the Tewa Area"; Tyler, "Ejido Lands in New Mexico."

52. Carlson, "Spanish-American Acquisition of Cropland," 96; Dunbar-Ortiz, *Roots of Resistance*, 64–65; Matthews-Lamb, "'Designing and Mischievous Individuals,'" 343.

53. Ebright, *Land Grants and Lawsuits*, 24–25; Jenkins, "Spanish Land Grants in the Tewa Area"; Matthews-Lamb, "'Designing and Mischievous Individuals'"; Dunbar-Ortiz, *Roots of Resistance*, 37–38, 52, 64, 66–67, 93; Tyler, "Ejido Lands in New Mexico," 24, 25.

54. Carlson, "Spanish-American Acquisition of Cropland," 99–103; Klein, "Treaties of Conquest," 236.

55. Clara D. True to C. J. Crandall, "Letter to the Superintendent about Pupils in the School," September 5, 1902, NARA—True.

56. C. J. Crandall to Clara D. True, "Letter to Clara D. True regarding a Stray Cow, Diphtheria, and Enrollment," September 5, 1902, vol. 3, p. 98, Press Copies of Letters Sent to the Commissioner of Indian Affairs, February 1900–November 1913, Records of the Bureau of Indian Affairs, RG 75, entry 34, National Archives and Records Administration, Rocky Mountain Region, Denver, Colo. (hereafter cited as NARA—Commissioner).

57. Laura E. Gomez notes that Hispanos typically held justice of the peace positions in the New Mexican legal system at this time. Anglos held district and supreme court–level judgeships. "Off-White in an Age of White Supremacy," 53.

58. Cutting fence around cultivated land ran contrary to Spanish and Mexican law, according to Daniel Tyler. U.S. law, however, does not appear to have addressed this directly. Tyler, "Ejido Lands in New Mexico," 28.

59. Clara D. True to C. J. Crandall, "Letter to Superintendent concerning Relations with the Governor and the Neighboring Mexicans," November 4, 1902, NARA—True.

60. "Court Document Alleging Illegal Cattle Grazing Santa Clara Lands, in English," 1902, box 2, folder 6, Indian Affairs Collection, Center for Southwest Research, University of New Mexico, Albuquerque, http://econtent.unm.edu/cdm4/document.php?CISOROOT=/indaffairs&CISOPTR=666&CISOSHOW=663. It is not clear whether or not this affidavit was submitted to the justice of the peace or another judicial body.

61. Clara D. True to C. J. Crandall, "Letter to Superintendent concerning Problems with Tools and Local Mexicans," November 5, 1902, NARA—True.

62. G. Hill Howard, "Opinion Report No. 133," July 22, 1854, MSS 29BC, series 301, case #17, folder 1, U.S. Soil Conservation Service Region Eight

Records, Center for Southwest Research, University of New Mexico, Albuquerque, http://econtent.unm.edu/cdm4/document.php?CISOROOT=/cat
ron&CISOPTR=54&REC=4; D. H. Smith, "Petition, Pueblo of Santa Clara v.
United States," June 18, 1892, Thomas B. Catron Papers, Center for Southwest Research, University of New Mexico, Albuquerque, http://econtent.
unm.edu/cdm4/document.php?CISOROOT=/catron&CISOPTR=36&REC
=6&CISOSHOW.

63. "Translations of Santa Clara Pueblo Papers, Decrees, etc.," n.d., box
44, folder 300, Northern Pueblos Agency, General Correspondence File,
1904–1937, Records of the Bureau of Indian Affairs, RG 75, entry 83, National
Archives and Records Administration, Rocky Mountain Region, Denver,
Colo.; Howard, "Opinion Report No. 133."

64. "Translations of Santa Clara Pueblo Papers, Decrees, etc." Sandra K.
Matthews-Lamb adds that this particular Spanish law ensured "ample water,
lands, woodlands, access routes, and farmlands and an *ejido* one league long
where the Indians can have their livestock without having them intermingle
with others belonging to Spaniards." "'Designing and Mischievous Individuals,'" 343.

65. Howard, "Opinion Report No. 133."

66. Ebright, *Land Grants and Lawsuits,* 40; Matthews-Lamb, "'Designing
and Mischievous Individuals,'" 349.

67. Howard, "Opinion Report No. 133"; Smith, "Petition, Pueblo of Santa
Clara v. United States"; "Pueblo of Santa Clara vs. United States Exhibit
No.2," July 28, 1894, MSS 29BC, series 301, case #17, folder 1, Catron Papers,
http://econtent.unm.edu/cdm4/document.php?CISOROOT=/catron&
CISOPTR=90&REC=5; D. H. Smith, "Pueblo of Santa Clara v. United
States Exhibit No.3," n.d, MSS 29, series 301, case #17, Catron Papers,
http://econtent.unm.edu/cdm4/document.php?CISOROOT=/catron&
CISOPTR=31&REC=16; D. H. Smith, "Memorandum, Pueblo of Santa Clara
vs. United States," n.d., MSS 29BC, series 301, case #17, folder 1, Catron Pa-
pers, http://econtent.unm.edu/cdm4/document.php?CISOROOT=/catron
&CISOPTR=177&REC=11.

68. G. H. Howard to N. C. Walpole, "Letter from G. H. Howard to
N.C. Walpole regarding Juan de Tafoya Grant," September 30, 1898, box 2,
folder 6, Indian Affairs Collection, http://econtent.unm.edu/cdm4/docu
ment.php?CISOROOT=/indaffairs&CISOPTR=454&CISOSHOW=446;
H. C. Sluss, James H. Reeder, and Quimby Vance, "Special Instructions for

the Correction Survey of the 'Pueblo of Santa Clara' Grant," September 20, 1898, box 5, Santa Clara Grant 1898 folder, Wendall V. Hall Collection, Center for Southwest Research, University of New Mexico, Albuquerque.

69. A full discussion of the tax case can be found in chapter 3, "Citizen."

70. C. J. Crandall to Santa Clara governor, "Letter to the Governor of the Santa Clara Pueblo regarding the Creation of the Santa Clara Reservation," August 29, 1905, p. 327, Press Copies of Letters Sent ("Miscellaneous Letters"), June 1890–December 1913, Records of the Bureau of Indian Affairs, RG 75, entry 32, National Archives and Records Administration, Rocky Mountain Region, Denver, Colo. (hereafter cited as NARA—Miscellaneous).

71. Carl Schurz, "Secretary of the Interior Schurz on Reservation Policy, November 1, 1880," in *Documents of United States Indian Policy*, ed. Francis Paul Prucha, 3rd ed. (Lincoln: University of Nebraska Press, 2000), 152.

72. Carlson, "Spanish-American Acquisition of Cropland," 96.

73. See Hill, *An Ethnography of Santa Clara Pueblo*, 20.

74. Ebright, *Land Grants and Lawsuits*, 20–21; Hill, *An Ethnography of Santa Clara Pueblo*, 20; Tyler, "Ejido Lands in New Mexico," 28. How Santa Clarans conceptualized land ownership over time is somewhat unclear. Hill outlines Santa Clara land ownership based on field notes collected during episodes throughout the twentieth century. This does not mean, however, that these customs were the same under the Spanish and Mexican regimes. See Hill, *An Ethnography of Santa Clara Pueblo*, 105–106.

75. C. J. Crandall to William A. Jones, "Letter to the Commissioner of Indian Affairs regarding Timber on Santa Clara land," April 30, 1903, vol. 3, p. 345, NARA—Commissioner; C. J. Crandall to William A. Jones, "Letter to the Commissioner of Indian Affairs regarding the Inspection of Land in Santa Clara Canyon," October 29, 1903, vol. 4, p. 136, NARA—Commissioner; C. J. Crandall to Commissioner of Indian Affairs, "Letter to the Commissioner of Indian Affairs Requesting an Additional Farmer if the Santa Clara Reservation Is Created," June 20, 1905, vol. 6, p. 4, NARA—Commissioner.

76. Crandall identifies all three of these men as living in Española. Other letters from both True and Crandall suggest that Anastacio and Desidero Naranjo were both originally from Santa Clara.

77. C. J. Crandall to Francis E. Leupp, "Letter to the Commissioner of Indian Affairs Reporting on Trespassers in the Santa Clara Reservation," October 25, 1905, vol. 6, p. 246, NARA—Commissioner.

78. C. J. Crandall to Francis E. Leupp, "Letter to the Commissioner of

Indian Affairs Requesting Advice about How to Handle Trespassers Who Take out Claims against the Additional Farmer at Santa Clara," October 25, 1905, vol. 6, p. 247–248, NARA—Commissioner.

79. See Gomez, "Off-White in an Age of White Supremacy," 52–54.

80. Dunbar-Ortiz, *Roots of Resistance,* 95–96.

81. Frances Leon Quintana, "Land, Water, and Pueblo-Hispanic Relations in Northern New Mexico," *Journal of the Southwest* 32, no. 3 (1990): 288–299.

82. Carlson, "Spanish-American Acquisition of Cropland," 97.

83. Diego Naranjo to C. J. Crandall, "Letter to Superintendent from Governor of Pueblo concerning Lands Claimed by a Mexican," September 9, 1903, NARA—True. Diego Naranjo did not appear to write this letter himself, as his "mark" was an "X" in the middle of his name at the end of the letter. Most communications from the Pueblo's governor went through True, who would either transcribe or summarize the request and add her commentary on the matter at hand.

84. C. J. Crandall to Diego Naranjo, "Letter to Gov. Diego Naranjo regarding Sanchez's Land Claim Adjacent to the Santa Clara Pueblo," September 9, 1903, vol. 18, p. 186, NARA—Miscellaneous.

85. Clara D. True and Santiago Naranjo to C. J. Crandall, "Letter to Superintendent concerning Removal of Mexican Cattle from Indian Lands," November 4, 1904, NARA—True.

86. George B. Haggett, "Letter to Clara D. True regarding Trespassing Livestock at Santa Clara," November 5, 1904, roll 26, NARA—Pueblo Day Schools.

87. C. J. Crandall to Francis E. Leupp, "Letter to the Commissioner of Indian Affairs regarding Contested Land Claims and Road Access on the Santa Clara Reservation," November 8, 1905, vol. 6, pp. 282–284, NARA—Commissioner.

88. C. J. Crandall to Francis E. Leupp, "Report on Hispano Squatters in Santa Clara Reservation," November 3, 1905, vol. 6, pp. 262–270, NARA—Commissioner.

89. Crandall to Leupp, "Letter to the Commissioner of Indian Affairs regarding Contested Land Claims and Road Access."

90. C. J. Crandall to Leandro Tafoya, "Letter to Leandro Tafoya regarding Squatters on the Santa Clara Reservation and the Pending National Park," June 18, 1906, vol. 24, p. 304, NARA—Miscellaneous.

91. C. J. Crandall to Samuel S. McKibben, "Letter to Samuel S. McKibbin

regarding the Removal of Squatters on the Santa Clara Reservation," July 11, 1906, vol. 24, p. 402, NARA—Miscellaneous.

92. Gomez, "Off-White in an Age of White Supremacy," 18, 25, 27.

93. Dozier, *The Pueblo Indians of North America*, 82–86.

94. Clara D. True to C. J. Crandall, "Letter to Superintendent Requesting Advice on Timber Cutting on Reservation Lands," February 16, 1906, NARA—True.

95. C. J. Crandall to Clara D. True, "Letter to Clara D. True regarding Judge Abbott's Advice on Trespassing Stock," February 16, 1906, roll 27, NARA—Pueblo Day Schools.

96. Clara D. True to C. J. Crandall, "Letter to Superintendent Requesting a Letter from Judge Abbott regarding Mexican Stock Trespassing on Indian Lands," February 19, 1906, NARA—True.

97. C. J. Crandall to Clara D. True, "Letter to Clara D. True regarding What to Do about Trespassing Stock," February 23, 1906, roll 27, NARA—Pueblo Day Schools.

98. C. J. Crandall to Leandro Tafoya, "Letter to Leandro Tafoya regarding Authority on the Santa Clara Reservation," February 28, 1906, vol. 23, p. 23, NARA—Miscellaneous.

99. Ferdinand Cowle Iglehart, *Theodore Roosevelt: The Man as I Knew Him* (New York: Christian Herald, 1919), 218–219; Theodore Roosevelt, *Theodore Roosevelt: An Autobiography* (New York: Macmillan, 1913), 435–436.

100. See, for example, Iglehart, *Theodore Roosevelt*, 218–222; John Muir, *Our National Parks* (Berkeley: University of California Press, 1900), 1–27; Roosevelt, *Theodore Roosevelt*, 408–436.

101. Thomas L. Altherr, "The Pajarito or Cliff Dwellers' National Park Proposal, 1900–1920," *New Mexico Historical Review* 60, no. 3 (1985): 277. See also Hal Rothman, "Chapter 1: The Open Plateau," in *Bandelier, NM: An Administrative History*, February 4, 2001, http://www.nps.gov/band/adhi/adhi1b.htm.

102. C. J. Crandall to William A. Jones, "Letter to the Commissioner regarding the Creation of the Santa Clara Reservation," January 3, 1903, vol. 3, pp. 236–238, NARA—Commissioner. This was before his investigation into squatters' claims and the volatile incidents with Hispanos who cut timber in the cañon.

103. C. J. Crandall to Clara D. True, "Letter to Clara D. True regarding the Failure of the Proposed Santa Clara Reservation," January 23, 1903, roll 25, NARA—Pueblo Day Schools.

104. C. J. Crandall to William A. Jones, "Letter to the Commissioner of Indian Affairs regarding Reservation Land for the Santa Clara Pueblo," April 25, 1903, vol. 3, p. 344, NARA—Commissioner.

105. C. J. Crandall to William A. Jones, "Letter to the Commissioner of Indian Affairs regarding the Cliff Dwellings Near the Santa Clara Pueblo," May 22, 1903, vol. 3, pp. 361–363, NARA—Commissioner.

106. Rothman, "Chapter 1: The Open Plateau"; Altherr, "The Pajarito or Cliff Dwellers' National Park Proposal," 280–281; C. J. Crandall to Robert E. Bradford, "Letter to Additional Farmer regarding Ditching and National Park, 07/18/1903," July 18, 1903, vol. 17, p. 451, NARA—Miscellaneous; R. F. Lee, "Creating Mesa Verde National Park and Chartering the Archeological Institute, 1906," June 18, 2006, http://www.cr.nps.gov/archeology/PUBS/LEE/Lee_CH7.htm.

107. C. J. Crandall to William A. Jones, "Letter to the Commissioner of Indian Affairs regarding the Survey of Land Near the Santa Clara Canyon and the Santa Clara Reservation," December 25, 1903, vol. 4, pp. 205–206, NARA—Commissioner.

108. C. J. Crandall to Clara D. True, "Letter to Clara D. True regarding Land Near Santa Clara Canyon," December 26, 1903, roll 26, NARA—Pueblo Day Schools.

109. Clara D. True to C. J. Crandall, "Letter to Superintendent concerning His Visit to the Santa Clara Canyon," December 29, 1903, NARA—True.

110. C. J. Crandall to William A. Jones, "Letter to the Commissioner of Indian Affairs regarding the Creation of a Reservation for the Santa Clara Indians," January 7, 1904, vol. 4, pp. 213–215, NARA—Commissioner. Historians disagree about Holsinger's report. National Park historian Ronald F. Lee, who wrote about the anthropology program and the Antiquities Act, contends that Holsinger's findings effectively defeated Lacey's bill to create Pajarito National Park as Holsinger recommended that much of the timberlands in question go to the Jemez Forest Reserve. Hal Rothman, the author of *Bandelier, NM: An Administrative History,* argues that Holsinger favored park advocates and did not think that Santa Clarans needed more land for agriculture. The author does not indicate what he or she means by "agriculture." Although it is not clear what Crandall told Holsinger as they surveyed the land together, Crandall's letters to Commissioner Jones recommend that the Santa Clara Cañon land be used for timber, water, and pasture, not for farming. Rothman, "Chapter 1: The Open Plateau"; Lee, "Creating Mesa Verde

National Park." See also Altherr, "The Pajarito or Cliff Dwellers' National Park Proposal," 280–281; Crandall to Jones, "Letter to the Commissioner of Indian Affairs regarding the Cliff Dwellings Near the Santa Clara Pueblo"; Crandall to Jones, "Letter to the Commissioner of Indian Affairs regarding the Survey of Land Near the Santa Clara Canyon and the Santa Clara Reservation"; Crandall to Jones, "Letter to the Commissioner of Indian Affairs regarding the Creation of a Reservation for the Santa Clara Indians."

111. This case is discussed fully in chapter 3, "Citizen."

112. Altherr, "The Pajarito or Cliff Dwellers' National Park Proposal," 283–285; C. J. Crandall to Francis E. Leupp, "Letter to the Commissioner of Indian Affairs regarding the Boundaries of the Santa Clara Reservation," September 27, 1905, vol. 5, p. 198, NARA—Commissioner.

113. Crandall to Tafoya, "Letter to Leandro Tafoya regarding Squatters on the Santa Clara Reservation and the Pending National Park."

114. Altherr, "The Pajarito or Cliff Dwellers' National Park Proposal," 285; John F. Lacey, *Act for the Preservation of American Antiquities, U.S. Statutes at Large* 34 (1906): 225; Lee, "Creating Mesa Verde National Park"; Woodrow Wilson, *Bandelier National Monument Proclamation, U.S. Statutes at Large* 39 (1916): 1764.

CHAPTER TWO. DISEASE; OR, THE INITIATION OF CLARA D. TRUE

1. Although the literature about True is limited, there are several brief articles that convey True's alliance. See Margaret D. Jacob, "Making Savages of Us All: White Women, Pueblo Indians, and the Controversy over Indian Dances in the 1920s," *Frontiers: A Journal of Women Studies* 17, no. 3 (1996): 178–209; Margaret D. Jacobs, "Clara True and Female Moral Authority," *Faculty Publications, Department of History* (2002), http://digitalcommons.unl .edu/historyfacpub/24; Cheryl J. Foote, *Women of the New Mexico Frontier, 1846–1912* (Albuquerque: University of New Mexico Press, 2005), 117–146.

2. Clara D. True to C. J. Crandall, "Letter to the Superintendent about Pupils in the School," September 5, 1902, Letters Received from Day School Teacher Clara D. True, 1902–1907, Records of the Bureau of Indian Affairs, RG 75, entry 38, National Archives and Records Administration, Rocky Mountain Region, Denver, Colo. (hereafter cited as NARA—True); C. J. Crandall to Clara D. True, "Letter to Clara D. True regarding a Stray Cow, Diphtheria, and Enrollment," September 5, 1902, vol. 3, p. 98, Press Copies of Letters

Sent to the Commissioner of Indian Affairs, February 1900–November 1913, Records of the Bureau of Indian Affairs, RG 75, entry 34, National Archives and Records Administration, Rocky Mountain Region, Denver, Colo. (hereafter cited as NARA—Commissioner).

3. C. J. Crandall to Clara D. True, "Letter to True regarding Diphtheria Breakout," December 8, 1902, roll 25, Press Copies of Letters Sent concerning Pueblo Day Schools, March 1900–June 1911, Records of the Bureau of Indian Affairs, RG 75, M1473, National Archives and Records Administration, Washington, D.C. (hereafter cited as NARA—Pueblo Day Schools).

4. Francis J. McCormick to Mary Dissette, "Letter to Miss Dissette regarding Diphtheria at the Santa Clara Pueblo," January 13, 1903, roll 25, NARA—Pueblo Day Schools; Francis J. McCormick to Clara D. True, "Letter to Clara D. True regarding What the Indian Office Will and Will Not Spend Money on during Diphtheria Quarantine," January 13, 1903, roll 25, NARA—Pueblo Day Schools.

5. Clara D. True to Francis J. McCormick, "Letter to Francis McCormick, Clerk-in-Charge, Indian Schools, Santa Fe, NM regarding Diphtheria Outbreak, Quarantine and Anti-toxin," January 14, 1903, NARA—True.

6. Francis J. McCormick to Clara D. True, "Letter to Clara D. True regarding the Enforcement of the Diphtheria Quarantine," January 16, 1903, roll 25, NARA—Pueblo Day Schools.

7. McCormick to Dissette, "Letter to Miss Dissette regarding Diphtheria at the Santa Clara Pueblo"; Clara D. True to Francis J. McCormick, "Letter to Clerk-in-Charge, Santa Fe Indian School, concerning Difficulties among the Santa Clara Pueblo Indians Accepting Vaccinations," January 21, 1903, NARA—True.

8. Clara D. True to Francis J. McCormick, "Letter to Clerk-in-Charge, Santa Fe Indian School, concerning Problems in Vaccinating the Indians in the Pueblo," January 20, 1903, NARA—True.

9. Clara D. True to C. J. Crandall, "Letter to Superintendent concerning Difficulties in Controlling the Diphtheria Outbreak," January 26, 1903, NARA—True.

10. For a parallel discussion of quarantine in the midst of a localized epidemic, see Robert A. Trennert, "White Man's Medicine vs. Hopi Tradition: The Smallpox Epidemic of 1899," *Journal of Arizona History* 33, no. 4 (1992): 349–366.

11. Barbara Aitken, "Temperament in Native American Religion," *Journal of the Royal Anthropological Institute* 60 (1930): 364.

12. Elsie Clews Parsons, "Relations between Ethnology and Archaeology in the Southwest," *American Antiquity* 5, no. 3 (January 1940): 214–220. See also Patricia A. Carter, "'completely discouraged': Women Teachers' Resistance in the Bureau of Indian Affairs Schools, 1900–1910," *Frontiers: A Journal of Women Studies* 15, no. 3 (1995): 53–86.

13. Aitken, "Temperament in Native American Religion," 384; Edward P. Dozier, *The Pueblo Indians of North America* (New York: Holt, Rinehart & Winston, 1970), 25–26; Edward P. Dozier, "The Pueblo Indians of the Southwest: A Survey of the Anthropological Literature and a Review of Theory, Method, and Results," *Current Anthropology* 5, no. 2 (April 1964): 85–86; W. W. Hill, *An Ethnography of Santa Clara Pueblo, New Mexico* (Albuquerque: University of New Mexico Press, 1982), 182; Jean Allard Jeançon Papers, n.d., folder 11, Western History and Genealogy, Denver Public Library, Denver, Colo.; Alfonso Ortiz, *The Tewa World: Space, Time, Being, and Becoming in a Pueblo Society* (Chicago: University of Chicago Press, 1969), 3–5.

14. Hill, *An Ethnography of Santa Clara Pueblo*, 166; Dozier, *The Pueblo Indians of North America*, 179–181; Edward P. Dozier, "Factionalism at Santa Clara Pueblo," *Ethnology* 5, no. 2 (April 1966): 174–175.

15. Jeançon Papers, folder 11.

16. Edward P. Dozier, "The Pueblos of the South-western United States," *Journal of the Royal Anthropological Institute of Great Britain and Ireland* 90, no. 1 (June 1960): 148–149, 152; Dozier, *The Pueblo Indians of North America*, 168, 172; Ortiz, *The Tewa World*, 44.

17. Edward P. Dozier, "The Pueblos of the South-western United States," 155–156; Dozier, *The Pueblo Indians of North America*, 170–172; Hill, *An Ethnography of Santa Clara Pueblo*, 148, 208–210.

18. Dozier, *The Pueblo Indians of North America*, 189–191; Edward P. Dozier, *Hano: A Tewa Indian Community in Arizona* (New York: Holt, Rinehart & Winston, 1966), 12; Dozier, "The Pueblos of the South-western United States," 153; Dozier, "The Pueblos of the South-western United States," 153; Hill, *An Ethnography of Santa Clara Pueblo*, 97, 188–189; Ortiz, *The Tewa World*, 60, 62, 64, 69, 71, 72; B. M. Pritzker, *A Native American Encyclopedia: History, Culture, and Peoples* (Oxford: Oxford University Press, 2000), 86; Joe S. Sando, *Pueblo Nations: Eight Centuries of Pueblo Indian History* (Santa Fe, N.Mex.: Clear Light, 1992), 14–15, 172.

19. Aitken, "Temperament in Native American Religion," 385–387; Dozier, "The Pueblos of the South-western United States," 154; Dozier, "Factionalism at Santa Clara Pueblo," 177; Hill, *An Ethnography of Santa Clara Pueblo,* 195–196.

20. Dozier, "Factionalism at Santa Clara Pueblo"; Hill, *An Ethnography of Santa Clara Pueblo,* 196; Ortiz, *The Tewa World,* 66–67.

21. Hill, *An Ethnography of Santa Clara Pueblo,* 195–196.

22. Dozier, "Factionalism at Santa Clara Pueblo"; Hill, *An Ethnography of Santa Clara Pueblo,* 196; Pritzker, *A Native American Encyclopedia,* 86.

23. Aitken, "Temperament in Native American Religion," 386; Dozier, "Factionalism at Santa Clara Pueblo," 178–179; Hill, *An Ethnography of Santa Clara Pueblo,* 97, 320.

24. Virgil J. Vogel, "American Indian Foods Used as Medicine," in *American Folk Medicine: A Symposium,* ed. Wayland D. Hand (Berkeley: University of California Press, 1976), 126.

25. *Civilization Fund Act, U.S. Statues at Large* 3 (1819): 516.

26. Felix S. Cohen, "Federal Services for Indians," in *Handbook of Federal Indian Law,* 4th ed. (Washington, D.C.: Government Printing Office, 1941), 243.

27. *Civilization Fund Act,* 516; Ruth M. Raup, *The Indian Health Program from 1800–1955* (Washington, D.C.: Indian Health Services, 1959).

28. C. Massing, "The Development of the United States Government Policy toward Indian Health Care, 1850–1900," *Past Imperfect* 3 (1994): 135.

29. Raup, *The Indian Health Program,* 2–3; Cohen, "Federal Services for Indians," 243.

30. Raup, *The Indian Health Program,* 5; Brookings Institution and Lewis Meriam, *The Problem of Indian Administration: Report of a Survey Made at the Request of Hubert Work, Secretary of the Interior, and Submitted to Him, February 21, 1928* (Washington, D.C.: Brookings Institution, 1928), 191, 229–234, 359–370; Cohen, "Federal Services for Indians," 243; Massing, "The Development of the United States Government Policy toward Indian Health Care," 145; Paul Stuart, *The Indian Office: Growth and Development of an American Institution, 1865–1900* (Ann Arbor, Mich.: UMI Research, 1979), 50–51.

31. J. G. Townsend, "Disease and the Indian," *Scientific Monthly,* December 1938, 484.

32. Brenda J. Child, *Boarding School Seasons: American Indian Families, 1900–1940* (Lincoln: University of Nebraska Press, 1998), 56; Jean A. Keller, *Empty*

Beds: Indian Student Health at Sherman Institute, 1902–1922, Native American Series (East Lansing: Michigan State University Press, 2002), 47; Diane T. Putney, "Fighting the Scourge: American Indian Morbidity and Federal Policy, 1897–1928" (Ph.D diss., Marquette University, 1980), 2.

33. Keller, *Empty Beds*, 8.

34. David Wallace Adams, *Education for Extinction: American Indians and the Boarding School Experience, 1875–1928* (Lawrence: University Press of Kansas, 1997), 131; David H. DeJong, "'Unless They Are Kept Alive': Federal Indian Schools and Student Health, 1878–1918," *American Indian Quarterly* 31, no. 2 (2007): 265; Richard M. Frost, "The Pueblo Indian Smallpox Epidemic in New Mexico, 1898–1899," *Bulletin of the History of Medicine* 64, no. 3 (1990): 423; Keller, *Empty Beds*, 47.

35. Keller, *Empty Beds*, 16–39.

36. Ibid., 47.

37. Emily K. Abel, "'Only the Best Class of Immigration': Public Health Policy toward Mexicans and Filipinos in Los Angeles, 1910–1940," *Public Health Then and Now* 94, no. 6 (2004): 932–939; A. M. Brandt and M. Gardner, "Antagonism and Accommodation: Interpreting the Relationship between Public Health and Medicine in the United States during the 20th Century," *American Journal of Public Health* 90, no. 5 (2000): 707–715; Beatrix Hoffman, "Health Care Reform and Social Movements in the United States," *Public Health Then and Now* 93, no. 1 (2003): 75–85.

38. David H. DeJong, *"If You Knew the Conditions": A Chronicle of the Indian Medical Service and American Indian Health Care, 1908–1955* (Lanham, Md.: Rowman & Littlefield, 2008), 28–29.

39. Treacher Collins, "Introductory Chapter," in *Trachoma*, ed. Julius Boldt (London: Hodder & Stoughton, 1904), xvi–xvii; Putney, "Fighting the Scourge," 141–142; Robert A. Trennert, "Indian Sore Eyes: The Federal Campaign to Control Trachoma in the Southwest, 1910–1940," *Journal of the Southwest* 32, no. 2 (1990): 121–122.

40. Julius Boldt, ed., *Trachoma* (Hodder & Stoughton, 1904), 173–174.

41. Keller, *Empty Beds*, 185–186; "Trachoma: MedlinePlus Medical Encyclopedia," n.d., http://www.nlm.nih.gov/medlineplus/ency/article/001486 .htm. Townsend writes that some believe trachoma came with Coronado's expeditions into the Southwest in the 1500s. He notes that this is "purely conjecture" as evidence has not been found to corroborate or refute this idea. See Townsend, "Disease and the Indian," 488. For a thorough discussion of

the history of trachoma and its treatment among American Indian populations, see Trennert, "Indian Sore Eyes."

42. H. Emerson, "Morbidity of the American Indians," *Science*, February 26, 1926, 230; Townsend, "Disease and the Indian," 488–489.

43. Estelle Reel, *Course of Study for the Indian Schools of the United States, Industrial and Literary* (Washington, D.C.: Government Printing Office, 1901), 201.

44. Brookings Institution and Meriam, *The Problem of Indian Administration*, 220.

45. Dozier, *The Pueblo Indians of North America*, 23–24; Trennert, "Indian Sore Eyes," 142.

46. Brookings Institution and Meriam, *The Problem of Indian Administration*, 220; Reel, *Course of Study*, 197.

47. "WHO: Diphtheria," n.d., http://www.who.int/mediacentre/fact sheets/fs089/en/; Thomas Morgan Rotch, *Pediatrics* (Philadelphia: Lippincott, 1901), 460; W. Gilman Thompson, "Diphtheria," in *A Textbook of the Theory and Practice of Medicine by American Teachers*, ed. William Pepper (London: F. J. Rebman, 1893), 1:377.

48. Rotch, *Pediatrics*, 460; Thompson, "Diphtheria," 1:373–374, 377–378.

49. "Diphtheria—MayoClinic.com," n.d., http://www.mayoclinic.com/health/diphtheria/DS00495; "WHO: Diphtheria"; Rotch, *Pediatrics*, 469. Dr. Anna Wessels Williams developed the antitoxin treatment in 1894.

50. Thompson, "Diphtheria," 389–393, 396.

51. Ibid., 389.

52. Richard I. Ford, "Communication Networks and Information Hierarchies in Native American Folk Medicine: Tewa Pueblos, New Mexico," in *American Folk Medicine: A Symposium*, ed. Wayland D. Hand (Berkeley: University of California Press, 1976), 146, 149, 150–151.

53. Malcolm Ebright and Rick Hendricks, *The Witches of Abiquiu: The Governor, the Priest, the Genizaro Indians, and the Devil* (Albuquerque: University of New Mexico Press, 2006).

54. Ford, "Communication Networks and Information Hierarchies," 147.

55. Frost, "The Pueblo Indian Smallpox Epidemic," 422.

56. Reel, *Course of Study*, 149–150.

57. Ibid., 196, 150, 197.

58. Ford, "Communication Networks and Information Hierarchies," 254.

59. True's letter does not indicate whether these men were principales, the governor, or the caciques.

60. Dozier, "The Pueblos of the South-western United States," 155; Jean-çon Papers, folder 11; Hill, *An Ethnography of Santa Clara Pueblo*, 169, 170, 348.

61. Ortiz, *The Tewa World*, 36, 81, 82.

62. True to McCormick, "Letter to Clerk-in-Charge, Santa Fe Indian School, concerning Difficulties among the Santa Clara Pueblo Indians Accepting Vaccinations."

63. According to the genealogical charts of Santa Clara in Hill's ethnography of the Pueblo, Thomas Dozier was the father of Edward P. Dozier the anthropologist.

64. True to McCormick, "Letter to Clerk-in-Charge, Santa Fe Indian School, concerning Difficulties among the Santa Clara Pueblo Indians Accepting Vaccinations."

65. Frost, "The Pueblo Indian Smallpox Epidemic," 429; Trennert, "White Man's Medicine vs. Hopi Tradition," 353; "Minor City Topics," *Santa Fe New Mexican,* November 16, 1898, sec. News/Opinion.

66. Frost, "The Pueblo Indian Smallpox Epidemic," 429.

67. Trennert, "White Man's Medicine vs. Hopi Tradition," 350–352, 354–355, 359.

68. Frost, "The Pueblo Indian Smallpox Epidemic," 435–440.

69. "A Fearful Epidemic: Terrible Ravages of Small-Pox in New Mexico," *San Francisco Daily Evening Bulletin,* February 7, 1878, sec. News/Opinion.

70. Frost, "The Pueblo Indian Smallpox Epidemic," 441.

71. Clara D. True to C.J. Crandall, "Letter to Superintendent regarding Enrolled Students and Dealings with the Indians in the Pueblo," November 28, 1902, NARA—True.

72. True to Crandall, "Letter to Superintendent concerning Difficulties in Controlling the Diphtheria Outbreak."

73. Clara D. True to C. J. Crandall, "Letter to Superintendent concerning a Possible Outbreak of Small-Pox," February 2, 1904, NARA—True.

74. Clara D. True to C. J. Crandall, "Letter to Superintendent regarding Deaths Due to Diphtheria and Problems Enforcing Vaccinations and Disinfectants," January 28, 1903, NARA—True.

75. David Wallace Adams, "Fundamental Considerations: The Deep Meaning of Native American Schooling, 1880–1900," *Harvard Educational Review* 58, no. 1 (February 1988): 1–28; Adams, *Education for Extinction;* Helen M. Bannan, "The Idea of Civilization and American Indian Policy Reformers in the 1880s," *Journal of American Culture* 1, no. 4 (1978): 787–799; Francis

Paul Prucha, ed., *Americanizing the American Indians: Writings by the "Friends of the Indian," 1880–1900* (Cambridge, Mass.: Harvard University Press, 1973); Child, *Boarding School Seasons;* Matthew L. M. Fletcher, *American Indian Education: Counternarratives in Racism, Struggle, and the Law,* Critical Educator (New York: Routledge, 2008); K. Tsianina Lomawaima, *They Called It Prairie Light: The Story of Chilocco Indian School* (Lincoln: University of Nebraska Press, 1994); K. Tsianina Lomawaima and Teresa L. McCarty, *"To Remain an Indian": Lessons in Democracy from a Century of Native American Education* (New York: Teachers College Press, 2006); Jon Allan Reyhner and Jeanne M. Oyawin Eder, *American Indian Education: A History* (Norman: University of Oklahoma Press, 2006).

76. See Prucha, *Americanizing the American Indians.*

77. Clara D. True to C. J. Crandall, "Letter to Superintendent Reporting the Death of Another Child and Problems in Sanitation Which Contributes to Greater Problems with Diphtheria," February 9, 1903, NARA—True.

78. Clara D. True to C. J. Crandall, "Letter to Superintendent concerning Doctor's Report on the Death of Another Child Due to Diphtheria and His Recommendations," February 10, 1903, NARA—True.

79. A. Holterman to C. J. Crandall, "Letter to Superintendent from the Doctor Reporting on His Findings and Recommendations for the Santa Clara Pueblo," February 20, 1903, NARA—True.

80. True to Crandall, "Letter to Superintendent concerning Doctor's Report on the Death of Another Child Due to Diphtheria and His Recommendations."

81. Dozier, "The Pueblos of the South-western United States," 156; Hill, *An Ethnography of Santa Clara Pueblo,* 173–174; Jeançon Papers, folder 16; Ortiz, *The Tewa World,* 50–57.

82. Ford, "Communication Networks and Information Hierarchies," 154; Jeançon Papers, folder 16.

83. C. J. Crandall to Clara D. True, "Letter to Clara D. True regarding the Lack of a Diphtheria Epidemic at Santa Clara Pueblo," January 29, 1903, roll 25, NARA—Pueblo Day Schools.

84. True to Crandall, "Letter to Superintendent regarding Deaths Due to Diphtheria and Problems Enforcing Vaccinations and Disinfectants."

85. Clara D. True to C. J. Crandall, "Letter to Superintendent regarding Internal Politics in the Santa Clara Pueblo and Problems with the 'Medicine Men,'" January 30, 1903, NARA—True.

86. Carter, "'completely discouraged.'"

87. True to Crandall, "Letter to Superintendent Reporting the Death of Another Child and Problems in Sanitation Which Contributes to Greater Problems with Diphtheria."

88. C. J. Crandall to Clara D. True, "Letter to Clara D. True regarding the Number of Diphtheria Cases and the Closing of the Day School, 02/10/1903," February 10, 1903, roll 25, NARA—Pueblo Day Schools.

89. C. J. Crandall to Diego Naranjo, "Letter to Diego Naranjo regarding Treatment of Children with Diphtheria and Disinfecting Houses," February 19, 1903, vol. 17, p. 77, Press Copies of Letters Sent ("Miscellaneous Letters"), June 1890–December 1913, Records of the Bureau of Indian Affairs, RG 75, entry 32, National Archives and Records Administration, Rocky Mountain Region, Denver, Colo. (hereafter cited as NARA—Miscellaneous).

90. Holterman to Crandall, "Letter to Superintendent from the Doctor Reporting on His Findings and Recommendations for the Santa Clara Pueblo."

91. C. J. Crandall to Mary Dissette, "Letter to Miss Dissette regarding Conditions at Santa Clara Pueblo," February 21, 1903, vol. 17, p. 78, NARA—Miscellaneous.

92. After True moved back to the Española valley in 1910, her ranch abutted that of Stevenson. They shared a ditch and had frequent disagreements over water rights, which eventually landed them in court. See Matilda Coxe Stevenson, "Praecipe, 1914," 1914, M386, Denver Public Library, Denver, Colo.

93. Clara Kern Bayliss, "A Tewa Sun Myth," *Journal of American Folklore* 22, no. 85 (September 1909): 333–335; Clara D. True, "The Experiences of a Woman Indian Agent," *Outlook (1893–1924)*, June 5, 1909, 331; Jacobs, "Clara True and Female Moral Authority" Margaret D. Jacobs, *Engendered Encounters: Feminism and Pueblo Cultures, 1879–1934* (Lincoln: University of Nebraska Press, 1999), 30–46.

CHAPTER THREE. CITIZEN; OR, THE LEGAL EDUCATION OF CLINTON J. CRANDALL

1. Generally though, before Congress made all American Indians citizens in 1924, many Indigenous individuals became legal citizens through the allotment process. This did not preclude the U.S. government, however, from continuing to regard American Indians as wards. See Frederick E. Hoxie, *A Final Promise: The Campaign to Assimilate the Indians, 1880–1920* (Lincoln:

University of Nebraska Press, 2001), 211–238; *Indian Citizenship Act, U.S. Statutes at Large* 43 (1924): 253.

2. G. Hill Howard, "Opinion Report No. 133," July 22, 1854, U.S. Soil Conservation Service Region Eight Records, MSS 29BC, series 301, case #17, folder 1, Center for Southwest Research, University of New Mexico, Albuquerque, http://econtent.unm.edu/cdm4/document.php?CISOROOT=/catron&CISOPTR=54&REC=4; "Handwritten Patent of Santa Clara Pueblo," (1861), Indian Affairs Collection, MSS 16BC, box 2, folder 6, Center for Southwest Research, University of New Mexico, Albuquerque, http://econtent.unm.edu/cdm4/document.php?CISOROOT=/indaffairs&CISOPTR=465&REC=20&CISOSHOW.

3. Alvar W. Carlson, "Spanish-American Acquisition of Cropland within the Northern Pueblo Indian Grants, New Mexico," *Ethnohistory* 22, no. 2 (Spring 1975): 96. This is worth emphasizing because the federal government did not work to protect the lands of neighboring Hispanos who opted to remain in the United States. "Treaty of Guadalupe Hidalgo and Protocol of Querétaro," May 30, 1848, in *1873 Treaties and Conventions Concluded between the United States of America and Other Powers* (1873), 562–578.

4. "Handwritten Patent of Santa Clara Pueblo."

5. Carl Schurz, "Secretary of the Interior Schurz on Reservation Policy, November 1, 1880," in *Documents of United States Indian Policy*, ed. Francis Paul Prucha, 3rd ed. (Lincoln: University of Nebraska Press, 2000), 153; Friends of the Indian, "Program of the Lake Mohonk Conference, September 1884," in Prucha, *Documents of United States Indian Policy*, 162.

6. *The General Allotment Act of 1887, U.S. Code*, vol. 25, sec. 331 (1887).

7. *Burke Act, U.S. Statutes at Large* 34 (1906): 183.

8. For a detailed discussion and deconstruction of the Dawes Act in light of a Hopi response to it, see Adrea Lawrence and Brec Cooke, "Law, Language, and Land: A Multi-method Analysis of the General Allotment Act and Its Discourses," *Qualitative Inquiry* 16, no. 3 (2010): 217–229.

9. Many Indian tribes also lost acres upon acres of territory, as unallotted land was frequently settled by non-Natives. Historian Frederick Hoxie writes that the problem for OIA agents "was to devise a means of providing greater federal protection without appearing to retreat from the government's commitment to Indian citizenship." *A Final Promise*, 213.

10. *Johnson v. M'Intosh*, 21 U.S. 543 (1823); *Cherokee Nation v. Georgia*, 30 U.S. 1 (1831); *Worcester v. Georgia*, 31 U.S. 515 (1832).

11. *Johnson v. M'Intosh,* 573–574, 579, 586, 587–588, 590–591, 603.

12. Vine Deloria Jr. and Clifford M. Lytle, *American Indians, American Justice* (Austin: University of Texas Press, 1983), 26–27.

13. *Cherokee Nation v. Georgia,* 17.

14. *U.S. v. José Juan Lucero,* 1 N.M. Sup. Ct. 422 (1869), 441–442.

15. Ibid., 425, 441–445.

16. *Pueblo Indian Communities; Bodies Corporate; Powers, N.M. Stat. Ann.* §53-9-1 (1847).

17. *U.S. v. Lucero,* 444.

18. Ibid., 434, 435, 458; see also Felix S. Cohen, *Cohen's Handbook of Federal Indian Law* (Newark, N.J.: LexisNexis, 2005), 323. For an extended discussion of how *U.S. v. Lucero* compares to other cases that delimited racial classification, see Michael A. Elliott, "Telling the Difference: Nineteenth-Century Legal Narratives of Racial Taxonomy," *Law and Social Inquiry* 24 (1999): 611–636. David E. Wilkins and Felix S. Cohen argue that American Indian tribes did not begin to incorporate in a widespread fashion until Congress passed the Indian Reorganization Act of 1934. See David Wilkins, "The Manipulation of Indigenous Status: The Federal Government as Shape-Shifter," *Stanford Law & Policy Review* 12 (2001): 229; Cohen, *Cohen's Handbook,* 255–256.

19. *U.S. v. Joseph,* 94 U.S. 614 (1876), 617–618.

20. U.S. Constitution, art. I, § 2.

21. For a detailed discussion of the different types of plenary power, see David Wilkins, "The U.S. Supreme Court's Explication of 'Federal Plenary Power': An Analysis of Case Law Affecting Tribal Sovereignty, 1886–1914," *American Indian Quarterly* 18, no. 3 (Summer 1994): 349–368; David E. Wilkins and K. Tsianina Lomawaima, *Uneven Ground: American Indian Sovereignty and Federal Law* (Norman: University of Oklahoma Press, 2001), 99–112; Wilkins, "The Manipulation of Indigenous Status," 232.

22. Deloria and Lytle, *American Indians,* 44–45; Wilkins, "The U.S. Supreme Court's Explication of 'Federal Plenary Power,'" 350–351, 352–353, 357; Wilkins and Lomawaima, *Uneven Ground,* 109–112. See also *U.S. v. Kagama and Another, Indians,* 118 U.S. 375 (1886); *Lone Wolf v. Hitchcock,* 187 U.S. 553 (1903).

23. It is entirely possible that there was dissension between the Summer and Winter People over whether the Santa Clara land grants should be converted into a reservation. The documentary record is silent on this point, however.

24. Theodore Roosevelt, "Executive Order—Santa Clara Pueblo, New

Mexico, July 29, 1905," ed. John T. Woolley and Gerhard Peters, *The American Presidency Project,* http://www.presidency.ucsb.edu/ws/index.php?pid =76703.

25. C. J. Crandall to Santa Clara governor, "Letter to the Governor of the Santa Clara Pueblo regarding the Creation of the Santa Clara Reservation," August 29, 1905, vol. 22, p. 327, Press Copies of Letters Sent ("Miscellaneous Letters"), June 1890–December 1913, Records of the Bureau of Indian Affairs, RG 75, entry 32, National Archives and Records Administration, Rocky Mountain Region, Denver, Colo. (hereafter cited as NARA—Miscellaneous).

26. Hoxie, *A Final Promise,* 213.

27. Crandall to Santa Clara governor, "Letter to the Governor of the Santa Clara Pueblo regarding the Creation of the Santa Clara Reservation."

28. Ibid.

29. U.S. Constitution, art. I, § 2.

30. T. A. Finical, "Document regarding Bernalillo County Tax Delinquency," 1899, Indian Affairs Collection, MSS 16BC, box 1, folder 5, http://econtent.unm.edu/cdm4/document.php?CISOROOT=/indaffairs&CISOPTR=180&CISOSHOW=176.

31. G. Hill Howard to T. A. Finical, "Letter from Pueblo Attorney regarding Pueblo Tax Delinquency," December 14, 1899, Indian Affairs Collection, MSS 16BC, box 1, folder 5, http://econtent.unm.edu/cdm4/item_viewer .php?CISOROOT=/indaffairs&CISOPTR=882.

32. C. J. Crandall to William A. Jones, "Letter to the Commissioner of Indian Affairs regarding the Citizenship of Pueblo Indians in the New Mexico Territory," March 12, 1904, vol. 4, pp. 297–298, Press Copies of Letters Sent to the Commissioner of Indian Affairs, February 1900–November 1913, Records of the Bureau of Indian Affairs, RG 75, entry 34, National Archives and Records Administration, Rocky Mountain Region, Denver, Colo. (hereafter cited as NARA—Commissioner).

33. *Territory of New Mexico v. The Persons, Real Estate, Land and Property Described Delinquent Tax List of the County of Bernalillo for the First Half of the Year 1899,* 12 N.M. Sup. Ct. 139 (1904).

34. Ibid., 140, 144, 145.

35. Ibid., 147.

36. Crandall to Jones, "Letter to the Commissioner of Indian Affairs regarding the Citizenship of Pueblo Indians in the New Mexico Territory."

37. C. J. Crandall to William A. Jones, "Letter to the Commissioner of

Indian Affairs regarding Pueblo Indians' Status as Citizens," March 28, 1904, vol. 4, pp. 323–324, NARA—Commissioner.

38. "All Pueblos Council to the President of the United States," April 6, 1904, box 44, folder 300, Northern Pueblos Agency, General Correspondence File, 1904–1937, Records of the Bureau of Indian Affairs, RG 75, entry 83, National Archives and Records Administration, Rocky Mountain Region, Denver, Colo.

39. Lauren Benton, "Symposium Introduction: Colonialism, Culture, and the Law; Making Order out of Trouble—Jurisdictional Politics in the Spanish Colonial Borderlands," *Law and Social Inquiry* 26 (2001): 377, 384.

40. J. G. Bourke, "The Laws of Spain in Their Application to the American Indians," *American Anthropologist* 7, no. 2 (April 1894): 193–201; Herbert O. Brayer, in Felix S. Cohen, *Handbook of Federal Indian Law*, 4th ed. (Washington, D.C.: Government Printing Office, 1941), 383–384, http://thorpe.ou.edu/cohen.html.

41. Cohen, *Handbook of Federal Indian Law*, 385–388.

42. Laura E. Gomez, "Off-White in an Age of White Supremacy: Mexican Elites and the Rights of Whites and Blacks in Nineteenth-Century New Mexico," *Chicano-Latin Law Review* 25 (Spring 2005): 16; *Territory of New Mexico v. The Persons, Real Estate, Land and Property Described Delinquent Tax List of the County of Bernalillo for the First Half of the Year 1899*, 12:142; *U.S. v. Lucero*, 1:433. Neither the court records nor Gomez give any indication whether citizenship rights differed for men and women. Hill notes that Santa Clara women could and did own houses and land. W. W. Hill, *An Ethnography of Santa Clara Pueblo, New Mexico* (Albuquerque: University of New Mexico Press, 1982), 20.

43. Cohen, *Handbook of Federal Indian Law*, 383–384.

44. The Treaty of Guadalupe Hidalgo does not distinguish between Pueblo Indians and other Indians; however, the New Mexico Supreme Court relied on this distinction in *New Mexico v. Persons on the Delinquent Tax List* (1904) and *U.S. v. Lucero* (1869).

45. Crandall to Jones, "Letter to the Commissioner of Indian Affairs regarding Pueblo Indians' Status as Citizens."

46. C. J. Crandall, "Letter to the Governor of Santa Clara Pueblo regarding the Tax-Exempt Status of Pueblo Indians," March 11, 1905, vol. 21, p. 266, NARA—Miscellaneous; *Making Appropriations for the Current and Contingent Expenses of the Indian Department and for Fulfilling Treaty Stipulations with*

Various Indian Tribes for the Fiscal Year Ending June Thirtieth, Nineteen Hundred and Six, and for Other Purposes, U.S. Statues at Large 33 (1905): 1069.

47. Crandall to Jones, "Letter to the Commissioner of Indian Affairs regarding the Citizenship of Pueblo Indians in the New Mexico Territory."

48. Reginald Horsman, "Scientific Racism and the American Indian in the Mid-Nineteenth Century," *American Quarterly* 27, no. 2 (1975): 164–167.

49. Gomez, "Off-White in an Age of White Supremacy," 21, 25.

50. John Nieto-Phillips, "Mexican Yankees and American Jibaros: The Americanization of Schoolchildren in New Mexico and Puerto Rico" (lecture, Indiana University, Bloomington, November 19, 2004); Manuel G. Gonzales, *Mexicanos: A History of Mexicans in the United States* (Bloomington: Indiana University Press, 1999); Mario T. García and Frances Equibel Tywoniak, *Migrant Daughter: Coming of Age as a Mexican American Woman* (Berkeley: University of California Press, 2000).

51. Gomez, "Off-White in an Age of White Supremacy," 53–54.

52. Izumi Ishii, "Alcohol and Politics in the Cherokee Nation before Removal," *Ethnohistory* 50, no. 4 (2003): 676; Peter C. Mancall, *Deadly Medicine: Indians and Alcohol in Early America* (Ithaca, N.Y.: Cornell University Press, 1995), 12–13.

53. Bourke, "The Laws of Spain," 199.

54. Thomas Jefferson, "President Jefferson on the Liquor Trade," in *Documents of United States Indian Policy,* ed. Francis Paul Prucha (Lincoln: University of Nebraska Press, 2000), 24.

55. *Trade and Intercourse Act, U.S. Statutes at Large* 4 (1834): 729–730, 732.

56. *Intoxicating Drinks to Indians Act, U.S. Statutes at Large* 29 (1897): 506.

57. Cohen, *Cohen's Handbook,* 324–325; *New Mexico Enabling Act, U.S. Statutes at Large* 36 (1910): 558, 560.

58. C. J. Crandall to William A. Jones, "Letter to the Commissioner of Indian Affairs Describing the Santa Clara Festival," August 12, 1902, vol. 3, pp. 42–44, NARA—Commissioner.

59. C. J. Crandall to William A. Jones, "Letter regarding Armed Apaches at the Santa Clara Festival," August 20, 1902, vol. 3, p. 49, NARA—Commissioner.

60. Edward P. Dozier, "Problem Drinking among American Indians: The Role of Sociocultural Deprivation," *Quarterly Journal of Studies on Alcohol* 27, no. 1 (1966): 73.

61. Michael D. Heaston, "Whiskey Regulation and Indian Land Titles in New Mexico Territory: 1851–1861." *Journal of the West* 10, no. 3 (1971): 474–475.

62. Mancall, *Deadly Medicine*, 133.

63. C. J. Crandall to William A. Jones, "Letter to the Commissioner of Indian Affairs Requesting Law Enforcement for the San Geronimo Fiesta at Taos," September 18, 1902, vol. 3, p. 120, NARA—Commissioner.

64. Gary Clayton Anderson, *The Indian Southwest, 1580–1830: Ethnogenesis and Reinvention* (Norman: University of Oklahoma Press, 1999), 95–96, 97, 106–107, 109–110; James F. Brooks, *Captives and Cousins: Slavery, Kinship, and Community in the Southwest Borderlands*, Omohundro Institute of Early American History and Culture (Chapel Hill: University of North Carolina Press, 2002), 37, 58–59; Dolores A. Gunnerson, *The Jicarilla Apaches: A Study in Survival* (DeKalb: Northern Illinois University Press, 1974), 90–92, 95–99, 122–126; Pekka Hämäläinen, *The Comanche Empire*, Lamar Series in Western History (New Haven, Conn.: Yale University Press, 2008), 72, 206; Veronica Velarde Tiller, *The Jicarilla Apache Tribe: A History, 1846–1970*, rev ed. (Albuquerque, N.Mex.: BowArrow, 2000), 5.

65. C. J. Crandall to William A. Jones, "Letter to the Commissioner of Indian Affairs Requesting a U.S. Marshall for the San Geronimo Fiesta at Taos," August 14, 1903, vol. 4, pp. 26–27, NARA—Commissioner.

66. C. J. Crandall to Francis E. Leupp, "Letter to the Commissioner of Indian Affairs regarding Liquor at the Jicarilla Apache Reservation," August 7, 1907, vol. 8, pp. 358–359, NARA—Commissioner.

67. C. J. Crandall to Francis E. Leupp, "Letter to the Commissioner of Indian Affairs regarding Legal Representation for Pueblo Indians in Enforcing Laws," December 20, 1906, vol. 7, pp. 422–423, NARA—Commissioner.

68. Pedro Baca to Rev. Father William Ketcham, "Letter regarding the Administration of C. J. Crandall," October 13, 1908, Bureau of Catholic Indian Missions, series 1-1: Correspondence, reel 43, Marquette University, Milwaukee, Wis.; William E. Johnson, "Letter to the Editor, *New York Times*," Edgar Lee Hewett Collection, 89ELH.048, box 4, Museum of Indian Arts and Culture, Santa Fe, N.Mex.; William Eugene Johnson, *The Federal Government and the Liquor Traffic* (Westerville, Ohio: American Issue, 1911); William E. Johnson, *The Story of Juan Cruz* (Washington, D.C.: H. A. Eby, 1912), http://www.archive.org/details/storyofjuanoojohnson.

69. *Matter of Heff*, 197 U.S. 488 (1905), 508.

70. *U.S. v. Benito Mares*, 14 N.M. Sup. Ct. 1 (1907), 4.

71. C. J. Crandall to Francis E. Leupp, "Letter to the Commissioner of Indian Affairs regarding the New Mexico Supreme Court's Decision on

Alcohol Sales among the Pueblo Indians," January 21, 1907, vol. 7, pp. 475–476, NARA—Commissioner.

72. C. J. Crandall, "Letter to the Commissioner of Indian Affairs regarding the Sale of Alcohol to Pueblo Indians," April 9, 1907, vol. 8, p. 111, NARA—Commissioner.

73. *U.S. v. Felipe Sandoval*, 231 U.S. 28 (1913).

74. In 1924, Congress passed the Indian Citizenship Act, which made all individuals of American Indian descent born in the United States U.S. citizens. The act did not resolve citizenship issues associated with property rights, however. Hoxie, *A Final Promise*, 211–238; *Indian Citizenship Act*.

75. C. J. Crandall, "Letter to Saloon Owners and Managers regarding the Sale of Alcohol to Indians, 04/13/1903," April 13, 1903, roll 25, Press Copies of Letters Sent concerning Pueblo Day Schools, March 1900–June 1911, Records of the Bureau of Indian Affairs, RG 75, M1473, National Archives and Records Administration, Washington, D.C. (hereafter cited as NARA—Pueblo Day Schools).

76. Clara D. True to C. J. Crandall, "Letter to Superintendent Expressing Anger over the Sale of Liquor to the Indians," October 4, 1904, Letters Received from Day School Teacher Clara D. True, 1902–1907, Records of the Bureau of Indian Affairs, RG 75, entry 38, National Archives and Records Administration, Rocky Mountain Region, Denver, Colo. (hereafter cited as NARA—True).

77. Henry K. Street, *The History of Wine in New Mexico: 400 Years of Struggle* (Ponderosa, N.Mex.: Ponderosa Valley Vineyards and Winery, 1997), 2–4.

78. Francisco Atanasio Domínguez, *The Missions of New Mexico, 1776: A Description, with Other Contemporary Documents* (Albuquerque: University of New Mexico Press, 1956), 50–51, 59, 71, 83, 119, 151, 207.

79. Heaston, "Whiskey Regulation and Indian Land Titles in New Mexico Territory," 475.

80. Mancall, *Deadly Medicine*, 82.

81. Peter C. Mancall, "Men, Women, and Alcohol in Indian Villages in the Great Lakes Region in the Early Republic," *Journal of the Early Republic* 15, no. 3 (Autumn 1995): 425–448.

82. Kathryn A. Abbott, "Alcohol and the Anishinaabeg of Minnesota in the Early Twentieth Century," *Western Historical Quarterly* 30 (Spring 1999): 31; Mancall, "Men, Women, and Alcohol," 433; Mancall, *Deadly Medicine*, 12–13.

83. Abbott, "Alcohol and the Anishinaabeg," 27; Ishii, "Alcohol and Politics in the Cherokee Nation," 672; Mancall, *Deadly Medicine*, 7; Gilbert Quintero, "Making the Indian: Colonial Knowledge, Alcohol, and Native Americans," *American Indian Culture & Research Journal* 25, no. 4 (2001): 59–60.

84. C. J. Crandall to Clara D. True, "Letter to Clara D. True regarding Drunkenness at Santa Clara Pueblo," October 5, 1904, vol. 20, pp. 376–377, NARA—Miscellaneous.

85. Mancall, "Men, Women, and Alcohol," 427–428; Abbott, "Alcohol and the Anishinaabeg," 34–35.

86. C. J. Crandall to William A. Jones, "Letter Reporting on the Santa Clara festival, 08/12/1902," August 12, 1902, vol. 3, p. 42, NARA—Commissioner.

87. True to Crandall, "Letter to Superintendent Expressing Anger over the Sale of Liquor to the Indians."

88. Clara D. True to C. J. Crandall, "Letter to Superintendent concerning 2 Girls Who Want to Enroll in the Santa Fe Indian Boarding School," September 14, 1904, NARA—True.

89. C. J. Crandall to Clara D. True, "Letter to Clara D. True regarding Payment to Pedro Cajete and the Enrollment of Two Girls at the Santa Fe Indian School," September 15, 1904, vol. 20, p. 307, NARA—Miscellaneous.

90. Clara D. True to C. J. Crandall, "Letter to Superintendent Requesting That a Student at the Santa Fe School Be Allowed to Come Home for Christmas," December 21, 1903, NARA—True.

91. C. J. Crandall to Clara D. True, "Letter to Clara D. True regarding Home Visits during the Christmas Holiday," December 22, 1903, roll 26, NARA—Pueblo Day Schools.

92. Several months after the diphtheria outbreak, Crandall does not appear to have regained faith in True's observations and reports of goings-on at Santa Clara. True, on the other hand, stood by her word, and she no doubt remembered this incident when she returned to the Española valley in 1910 after a brief stint as the superintendent of the Potrero School on the Morongo (Malki) Reservation in southern California. Eight years after True's initial veiled claim that Crandall had aided Benjamin and Severiano in obtaining liquor, the Indian Office investigated Crandall for running a liquor ring out of a drugstore he owned in Santa Fe. In a 1911 article that appeared in the *Morning Oregonian,* W. E. "Pussyfoot" Johnson, a former OIA special chief officer, wrote that he had worked with a group of Santa Clara Indians from 1909 to 1911 to identify and expose illicit liquor vendors in northern

New Mexico. Johnson specifically named Crandall in the article and accused him of a cover-up that went all the way up the chain of command in the Indian Office. By September 1911, one month before Johnson's article was published, correspondence in Crandall's personnel file indicates that the OIA investigation cleared Crandall of the charges Johnson brought against him. The commissioner of Indian Affairs, Robert A. Valentine, nevertheless transferred Crandall to the Pierre School in South Dakota in December 1911. The possibility that Crandall was clandestinely involved in the very practices he claimed to be rooting out suggests either a profound example of duplicity or a frame-up. Regardless, the commissioner of Indian Affairs did not believe Crandall should continue to work for the Indian Office in Santa Fe.

CHAPTER FOUR. INSTITUTIONS; OR, GETTING SCHOOLED
BY THE U.S. COLONIAL SYSTEM

1. Lyman Abbott, "Education for the Indian, from 'Proceedings of the Sixth Annual Meeting of the Lake Mohonk Conference of Friends of the Indian, 1888, pp. 11–16,'" in *Americanizing the American Indians: Writings by the "Friends of the Indian," 1880–1900*, ed. Francis Paul Prucha (Cambridge, Mass.: Harvard University Press, 1973), 212–213.

2. Seth Low, "Comments on Lyman Abbott's paper," in Prucha, *Americanizing the American Indians*, 219.

3. Francis E. Leupp, "Annual Report of the Commissioner of Indian Affairs," in *Documents of United States Indian Policy* (Lincoln: University of Nebraska Press, 1905), 3:202.

4. Abbott, "Education for the Indian," 212–213; David Wallace Adams, "Fundamental Considerations: The Deep Meaning of Native American Schooling, 1880–1900," *Harvard Educational Review* 58, no. 1 (February 1988): 10; David Wallace Adams, *Education for Extinction: American Indians and the Boarding School Experience, 1875–1928* (Lawrence: University Press of Kansas, 1997), 5–27; Wilbert H. Ahern, "An Experiment Aborted: Returned Indian Students in the Indian School Service, 1881–1908," *Ethnohistory* 44, no. 2 (Spring 1997): 266; Board of Indian Commissioners, "Indian Education: Twelfth Annual Report of the Board of Indian Commissioners (1880)," in Prucha, *Americanizing the American Indians*, 194; Michael C. Coleman, "The Responses of American Indian Children to Presbyterian Schooling in the Nineteenth Century: An Analysis through Missionary Sources," *History of Education Quarterly* 27, no. 4 (Winter 1987): 474–478; K. Tsianina Lomawaima

and Teresa L. McCarty, *"To Remain an Indian": Lessons in Democracy from a Century of Native American Education* (New York: Teachers College Press, 2006), 4–6; Jon Allan Reyhner and Jeanne M. Oyawin Eder, "A History of Indian Education," in *Teaching American Indian Students*, ed. Jon Allan Reyhner (Norman: University of Oklahoma Press, 1992), 33; Jon Allan Reyhner and Jeanne M. Oyawin Eder, *American Indian Education: A History* (Norman: University of Oklahoma Press, 2006), 142–146, 149–157.

5. See, for example, John L. O'Sullivan's article on the annexation of Texas, California, and the Southwest in which he coined the term "Manifest Destiny." "Annexation," *United States Magazine and Democratic Review*, July–August 1845, 5–10.

6. Thomas J. Morgan, "Supplemental Report on Indian Education, 1889," in Prucha, *Americanizing the American Indians*, 177. For a discussion of Morgan's treatise, *Ancient Society; or, Researches in the Lines of Human Progress from Savagery through Barbarism to Civilization*, within the context of Indian reform efforts, see Adams, *Education for Extinction*, 14–15.

7. Abbott, "Education for the Indian," 212–213; Adams, "Fundamental Considerations," 2, 10; Adams, *Education for Extinction*, 21–24; Ahern, "An Experiment Aborted," 266; Helen M. Bannan, "The Idea of Civilization and American Indian Policy Reformers in the 1880s," *Journal of American Culture* 1, no. 4 (1978): 787–799; Board of Indian Commissioners, "Indian Education"; Coleman, "The Responses of American Indian Children to Presbyterian Schooling in the Nineteenth Century," 474–478; Edgar L. Hewett, "Ethnic Factors in Education," *American Anthropologist*, n.s., 7, no. 1 (March 1905): 3; Reyhner and Eder, "A History of Indian Education," 33; James D. Anderson, "Race-Conscious Educational Policies versus a 'Color-blind Constitution': A Historical Perspective," *Educational Researcher* 36, no. 5 (July 2007): 249–257; Elliott West, "Reconstructing Race," *Western Historical Quarterly* 34, no. 1 (Spring 2003), http://www.historycooperative.org.proxyau.wrlc.org/jour nals/whq/34.1/west.html.

8. Adams, "Fundamental Considerations," 8; Adams, *Education for Extinction*, 5–27; Donna Deyhle and Karen Swisher, "Research in American Indian and Alaska Native Education: From Assimilation to Self-Determination," *Review of Research in Education* 22 (1997), 114–115; Christine A. Klein, "Treaties of Conquest: Property Rights, Indian Treaties, and the Treaty of Guadalupe Hidalgo," *New Mexico Law Review* 26 (1996): 207. As discussed in chapter 3, assumed guardianship over Indian wards followed the U.S. Supreme Court's

rulings in *Johnson v. M'Intosh* (1823), *Cherokee Nation v. Georgia* (1831), and *Worcester v. Georgia* (1832). These cases established that Indigenous people were wards of the U.S. government since a trust relationship existed between the federal government and individual tribes.

9. Morgan, "Supplemental Report on Indian Education, 1889," 233–234.

10. Abbott, "Education for the Indian"; Michael C. Coleman, "The Symbiotic Embrace: American Indians, White Educators and the School, 1820s-1920s," in *The RoutledgeFalmer Reader in History of Education*, ed. Gary McCulloch (London and New York: Routledge, 2005), 201; Lomawaima and McCarty, *"To Remain Indian,"* 49.

11. *Regulations for Withholding Rations for Nonattendance at Schools, U.S. Statutes at Large* 27 (1893): 628, 635; *An Act Making Appropriations for Current and Contingent Expenses of the Indian Department, U.S. Statutes at Large* 28 (1894): 313–314.

12. Adams, "Fundamental Considerations," 3; Adams, *Education for Extinction*, 58–59, 65; Lomawaima and McCarty, *"To Remain an Indian,"* 46–47.

13. Coleman, "The Symbiotic Embrace," 201.

14. C. J. Crandall to William A. Jones, "Letter to the Commissioner of Indian Affairs Recommending Compulsory Schooling for Indian Students," October 4, 1901, vol. 2, pp. 117–118, Press Copies of Letters Sent to the Commissioner of Indian Affairs, February 1900–November 1913, Records of the Bureau of Indian Affairs, RG 75, entry 34, National Archives and Records Administration, Rocky Mountain Region, Denver, Colo. (hereafter cited as NARA—Commissioner).

15. Estelle Reel to C. J. Crandall, "Letter regarding Idaho's Compulsory Attendance Law," November 4, 1902, box 1, folder 1902, Correspondence and Other Records relating to Finance and Administration, 1902, 1905–1911, 1913–1925, Records of the Bureau of Indian Affairs, RG 75, entry 39, National Archives and Records Administration, Rocky Mountain Region, Denver, Colo. (hereafter cited as NARA—Finance).

16. C. J. Crandall to Clara D. True, "Letter to True regarding a Mentally Ill Indian, Enrollment, and Marriage," November 29, 1902, roll 25, Press Copies of Letters Sent concerning Pueblo Day Schools, March 1900–June 1911, Records of the Bureau of Indian Affairs, RG 75, M1473, National Archives and Records Administration, Washington, D.C. (hereafter cited as NARA—Pueblo Day Schools).

17. C. J. Crandall to William A. Jones, "Letter to Commissioner

regarding Compulsory Education," December 17, 1902, vol. 3, pp. 219–220, NARA—Commissioner.

18. C. J. Crandall to William A. Jones, "Letter to the Commissioner of Indian Affairs regarding a Territorial Compulsory Education Law for American Indians," February 10, 1903, vol. 3, pp. 259–260, NARA—Commissioner. The territorial supreme court indirectly addressed this when it issued its opinion in *New Mexico v. Persons on the Delinquent Tax List* (1904), determining that Pueblo Indians were full citizens of the territory and the United States.

19. Julius Seligman to C. J. Crandall, "Letter regarding Children from Santo Domingo Pueblo," August 24, 1906, box 59, folder 721.1, Northern Pueblos Agency, General Correspondence File, 1904–1937, Records of the Bureau of Indian Affairs, RG 75, entry 83, National Archives and Records Administration, Rocky Mountain Region, Denver, Colo. (hereafter cited as NARA—NPA).

20. C. J. Crandall to Francis E. Leupp, "Letter to the Commissioner of Indian Affairs regarding the Status of Compulsory Schooling in New Mexico," May 25, 1907, vol. 8, pp. 177–178, NARA—Commissioner.

21. See, for example, Coleman, "The Symbiotic Embrace," 201; Lomawaima and McCarty, *"To Remain Indian,"* 49.

22. W. W. Hill, *An Ethnography of Santa Clara Pueblo, New Mexico* (Albuquerque: University of New Mexico Press, 1982), 169; Jean Allard Jeançon Papers, n.d., folder 11, Western History and Genealogy, Denver Public Library, Denver, Colo.

23. Clara D. True to C. J. Crandall, "Letter to Superintendent concerning Relations with the Governor and the Neighboring Mexicans," November 4, 1902, Letters Received from Day School Teacher Clara D. True, 1902–1907, Records of the Bureau of Indian Affairs, RG 75, entry 38, National Archives and Records Administration, Rocky Mountain Region, Denver, Colo. (hereafter cited as NARA—True); Clara D. True to C. J. Crandall, "Letter to Superintendent Expressing Need for Judge Abbott to Come to Santa Clara Pueblo," November 21, 1902, NARA—True.

24. See, for example, Brenda J. Child, *Boarding School Seasons: American Indian Families, 1900–1940* (Lincoln: University of Nebraska Press, 1998); Coleman, "The Symbiotic Embrace"; Deyhle and Swisher, "Research in American Indian and Alaska Native Education"; Ohíye S'a [Charles A. Eastman], *Indian Boyhood* (New York: McClure, Phillips, 1902; repr., New York: Dover, 1971); Amelia V. Katanski, *Learning to Write "Indian": The Boarding-*

School Experience and American Indian Literature (Norman: University of Oklahoma Press, 2005); Francis La Flesche, *The Middle Five: Indian Schoolboys of the Omaha Tribe* (1900; repr., Lincoln: University of Nebraska Press, 1978); K. Tsianina Lomawaima, "American Indian Education: By Indians for Indians," in *A Companion to American Indian History,* ed. Philip J. Deloria and Neal Salisbury, Blackwell Companions to American History (Malden, Mass.: Blackwell, 2002), 422–440; Reyhner and Eder, "A History of Indian Education"; Reyhner and Eder, *American Indian Education;* Clifford E. Trafzer, Jean A. Keller, and Lorene Sisquoc, *Boarding School Blues: Revisiting American Indian Educational Experiences* (Lincoln: Bison Books, University of Nebraska Press, 2006).

25. C. J. Crandall to Francis E. Leupp, "Annual Report to the Commissioner of Indian Affairs," August 19, 1905, vol. 6, pp. 114–129, NARA—Commissioner.

26. C. J. Crandall to Francis E. Leupp, "Annual Report to the Commissioner of Indian Affairs," August 19, 1907, vol. 8, p. 370, NARA—Commissioner.

27. Clara D. True to C. J. Crandall, "Letter to Superintendent concerning 2 Girls Who Want to Enroll in the Santa Fe Indian Boarding School," September 14, 1904, NARA—True; C. J. Crandall to Clara D. True, "Letter to Clara D. True regarding Payment to Pedro Cajete and the Enrollment of Two Girls at the Santa Fe Indian School," September 15, 1904, vol. 20, p. 307, Press Copies of Letters Sent ("Miscellaneous Letters"), June 1890–December 1913, Records of the Bureau of Indian Affairs, RG 75, entry 32, National Archives and Records Administration, Rocky Mountain Region, Denver, Colo. (hereafter cited as NARA—Miscellaneous).

28. C. J. Crandall to Clara D. True, "Letter to Clara D. True regarding the Enrollment of Two Santa Clara Girls in the Santa Fe Indian School," September 12, 1905, roll 27, NARA—Pueblo Day Schools.

29. Swaso's last name has multiple spellings in the primary and secondary source material, including "Swaso," "Swazo," "Suazo," and "Sousea." C. J. Crandall to Clara D. True, "Letter to Clara D. True regarding the Wellbeing of Brigida Sousea," January 23, 1906, roll 27, NARA—Pueblo Day Schools; C. J. Crandall to Francis E. Leupp, "Letter to the Commissioner of Indian Affairs regarding the Appointment of Indian Girls to Indian Schools," December 8, 1905, vol. 6, p. 319, NARA—Commissioner; Clara D. True to C. J. Crandall, "Letter to Superintendent concerning the Placement of Pupils, Enrollment at Santa Clara School and a Visit of the Sisters of St. Catherine's

School," September 2, 1903, NARA—True; Clara D. True to C. J. Crandall, "Letter to Superintendent Requesting That a Student at the Santa Fe Indian Boarding School Be Sent Home," October 31, 1904, NARA—True.

30. Hill, *An Ethnography of Santa Clara Pueblo,* 161; True to Crandall, "Letter to Superintendent concerning the Placement of Pupils, Enrollment at Santa Clara School and a Visit of the Sisters of St. Catherine's School"; C. J. Crandall to Francisco Naranjo et al., "Letter to Francisco Naranjo, Pedro Ignasio Gutierres, Jose Manuel Naranjo, and Rafael Vigil regarding the Progressive Party at Santa Clara," February 27, 1904, vol. 19, pp. 200–201, NARA—Miscellaneous; Clara D. True to Francis J. McCormick, "Letter to Clerk-in-Charge, Santa Fe Indian School, concerning Difficulties among the Santa Clara Pueblo Indians Accepting Vaccinations," January 21, 1903, NARA—True; Clara D. True to Francis J. McCormick, "Letter to Clerk-in-Charge, Santa Fe Indian School, concerning Problems in Vaccinating the Indians in the Pueblo," January 20, 1903, NARA—True.

31. William A. Jones, "Indian Commissioner Jones on Indian Self-Support, October 15, 1901," in *Documents of United States Indian Policy,* ed. Francis Paul Prucha, 3rd ed. (Lincoln: University of Nebraska Press, 2000), 200.

32. Estelle Reel, *Course of Study for the Indian Schools of the United States, Industrial and Literary* (Washington, D.C.: Government Printing Office, 1901), 5.

33. Indeed, the similarities between American Indian and Black schooling experiences were striking in terms of their subordinate position in relation to the dominant Anglo population and their industrial training. Carter G. Woodson, a noted scholar of African American history, argued in 1933 that both industrial and classical schooling models had failed Blacks in part because "the 'friend' of the Negro" premised Black schooling on "controlling the underprivileged classes." Much of this "control" or "training" directly reflected both dominant views of racial hierarchy and what constituted viable citizenship practices in the late nineteenth and early twentieth centuries. More recently, historian Irving G. Hendrick writes that as the federal government phased out organizations for ex-slaves, such as the Freedman's Bureau, which were established in the wake of the Civil War to prepare newly free Blacks for citizenship, it likewise focused attention on transforming American Indians into U.S. citizens. For reformers, schooling—with a heavily practical and economically grounded focus—appeared to be the panacea

that would instill Anglo values about work and citizenship and simultaneously prepare American Indians and Blacks to participate as viable members in the U.S. economy, albeit in lower positions than whites. See Woodson, *The Mis-education of the Negro* (Trenton, N.J.: Africa World Press, 1933), 30; Hendrick, "Federal Policy Affecting the Education of Indians in California, 1849–1934," *History of Education Quarterly* 16, no. 2 (Summer 1976): 166, 170; Adams, *Education for Extinction*, 145–149; Ahern, "An Experiment Aborted," 266, 272–274, 280–285; K. Tsianina Lomawaima, "Estelle Reel, Superintendent of Indian Schools, 1898–1910: Politics, Curriculum, and Land," *Journal of American Indian Education* 35, no. 3 (May 1996); Lomawaima and McCarty, *"To Remain an Indian,"* 49; Richard Henry Pratt, "The Advantages of Mingling Indians with Whites, 1892," in Prucha, *Americanizing the American Indians,* 262. Alice Littlefield has written about American Indian industrial schools as a means to "proletarianize" Native students. See "Learning to Labor: Native American Education in the United States, 1880–1930," in *The Political Economy of North American Indians,* ed. John H. Moore (Norman: University of Oklahoma Press, 1993), 43–59.

34. Lomawaima, "Estelle Reel"; Lomawaima and McCarty, *"To Remain an Indian,"* 51–53.

35. Reel, *Course of Study,* 54–55.

36. C. J. Crandall to William A. Jones, "Letter to the Superintendent of Indian Schools regarding the Receipt of the Course of Study for Indian Schools," November 19, 1901, vol. 2, p. 169, NARA—Commissioner; Hill, *An Ethnography of Santa Clara Pueblo,* 106.

37. Crandall to Leupp, "Annual Report to the Commissioner of Indian Affairs," August 19, 1905. For a thorough discussion of the economic self-reliance of off-reservation boarding schools, see Adams, *Education for Extinction,* 149–156.

38. Morgan, "Supplemental Report on Indian Education, 1889," 226.

39. C. J. Crandall to William A. Jones, "Letter to the Commissioner of Indian Affairs regarding Indian Boys Who Are 'Outing' on Farms in Colorado," June 30, 1904, vol. 4, p. 475, NARA—Commissioner; C. J. Crandall to Francis E. Leupp, "Letter to the Commissioner of Indian Affairs regarding Students Participating in Outing Program," June 30, 1905, vol. 6, p. 39, NARA—Commissioner; Crandall to Leupp, "Annual Report to the Commissioner of Indian Affairs," August 19, 1905; Crandall to Leupp, "Annual Report to the Commissioner of Indian Affairs" August 17, 1906; C. J. Crandall to Francis E.

Leupp, "Annual Report to the Commissioner of Indian Affairs," August 19, 1907, vol. 8, pp. 369–377, NARA—Commissioner.

40. Crandall to Leupp, "Annual Report to the Commissioner of Indian Affairs," August 19, 1907. Adams provides a lucid account of how students at Carlisle experienced the outing system in *Education for Extinction*, 156–163.

41. Hill, *An Ethnography of Santa Clara Pueblo*, 166.

42. Abbott, "Education for the Indian," 213; Adams, "Fundamental Considerations," 9–10, 18–19, 20; Adams, *Education for Extinction*, 191–206; Ahern, "An Experiment Aborted," 284; J. D. C. Atkins, "The English Language in Indian Schools," in Prucha, *Americanizing the American Indians*, 199–203; Deyhle and Swisher, "Research in American Indian and Alaska Native Education," 124; Morgan, "Supplemental Report on Indian Education, 1889," 222–224.

43. A. C. Tonner to B. S. Rodey, "Letter regarding the Use of Rifles in Military Drills at the Santa Fe Indian School," April 16, 1902, box 1, folder 1902, NARA—Finance.

44. Frank D. Baldwin, "Letter regarding Guns for Military Drills at the Santa Fe Indian School," May 5, 1906, box 61, folder 806, NARA—NPA.

45. Crandall to Leupp, "Annual Report to the Commissioner of Indian Affairs," August 17, 1906; C. J. Crandall to Clara D. True, "Letter to Clara D. True regarding Her Report on Memorial Day Activities at Santa Clara," June 5, 1906, roll 27, NARA—Pueblo Day Schools.

46. Clara D. True to C. J. Crandall, "Letter to Superintendent concerning Personnel Problems with the Interpreter and the Governor," December 27, 1902, NARA—True; Clara D. True to C. J. Crandall, "Letter to Superintendent regarding Internal Politics in the Santa Clara Pueblo and Problems with the 'Medicine Men,'" January 30, 1903, NARA—True; Clara D. True to C. J. Crandall, "Letter to Superintendent Requesting a Letter from Judge Abbott regarding Mexican Stock Trespassing on Indian Lands," February 19, 1906, NARA—True.

47. C. J. Crandall to Francisco Naranjo, "Letter to Francisco Naranjo regarding a Complaint against the Santa Clara Governor and the Pueblos Citizenship Status," March 14, 1904, vol. 19, p. 239, NARA—Miscellaneous; C. J. Crandall to Francisco Naranjo, "Letter to Francisco Naranjo et al. regarding Individual Land Claims within the Pueblo Holding," May 1, 1905, vol. 21, p. 412, NARA—Miscellaneous.

48. Adams, "Fundamental Considerations," 13; Adams, *Education for Extinction*, 55–59; Brookings Institution and Lewis Meriam, *The Problem of*

Indian Administration: Report of a Survey Made at the Request of Hubert Work, Secretary of the Interior, and Submitted to Him, February 21, 1928 (Washington, D.C.: Brookings Institution, 1928), 405–411; Morgan, "Supplemental Report on Indian Education, 1889," 227.

49. Friends of the Indian, "Program of the Lake Mohonk Conference, September 1884," in Prucha, *Documents of United States Indian Policy*, 162.

50. Adams, "Fundamental Considerations," 3.

51. Adams, *Education for Extinction*, 58.

52. Abbott, "Education for the Indian," 213; Coleman, "The Symbiotic Embrace," 197–199; Margaret Connell Szasz, *Indian Education in the American Colonies, 1607–1783* (Lincoln: Bison Books, University of Nebraska Press, 2007), 5, 54; T. Smith to C. E. Nordstrom, "Letter to C. E. Nordstrom, Acting Agent of the Pueblo and Jicarilla Agency, regarding Educational Practices and Goals at Indian Schools, Education 22474–1897," June 10, 1897, box 7, folder 131, Northern Pueblos Agency, Miscellaneous Correspondence and Reports, 1868–1904, Records of the Bureau of Indian Affairs, RG 75, 8NN-075-88-073, National Archives and Records Administration, Rocky Mountain Region, Denver, Colo. (hereafter cited as NARA—NPA Misc.).

53. Morgan, "Supplemental Report on Indian Education, 1889," 234–235.

54. Crandall to Leupp, "Annual Report to the Commissioner of Indian Affairs," August 19, 1907.

55. Adams, *Education for Extinction*, 63, 70; Paul Stuart, "Administrative Reform in Indian Affairs," *Western Historical Quarterly* 16, no. 2 (April 1985): 138–139; Paul Stuart, *The Indian Office: Growth and Development of an American Institution, 1865–1900* (Ann Arbor, Mich.: UMI Research, 1979), 2, 13.

56. U.S. Congress, "Authorization of Indian Agents, 1818," in Prucha, *Documents of United States Indian Policy*, 30; U.S. Congress, "Creation of a Bureau of Indian Affairs in the War Department, March 11, 1824," in Prucha, *Documents of United States Indian Policy*, 37–38; U.S. Congress, "Authorization of a Commissioner of Indian Affairs, July 9, 1832," in Prucha, *Documents of United States Indian Policy*, 62; U.S. Congress, "Organization of the Department of Indian Affairs, June 30, 1834," in Prucha, *Documents of United States Indian Policy*, 68–70; U.S. Congress, "Transfer of Indian Affairs to the Department of the Interior, March 3, 1849," in Prucha, *Documents of United States Indian Policy*, 79–80; U.S. Congress, "Modifications in the Indian Department, February 27, 1851," in Prucha, *Documents of United States Indian Policy*, 83. See also

Adams, *Education for Extinction,* 60–71. The organizational chart on p. 71 is especially helpful.

57. Daniel M. Browning, "Extension of Civil Service Rules, September 15, 1896," in Prucha, *Documents of United States Indian Policy,* 194–195; John W. Noble and Benjamin Harrison, "Civil Service Classifications in the Indian Service, April 13, 1891," in Prucha, *Documents of United States Indian Policy,* 180; Stuart, *The Indian Office,* 40–41.

58. Adams, *Education for Extinction,* 89; Brookings Institution and Meriam, *The Problem of Indian Administration,* 359–370; Patricia A. Carter, "'completely discouraged': Women Teachers' Resistance in the Bureau of Indian Affairs Schools, 1900–1910," *Frontiers: A Journal of Women Studies* 15, no. 3 (1995): 69, 73–75; Coleman, "The Symbiotic Embrace," 200.

59. Adams, *Education for Extinction,* 82–94; Carter, "'completely discouraged'"; Catharine E. Beecher, "Catharine E. Beecher: An Essay on the Education of Female Teachers for the United States, 1835," in *The School in the United States: A Documentary History,* ed. James W. Fraser (New York: McGraw-Hill, 2001), 61–66; Anne Ruggles Gere, "Indian Heart/White Man's Head: Native-American Teachers in Indian Schools, 1880–1930," *History of Education Quarterly* 45, no. 1 (Summer 2005): 38–65.

60. Clara D. True to C. J. Crandall, "Letter to Superintendent concerning the Enrollment Capacity of the Santa Clara Day School," November 4, 1903, NARA—True.

61. C. J. Crandall to Clara D. True, "Letter to Clara D. True regarding Sewing Machine Needles She Requested," November 3, 1903, roll 26, NARA—Pueblo Day Schools; C. J. Crandall to Clara D. True, "Letter to Clara D. True regarding Seed for the Santa Clara Pueblo," April 30, 1904, roll 26, NARA—Pueblo Day Schools; Clara D. True to C. J. Crandall, "Letter to Superintendent Requesting Grass Seed for Improvement and to Report on Health Conditions," March 30, 1903, NARA—True; Clara D. True to C. J. Crandall, "Letter to Superintendent Expressing Need for Seeds," April 30, 1904, NARA—True.

62. C. J. Crandall to Clara D. True, "Letter to Clara D. True Regarding a Stray Cow, Diphtheria, and Enrollment," September 5, 1902, vol. 3, p. 98, NARA—Commissioner; Crandall to True, "Letter to True regarding a Mentally Ill Indian, Enrollment, and Marriage"; C. J. Crandall to Clara D. True, "Letter to Clara D. True regarding Student Enrollment," August 31, 1903, roll 25, NARA—Pueblo Day Schools; C. J. Crandall to Clara D. True, "Letter to

Clara D. True regarding Young Students at the Santa Fe Indian School," September 15, 1903, roll 25, NARA—Pueblo Day Schools; Clara D. True to C. J. Crandall, "Letter to Superintendent regarding Enrolled Students and Dealings with the Indians in the Pueblo," November 28, 1902, NARA—True; Clara D. True to C. J. Crandall, "Letter to Superintendent concerning Enrollment of Students," August 28, 1904, NARA—True; Clara D. True to C. J. Crandall, "Letter to Superintendent concerning a Sick Pupil from the Santa Fe Indian Boarding School," October 27, 1904, NARA—True.

63. Crandall to True, "Letter to Clara D. True regarding a Stray Cow, Diphtheria, and Enrollment"; Clara D. True to C. J. Crandall, "Letter to Superintendent concerning Daily Activities at the School," September 6, 1902, NARA—True.

64. C. J. Crandall to Clara D. True, "Letter to Clara D. True regarding Student Transfers to Haskell," September 4, 1903, roll 25, NARA—Pueblo Day Schools.

65. C. J. Crandall to Clara D. True, "Letter to Clara D. True regarding Pupils Who Are to Go to the Santa Fe Indian School," August 16, 1904, vol. 20, p. 186, NARA—Miscellaneous.

66. C. J. Crandall to Clara D. True, "Letter to Clara D. True regarding the Enrollment of Santa Clara Students at the Santa Fe Indian School," September 15, 1904, roll 26, NARA—Pueblo Day Schools.

67. Clara D. True to C. J. Crandall, "Letter to Superintendent concerning Getting Santa Fe Indian School Students to Leave Home with a Large Harvest Being Conducted," September 21, 1904, NARA—True.

68. Minnie Crandall to Clara D. True, "Contract to Return Cesaria Tafoya to the Santa Fe Indian School in September," June 22, 1905, box 8, folder 168, NARA—NPA Misc.; George B. Haggett to Clara D. True, "Note regarding the Return of Monica Silva to the Santa Fe Indian School," June 26, 1905, box 8, folder 168, NARA—NPA Misc.; C. J. Crandall to Clara D. True, "Letter to Clara D. True regarding Students Who Have Yet to Return to the Santa Fe Indian School," September 12, 1907, roll 28, NARA—Pueblo Day Schools.

69. Crandall to Leupp, "Annual Report to the Commissioner of Indian Affairs," August 19, 1907.

70. Abbott, "Education for the Indian."

71. Gere, "Indian Heart/White Man's Head," 39, 57; Lomawaima, "Estelle Reel"; Ahern, "An Experiment Aborted," 273–279, 278, 280–283, 290.

72. Harwood Hall to C. J. Crandall, "Letter to C. J. Crandall regarding the

Transfer of Sallie B. Neal," June 6, 1903, box 7, folder 156, NARA—NPA Misc.; Clara D. True to C. J. Crandall, "Letter to Superintendent Recommending Sallie B. Neal for Teaching Position in the Indian School Service," June 18, 1903, NARA—True; C. J. Crandall to Charles H. Dickson, "Letter to Chas. H. Dickson regarding Teachers at Northern Pueblo Day Schools," June 22, 1903, vol. 17, pp. 360–364, NARA—Miscellaneous; Clara D. True to C. J. Crandall, "Letter to Superintendent concerning Lack of a Position for Sallie Neal in the Indian School Service," June 23, 1903, NARA—True.

73. Clara D. True to C. J. Crandall, "Letter to the Superintendent Recommending a Housekeeper for Sallie Neal at the San Juan Day School," October 8, 1903, NARA—True; Clara D. True to C. J. Crandall, "Letter to Superintendent concerning the Visit of Mrs. Neal and Tourists from Illinois," October 23, 1903, NARA—True.

74. C. J. Crandall to William A. Jones, "Letter to the Commissioner of Indian Affairs regarding the Teaching Position at San Juan Day School," October 24, 1903, vol. 4, p. 128, NARA—Commissioner.

75. C. J. Crandall to Clara D. True, "Letter to Clara D. True regarding the Possible Vacancy at San Juan Pueblo Day School," October 22, 1903, roll 26, NARA—Pueblo Day Schools.

76. Clara D. True to C. J. Crandall, "Letter to Superintendent concerning Mrs. S. B. Neal Remaining in the Area to See if There Are Any Positions Available," October 28, 1903, NARA—True.

77. Pedro Baca to Rev. Father William Ketcham, "Letter regarding the Administration of C. J. Crandall," October 13, 1908, Bureau of Catholic Indian Missions, series 1-1: Correspondence, reel 43, Marquette University, Milwaukee, Wis.

78. Mary Dissette to W. H. Pope, "Letter from Mary E. Dissette to W. H. Pope Criticizing the Indian Service and Requesting to be Independent of Crandall," January 1, 1902, Indian Affairs Collection, box 1, folder 4, Center for Southwest Research, University of New Mexico, Albuquerque, http://econtent.unm.edu/cdm4/document.php?CISOROOT=/indaffairs&CISOPTR=877&CISOSHOW=. Dissette's claims lend credence to charges brought against Crandall in 1911 that he ran an illicit liquor ring out of a drugstore he co-owned in Santa Fe.

79. C. J. Crandall to Clara D. True, "Letter to Clara D. True regarding Books Included for Disposal," October 11, 1904, roll 26, NARA—Pueblo Day Schools.

80. Clara D. True to C. J. Crandall, "Letter to Superintendent Accounting for Books and Other Supplies," October 12, 1904, NARA—True.

81. Ibid.

82. C. J. Crandall to Clara D. True, "Letter to Clara D. True regarding Government Property She Reportedly Gave to the School in Espanola," May 6, 1905, roll 27, NARA—Pueblo Day Schools.

CHAPTER FIVE. EDUCATION; OR, LEARNING WITHIN A
COLONIAL REGIME

1. David F. Labaree, *How to Succeed in School without Really Learning: The Credentials Race in American Education* (New Haven, Conn.: Yale University Press, 1997); John Dewey, *Democracy and Education* (New York: Macmillan, 1916); John Dewey, *How We Think: A Restatement of the Relation of Reflective Thinking to the Educative Process* (Boston: D. C. Heath, 1933); Bernard Bailyn, *Education in the Forming of American Society: Needs and Opportunities for Study* (New York: Vintage, 1960); Lawrence A. Cremin, *The Wonderful World of Ellwood Patterson Cubberley: An Essay on the Historiography of American Education* (New York: Bureau of Publications, Teachers College, Columbia University, 1965); Richard J. Storr, "The Education of History: Some Impressions," *Harvard Educational Review* 31, no. 2 (Spring 1961): 124–135; Richard J. Storr, "The Role of Education in American History: A Memorandum for the Committee Advising the Fund for the Advancement of Education in Regard to This Subject," *Harvard Educational Review* 46, no. 3 (August 1976): 331–354.

2. Bailyn, *Education in the Forming of American Society*, 13, 14; Lawrence A. Cremin, *Traditions of American Education* (New York: Basic, 1977), 134; Storr, "The Role of Education in American History," 334; Storr, "The Education of History," 124.

3. John Dewey, *My Pedagogic Creed* (New York: E. L. Kellogg, 1897), 4, 8; Dewey, *Democracy and Education*, 6, 26, 89–90.

4. Dewey, *Democracy and Education*, 63, 79; Dewey, *How We Think*, 78.

5. Bailyn, *Education in the Forming of American Society*, 48.

6. William F. Slocum, "The World's Fair as an Educative Force," *Outlook*, August 6, 1904, 785–805; Ernest Hamlin Abbott, "The Fair at St. Louis," *Outlook*, July 4, 1903, 560. See also "The St. Louis Fair," *Outlook*, April 25, 1903, 952–953; "Educational Progress of the Year," *Outlook*, August 6, 1904, 776–781.

7. Nancy J. Parezo and Don D. Fowler, *Anthropology Goes to the Fair: The*

1904 Louisiana Purchase Exposition (Lincoln: University of Nebraska Press, 2007), 2; Robert A. Trennert Jr., "Selling Indian Education at World's Fairs and Expositions, 1893–1904" *American Indian Quarterly* 11, no. 3 (Summer 1987): 203, 211–212, 213, 217–218.

8. Parezo and Fowler, *Anthropology Goes to the Fair,* 55, 59.

9. Samuel M. McCowan to C. J. Crandall, "Letter to C. J. Crandall regarding the Participation of Pueblo Indians in the 1904 St. Louis Expo," May 14, 1903, box 7, folder 160, Northern Pueblos Agency, Miscellaneous Correspondence and Reports, 1868–1904, Records of the Bureau of Indian Affairs, RG 75, 8NN-075-88-073, National Archives and Records Administration, Rocky Mountain Region, Denver, Colo.

10. Parezo and Fowler, *Anthropology Goes to the Fair,* 55, 59, 154–157.

11. Clara D. True to C. J. Crandall, "Letter to Superintendent concerning a Santa Clara Pueblo Woman Attending the St. Louis Exposition to Demonstrate Her Pottery," January 20, 1904, Letters Received from Day School Teacher Clara D. True, 1902–1907, Records of the Bureau of Indian Affairs, RG 75, entry 38, National Archives and Records Administration, Rocky Mountain Region, Denver, Colo. (hereafter cited as NARA—True).

12. C. J. Crandall to Clara D. True, "Letter to Clara D. True regarding the Potter Going to the St. Louis Expo," January 22, 1904, roll 26, Press Copies of Letters Sent concerning Pueblo Day Schools, March 1900–June 1911, Records of the Bureau of Indian Affairs, RG 75, M1473, National Archives and Records Administration, Washington, D.C. (hereafter cited as NARA—Pueblo Day Schools); C. J. Crandall to Clara D. True, "Letter to Clara D. True regarding Potters Going to the St. Louis Expo," February 15, 1904, roll 26, NARA—Pueblo Day Schools; Clara D. True to C. J. Crandall, "Letter to Superintendent concerning Additional Women Potters to Go to St. Louis Exposition," February 18, 1904, NARA—True; Clara D. True to C. J. Crandall, "Letter to Superintendent Pertains to the Woman Potter and Her Husband and Their Trip to the St. Louis Exposition," March 31, 1904, NARA—True. Neither True nor Crandall name Martinez, of San Ildefonso Pueblo, in their letters. Rather, when I shared information about Santa Claran attendance at the expo with Diane Bird, a state archivist at the Laboratory of Anthropology at the Museum of Indian Arts and Culture in Santa Fe, she recognized that Martinez was indeed the potter to whom True and Crandall referred. Bird confirmed her hypothesis with Tony Chavarria, the curator of the Museum of Ethnology, who is also Santa Claran. In addition to her sheer skill and

grace as a potter, Martinez is known for reconstructing the firing process used to produce the ancient black-on-black pottery for which Santa Clara and San Ildefonso potters are known. Diane Bird, e-mail messages to Adrea Lawrence, January 7, 2010, January 11, 2010, January 12, 2010. See also Parezo and Fowler, *Anthropology Goes to the Fair,* 251, 387.

13. C. J. Crandall to Clara D. True, "Letter to Clara D. True regarding Crandall's Non-participation in the St. Louis Expo," February 29, 1904, roll 26, NARA—Pueblo Day Schools.

14. Parezo and Fowler, *Anthropology Goes to the Fair,* 61.

15. Ibid., 100–134. It is worth noting that Maria Martinez, the skilled potter whom Crandall was delighted to send to the expo, re-created the ancient black ware that had stumped anthropologists such as Edgar Lee Hewett. Certainly, if Martinez was wedded to the styles and practices current in the late nineteenth and early twentieth centuries, she would not have attempted something different. In other words, Pueblo Indian potters were dynamic artists who modified their methods at will; they were not necessarily interested in exclusively reproducing the same works over and over again.

16. True to Crandall, "Letter to Superintendent concerning Additional Women Potters to Go to St. Louis Exposition" February 18, 1904, NARA—True.

17. W. W. Hill, *An Ethnography of Santa Clara Pueblo, New Mexico* (Albuquerque: University of New Mexico Press, 1982), 140.

18. Clara D. True to C. J. Crandall, "Letter to Superintendent Requesting Permission to Allow Pedro Chiquito Cajete and His Daughter to Go to the St. Louis Exposition," April 14, 1904, NARA—True.

19. Ibid.

20. Hill, *An Ethnography of Santa Clara Pueblo,* 166. W. E. B. DuBois discussed the notion of double consciousness, or the Veil, at length in his seminal work, *The Souls of Black Folk* (New York: Modern Library, 1903).

21. Parezo and Fowler, *Anthropology Goes to the Fair,* 143–150, 161.

22. Trennert, "Selling Indian Education," 211–212, 213, 217–218.

23. "Correspondence," *Outlook,* October 31, 1903, 519.

24. Parezo and Fowler, *Anthropology Goes to the Fair,* 246–252; Trennert, "Selling Indian Education," 216; Crandall to True, "Letter to Clara D. True regarding the Potter Going to the St. Louis Expo."

25. Parezo and Fowler, *Anthropology Goes to the Fair,* 128–129. Clara D. True

to C. J. Crandall, "Letter to the Superintendent concerning the Santa Claran Indians at the St. Louis Exposition," May 17, 1904, NARA—True.

26. C. J. Crandall to Pedro Cajete, "Letter to Pedro Cajete regarding Recruiting Pueblo Students to the Chilocco Indian School," June 25, 1904, vol. 20, p. 100, Press Copies of Letters Sent ("Miscellaneous Letters"), June 1890–December 1913, Records of the Bureau of Indian Affairs, RG 75, entry 32, National Archives and Records Administration, Rocky Mountain Region, Denver, Colo.

27. Adolph Francis Alphonse Bandelier, "The Siege of Santa Fe by the Insurgent Indians of the Pueblos in the Year 1680," *New Mexican*, June 28, 1890, sec. News/Opinion; Bandelier, *Final Report of Investigations among the Indians of the Southwestern United States, Carried on Mainly in the Years from 1880 to 1885* (1890); Bandelier and Edgar L. Hewett, *Indians of the Rio Grande Valley*, Handbooks of Archeological History (New York: Cooper Square, 1973); Bandelier, "Documentary History of the Rio Grande Pueblos, New Mexico, Part I: 1536–1542," *New Mexico Historical Review* 5, no. 1 (1930): 38; Bandelier, "Documentary History of the Rio Grande Pueblos, New Mexico, Part III: 1581–1584," *New Mexico Historical Review* 5, no. 4 (October 1, 1930): 333. For a present-day discussion of cultural tourism and how Pueblo Indians have learned to mediate it, see Deirdre Evans-Pritchard, "The Portal Case: Authenticity, Tourism, Traditions, and the Law," *Journal of American Folklore* 100, no. 397 (September 1987): 287–296; Deirdre Evans-Pritchard, "How 'They' See 'Us': Native American Images of Tourists," *Annals of Tourism Research* 16 (1989): 89–106; Amanda Stronza, "Anthropology of Tourism: Forging New Ground for Ecotourism and Other Alternatives," *Annual Review of Anthropology* 30 (2001): 261–284; Jill D. Sweet, "The Portals of Tradition: Tourism in the American Southwest," *Cultural Survival Quarterly* 14, no. 2 (1990): 6–8; Jill D. Sweet, "'Let 'em Loose': Pueblo Indian Management of Tourism," *American Indian Culture & Research Journal* 15, no. 4 (1991): 59–74.

28. "A Vacation among the Cliff-Ruins," *Friend: A Religious and Literary Journal*, March 2, 1895; "The Cliff Dwellers: A Visit to the Interesting Santa Clara Ruins by an Archaeologist," *Santa Fe New Mexican*, March 22, 1900, sec. News/Opinion; "The Cliff Dwellers: An Interesting Visit and Excavations Made in Pajarito Canon by California People," *Santa Fe New Mexican*, September 4, 1900, sec. News/Opinion; Frederick Schwatka, "The Ancient Cliff and Cave-Dwellers," *Independent*, April 17, 1890.

29. "A Vacation among the Cliff-Ruins." What this author might not have known, but which many anthropologists in the early twentieth century readily observed at many Indian Pueblos, was that women were often the home builders within a village.

30. "The Cliff Dwellers: A Visit to the Interesting Santa Clara Ruins by an Archaeologist."

31. Ad. F. [Bandelier], "Kingdom of New Mexico: Its Antiquities and Population of the Pueblos," *Santa Fe Daily New Mexican*, May 3, 1890, sec. News/Opinion.

32. "An Exploring Party: Scientists Are Examining Indian Pueblos and Ruins of Ancient Cliff Dwellers," *Santa Fe New Mexican*, July 28, 1899, sec. News/Opinion.

33. "The Cliff Dwellers: An Interesting Visit and Excavations Made in Pajarito Canon by California People"; "A Vacation among the Cliff-Ruins."

34. Charles S. Rawles to C. J. Crandall, "Letter to Superintendent regarding Placards for Santa Clara Cañon," August 14, 1910, box 8, folder 161, Northern Pueblos Agency, General Correspondence File, 1904–1937, Records of the Bureau of Indian Affairs, RG 75, entry 83, National Archives and Records Administration, Rocky Mountain Region, Denver, Colo.

35. Schwatka, "The Ancient Cliff and Cave-Dwellers."

36. Charles Fletcher Lummis, "A Spring Medicine-Making," *Youth's Companion*, July 28, 1892.

37. William E. Curtis, "Want to Remain Indians: The Pueblos Impervious to the Influence of Civilization and Adhere to Their Ancient Customs—A Curious People," *Lexington (Ky.) Morning Herald*, May 11, 1899, sec. News/Opinion; F. S. Dellenbaugh, "The First Americans," *St. Nicholas: An Illustrated Magazine for Young Folks*, October 1889.

38. George Thomas Dowling, "A Song of the Ancient People," *Independent*, December 8, 1892.

39. "New Mexico Indians: A General Statement as to Their Education, Condition, Water Rights, etc.," *Santa Fe New Mexican*, September 15, 1900, sec. News/Opinion; "A Vacation among the Cliff-Ruins."

40. Curtis, "Want to Remain Indians."

41. "New Mexico Indians."

42. William E. Curtis, "The New Mexico of 1905," *Dallas Morning News*, September 10, 1905, sec. News/Opinion.

43. R. W. Shufelt, "Beauty from an Indian's Point of View," *Cosmopolitan: A Monthly Illustrated Magazine*, March 1895.

44. Edith Sessions Tupper, "The Land of Tomorrow," *Zion's Herald*, August 18, 1897.

45. Shufelt, "Beauty."

46. Tupper, "The Land of Tomorrow"; Edward Coale, "Edward Coale on New Mexico," *Friends' Intelligencer* (Ill.), November 14, 1896.

47. Virginia Conser Shaffer, "The Penitentes," *Peterson Magazine*, May 1895.

48. Tupper, "The Land of Tomorrow"; Coale, "Edward Coale on New Mexico"; Ellenore Dutcher, "Way Down in New Mexico: Life as Seen by an Omaha Girl Visiting in the Southern Territory," *Omaha Sunday World-Herald*, August 24, 1890, sec. News/Opinion.

49. Joseph E. Wing, "Life in New Mexico: It Is Peculiar but at the Same Time Has Some Pleasant and Pretty Features," *Willes-Barré* [sic] *(Pa.) Weekly Times*, April 1, 1899, sec. News/Opinion; "The Mexicans of New Mexico: A Citizen of Santa Fe Who Has a High Opinion of Them," *San Francisco Evening Bulletin*, September 3, 1881, sec. News/Opinion; Curtis, "The New Mexico of 1905."

50. Dutcher, "Way Down in New Mexico"; Frederic J. Haskins, "New Mexico," *Duluth News-Tribune*, February 2, 1910.

51. "New Discoveries: The Cochiti Mineral Belt Located Twenty Miles to the North—Mine Echoes from the Hills," *Santa Fe New Mexican*, March 31, 1894, sec. News/Opinion; Old Rustler, "Cochiti Cullings," *Albuquerque Morning Democrat*, July 3, 1894, sec. News/Opinion.

52. For further elaboration on this point from an Indigenous perspective, see Vine Deloria Jr., *God Is Red: A Native View of Religion*, 2nd ed. (Golden, Colo.: Fulcrum, 1992), 62–77.

53. Frederick Jackson Turner, *The Frontier in American History* (New York: H. Holt, 1921), 2.

54. See, for example, Margaret D. Jacobs, "Clara True and Female Moral Authority," *Faculty Publications, Department of History* (2002), http://digitalcommons.unl.edu/historyfacpub/24. Though Jacobs presents a very different characterization of True than the one presented here, True's friendships with individual Santa Clarans who were Winter People nevertheless come through.

55. Clara D. True, "The Experiences of a Woman Indian Agent," *Outlook*, June 5, 1909, 336.

56. G. Emlen Hall, "Land Litigation and the Idea of New Mexico Progress," *Journal of the West* 27, no. 3 (1988): 48–58; Jacobs, "Clara True and Female Moral Authority"; Margaret D. Jacobs, "Making Savages of Us All: White Women, Pueblo Indians, and the Controversy over Indian Dances in the 1920s," *Frontiers: A Journal of Women Studies* 17, no. 3 (1996): 178–209; Clara D. True, "No Place Like Home," *Independent Woman*, December 1914.

EPILOGUE

1. David J. Weber, "The Spanish Borderlands of North America: A Historiography," *OAH Magazine of History* 14, no. 4 (Summer 2000): 5–11; Herbert Eugene Bolton, *The Spanish Borderlands: A Chronicle of Old Florida and the Southwest,* Chronicles of America Series, 23 (New Haven, Conn.: Yale University Press, 1921).

2. Weber, "The Spanish Borderlands of North America"; David J. Weber, *The Spanish Frontier in North America*, Yale Western Americana Series (New Haven, Conn.: Yale University Press, 1992); Linda Gordon, *The Great Arizona Orphan Abduction* (Cambridge, Mass.: Harvard University Press, 2001); Eric V. Meeks, *Border Citizens: The Making of Indians, Mexicans, and Anglos in Arizona* (Austin: University of Texas Press, 2007); Samuel Truett, *Fugitive Landscapes: The Forgotten History of the U.S.-Mexico Borderlands* (New Haven, Conn.: Yale University Press, 2008); Meredith I. Honig, *New Directions in Education Policy Implementation: Confronting Complexity* (Albany: State University of New York Press, 2006); Margaret Sutton and Bradley A. U. Levinson, *Policy as Practice: Toward a Comparative Sociocultural Analysis of Educational Policy,* Sociocultural Studies in Educational Policy Formation and Appropriation (Westport, Conn.: Ablex, 2001); Allan R. Odden, *Education Policy Implementation* (Albany: State University of New York Press, 1991).

3. See, for example, David Wallace Adams, *Education for Extinction: American Indians and the Boarding School Experience, 1875–1928* (Lawrence: University Press of Kansas, 1997); Brenda J. Child, *Boarding School Seasons: American Indian Families, 1900–1940* (Lincoln: University of Nebraska Press, 1998); Michael C. Coleman, *American Indian Children at School, 1850–1930* (Jackson: University Press of Mississippi, 1993); Matthew L. M. Fletcher, *American Indian Education: Counternarratives in Racism, Struggle, and the Law,* Critical Educator (New York: Routledge, 2008); Amelia V. Katanski, *Learning to Write "Indian": The Boarding-School Experience and American Indian Literature* (Norman: University of Oklahoma Press, 2005); K. Tsianina Lomawaima,

They Called It Prairie Light: The Story of Chilocco Indian School (Lincoln: University of Nebraska Press, 1994); Jon Allan Reyhner and Jeanne M. Oyawin Eder, *American Indian Education: A History* (Norman: University of Oklahoma Press, 2006); Margaret Connell Szasz, *Indian Education in the American Colonies, 1607–1783* (Lincoln: Bison Books, University of Nebraska Press, 2007); Clifford E. Trafzer, Jean A. Keller, and Lorene Sisquoc, *Boarding School Blues: Revisiting American Indian Educational Experiences* (Lincoln: Bison Books, University of Nebraska Press, 2006).

4. Margaret Connell Szasz, ed., *Between Indian and White Worlds: The Cultural Broker* (Norman: University of Oklahoma Press, 1994); Coleman, *American Indian Children at School;* Lomawaima, *They Called It Prairie Light.* See also Patricia A. Carter, "'completely discouraged': Women Teachers' Resistance in the Bureau of Indian Affairs Schools, 1900–1910," *Frontiers: A Journal of Women Studies* 15, no. 3 (1995): 53–86; Anne Ruggles Gere, "Indian Heart/White Man's Head: Native-American Teachers in Indian Schools, 1880–1930," *History of Education Quarterly* 45, no. 1 (Summer 2005): 38–65; Katanski, *Learning to Write "Indian."*

5. Jean A. Keller, *Empty Beds: Indian Student Health at Sherman Institute, 1902–1922,* Native American Series (East Lansing: Michigan State University Press, 2002).

6. See, for example, Ira Berlin, *Generations of Captivity: A History of African-American Slaves* (Cambridge, Mass.: Belknap Press of Harvard University Press, 2003); Charles B. Dew, *Bond of Iron: Master and Slave at Buffalo Forge* (New York: W. W. Norton, 1994); W. E. B. DuBois, *The Souls of Black Folk* (New York: Modern Library, 1903); Steven Hahn, *A Nation under Our Feet: Black Political Struggles in the Rural South, from Slavery to the Great Migration* (Cambridge, Mass.: Belknap Press of Harvard University Press, 2003); Child, *Boarding School Seasons;* Christopher J. Frey, "Ainu Schools and Education Policy in Nineteenth-Century Hokkaido, Japan" (Ph.D. diss., Indiana University, 2007); Keller, *Empty Beds;* Lomawaima, *They Called It Prairie Light;* Glen P. Lauzon, "Civic Learning through Agricultural Improvement: Bringing the 'Loom and the Anvil into Proximity with the Plow' in Nineteenth-Century Indiana" (Ph.D. diss., Indiana University, 2007); Eileen H. Tamura, "Value Messages Collide with Reality: Joseph Kurihara and the Power of Informal Education," *History of Education Quarterly* 50, no. 1 (2010): 1–33.

Bibliography

PRIMARY SOURCES

Archival Sources

Bureau of Catholic Indian Missions. Series 1-1: Correspondence, reel 43. Marquette University, Milwaukee, Wis.

Thomas B. Catron Papers. Center for Southwest Research. University of New Mexico, Albuquerque.

Correspondence and Other Records relating to Finance and Administration, 1902, 1905–1911, 1913–1925. Records of the Bureau of Indian Affairs, RG 75, entry 39. National Archives and Records Administration, Rocky Mountain Region, Denver, Colo.

Wendall V. Hall Collection. Center for Southwest Research. University of New Mexico, Albuquerque.

Edgar Lee Hewett Collection. 89ELH.048, box 4. Museum of Indian Arts and Culture, Santa Fe, N.Mex.

Indian Affairs Collection. Center for Southwest Research. University of New Mexico, Albuquerque.

Jean Allard Jeançon Papers. Western History and Genealogy. Denver Public Library, Denver, Colo.

Letters Received from Day School Teacher Clara D. True, 1902–1907. Records of the Bureau of Indian Affairs, RG 75, entry 38. National Archives and Records Administration, Rocky Mountain Region, Denver, Colo.

Northern Pueblos Agency, General Correspondence File, 1904–1937. Records of the Bureau of Indian Affairs, RG 75, entry 83. National Archives and Records Administration, Rocky Mountain Region, Denver, Colo.

Northern Pueblos Agency, Miscellaneous Correspondence and Reports, 1868–1904. Records of the Bureau of Indian Affairs, RG 75, 8NN-075-88-073. National Archives and Records Administration, Rocky Mountain Region, Denver, Colo.

Press Copies of Letters Sent concerning Pueblo Day Schools, March 1900–June 1911. Records of the Bureau of Indian Affairs, RG 75, M1473. National Archives and Records Administration, Washington, D.C.

Press Copies of Letters Sent ("Miscellaneous Letters"), June 1890–December 1913. Records of the Bureau of Indian Affairs, RG 75, entry 32. National Archives and Records Administration, Rocky Mountain Region, Denver, Colo.

Press Copies of Letters Sent to the Commissioner of Indian Affairs, February 1900–November 1913. Records of the Bureau of Indian Affairs, RG 75, entry 34. National Archives and Records Administration, Rocky Mountain Region, Denver, Colo.

Clara D. True Employment File. National Personnel Records Center. National Archives and Records Administration, St. Louis, Mo.

U.S. Soil Conservation Service Region Eight Records. Center for Southwest Research. University of New Mexico, Albuquerque.

Published Sources

Abbott, Ernest Hamlin. "The Fair at St. Louis." *Outlook*, July 4, 1903, 552–563.

Abbott, Lyman. "Education for the Indian, from 'Proceedings of the Sixth Annual Meeting of the Lake Mohonk Conference of Friends of the Indian, 1888, pp. 11–16.'" In *Americanizing the American Indians: Writings by the "Friends of the Indian," 1880–1900*, edited by Francis Paul Prucha, 207–215. Cambridge, Mass.: Harvard University Press, 1973.

Atkins, J. D. C. "The English Language in Indian Schools." In *Americanizing the American Indians: Writings by the "Friends of the Indian," 1880–1900*, edited by Francis Paul Prucha, 197–206. Cambridge, Mass.: Harvard University Press, 1973.

Bandelier, Adolph Francis Alphonse. "Documentary History of the Rio Grande Pueblos, New Mexico, Part I: 1536–1542." *New Mexico Historical Review* 5, no. 1 (1930): 38.

———. "Documentary History of the Rio Grande Pueblos, New Mexico, Part III: 1581–1584." *New Mexico Historical Review* 5, no. 4 (October 1, 1930): 333.

———. *Final Report of Investigations among the Indians of the Southwestern United States, Carried on Mainly in the Years from 1880 to 1885*. 1890.

———. "Kingdom of New Mexico. Its Antiquities and Population of the Pueblos." *Santa Fe Daily New Mexican*, May 3, 1890, sec. News/Opinion.

———. "The Siege of Santa Fe by the Insurgent Indians of the Pueblos in the Year 1680." *New Mexican*, June 28, 1890, sec. News/Opinion.

Bandelier, Adolph Francis Alphonse, and Edgar L. Hewett. *Indians of the Rio*

Grande Valley. Handbooks of Archeological History. New York: Cooper Square, 1973.

Bayliss, Clara Kern. "A Tewa Sun Myth." *Journal of American Folklore* 22, no. 85 (September 1909): 333–335.

Beecher, Catharine E. "Catharine E. Beecher: An Essay on the Education of Female Teachers for the United States, 1835." In *The School in the United States: A Documentary History*, edited by James W. Fraser, 61–66. New York: McGraw-Hill, 2001.

Board of Indian Commissioners. "Indian Education: Twelfth Annual Report of the Board of Indian Commissioners (1880)." In *Americanizing the American Indians: Writings by the "Friends of the Indian," 1880–1900*, edited by Francis Paul Prucha, 193–196. Cambridge, Mass.: Harvard University Press, 1973.

Boldt, Julius, ed. *Trachoma*. London: Hodder & Stoughton, 1904.

Brookings Institution and Lewis Meriam. *The Problem of Indian Administration: Report of a Survey Made at the Request of Hubert Work, Secretary of the Interior, and Submitted to Him, February 21, 1928*. Washington, D.C.: Brookings Institution, 1928.

Browning, Daniel M. "Extension of Civil Service Rules, September 15, 1896." In *Documents of United States Indian Policy*, edited by Francis Paul Prucha, 194–195. 3rd ed. Lincoln: University of Nebraska Press, 2000.

"The Cliff Dwellers: An Interesting Visit and Excavations Made in Pajarito Canon by California People." *Santa Fe New Mexican*, September 4, 1900, sec. News/Opinion.

"The Cliff Dwellers: A Visit to the Interesting Santa Clara Ruins by an Archaeologist." *Santa Fe New Mexican*, March 22, 1900, sec. News/Opinion.

Coale, Edward. "Edward Coale on New Mexico." *Friends' Intelligencer* (Ill.), November 14, 1896.

Collins, Treacher. "Introductory Chapter." In *Trachoma*, edited by Julius Boldt, xi–lii. London: Hodder & Stoughton, 1904.

"Correspondence." *Outlook*, October 31, 1903, 519.

Curtis, William E. "The New Mexico of 1905." *Dallas Morning News*, September 10, 1905, sec. News/Opinion.

———. "Want to Remain Indians: The Pueblos Impervious to the Influence of Civilization and Adhere To Their Ancient Customs—A Curious People." *Lexington (Ky.) Morning Herald*, May 11, 1899, sec. News/Opinion.

Dawes, Henry L. "Solving the Indian Problem, 1883." In *Americanizing the American Indians: Writings by the "Friends of the Indian," 1880–1900*, edited by Francis Paul Prucha, 27–30. Cambridge, Mass.: Harvard University Press, 1973.

Dellenbaugh, F.S. "The First Americans." *St. Nicholas: An Illustrated Magazine for Young Folks*, October 1889, 935.

Domínguez, Francisco Atanasio. *The Missions of New Mexico, 1776: A Description, with Other Contemporary Documents*. Albuquerque: University of New Mexico Press, 1956.

Dowling, George Thomas. "A Song of the Ancient People." *Independent*, December 8, 1892.

Dutcher, Ellenore. "Way Down in New Mexico: Life as Seen by an Omaha Girl Visiting in the Southern Territory." *Omaha Sunday World-Herald*, August 24, 1890, sec. News/Opinion.

"Educational Progress of the Year." *Outlook*, August 6, 1904, 776–781.

Emerson, H. "Morbidity of the American Indians." *Science*, February 26, 1926, 229–231.

"An Exploring Party: Scientists Are Examining Indian Pueblos and Ruins of Ancient Cliff Dwellers." *Santa Fe New Mexican*, July 28, 1899, sec. News/Opinion.

"A Fearful Epidemic: Terrible Ravages of Small-Pox in New Mexico." *San Francisco Daily Evening Bulletin*, February 7, 1878, sec. News/Opinion.

Friends of the Indian. "Program of the Lake Mohonk Conference, September 1884." In *Documents of United States Indian Policy*, edited by Francis Paul Prucha, 161–164. 3rd ed. Lincoln: University of Nebraska Press, 2000.

Haskins, Frederic J. "New Mexico." *Duluth News-Tribune*, February 2, 1910.

Hewett, Edgar L. "Ethnic Factors in Education." *American Anthropologist*, n.s., 7, no. 1 (March 1905): 1–16.

Hewett, Edgar L., and Bertha P. Dutton. *The Pueblo Indian World*. Handbooks of Archaeological History. Albuquerque: University of New Mexico Press, 1945.

Iglehart, Ferdinand Cowle. *Theodore Roosevelt: The Man as I Knew Him*. New York: Christian Herald, 1919.

Jefferson, Thomas. "President Jefferson on the Liquor Trade." In *Documents of United States Indian Policy*, edited by Francis Paul Prucha, 24. 3rd ed. Lincoln: University of Nebraska Press, 2000.

Johnson, William Eugene. *The Federal Government and the Liquor Traffic*. Westerville, Ohio: American Issue, 1911.

———. *The Story of Juan Cruz*. Washington, D.C.: H. A. Eby, 1912. http://www.archive.org/details/storyofjuanoojohnson.

Jones, William A. "Indian Commissioner Jones on Indian Self-Support, October 15, 1901." In *Documents of United States Indian Policy*, edited by Francis Paul Prucha, 198–201. 3rd ed. Lincoln: University of Nebraska Press, 2000.

La Flesche, Francis. *The Middle Five: Indian Schoolboys of the Omaha Tribe*. 1900. Reprint, Lincoln: University of Nebraska Press, 1978.

Leupp, Francis E. "Annual Report of the Commissioner of Indian Affairs." In *Documents of United States Indian Policy*, edited by Francis Paul Prucha, 3:202–205. 3rd ed. Lincoln: University of Nebraska Press, 2000.

Low, Seth. "Comments on Lyman Abbott's paper." In *Americanizing the American Indians: Writings by the "Friends of the Indian," 1880–1900*, edited by Francis Paul Prucha, 219–220. Cambridge, Mass.: Harvard University Press, 1973.

Lummis, Charles Fletcher. "A Spring Medicine-Making." *Youth's Companion*, July 28, 1892, 378.

"The Mexicans of New Mexico: A Citizen of Santa Fe Who Has a High Opinion of Them." *San Francisco Evening Bulletin*, September 3, 1881, sec. News/Opinion.

"Minor City Topics." *Santa Fe New Mexican*, November 16, 1898, sec. News/Opinion.

Morgan, Thomas J. "Supplemental Report on Indian Education, 1889." In *Americanizing the American Indians: Writings by the "Friends of the Indian," 1880–1900*, edited by Francis Paul Prucha, 221–238. Cambridge, Mass.: Harvard University Press, 1973.

Muir, John. *Our National Parks*. Berkeley: University of California Press, 1900.

"New Discoveries: The Cochiti Mineral Belt Located Twenty Miles to the North—Mine Echoes from the Hills." *Santa Fe New Mexican*, March 31, 1894, sec. News/Opinion.

"New Mexico Indians: A General Statement as to Their Education, Condition, Water Rights, etc." *Santa Fe New Mexican*, September 15, 1900, sec. News/Opinion.

Noble, John W., and Benjamin Harrison. "Civil Service Classifications in the Indian Service, April 13, 1891." In *Documents of United States Indian Policy*, edited by Francis Paul Prucha, 180. 3rd ed. Lincoln: University of Nebraska Press, 2000.

Ohíye S'a [Charles A. Eastman]. *Indian Boyhood*. New York: McClure, Phillips, 1902. Reprint, New York: Dover, 1971.

Old Rustler. "Cochiti Cullings." *Albuquerque Morning Democrat*, July 3, 1894, sec. News/Opinion.

O'Sullivan, John L. "Annexation." *United States Magazine and Democratic Review*, July–August 1845, 5–10.

Parsons, Elsie Clews. *Tewa Tales*. Tucson and London: University of Arizona Press, 1994.

Pepper, William, ed. *A Textbook of the Theory and Practice of Medicine by American Teachers*. Vol. 1. London: F. J. Rebman, 1893.

Pratt, Richard Henry. "The Advantages of Mingling Indians with Whites, 1892." In *Americanizing the American Indians: Writings by the "Friends of the Indian," 1880–1900*, edited by Francis Paul Prucha, 260–271. Cambridge, Mass.: Harvard University Press, 1973.

Reel, Estelle. *Course of Study for the Indian Schools of the United States, Industrial and Literary*. Washington, D.C.: Government Printing Office, 1901.

Roosevelt, Theodore. *Theodore Roosevelt: An Autobiography*. New York: Macmillan, 1913.

Rotch, Thomas Morgan. *Pediatrics*. Philadelphia: Lippincott, 1901.

Schurz, Carl. "Present Aspects of the Indian Problem, 1881." In *Americanizing the American Indians: Writings by the "Friends of the Indian," 1880–1900*, edited by Francis Paul Prucha, 13–26. Cambridge, Mass.: Harvard University Press, 1973.

———. "Secretary of the Interior Schurz on Reservation Policy, November 1, 1880." In *Documents of United States Indian Policy*, edited by Francis Paul Prucha, 152–154. 3rd ed. Lincoln: University of Nebraska Press, 2000.

Schwatka, Frederick. "The Ancient Cliff and Cave-Dwellers." *Independent*, April 17, 1890, 1.

Shaffer, Virginia Conser. "The Penitentes." *Peterson Magazine*, May 1895, 540.

Shufelt, R. W. "Beauty from an Indian's Point of View." *Cosmopolitan: A Monthly Illustrated Magazine*, March 1895, 591–598.

Slocum, William F. "The World's Fair as an Educative Force." *Outlook*, August 6, 1904, 785–805.

"The St. Louis Fair." *Outlook,* April 25, 1903, 952–953.

Thompson, W. Gilman. "Diphtheria." In *A Textbook of the Theory and Practice of Medicine by American Teachers*, 1:373–396. London: F. J. Rebman, 1893.

Tocqueville, Alexis de. *Democracy in America*. Chicago: University of Chicago Press, 2000.

Townsend, J. G. "Disease and the Indian." *Scientific Monthly,* December 1938, 479–495.

True, Clara D. "The Experiences of a Woman Indian Agent." *Outlook,* June 5, 1909, 331–336.

———. "No Place Like Home." *Independent Woman,* December 1914, 365, 382–383.

Tupper, Edith Sessions. "The Land of Tomorrow." *Zion's Herald,* August 18, 1897, 515.

Turner, Frederick Jackson. *The Frontier in American History*. New York: H. Holt, 1921.

U.S. Bureau of the Census. "1870 United States Census, Rockford, Wright, Minnesota." 1870. http://search.ancestrylibrary.com/cgi-bin/sse.dll?db=1870usfedcen%2c&gsfn=Clinton&gsl....

———. "1880 United States Census, Fulton, Callaway, Missouri." 1880. http://www.familysearch.org/Eng/search/frameset_search.asp?PAGE=ancestorsearchresults.asp.

———. "1900 United States Census, Santa Fe Ward 1, U.S. Indian Industrial School, Santa Fe, New Mexico." 1900. http://search.ancestrylibrary.com/cgi-bin/sse.dll?db=1900usfedcen%2c&gsfn=Clinton&gsl....

"A Vacation among the Cliff-Ruins." *Friend: A Religious and Literary Journal,* March 2, 1895, 250.

Wing, Joseph E. "Life in New Mexico: It Is Peculiar but at the Same Time Has Some Pleasant and Pretty Features." *Willes-Barré [sic] (Pa.) Weekly Times,* April 1, 1899, sec. News/Opinion.

Legal Documents

An Act Making Appropriations for Current and Contingent Expenses of the Indian Department. U.S. Statutes at Large 28 (1894): 286.

An Act Making Appropriations for the Current and Contingent Expenses of the Indian Department and for Fulfilling Treaty Stipulations with Various Indian Tribes for the Fiscal Year Ending June Thirtieth, Nineteen Hundred and Six, and for Other Purposes. U.S. Statues at Large 33 (1905): 1048–1082.

Burke Act. U.S. Statutes at Large 34 (1906): 182.

Cherokee Nation v. Georgia. 30 U.S. 1 (1831).

Civilization Fund Act. U.S. Statues at Large 3 (1819): 515–517.

The General Allotment Act of 1887. U.S. Code, vol. 25, sec. 331 (1887).

Indian Citizenship Act. U.S. Statutes at Large 43 (1924): 253.

Intoxicating Drinks to Indians Act. U.S. Statutes at Large 29 (1897): 506.

Johnson v. M'Intosh. 21 U.S. 543 (1823).

Lacey, John F. *Act for the Preservation of American Antiquities. U.S. Statutes at Large* 34 (1906): 225.

Lone Wolf v. Hitchcock. 187 U.S. 553 (1903).

Matter of Heff. 197 U.S. 488 (1905).

New Mexico Enabling Act. U.S. Statutes at Large 36 (1910): 557.

Pueblo Indian Communities; Bodies Corporate; Powers. N.M. Stat. Ann. §53-9-1 (1847).

Regulations for Withholding Rations for Nonattendance at Schools. U.S. Statutes at Large 27 (1893): 612–646.

Roosevelt, Theodore. "Executive Order—Santa Clara Pueblo, New Mexico, July 29, 1905." In *The American Presidency Project,* edited by John T. Woolley and Gerhard Peters. n.d. http://www.presidency.ucsb.edu/ws/index.php?pid=76703.

Stevenson, Matilda Coxe. "Praecipe, 1914." 1914. M386. Denver Public Library, Denver, Colo.

Territory of New Mexico v. The Persons, Real Estate, Land and Property Described Delinquent Tax List of the County of Bernalillo for the First Half of the Year 1899. 12 N.M. Sup. Ct. 139 (1904).

Trade and Intercourse Act. U.S. Statutes at Large 4 (1834): 729–735.

"Treaty of Guadalupe Hidalgo and Protocol of Querétaro." May 30, 1848. In *1873 Treaties and Conventions Concluded between the United States of America and Other Powers* (1873), 562–578. Washington, D.C.: Government Printing Office.

U.S. Congress. "Authorization of a Commissioner of Indian Affairs, July 9, 1832." In *Documents of United States Indian Policy,* edited by Francis Paul Prucha, 62. 3rd ed. Lincoln: University of Nebraska Press, 2000.

———. "Authorization of Indian Agents, 1818." In *Documents of United States Indian Policy,* edited by Francis Paul Prucha, 30. 3rd ed. Lincoln: University of Nebraska Press, 2000.

———. "Creation of a Bureau of Indian Affairs in the War Department,

March 11, 1824." In *Documents of United States Indian Policy*, edited by
Francis Paul Prucha, 37–38. 3rd ed. Lincoln: University of Nebraska Press,
2000.

———. "Modifications in the Indian Department, February 27, 1851." In
Documents of United States Indian Policy, edited by Francis Paul Prucha, 83.
3rd ed. Lincoln: University of Nebraska Press, 2000.

———. "Organization of the Department of Indian Affairs, June 30, 1834."
In *Documents of United States Indian Policy*, edited by Francis Paul Prucha,
68–70. 3rd ed. Lincoln: University of Nebraska Press, 2000.

———. "Transfer of Indian Affairs to the Department of the Interior, March
3, 1849." In *Documents of United States Indian Policy*, edited by Francis Paul
Prucha, 79–80. 3rd ed. Lincoln: University of Nebraska Press, 2000.

U.S. v. Benito Mares. 14 N.M. Sup. Ct. 1 (1907).

U.S. v. Felipe Sandoval. 231 U.S. 28 (1913).

U.S. v. José Juan Lucero. 1 N.M. Sup. Ct. 422 (1869).

U.S. v. Joseph. 94 U.S. 614 (1876).

U.S. v. Kagama and Another, Indians. 118 U.S. 375 (1886).

Wilson, Woodrow. *Bandelier National Monument Proclamation. U.S. Statutes at
Large* 39 (1916): 1764.

Worcester v. Georgia. 31 U.S. 515 (1832).

SECONDARY SOURCES

Abbott, Kathryn A. "Alcohol and the Anishinaabeg of Minnesota in the
Early Twentieth Century." *Western Historical Quarterly* 30 (Spring 1999):
25–43.

Abel, Emily K. "'Only the Best Class of Immigration': Public Health Policy
toward Mexicans and Filipinos in Los Angeles, 1910–1940." *Public Health
Then and Now* 94, no. 6 (2004): 932–939.

Adams, David Wallace. *Education for Extinction: American Indians and the
Boarding School Experience, 1875–1928.* Lawrence: University Press of
Kansas, 1997.

———. "Fundamental Considerations: The Deep Meaning of Native
American Schooling, 1880–1900." *Harvard Educational Review* 58, no. 1
(February 1988): 1–28.

Adelman, J., and S. Aron. "From Borderlands to Borders: Empires, Nation-
States, and the Peoples in between in North American History." *American
Historical Review* 104, no. 3 (1999): 814–841.

Ahern, Wilbert H. "An Experiment Aborted: Returned Indian Students in the Indian School Service, 1881–1908." *Ethnohistory* 44, no. 2 (Spring 1997): 263–304.

Aitken, Barbara. "Temperament in Native American Religion." *Journal of the Royal Anthropological Institute* 60 (1930): 363–387.

Altherr, Thomas L. "The Pajarito or Cliff Dwellers' National Park Proposal, 1900–1920." *New Mexico Historical Review* 60, no. 3 (1985): 271–294.

Anderson, Gary Clayton. *The Indian Southwest, 1580–1830: Ethnogenesis and Reinvention.* Norman: University of Oklahoma Press, 1999.

Anderson, James D. "Race-Conscious Educational Policies versus a 'Color-blind Constitution': A Historical Perspective." *Educational Researcher* 36, no. 5 (July 2007): 249–257.

Andrews, Thomas G. "Turning the Tables on Assimilation: Oglala Lakotas and the Pine Ridge Day Schools, 1889–1920s." *Western Historical Quarterly* 33, no. 4 (Winter 2002): 407–430.

Bailyn, Bernard. *Education in the Forming of American Society: Needs and Opportunities for Study.* New York: Vintage, 1960.

Bannan, Helen M. "The Idea of Civilization and American Indian Policy Reformers in the 1880s." *Journal of American Culture* 1, no. 4 (1978): 787–799.

Basso, Keith H. "Stalking with Stories." In *Schooling the Symbolic Animal: Social and Cultural Dimensions of Education*, edited by Bradley A. U. Levinson, 41–52. Lanham, Md.: Rowman & Littlefield, 2000.

———. "Wisdom Sits in Places: Notes on a Western Apache Landscape." In *Senses of Place*, 53–90. School of American Research Advanced Seminar Series. Santa Fe, N.Mex.: School of American Research Press, 1996.

Benton, Lauren. "Symposium Introduction: Colonialism, Culture, and the Law; Making Order out of Trouble—Jurisdictional Politics in the Spanish Colonial Borderlands." *Law and Social Inquiry* 26 (2001): 373–401.

Berlin, Ira. *Generations of Captivity: A History of African-American Slaves.* Cambridge, Mass.: Belknap Press of Harvard University Press, 2003.

Bolton, Herbert Eugene. *The Spanish Borderlands: A Chronicle of Old Florida and the Southwest.* Chronicles of America Series, 23. New Haven, Conn.: Yale University Press, 1921.

Bourke, J. G. "The Laws of Spain in Their Application to the American Indians." *American Anthropologist* 7, no. 2 (April 1894): 193–201.

Brandt, A. M., and M. Gardner. "Antagonism and Accommodation:

Interpreting the Relationship between Public Health and Medicine in the United States During the 20th Century." *American Journal of Public Health* 90, no. 5 (2000): 707–715.

Brooks, James F. *Captives and Cousins: Slavery, Kinship, and Community in the Southwest Borderlands*. Omohundro Institute of Early American History and Culture. Chapel Hill: University of North Carolina Press, 2002.

Brown, Tracy. "Tradition and Change in Eighteenth-Century Pueblo Indian Communities." *Journal of the Southwest* 46, no. 3 (Autumn 2004): 463–500.

Burke, Ruth. "Devil of the Rio Grande." *True West* 48, no. 1 (January 2001): 36–40.

Carlson, Alvar W. "Spanish-American Acquisition of Cropland within the Northern Pueblo Indian Grants, New Mexico." *Ethnohistory* 22, no. 2 (Spring 1975): 95–110.

Carter, Patricia A. "'completely discouraged': Women Teachers' Resistance in the Bureau of Indian Affairs Schools, 1900–1910." *Frontiers: A Journal of Women Studies* 15, no. 3 (1995): 53–86.

Child, Brenda J. *Boarding School Seasons: American Indian Families, 1900–1940*. Lincoln: University of Nebraska Press, 1998.

Chronic, Halka. *Roadside Geology of New Mexico*. Missoula, Mont.: Mountain Press, 1987.

Cohen, Felix S. *Cohen's Handbook of Federal Indian Law*. Newark, N.J.: LexisNexis, 2005.

———. *Handbook of Federal Indian Law*. 4th ed. Washington, D.C.: Government Printing Office, 1941.

Coleman, Michael C. *American Indian Children at School, 1850–1930*. Jackson: University Press of Mississippi, 1993.

———. "The Responses of American Indian Children to Presbyterian Schooling in the Nineteenth Century: An Analysis through Missionary Sources." *History of Education Quarterly* 27, no. 4 (Winter 1987): 473–497.

———. "The Symbiotic Embrace: American Indians, White Educators and the School, 1820s–1920s." In *The RoutledgeFalmer Reader in History of Education*, edited by Gary McCulloch, 195–213. London and New York: Routledge, 2005.

Cremin, Lawrence A. *Traditions of American Education*. New York: Basic, 1977.

———. *The Wonderful World of Ellwood Patterson Cubberley: An Essay on the Historiography of American Education*. New York: Bureau of Publications, Teachers College, Columbia University, 1965.

Cronon, William. *Changes in the Land: Indians, Colonists, and the Ecology of New England*. Rev. ed. New York: Hill & Wang, 2003.

DeJong, David H. *"If You Knew the Conditions": A Chronicle of the Indian Medical Service and American Indian Health Care, 1908–1955*. Lanham, Md.: Rowman & Littlefield, 2008.

———. "'Unless They Are Kept Alive': Federal Indian Schools and Student Health, 1878–1918." *American Indian Quarterly* 31, no. 2 (2007): 256–282.

Deloria, Vine, Jr. *God Is Red: A Native View of Religion*. 2nd ed. Golden, Colo.: Fulcrum, 1992.

Deloria, Vine, Jr., and Clifford M. Lytle. *American Indians, American Justice*. Austin: University of Texas Press, 1983.

Deloria, Vine, Jr., and Daniel R. Wildcat. *Power and Place: Indian Education in America*. Golden, Colo.: Fulcrum, 2001.

Dew, Charles B. *Bond of Iron: Master and Slave at Buffalo Forge*. New York: W. W. Norton, 1994.

Dewey, John. *Democracy and Education*. New York: Macmillan, 1916.

———. *How We Think: A Restatement of the Relation of Reflective Thinking to the Educative Process*. Boston: D. C. Heath, 1933.

———. *My Pedagogic Creed*. New York: E. L. Kellogg, 1897.

Deyhle, Donna, and Karen Swisher. "Research in American Indian and Alaska Native Education: From Assimilation to Self-Determination." *Review of Research in Education* 22 (1997): 113–194.

"Diphtheria—MayoClinic.com." n.d. http://www.mayoclinic.com/health/diphtheria/DS00495.

Dozier, Edward P. "Factionalism at Santa Clara Pueblo." *Ethnology* 5, no. 2 (April 1966): 172–185.

———. *Hano: A Tewa Indian Community in Arizona*. New York: Holt, Rinehart & Winston, 1966.

———. "Problem Drinking among American Indians: The Role of Sociocultural Deprivation." *Quarterly Journal of Studies on Alcohol* 27, no. 1 (1966): 72–87.

———. *The Pueblo Indians of North America*. New York: Holt, Rinehart & Winston, 1970.

———. "The Pueblo Indians of the Southwest: A Survey of the Anthropological Literature and a Review of Theory, Method, and Results." *Current Anthropology* 5, no. 2 (April 1964): 79–97.

———. "The Pueblos of the South-western United States." *Journal of the*

Royal Anthropological Institute of Great Britain and Ireland 90, no. 1 (June 1960): 146–160.

DuBois, W. E. B. *The Souls of Black Folk*. New York: Modern Library, 1903.

Dunbar-Ortiz, Roxanne. *Roots of Resistance: A History of Land Tenure in New Mexico*. Norman: University of Oklahoma Press, 2007.

Ebright, Malcolm. *Land Grants and Lawsuits in Northern New Mexico*. Santa Fe, N.Mex.: Center for Land Grant Studies Press, 2008.

Ebright, Malcolm, and Rick Hendricks. *The Witches of Abiquiu: The Governor, the Priest, the Genizaro Indians, and the Devil*. Albuquerque: University of New Mexico Press, 2006.

Elliott, Michael A. "Telling the Difference: Nineteenth-Century Legal Narratives of Racial Taxonomy." *Law and Social Inquiry* 24 (1999): 611–636.

Ellis, Clyde. *To Change Them Forever: Indian Education at the Rainy Mountain Boarding School, 1893–1920*. Norman: University of Oklahoma Press, 1996.

Evans-Pritchard, Deirdre. "How 'They' See 'Us': Native American Images of Tourists." *Annals of Tourism Research* 16 (1989): 89–106.

———. "The Portal Case: Authenticity, Tourism, Traditions, and the Law." *Journal of American Folklore* 100, no. 397 (September 1987): 287–296.

Fear-Segal, Jacqueline. *White Man's Club: Schools, Race, and the Struggle of Indian Acculturation*. Lincoln: University of Nebraska Press, 2007.

Fixico, Donald Lee. *The American Indian Mind in a Linear World: American Indian Studies and Traditional Knowledge*. New York: Routledge, 2003.

Fletcher, Matthew L. M. *American Indian Education: Counternarratives in Racism, Struggle, and the Law*. Critical Educator. New York: Routledge, 2008.

Foote, Cheryl J. *Women of the New Mexico Frontier, 1846–1912*. Albuquerque: University of New Mexico Press, 2005.

Ford, Richard I. "Communication Networks and Information Hierarchies in Native American Folk Medicine: Tewa Pueblos, New Mexico." In *American Folk Medicine: A Symposium*, edited by Wayland D. Hand, 143–157. Berkeley: University of California Press, 1976.

Frey, Christopher J. "Ainu Schools and Education Policy in Nineteenth-Century Hokkaido, Japan." Ph.D. diss., Indiana University, 2007.

Frost, Richard M. "The Pueblo Indian Smallpox Epidemic in New Mexico, 1898–1899." *Bulletin of the History of Medicine* 64, no. 3 (1990): 417–445.

Galgano, Robert C. *Feast of Souls: Indians and Spaniards in the Seventeenth-*

Century Missions of Florida and New Mexico. Albuquerque: University of New Mexico Press, 2005.

García, Mario T., and Frances Equibel Tywoniak. *Migrant Daughter: Coming of Age as a Mexican American Woman.* Berkeley: University of California Press, 2000.

Gere, Anne Ruggles. "Indian Heart/White Man's Head: Native-American Teachers in Indian Schools, 1880–1930." *History of Education Quarterly* 45, no. 1 (Summer 2005): 38–65.

Gomez, Laura E. "Off-White in an Age of White Supremacy: Mexican Elites and the Rights of Whites and Blacks in Nineteenth-Century New Mexico." *Chicano-Latin Law Review* 25 (Spring 2005): 9–59.

Gonzales, Manuel G. *Mexicanos: A History of Mexicans in the United States.* Bloomington: Indiana University Press, 1999.

Gordon, Linda. *The Great Arizona Orphan Abduction.* Cambridge, Mass.: Harvard University Press, 2001.

Gunnerson, Dolores A. *The Jicarilla Apaches: A Study in Survival.* DeKalb: Northern Illinois University Press, 1974.

Gutiérrez, Ramón A. *When Jesus Came, the Corn Mothers Went Away: Marriage, Sexuality, and Power in New Mexico, 1500–1846.* Stanford, Calif.: Stanford University Press, 1991.

Hahn, Steven. *A Nation under Our Feet: Black Political Struggles in the Rural South, from Slavery to the Great Migration.* Cambridge, Mass.: Belknap Press of Harvard University Press, 2003.

Hall, G. Emlen. "Land Litigation and the Idea of New Mexico Progress." *Journal of the West* 27, no. 3 (1988): 48–58.

Hämäläinen, Pekka. *The Comanche Empire.* Lamar Series in Western History. New Haven, Conn.: Yale University Press, 2008.

Heaston, Michael D. "Whiskey Regulation and Indian Land Titles in New Mexico Territory: 1851–1861." *Journal of the West* 10, no. 3 (1971): 474–483.

Hendrick, Irving G. "Federal Policy Affecting the Education of Indians in California, 1849–1934." *History of Education Quarterly* 16, no. 2 (Summer 1976): 163–185.

Hill, W. W. *An Ethnography of Santa Clara Pueblo, New Mexico.* Albuquerque: University of New Mexico Press, 1982.

Hoffman, Beatrix. "Health Care Reform and Social Movements in the United States." *Public Health Then and Now* 93, no. 1 (2003): 75–85.

Honig, Meredith I. *New Directions in Education Policy Implementation: Confronting Complexity*. Albany: State University of New York Press, 2006.

Horsman, Reginald. "Scientific Racism and the American Indian in the Mid-Nineteenth Century." *American Quarterly* 27, no. 2 (1975): 152–168.

Hoxie, Frederick E. *A Final Promise: The Campaign to Assimilate the Indians, 1880–1920*. Lincoln: University of Nebraska Press, 2001.

Ishii, Izumi. "Alcohol and Politics in the Cherokee Nation Before Removal." *Ethnohistory* 50, no. 4 (2003): 671–695.

Jacobs, Margaret D. "Clara True and Female Moral Authority." *Faculty Publications, Department of History* (2002). http://digitalcommons.unl .edu/historyfacpub/24.

———. *Engendered Encounters: Feminism and Pueblo Cultures, 1879–1934*. Lincoln: University of Nebraska Press, 1999.

———. "Making Savages of Us All: White Women, Pueblo Indians, and the Controversy over Indian Dances in the 1920s." *Frontiers: A Journal of Women Studies* 17, no. 3 (1996): 178–209.

———. *White Mother to a Dark Race: Settler Colonialism, Maternalism, and the Removal of Indigenous Children in the American West and Australia, 1880–1940*. Lincoln: University of Nebraska Press, 2009.

Jenkins, Myra Ellen. "Spanish Land Grants in the Tewa Area." *New Mexico Historical Review* 47, no. 2 (1972): 113–134.

Katanski, Amelia V. *Learning to Write "Indian": The Boarding-School Experience and American Indian Literature*. Norman: University of Oklahoma Press, 2005.

Keller, Jean A. *Empty Beds: Indian Student Health at Sherman Institute, 1902–1922*. Native American Series. East Lansing: Michigan State University Press, 2002.

Klein, Christine A. "Treaties of Conquest: Property Rights, Indian Treaties, and the Treaty of Guadalupe Hidalgo." *New Mexico Law Review* 26 (1996): 201–255.

Labaree, David F. *How to Succeed in School without Really Learning: The Credentials Race in American Education*. New Haven, Conn.: Yale University Press, 1997.

Lauzon, Glen P. "Civic Learning through Agricultural Improvement: Bringing the 'Loom and the Anvil into Proximity with the Plow' in Nineteenth-Century Indiana." Ph.D. diss., Indiana University, 2007.

Lavender, David. *The Southwest*. Albuquerque: University of New Mexico Press, 1980.

Lawrence, Adrea, and Brec Cooke. "Law, Language, and Land: A Multi-method Analysis of the General Allotment Act and Its Discourses." *Qualitative Inquiry* 16, no. 3 (2010): 217–229.

Lee, R. F. "Creating Mesa Verde National Park and Chartering the Archeological Institute, 1906." June 18, 2006. http://www.cr.nps.gov/archeology/PUBS/LEE/Lee_CH7.htm.

Littlefield, Alice. "Learning to Labor: Native American Education in the United States, 1880–1930." In *The Political Economy of North American Indians*, edited by John H. Moore, 43–59. Norman: University of Oklahoma Press, 1993.

Lomawaima, K. Tsianina. "American Indian Education: By Indians for Indians." In *A Companion to American Indian History*, edited by Philip J. Deloria and Neal Salisbury, 422–440. Blackwell Companions to American History. Malden, Mass.: Blackwell, 2002.

———. "Estelle Reel, Superintendent of Indian Schools, 1898–1910: Politics, Curriculum, and Land." *Journal of American Indian Education* 35, no. 3 (May 1996).

———. *They Called It Prairie Light: The Story of Chilocco Indian School*. Lincoln: University of Nebraska Press, 1994.

Lomawaima, K. Tsianina, and Teresa L. McCarty. *"To Remain an Indian": Lessons in Democracy from a Century of Native American Education*. New York: Teachers College Press, 2006.

Mancall, Peter C. *Deadly Medicine: Indians and Alcohol in Early America*. Ithaca, N.Y.: Cornell University Press, 1995.

———. "Men, Women, and Alcohol in Indian Villages in the Great Lakes Region in the Early Republic." *Journal of the Early Republic* 15, no. 3 (Autumn 1995): 425–448.

Massing, C. "The Development of the United States Government Policy toward Indian Health Care, 1850–1900." *Past Imperfect* 3 (1994): 129–158.

Matthews-Lamb, Sandra K. "'Designing and Mischievous Individuals': The Cruzate Grants and the Office of the Surveyor General." *New Mexico Historical Review* 71, no. 4 (October 1996): 341–359.

Meeks, Eric V. *Border Citizens: The Making of Indians, Mexicans, and Anglos in Arizona*. Austin: University of Texas Press, 2007.

Meinig, D. W. *The Southwest: Three Peoples in Geographical Change, 1600–1970*. New York: Oxford University Press, 1971.

Meyer, Manuali Aluli. "Indigenous and Authentic." In *Handbook of Critical and Indigenous Methodologies*, 217–232. Thousand Oaks, Calif.: Sage, 2008.

Nieto-Phillips, John M. *The Language of Blood: The Making of Spanish-American Identity in New Mexico, 1880s–1930s*. Albuquerque: University of New Mexico Press, 2004.

———. "Mexican Yankees and American Jibaros: The Americanization of Schoolchildren in New Mexico and Puerto Rico." Lecture, Indiana University, Bloomington, November 19, 2004.

Odden, Allan R. *Education Policy Implementation*. Albany: State University of New York Press, 1991.

Ortiz, Alfonso. *The Tewa World: Space, Time, Being, and Becoming in a Pueblo Society*. Chicago: University of Chicago Press, 1969.

Parezo, Nancy J., and Don D. Fowler. *Anthropology Goes to the Fair: The 1904 Louisiana Purchase Exposition*. Lincoln: University of Nebraska Press, 2007.

Parsons, Elsie Clews. "Relations between Ethnology and Archaeology in the Southwest." *American Antiquity* 5, no. 3 (January 1940): 214–220.

Peavy, Linda S., and Ursula Smith. *Full-Court Quest: The Girls from Fort Shaw Indian School, Basketball Champions of the World*. Norman: University of Oklahoma Press, 2008.

Poling, Susan A., and Alan R. Kasdan. *Treaty of Guadalupe Hidalgo: Definition and List of Community Land Grants in New Mexico, Exposure Draft*. Washington, D.C.: U.S. General Accountability Office, January 2001.

Pritzker, B. M. *A Native American Encyclopedia: History, Culture, and Peoples*. Oxford: Oxford University Press, 2000.

Prucha, Francis Paul, ed. *Americanizing the American Indians: Writings by the "Friends of the Indian," 1880–1900*. Cambridge, Mass.: Harvard University Press, 1973.

Putney, Diane T. "Fighting the Scourge: American Indian Morbidity and Federal Policy, 1897–1928." Ph.D diss., Marquette University, 1980.

Quintana, Frances Leon. "Land, Water, and Pueblo-Hispanic Relations in Northern New Mexico." *Journal of the Southwest* 32, no. 3 (1990): 288–299.

Quintero, Gilbert. "Making the Indian: Colonial Knowledge, Alcohol, and

Native Americans." *American Indian Culture & Research Journal* 25, no. 4 (2001): 57–71.

Raup, Ruth M. *The Indian Health Program from 1800–1955.* Washington, D.C.: Indian Health Services, 1959.

Reyhner, Jon Allan, and Jeanne M. Oyawin Eder. *American Indian Education: A History.* Norman: University of Oklahoma Press, 2006.

———. "A History of Indian Education." In *Teaching American Indian Students*, edited by Jon Allan Reyhner, 33–58. Norman: University of Oklahoma Press, 1992.

Roberts, David. *The Pueblo Revolt: The Secret Rebellion That Drove the Spaniards out of the Southwest.* New York: Simon & Schuster, 2004.

Rothman, Hal. "Chapter 1: The Open Plateau." In *Bandelier, NM: An Administrative History.* February 4, 2001. http://www.nps.gov/band/adhi/adhi1b.htm.

Sando, Joe S. *Pueblo Nations: Eight Centuries of Pueblo Indian History.* Santa Fe, N.Mex.: Clear Light, 1992.

Sawtelle, Susan D., Alan R. Kasdan, and Jeffrey D. Malcolm. *Treaty of Guadalupe Hidalgo: Findings and Possibly Options regarding Longstanding Community Land Grant Claims in New Mexico.* Washington, D.C.: U.S. General Accountability Office, June 2004.

Silko, Leslie Marmon. "Landscape, History, and the Pueblo Imagination." In *The Ecocriticism Reader: Landmarks in Literary Ecology*, edited by Cheryll Glotfelty and Harold Fromm, 264–275. Athens: University of Georgia Press, 1996.

Storr, Richard J. "The Education of History: Some Impressions." *Harvard Educational Review* 31, no. 2 (Spring 1961): 124–135.

———. "The Role of Education in American History: A Memorandum for the Committee Advising the Fund for the Advancement of Education in Regard to This Subject." *Harvard Educational Review* 46, no. 3 (August 1976): 331–354.

Street, Henry K. *The History of Wine in New Mexico: 400 Years of Struggle.* Ponderosa, N.Mex.: Ponderosa Valley Vineyards and Winery, 1997.

Stronza, Amanda. "Anthropology of Tourism: Forging New Ground for Ecotourism and Other Alternatives." *Annual Review of Anthropology* 30 (2001): 261–284.

Stuart, Paul. "Administrative Reform in Indian Affairs." *Western Historical Quarterly* 16, no. 2 (April 1985): 133–146.

————. *The Indian Office: Growth and Development of an American Institution, 1865–1900.* Ann Arbor, Mich.: UMI Research, 1979.

Sutton, Margaret, and Bradley A. U. Levinson. *Policy as Practice: Toward a Comparative Sociocultural Analysis of Educational Policy.* Sociocultural Studies in Educational Policy Formation and Appropriation. Westport, Conn.: Ablex, 2001.

Svenningsen, R. *Preliminary Inventory of the Pueblo Records Created by Field Offices of the Bureau of Indian Affairs, Record Group 75.* General Services Administration, Washington, D.C., 1980.

Sweet, Jill D. "'Let 'em Loose': Pueblo Indian Management of Tourism." *American Indian Culture & Research Journal* 15, no. 4 (1991): 59–74.

————. "The Portals of Tradition: Tourism in the American Southwest." *Cultural Survival Quarterly* 14, no. 2 (1990): 6–8.

Szasz, Margaret Connell, ed. *Between Indian and White Worlds: The Cultural Broker.* Norman: University of Oklahoma Press, 1994.

————. *Indian Education in the American Colonies, 1607–1783.* Lincoln: Bison Books, University of Nebraska Press, 2007.

Tamura, Eileen H. "Value Messages Collide with Reality: Joseph Kurihara and the Power of Informal Education." *History of Education Quarterly* 50, no. 1 (2010): 1–33.

Tiller, Veronica Velarde. *The Jicarilla Apache Tribe: A History, 1846–1970.* Rev. ed. Albuquerque, N.Mex.: BowArrow, 2000.

"Trachoma: MedlinePlus Medical Encyclopedia." n.d. http://www.nlm.nih.gov/medlineplus/ency/article/001486.htm.

Trafzer, Clifford E., Jean A. Keller, and Lorene Sisquoc. *Boarding School Blues: Revisiting American Indian Educational Experiences.* Lincoln: Bison Books, University of Nebraska Press, 2006.

Trennert, Robert A. "Indian Sore Eyes: The Federal Campaign to Control Trachoma in the Southwest, 1910–1940." *Journal of the Southwest* 32, no. 2 (1990): 121–149.

————. "Selling Indian Education at World's Fairs and Expositions, 1893–1904." *American Indian Quarterly* 11, no. 3 (Summer 1987): 203–220.

————. "White Man's Medicine vs. Hopi Tradition: The Smallpox Epidemic of 1899." *Journal of Arizona History* 33, no. 4 (1992): 349–366.

Truett, Samuel. *Fugitive Landscapes: The Forgotten History of the U.S.-Mexico Borderlands.* New Haven, Conn.: Yale University Press, 2008.

Tyler, Daniel. "Ejido Lands in New Mexico." In *Spanish and Mexican Land*

Grants and the Law, edited by Malcolm Ebright, 24–35. Manhattan, Kans.: Sunflower University Press, 1989.

Vogel, Virgil J. "American Indian Foods Used as Medicine." In *American Folk Medicine: A Symposium*, edited by Wayland D. Hand, 125–141. Berkeley: University of California Press, 1976.

Weber, David J. "The Spanish Borderlands of North America: A Historiography." *OAH Magazine of History* 14, no. 4 (Summer 2000): 5–11.

———. *The Spanish Frontier in North America*. Yale Western Americana Series. New Haven, Conn.: Yale University Press, 1992.

West, Elliott. "Reconstructing Race." *Western Historical Quarterly* 34, no. 1 (Spring 2003): 6–26.

"WHO: Diphtheria." n.d. http://www.who.int/mediacentre/factsheets/fs089/en/.

Wilkins, David. "The Manipulation of Indigenous Status: The Federal Government as Shape-Shifter." *Stanford Law & Policy Review* 12 (2001): 223–233.

———. "The U.S. Supreme Court's Explication of 'Federal Plenary Power': An Analysis of Case Law Affecting Tribal Sovereignty, 1886–1914." *American Indian Quarterly* 18, no. 3 (Summer 1994): 349–368.

Wilkins, David E., and K. Tsianina Lomawaima. *Uneven Ground: American Indian Sovereignty and Federal Law*. Norman: University of Oklahoma Press, 2001.

Woodson, Carter G. *The Mis-education of the Negro*. Trenton, N.J.: Africa World Press, 1933.

Index

women
  authority, 94, 96, 146
  facial features of Indians, 191–192
  laundresses at Indian schools, 148
  liquor consumption, 133–134
  potters, 176, 179
  property rights, 247n42
  teachers, 91–92, 158–160, 162–164
  See also gender roles

Women's Christian Temperance
  Union, 120
Women's Society, 73, 83
Worcester v. Georgia, 103, 104
World's Fair (1904). *See* Louisiana
  Purchase Exposition

Zuni Pueblo, 3, 85